C000125576

CURRENT LITERARY TERMS

CURRENT LITERARY TERMS

A Concise Dictionary of their Origin and Use

A. F. SCOTT, M.A.

MACMILLAN

First Edition 1965
Reprinted with revisions 1967, 1971
Reprinted 1973

Published by
THE MACMILLAN PRESS LTD
London and Basingstoke
Associated companies in New York Dublin
Melbourne Johannesburg and Madras

Library of Congress catalog card no. 65-24300

SBN 333 03566 6

Printed in Great Britain by
REDWOOD PRESS LIMITED
Trowbridge, Wiltshire

PREFACE

THIS is a complete reference-book, alphabetically arranged, carefully cross-referenced, giving the etymology and concise but comprehensive definition of the principal terms used in all branches of literature. Definitions are illustrated with extensive quotations, some in old forms, but mainly taken from recent texts. The book, which is international, includes descriptions of forms as various as Epic, Dadaism, and Kabuki, and provides scholarly information, with a clear critical line, on the techniques and complexities of expression in words.

Words are alive, and like all live things they grow, they change, they meet honour and disaster. Some remain puny, others stretch like giants. Perhaps few people know their story as far back as we can go.

The interested reader probably knows the origin of *carol* and *serenade* and *bucolic*, but what of *fustian* and *bombast* and *babery*, *doggerel* and *baroque* and *farce*? What was the original *caricature*, the original *maundy*, the original *leonine rhyme*? If 'slithy' means 'lithe and slimy' what does 'ordinailed ungles' mean? How and when was the first *clerihew* written, and how did the *limerick* get its name? Did science fiction really begin with Lucian's *Vera Historia* in the second century? We may know how Walter Mapes became the *Jovial Toper*, but wonder how Thomas Moore became *Anacreon*.

Is Goliardic really a corruption of Golias? Who was this Mrs. Grundy, whose name is uttered with distaste? And who (or what) are Dora and Aunt Edna and Andy Capp? Why did Tennyson kick the geese out of the boat, and what man adorned a sermon with kinquering congs? We may guess how the Grand Guignol was connected with Great Punch, but what was the Satanic School, and who boldly introduced Baby-Cake into a Christmas Masque?

We have heard the Buddhist proverb that the fallen flower never returns to the branch; but does the broken looking-glass never reflect again?

Many of us know Oscar Wilde said, 'I can resist everything except temptation', and that Robert Frost declared, 'Writing free verse is like playing tennis with the net down'; but we may not remember who said, speaking of Good Sense, that his son was Wit, who married Mirth, and Humour was their child.

Why did a Greek word linger in the mind of John Phillips when he wrote:

'Lewd did I live & evil I did dwell'?

Literary and critical terms can be treated in such a way as not only to help the student, but also to interest those readers who look upon literature as copious, vivid, and profound.

We know that many of these terms are unfamiliar and abstruse, many of them are Greek names, perhaps at first sight forbidding. To meet this problem in Elizabethan times, Richard Puttenham made a vigorous but unsuccessful attempt in his *Arte of English Poesie* to personify the terms themselves, or, as L. G. Salingar says, 'to anglicize them with the aid of homely illustrations'. *Zeugma* Puttenham names 'single supply'. We should not gain very much today by calling Irony 'the Dry mock' or Sarcasm 'the Bitter taunt' or *Micterismus* 'the Fleering frump'. But to know the true meaning of such words as *nemesis, plagiarism, catharsis,* and to realize more of their significance is of real value in literary elucidation.

'Poetry', Dr. Leavis once said, 'can communicate the actual quality of experience with a subtlety and precision unapproachable by any other means.' But we can only share this experience by an appreciation of the words, for it is the words which stand for all the poet has felt, for all that has passed through his imagination.

Coleridge had this in mind when, writing of poetry, he stated, 'Be it observed, however, that I include in the meaning of a word not only its correspondent object but likewise all the associations which it recalls'.

So the writer, in prose or verse, strong in the use of such associations, presenting the width and the profundities of life, makes demands upon the reader beyond the plain meaning of the words themselves — for a word, full of purpose, surpasses its mere definition.

This book, therefore, grew out of the need for something to meet these demands. It is a dictionary consisting of literary and critical terms used in explaining the unfamiliar forms, the varied techniques and larger aspects of the complex art of writing.

In the preparation of this glossary I am greatly indebted to the *Oxford English Dictionary*, H. C. Wyld's *Universal Dictionary of the English Language*, Ernest Weekley's *Concise Etymological Dictionary of Modern English*, Chambers's *Etymological English Dictionary*, H. W. Fowler's *Dictionary of Modern English Usage*, Sir Paul Harvey's *Oxford Companion to English Literature* and *Oxford Companion to Classical Literature*.

I owe more personal thanks to Dr. Frederick T. Wood, who read the first draft and made many valuable suggestions, to Mr. Kevin McGarry for his kindly assistance, and to my wife for constant interest and encouragement.

Finally I wish to express my indebtedness to Mr. T. M. Farmiloe for his most valued guidance and practical advice.   A. F. Scott

CONTENTS

A

ABBEY THEATRE. *See* IRISH DRAMATIC MOVEMENT.

ABECEDARIANS. The name, which is derived from the first four letters of the alphabet, of a small sect, followers of Storch, the German Anabaptist, in the sixteenth century. Abecedarians refused to read because they held that knowledge of the Scriptures communicated direct by the Holy Spirit was essential.

ABECEDARIUS. A composition in verse in which the initial letters of the words of each line are the same, and in which successive lines are in alphabetical order. Here are the opening lines from one by Alaric Watts:

> An Austrian army awfully array'd,
> Boldly by battery besieged Belgrade.
> Cossack commanders cannonading come
> Dealing destruction's devastating doom.

ABRACADABRA. A cabalistic word of obscure late Latin origin, first appearing in a poem by Q. Severus Sammonicus, in the second century B.C. Written in the form of a triangle and worn round the neck, it was used to cure agues and drive away evil spirits.

In *A Lay of St. Dunstan*, R. H. Barham makes fun of the word and says:

> For I'm told that most Cabalists use that identical
> Word, written thus, in what they call 'a Pentacle'.

ABRIDGED EDITION. Latin *abbreviāre*, to shorten. The reduced or condensed form of the original text of a book.

ABSOLUTE. Latin *absolūtus*, loosened or freed from. In a general sense, completely independent of anything else, or of something which might be expected to be of influence.

An absolute word is one which cannot be qualified, such as *unique*, or one which is without the part of speech that usually accompanies it, such as a transitive verb without an object, or an adjective without a noun. For example: If wishes could *destroy*. Fortune favours the *brave*.

Also, a clause out of ordinary syntactic relation to the other parts of the sentence, as in the Ablative Absolute, analogous to the

Ablative Absolute in Latin and the Genitive Absolute in Greek: *Night having fallen,* we decided to go.

ABSTRACT. Latin *abstrahĕre*; *abs,* away from, *trahĕre, tractum,* to draw. To form a general concept from consideration of particular instances.

> When an organic form is stabilized and repeated as a pattern, and the intention of the artist is no longer related to the inherent dynamism of an inventive art, but seeks to adapt content to predetermined structure, then the resulting form may be described as *abstract.*
>
> Herbert Read, *Collected Essays*

Abstract used of language means existing, or thought of as existing, apart from material objects, and is opposed to *concrete*; hence it is ideal, not practical.

The word *abstract* applied to art means 'non-representational', dissociated from theme.

'It is good to be honest and true' and 'Honesty is the best policy' are abstract statements.

ABSTRACTION. Latin *abstrahĕre,* to draw away. A process of the mind by which it directs its attention to particular attributes of an object or objects without regard for the other attributes which the object may possess. Thus in the objects *sugar, honey, syrup,* we see the quality *sweetness,* and this we may abstract from among the other attributes in the objects and consider it independently. The process by which general terms are used to classify all *ships* or all *trees* together is called *abstraction.*

> We make abstraction of certain attributes a noun possesses, leaving out others which would not fit; for instance in 'the *roses* of her cheeks', we think only of fragrance, pinkness and softness, not of thorns, leaves, yellowness or dark red.
>
> Christine Brooke-Rose, *A Grammar of Metaphor*

ACATALECTIC. From Greek *akatalēktós,* from *a-* (negating) and *katalêgein,* to leave off, stop. Of a verse it means complete, having the full number of feet or syllables.

If a verse is short of one or more unstressed syllables in its final foot, it is called *catalectic* or *truncated.* A line which lacks initial syllable or syllables is called *headless.*

This line from Dryden's *Alexander's Feast* is an example of *catalectic*:

Sweet is | Pleasure | after | Pain.

ACCENT. Latin *accentus*, the accentuation of a word, song added to speech. The modulation of the voice; tone of the voice. The stress on a syllable or word. A mark used to direct this stress. Any form of utterance characteristic of an individual, a class, or a region. On Carlyle's style, Meredith says this in *Beauchamp's Career*:

> A style resembling either early architecture or utter dilapidation, so loose and rough it seemed . . . learned dictionary words giving a hand to street-slang, and accents falling on them haphazard, like slant rays from driving clouds; all the pages in a breeze, the whole book producing a kind of electrical agitation in the mind and the joints.

ACCIDENCE. Latin *accidentia*, the things that befall (a word). That part of grammar dealing with inflexions (the accidents or non-essentials of words). The elements of any subject.

> *Mrs. Page:* Sir Hugh, my husband says my son profits nothing in the world at his book. I pray you, ask him some questions in his accidence. *The Merry Wives of Windsor*

ACRONYM. *See* ACROSTIC.

ACROSTIC. Greek *akrostíkhion*; *ákros*, extreme, *stikhos*, a line. A poem or puzzle in which the first, the middle, or the last letters of each line (or a combination of any two or of all three of these), when taken in order, spell a word or a sentence.

An interesting extension of the acrostic form is the use of the word *cabal*, as a kind of pun upon an already existing word. It came to mean a body of people engaged in intrigue, applied to five ministers of Charles II. These were Clifford, Arlington, Buckingham, Ashley, and Lauderdale, the initial letters of whose names form the word.

A single word, such as *cabal* in the above context, or Dora (Defence of the Realm Act), or the more modern Nato (North Atlantic Treaty Organization), or Pluto (pipe line under the ocean), formed from the initial letters of other words, is also known as an acronym.

ACT. Greek *ágein*, to put in motion. The main division of a play. Greek plays were continuous, the only pauses being marked by the chorus. Horace insisted on the importance of five acts. With the Renaissance this was accepted, taken by the French dramatists, and passed to England in the plays of Ben Jonson. In comedy, three acts became quite usual, and this division is now common in modern drama.

ACTION IN DRAMA. On this subject Dryden says in *An Essay of Dramatic Poesy*:

> 'Tis a great mistake in us to believe the French present no part
> of the action on the stage; every alteration or crossing of a
> design, every new-sprung passion and turn of it, is a part of
> the action, and much the noblest, except we conceive nothing
> to be action till the players come to blows; as if the painting
> of the hero's mind were not more properly the poet's work
> than the strength of his body.

ADAPTATION. Latin *adaptāre*; *ad*, to, *aptāre*, to fit. The modifying of a literary work to fit another medium, e.g. to change a novel into a play.

ADDENDUM: (pl.) ADDENDA. Latin *addĕre*, add. A thing or things to be added; an addition, or an appendix to a book.

AD LIBITUM: AD LIB. Latin, literally, at pleasure, to any extent. An *ad lib.* remark is one spoken off the cuff, spontaneously.

AD LOCUM: AD LOC. Latin, at the place.

AESTHETIC. Greek *aisthētikós*, perceptive; *aisthánesthai*, to feel, or to perceive. Connected with the appreciation or criticism of the beautiful. *Aesthetics* is the philosophy of the fine arts.

AESTHETIC MOVEMENT. A movement during the 1890s in which sentimental archaism was adopted as the ideal of beauty. 'Art for Art's Sake', claiming that art was independent of morality, became the doctrine, subscribed to by Oscar Wilde (following his master, Walter Pater), Ernest Dowson, Lionel Johnson. The movement was much ridiculed. Tennyson wrote:

> Art for Art's sake! Hail, truest lord of Hell!
> Hail Genius, Master of the Moral Will!
> 'The filthiest of all paintings painted well
> Is mightier than the purest painted ill!'
> Yes, mightier than the purest painted well,
> So prone are we toward the broad way to Hell.

AFFECTIVE FALLACY. W. K. Wimsatt and M. C. Beardsley in *The Verbal Icon* have defined the Affective Fallacy as 'a confusion between the poem and its *results* (what it *is* and what it *does*)'. They go on to say:

> It begins by trying to derive the standard of criticism from the
> psychological effects of the poem and ends in impressionism

and relativism . . . the poem itself, as an object of specially
critical judgment, tends to disappear . . .

AGE OF REASON, THE.   The term applies to the Restoration and
the Augustan Periods, extending between the years 1660 and 1750.
'Augustan' is characterized by a sense of form, balance, proportion,
by classical order and discipline.   It implies self-knowledge, self-
control, a sense of reality.   These qualities were offset by wide-
spread self-indulgence and excess; by material greed, by spiritual
lassitude.   It was an age which produced the philosophy of Hobbes
and Locke, the prose of Swift, Addison, Johnson, and Gibbon.
Pope spoke for it as a poet.   Hogarth exposed it in his paintings
and engravings.   The caricatures of Gillray and Rowlandson
attacked the human follies of the day.

AGON.   Greek *agón*, contest.   Aristophanic comedy contained these
parts:

(*a*) A Prologue (*prólogos*) or exposition
(*b*) A *párodos* or entry of the chorus
(*c*) An *agón* or vigorous dispute between two adversaries; this
provided the main subject of the play
(*d*) A *parábasis*, in which the chorus spoke to the audience in
the name of the poet.

AIODOS.   Greek.   The itinerant singer of songs and poetry.

ALAZON.   The name of the braggart captain appearing in Greek
comedy.   Such a stock character is found in *Miles Gloriosus* of
Plautus.   The influence of Plautus may be traced in many plays
from *Ralph Roister Doister* of Udall, *Mother Bombie* of Lyly, *The
Comedy of Errors* of Shakespeare, to the *Amphitryon* of Dryden.
The character of the braggart soldier, Ben Jonson's Bobadill, is
derived from Plautus.

ALCAIC.   Greek *Alkaikós*, from *Alkaîos*, *Alcaeus*, Greek lyric poet,
600 B.C.   Pertaining to Alcaeus, or to the metre invented by him.
This was used in a slightly altered form by Horace.   Tennyson
imitated the original alcaic metre in this way:

Ō | mīghtў-|mouth'd ĭn|ventŏr ŏf | harmŏn|ies,
Ō | skĭll'd tŏ | sīng ŏf | Tīme ŏr Ĕ|ternĭt|ȳ,
 God-|gīftĕd | ˙orgăn-|voice ŏf | Englănd,
  Mīltŏn, ă | name tŏ rĕ|sound fŏr | agĕs;

Milton, *Alcaics*

ALEXANDRINE. From the French *alexandrin*, perhaps because this twelve-syllable iambic line was used in the Old French in poems on Alexander the Great.

In English, an iambic *hexameter* verse is often called an *alexandrine*.

Dr. Johnson says:

> Cowley was, I believe, the first poet that mingled Alexandrines at pleasure with the common heroick of ten syllables, and from him Dryden borrowed the practice, whether ornamental or licentious. He considered the verse of twelve syllables as elevated and majestic, and has therefore deviated into that measure when he supposes the voice heard of the Supreme Being.

> God the first garden made, and the first city Cain.
> Abraham Cowley, The Garden

> And, like another Helen, fired another Troy.
> John Dryden, Alexander's Feast

ALLEGORY. Greek *allēgoría*; *állos*, other, and *agoreúein*, to speak. A description of one thing under the guise of another suggestively similar. Coleridge defines allegory as

> . . . the employment of a set of agents and images to convey in disguise a moral meaning — those agents and images being so combined as to form a homogeneous whole.

Following the *Roman de la Rose*, allegory is one accepted poetic form of the medieval poem, seen in Chaucer's *The Hous of Fame*. Perhaps the most obvious example in English is Bunyan's *The Pilgrim's Progress*, which describes the adventures of the human soul in the guise of a journey. The moral meaning of the allegory is clear in Spenser's *The Faerie Queene* and in the fifteenth-century play, *Everyman*.

ALLEGRO. Latin *alacer*, lively, brisk, spirited. A word denoting a brisk movement. Often used also as the title of a composition or movement in that style. Here are some lines from Milton's *L'Allegro*:

> Haste thee Nymph, and bring with thee
> Jest and youthful jollity,
> Quips and cranks, and wanton wiles,
> Nods, and becks, and wreathed smiles. . . .
> Sport that wrinkled Care derides,
> And Laughter holding both his sides.
> Come, and trip it as ye go
> On the light fantastic toe.

ALLITERATION. As if from Latin *ad literam*, according to the letter. This device, sometimes called head rhyme or initial rhyme, is the close repetition, not (as by the derivation of the word it ought to be) of the same letter, but of the same *sound*, usually at the beginning of words. A 'hard' and a 'soft' *c*, for instance, do not alliterate, but a 'hard' *c* and a *k* do, and so do a 'soft' *c* and an *s*.

The pattern of Anglo-Saxon verse depended on alliteration, and the repeated initial consonants marked the stressed syllables. Here are the opening lines in *Piers the Plowman* by William Langland, an important work in Middle English:

> In a somer seson · whan soft was the sonne,
> I shope me in shroudes · as I a shepe were,
> In habite as an heremite · vnholy of workes,
> Went wyde in þis world · wondres to here.

These well-known lines occur in Charles Churchill's *The Prophecy of Famine*:

> Who often, but without success, have prayed
> For apt Alliteration's artful aid.

Spenser makes use of unobtrusive alliteration in *The Faerie Queene*:

> Her angel's face
> As the great eye of heaven shined bright,
> And made a sunshine in the shady place;
> Did never mortal eye behold such heavenly grace.

> Sweet is the lily's silver bell,
> And sweet the wakeful taper's smell
> That watch for early prayer.
> Christopher Smart, *The Song to David*

ALLONYM. Greek *állos*, other; *ónoma*, name. The name of some-one else assumed by the author of a work. A work bearing such a name.

ALLUSION. Latin *allūděre*, to play with, to jest, to refer to. A reference to characters and events of mythology, legends, history.

Poetry relies upon all the qualities of words — meaning, sound, associations. Association is an essential part of allusion. Used by great writers, allusion brings a wide world of experience outside the limitations of plain statement. Here is an example in *Paradise Lost*:

> What resounds
> In fable or romance of Uther's son
> Begirt with British and Armoric knights;
> And all who since, baptized or infidel
> Jousted in Aspramont or Montalban,
> Damasco, or Marocco, or Trebisond,

> Or whom Biserta sent from Afric shore
> When Charlemain with all his peerage fell
> By Fontarabbia.

ALMANAC. Spanish *almanaque*, almanac. Annual calendar of months and days, with astronomical data and indications of feasts and holidays.

ALTAR POEM. A metrical composition, written or printed to form a design on the page, such as an altar or a cross. This type was common in the seventeenth century, as exemplified in George Herbert's *The Altar*:

> A broken ALTAR, Lord, thy servant reares,
> Made of a heart, and cemented with teares,
>   Whose parts are as thy hand did frame;
>   No workman's tool hath touch'd the same.
>   A HEART alone
>   Is such a stone,
>   As nothing but
>   Thy power doth cut.
>   Wherefore each part
>   Of my hard heart
>   Meets in this frame,
>   To praise thy name:
> That, if I chance to hold my peace,
> These stones to praise thee may not cease.
> O let thy blessed SACRIFICE be mine,
> And sanctifie this ALTAR to be thine.

ALTERNATE ALLITERATION. In *Literary Remains*, Coleridge called alternate alliteration 'a great secret in melody'. Here is an example from Shelley's *The Daemon of the World*:

> Though frosts may blight the freshness of its bloom.

ALTERNATE RHYME. This is the rhyme of the stanza form *a b a b*, such as in Gray's *Elegy*:

> The curfew tolls the knell of parting day,
>   The lowing herd wind slowly o'er the lea,
> The ploughman homeward plods his weary way,
>   And leaves the world to darkness and to me.

AMBIGUITY. Latin *ambiguus*, doubtful; from *ambigĕre*, *amb-*, both ways, *agĕre*, drive. Double meaning, or an expression capable of more than one meaning. In *Seven Types of Ambiguity*, William Empson says:

> The fundamental situation, whether it deserves to be called ambiguous or not, is that a word or a grammatical structure is effective in several ways at once. To take a famous example, there is no pun, double syntax, or dubiety of feeling in
>
> > Bare ruined choirs, where late the sweet birds sang,
>
> but the comparison holds for many reasons; because ruined monastery choirs are places in which to sing, because they involve sitting in a row, because they are made of wood, are carved into knots and so forth, because they used to be surrounded by a sheltering building crystallized out of the likeness of a forest, and coloured with stained glass and painting like flowers and leaves, because they are now abandoned by all but the grey walls coloured like the skies of winter, because the cold and Narcissistic charm suggested by choir-boys suits well with Shakespeare's feeling for the object of the Sonnets, and for various sociological and historical reasons (the protestant destruction of monasteries; fear of puritanism), which it would be hard now to trace out in their proportions; these reasons, and many more relating the simile to its place in the Sonnet, must all combine to give the line its beauty, and there is a sort of ambiguity in not knowing which of them to hold most clearly in mind. Clearly this is involved in all such richness and heightening of effect, and the machinations of ambiguity are among the very roots of poetry.

AMBIVALENCE.   Latin *ambo*, both, *valens* from *valēre*, to be strong.   The state of having opposing emotional attitudes towards the same object.   The capacity to see two or more sides to an issue.

AMPERSAND.   A corruption of *and per se and*; *per se*, 'standing by itself'; therefore, *and* standing by itself means *and*.   Children learning from the hornbook repeated aloud, 'A per se A, B per se B . . . *and per se and*'.   *Ampersand* is the old way of naming and spelling the sign &, formerly &, ligature of *et*.

AMPHIBOLY: AMPHIBOLOGY.   Greek *amphibolos*, attacked on both sides; doubtful, ambiguous.   A phrase or statement yielding sense in more than one way.   For example: I met my sister smiling.

AMPHIBRACH. Greek *amphibrakhus*, short at both ends; a metrical foot of three syllables, the first and third being short and the middle one long (ᴗ — ᴗ), as in *ĭntensĕlўˇ, ăttĕntĭŏn*.

AMPHIMACER. From Greek *makrós*, long (on both sides). A metrical foot consisting of a short syllable between two long syllables, as *mérchăndĭse*.

AMPHISBAENIC RHYMES: BACKWARD RHYMES. Greek *amphisbaina*, a fabled monster with a head at each end, and able to go in either direction. Now a poetical device. This way of writing verse was introduced by Edmund Wilson, and is illustrated by one of his quatrains:

> But tonight I come lone and belated —
> Foreseeing in every detail,
> And resolved for a day to sidestep
> My friends and their guests and their pets.

-ANA. Neuter plural of Latin adjectives in *-ānus* denoting connected with, of the nature of, coming from; added to names to form nouns meaning sayings of, personal anecdotes. Appended in England from the eighteenth century to denote a collection of memorable sayings by eminent people, as *Shakespeariana*, *Johnsoniana*. Also publications bearing on places, *Tunbrigiana*.

ANABASIS. Greek *anábasis*, a going up, from *aná-* and *básis*, a going. A military expedition, specifically that of the younger Cyrus against his brother Artaxerxes, and the retreat of his ten thousand Greeks, described by Xenophon in *Anabasis*.

> Your chronicler, in writing this,
> Had in his mind th' Anabasis.
> Longfellow, *The Wayside Inn*

ANACHRONISM. Greek *anakhronismós*, from *aná*, back, backwards, and *khrónos*, time. An error in chronology, placing an event in its wrong historical time. In *Julius Caesar*, Brutus says to Cassius, 'Peace! count the clock.' To which Cassius replies, 'The clock has stricken three.'

Clocks were not known to the Romans, and striking-clocks were not invented until some fourteen hundred years after the death of Caesar.

George Bernard Shaw makes deliberate use of anachronisms in *Saint Joan*.

ANACOLUTHON. Greek *anakólouthon* from *an-*, not, and *akólouthos*, following, agreeing with. A broken sentence construction, lacking a grammatical sequence. This example is taken from *King Lear*:

> Why I do trifle thus with his despair
> Is done to cure it.

ANACREONTIC. Anakreōn, the name of a Greek lyrical poet, *c.* 570 B.C. In the manner or metre of Anacreon's lyrics, celebrating wine, women, and the convivial life. Walter Mapes, 'the Jovial Toper', was known as the Anacreon of the twelfth century. His famous drinking-song, 'Meum est propositum . . .' has been translated by Leigh Hunt. The principal work of the fourteenth-century Persian poet Muhammad Hafiz called the 'Diwan' is of anacreontic character. Thomas Moore was called Anacreon from his translation of that Greek poet, and from his own anacreontic songs. Byron says in *Don Juan*:

> Described by Mahomet and Anacreon Moore.

Here are some lines from Anacreon's lyric *The Intruder*, translated by Thomas Stanley in 1651:

> 'Who's that,' said I, 'that does keep
> Such a noise, and breaks my sleep?'
> 'Ope,' saith Love, 'for pity hear;
> ''Tis a childe, thou need'st not fear,
> Wet and weary, from his way
> Led by this dark night astray.'
> . . . When well warm'd he was, and dry,
> 'Now,' saith he, ''tis time to try
> If my bow no hurt did get,
> For methinks the string is wet.'
> With that, drawing it, a dart
> He let fly that pierc'd my heart:
> Leaping then, and laughing said,
> 'Come, my friend, with me be glad;
> For my Bow thou see'st is sound
> Since thy heart hath got a wound.'

ANACRUSIS. Greek *anákrousis*, a pushing back, checking, from *anakroúein*, to thrust back. An unstressed syllable or group of syllables at the beginning of a verse which normally begins with a stress.

> Cléaręr | lóves sound | óthęr | wáys;
> I míss my | líttlĕ | húman | práise.

ANADIPLOSIS. Greek, literally, to double back. That kind of repetition in which the last words of one sentence, line or phrase, or any prominent word or phrase, are repeated, as in these lines from Sir Philip Sidney's *Astrophel and Stella*:

> O stealing time, the subject of delay,
> Delay the rack of unrefrain'd desire,
> What strange design hast thou my hopes to stay?
> My hopes which do but to mine own aspire?

ANAGNORISIS. Greek *anagnŏrisis*, recognition. Aristotle uses this term in *Poetics*. He is analysing the construction or plot of tragedy and makes use of 'discovery' and 'reversal of fortune'. When a character realizes the truth, this is the moment of recognition, *anagnŏrisis*; then the fortune is reversed, *peripéteia*. In Sophocles' *Oedipus Rex*, *anagnŏrisis* comes when Oedipus finds out that he is the man who killed Laius; from that moment the whole action of the tragedy is reversed.

ANAGRAM. From Greek *aná*, back, and *grámma*, a written character, a letter. A new word or phrase made out of a word or phrase by transposing the letters. Bunyan says that an anagram for *John Bunyan* is *nu hony in a B* (new honey in a bee). The title of Samuel Butler's novel *Erewhon* is an anagram of *nowhere*.

ANALECTS. Greek *análekta*, things gathered up, chosen. Collections of literary fragments.

ANALOGUE. Greek *análogon*, according to due proportion. A word or thing which resembles, or is compared with, another word or thing.

ANALOGY. Greek *analogía*, proportion. The process of reasoning from parallel cases (in its logical sense). In the literary way, it is the description of something known in order to suggest in certain respects something unknown. An *analogue* is a word or thing bearing analogy to, or resembling, another. The use of analogy is illustrated in Lyly's *Euphues*:

> But seeinge I see mine owne impietie, I wyll endevoure my selfe to amende all that is paste, and to be a myrrour of godlynes heereafter. The Rose though a lyttle it be eaten with the Canker yet beeing distilled yeeldeth sweete water, the yron thoughe fretted with the ruste yet beeing burnte in the fire shyneth brighter, and witte although it hath beene eaten with the canker of his own conceite, and fretted with the rust of vaine love, yet beeinge purified in the stille of wisedome, and tryed in the fire of zeale, will shine bright and smell sweete in the nosethrilles of all young nouises.

ANALYSED RHYME. This is elaboration of rhyme which must be analysed to be appreciated. Babette Deutsch, in *Poetry Handbook*, indicates the complexity of a quatrain by W. H. Auden exhibiting analysed rhyme:

> That night when joy began
> Our narrowest veins to flush,
> We waited for the flash
> Of morning's levelled gun.

Here the vowels of the end-rhymes in the first and third lines are identical, as are those in the second and fourth lines; while the consonants of the end-rhymes in the first and fourth lines are identical, as are those in the second and third lines.

In this quatrain, the rhyming vowels are 'beg*a*n : fl*a*sh' and 'fl*u*sh : g*u*n'. The rhyming consonants are 'bega*n* : gu*n*' and 'flu*sh* : fla*sh*'.

ANALYSIS. Greek *análusis, analúein,* to unloose; *aná,* up, *lúein,* to loose. A resolving or separating a work of art into its component parts. For example, the total meaning of a poem consists of thought, feeling, attitude, and intention. It is conveyed by the words and their arrangement. It is only by a close analysis of all the qualities of the words (meaning, sound, associations), and also of the ordering of the rhythm, that the poem can be understood, and its value estimated.

ANAPAEST. Latin *anapaestus,* from Greek *anápaistos,* struck back, rebounding. A metrical foot consisting of two short syllables followed by a long syllable.

Byron's *Destruction of Sennacherib* is a well-known poem in anapaestic tetrameters:

The Assŷr|ian came down | like the wolf | on the fold.

ANAPHORA. Greek from *aná,* back, and *phérein,* to bear. The repetition of words or phrases at the beginning of successive verses or clauses.

> And she forgot the stars, the moon, and sun,
> And she forgot the blue above the trees,
> And she forgot the dells where waters run,
> And she forgot the chilly autumn breeze;
> She had no knowledge when the day was done,
> And the new morn she saw not.
>
> Keats, *Isabella*

ANASTROPHE. Greek *anastrophé*, turning backwards, reversal. The inversion, for effect, of the normal order of words, the normal order being the preposition before the noun, the object after the verb.

> The eagle flew the cloud above.
>
> Long time the manxome foe he sought.

ANECDOTE. Greek *anékdota*, things unpublished. A brief account of a striking incident. Details of history hitherto unpublished.

ANDY CAPP. Reg Smythe's popular cartoon in the *Daily Mirror* of a hero of our times, for Andy Capp never intends to do a day's work in his life, and gets away with it. In *Drawing for Illustration*, Lynton Lamb says:

> Such cartoons are a daily experience of social conditions at first hand. We are not asked to see ourselves as others see us, but to see others as they see themselves.

ANGRY YOUNG MAN. This phrase was originally the title of an autobiography published by Leslie Paul in 1951. The best-known example is perhaps Jimmy Porter, the 'anti-hero' of John Osborne's play *Look Back in Anger* (1956). The author shows his hatred of outworn social and political attitudes, and strong reaction against 'bourgeois' values.

ANGST. German. Anxiety, anguish. The anxiety-neurosis of the years following the Second World War expressed in the works of such writers as Jean-Paul Sartre and Albert Camus.

ANIMADVERSION. Latin *animadvertĕre*, for *animum advertĕre*, to turn the mind to. Criticism; censure.

ANNALS. Latin *annālēs (librī)*, yearly (books); *annus*, a year. A narrative of events written year by year. Historical records generally. Annals are less extensive in use of material than chronicles. The *Annales* of Tacitus and *Annales Gentium* of Calpurnius Piso are famous examples.

ANNOTATION. Latin *annotāre*; *ad*, to, *notāre*, *-ātum*, to mark. The action of adding notes to a work or author, by way of explanation or comment. An annotated edition is one printed with comments by the author or an editor.

ANONYM. Greek *anónumos*, unnamed. A person who remains nameless. A pseudonym.

ANONYMOUS. Greek *anónumos*, nameless; *an-*, not, *ónoma*, name. Of unknown name; of unknown authorship. Generally abbreviated to *anon*.

ANONYMUNCULE. Latin *homunculus*, a little man. A petty anonymous writer. Charles Reade was said to be 'awfully hard on the criticasters and anonymuncules of the press'.

ANOPISTHOGRAPHIC. A term applied to the earliest printed block-books. These were printed on one side of the leaf only, and then consecutive leaves were pasted back to back.

ANTAGONIST. Greek *antagōnistés*, a rival; *antí*, against, *agón*, a contest. One who strives against another. The term is used for the main character opposing the hero or protagonist in drama. Iago is the antagonist in *Othello*.

ANTE-MASQUE. *See* ANTI-MASQUE.

ANTEPENULT. Latin *antepaenultima*; *paene*, almost, *ultima*, last. The last but two, originally and usually of syllables. In the word 'astronomical', *nom* is the antepenult.

ANTHOLOGY. Greek *anthologia*, a flower-gathering, a collection of choice poems; *ánthos*, flower, and *logía*, collection, from *légō*, I gather. The ancient Greek anthologies were collections of Greek epigrams. The modern 'Greek Anthology' consists of the 'Palatine Anthology', and contains over six thousand short poems composed over seventeen centuries. Anthology is now any collection of choice pieces of poetry or prose.

ANTICLIMAX. Greek *antí*, against, the reverse of, and *klímax*, a ladder, from *klínein*, to slope. The arrangements of words or phrases in descending order of importance; a sudden descent from the sublime to the ridiculous.

> I feasted like a king, like four kings, like a boy in the fourth form.   Kinglake, *Eōthen*

When an anticlimax is unintentional it is also called *bathos*. Here is an example in Tennyson's *Enoch Arden*:

> So passed the strong heroic soul away.
> And when they buried him the little port
> Had seldom seen a costlier funeral.

ANTIC MASQUE. *See* ANTI-MASQUE.

ANTI-HERO.   In *Tradition and Dream*, Walter Allen speaks of this
term:

> The anti-hero is indeed the other face of the hero. . . . He is
> consciously, even conscientiously, graceless. . . . One may
> speculate whence he derives.   The Services, certainly,
> helped to make him; but George Orwell, Dr. Leavis and the
> Logical Positivists — or, rather, the attitudes these represent
> — all contributed to his genesis.

In fiction he arrived as Charles Lumley, the central character of
John Wain's novel *Hurry on Down* (1953).   He turns up again as
Jim Dixon in Kingsley Amis's *Lucky Jim* (1954).

ANTI-MASQUE.   In *The Oxford Companion to the Theatre*, Phyllis
Hartnoll says:

> One of Ben Jonson's innovations was the anti-masque, which
> he first employed in 1609.   It introduced a grotesque
> element in contrast to the masque proper, as Hell before
> Heaven, Shipwreck before Peace, and was also known as the
> false masque.   The form ante-masque is also found, pre-
> sumably in reference to the fact that it preceded the main
> masque.   It was not entirely new, since the earlier masques
> made use of grotesque elements in dancing, known as the
> antic, whence the suggestion that Jonson's innovation
> should properly be known as the antic masque.   Whatever
> its origin, Jonson seems to have been the first to name it and
> make conscious use of it.

ANTIPHON.   Greek *antiphōna*, things sounding in response;
phōnḗ, vocal sound.   The verse of a psalm, or other traditional
passage, intoned or sung by alternating choirs during Divine
Office, before and after the psalm or canticle in the Roman Catholic
Church.

ANTISTROPHE.   Greek *antistrophḗ*, a turning back, counter-turn;
anti, against, *strophḗ*, a turning, twisting.   In ancient Greek drama,
the part of a Greek chorus chanted on returning from left to right
in reply to the strophe previously chanted when moving from right
to left.   This reply reproduces exactly the metre of the strophe.

ANTITHESIS.   Greek *anti*, against, *tithénai*, to place, to set against.
The choice or arrangement of words to emphasize the contrast and
give the effect of balance.   For example:

> Fools rush in where angels fear to tread.

Crafty men contemn studies; simple men admire
them; and wise men use them.

Francis Bacon, Of Studies

ANTITHETICAL PARALLELISM.   Greek *anti*, against, *tithénai*,
to place; *parállēlos*, beside one another.   A couplet in which the
idea expressed in the second line is in contrast with that in the first:

> Every good tree bringeth forth good fruit,
> But the corrupt tree bringeth forth evil fruit.

ANTONOMASIA.   Greek *antonomázein*, to name instead, to call by
a new name; from *anti*, against, and *ónoma*, name.   A figure of
speech in which a proper name is used to express a general idea.
An example occurs in Gray's *Elegy*:

> Some mute inglorious Milton here may rest,
> Some Cromwell guiltless of his country's blood.

'Milton' has stronger associations than the word 'poet', and
'Cromwell' than the word 'tyrant'.

Antonomasia is also the substitution of an epithet or descriptive
phrase for a proper name.   For example:

> *the Iron Duke* for Wellington
> *the little Corporal* for Napoleon.

ANTONYM.   Greek *anti*, against, *ónoma*, a name.   A word of
opposite meaning to another, as *light* to *heavy*, *bad* to *good*.

AORIST.   Greek *aóristos*, indefinite, undefined.   One of the past
tenses of a verb, especially in Greek, expressing simple past time,
with none of the limitations of the other past tenses.

A PER SE.   The letter A when it stands by itself; hence the first,
most distinguished person or thing.

> The floure and A per se of Troie and Grece.

Henryson, Testament of Cresseid

APHAERESIS.   Greek *aphaíresis*, a taking away; *apó*, away, and
hairéein, to take.   The loss of a letter or syllable at the beginning of
a word.   For example, *adder*, Old English *nædre*, was originally
a nadder; *special* was *especial*, an *apron* was *a naperon*, and *cute* was
acute.   *See also* APHESIS.

APHESIS.   Greek, letting go, from *aphíēmi*; *apó*, away, and *híēmi*,
send.   The gradual and unintentional loss of the unstressed vowel
at the beginning of a word, as in *squire* from *esquire*.

APHORISM.   Greek *aphorízein*, to mark off by boundaries; *apó*, from, and *hóros*, a limit.   A concise and pithy observation or statement of a truth or doctrine.   The term was first used by Hippocrates, who called his series of precepts *Aphorisms*.   One of these, 'Ars longa, vita brevis', was translated by Chaucer:

> The life so short, the craft so long to learn.

In a speech on 19th May 1856, Abraham Lincoln said:

> The ballot is stronger than the bullet.

Oscar Wilde in *The Importance of Being Earnest* says:

> Truth is never pure, and rarely simple.

Or to take a contemporary example, culled from a newspaper:

> Gossip is the art of saying very little in a way that leaves very little unsaid.

Finally:

> An aphorism is a witty, wise, and true remark which one can never remember at the moment when it would be most advantageous to repeat it.   Alan Brien

APOCALYPSE.   Greek *apokálupsis*, unveiling, from *kalúptein*, to cover.   The last book of the New Testament containing the revelation made to St. John on the island of Patmos.   Any revelation or disclosure of the future.

APOCALYPTIC.   Greek *apokálupsis*, unveiling, from *kalúptein*, to cover.   The word means 'connected with revelation'.

APOCOPATED RHYME.   Greek *apokóptein*, to cut off.   To cut off the end of one rhyming word.   This device is used in modern verse. It was also a feature of early ballads:

> Fly around, my pretty little Miss,
> Fly around, I say,
> Fly around, my pretty little Miss,
> You'll drive me almost crazy.

APOCOPE.   Greek, from *apokóptein*, to cut off.   The loss of a final letter or syllable or more.   H. W. Fowler gives as examples *my*, *curio*, *cinema*, which were formerly *mine*, *curiosity*, *cinematograph*.

APOCRYPHA.   Greek *apókruphos*, hidden away; *apo-*, from, *krúptein*, to hide.   Writings of uncertain or unknown authorship. Fourteen books in the Greek version of the Old Testament, but not in the Hebrew Bible, contained in the Septuagint were not regarded as part of the Canon.   There is also a New Testament Apocrypha, much less well known than that of the Old Testament. Writings doubtfully attributed to certain authors, Chaucer and Shakespeare, are called *apocryphal*. The adjective *apocryphal* is also used of stories and anecdotes about, or attributed to, a particular person, though probably not genuine. The adjective applied to the authenticated work of any author is *canonical*.

APODOSIS. Greek *apodidōmi*, give back. The concluding clause of a sentence. Now, the consequent clause, expressing the result, in a conditional sentence, as:

> If your opponent is wounded, revive him.

APOLLONIAN and DIONYSIAN. In *The Birth of Tragedy* (1872), Friedrich Nietzsche used these terms to show contrasting elements in ancient Greek tragedy. Apollo, the god of light and youth, stood for reason, culture, and moral excellence. Dionysus, the god of wine, represented the irrational, the frenzied, the undisciplined. Greek drama grew out of the dithyrambic choruses at the festival of Dionysus and the Apollonian dialogue. Dionysian has been associated with romanticism, and Apollonian with classicism.

APOLOGUE. Greek *apólogos*, fable; *apó*, from, and *lógos*, speech. A short allegorical tale intended to convey a moral; especially a tale in which the characters are animals or inanimate things. In Judges ix. there is an example, the story of the trees trying to choose a king:

> The trees went forth on a time to anoint a king over them; and they said unto the olive tree, Reign thou over us. But the olive tree said unto them, Should I leave my fatness, wherewith by me they honour God and man, and go to wave to and fro over the trees? And the trees said to the fig tree, Come thou, and reign over us. But the fig tree said unto them, Should I leave my sweetness, and my good fruit, and go to wave to and fro over the trees?

APOLOGY. Greek *apologia*, defence; *apó*, away, *logia*, speaking. A work written to defend or justify the writer's ideas or beliefs. In his *Apology*, Plato sets before us Socrates defending himself at his trial in a series of questions and answers. In *Apologie for Poetrie* (1580), Sir Philip Sidney makes a methodical examination of the art of poetry. In the eighteenth century *apology* came to be used loosely almost as a synonym for autobiography, without any suggestion of justifying or defending the writer's ideas or conduct. In 1740, Cibber published an autobiography entitled *Apology for the life of Mr. Colley Cibber, Comedian.* In 1864, appeared Newman's *Apologia pro Vita Sua* in answer to Charles Kingsley.

APOPHTHEGM.   Greek *apophthéggomai*, speak out plainly.   A terse, pithy saying.   More terse than an *aphorism* need be.   Francis Bacon wrote *Apophthegms New and Old*, and in the collection attributed these to Elizabeth I:

> Anger makes dull men witty, but it keeps them poor.
>
> Hope is a good breakfast, but it is a bad supper.

APOSIOPESIS.   Greek *aposiópēsis*, from *aposiōpáō*, I am silent; *siōpé*, silence.   A rhetorical device which consists in a sudden breaking off in speech leaving the sentence unfinished.   In *The Tatler*, Richard Steele gives this description of the death of two lovers in a fire:

> He catches her in his arms.   The fire surrounds them while —
>   I cannot go on.

Sometimes, beginning with an apostrophe, a following sentence completes the sense; or to express another urgent thought.

> *Hamlet:* A little month, or ere those shoes were old
>   With which she follow'd my poor father's body,
>   Like Niobe, all tears: — why she, even she, —
>   O God! a beast that wants discourse of reason
>   Would have mourn'd longer.

> Had ye been there — for what could that have done?
>
>   Milton, *Lycidas*

APOSTROPHE.   Greek *apostrophé*, a turning away.   A figure in rhetoric in which the orator turned away from the rest of the audience to address one person.   It is also an exclamatory address to some person or thing, absent or present, usually breaking the thread of speech.

> And couched her head upon her breast,
> And looked askance at Christabel —
> *Jesu, Maria, shield her well!*

APPENDIX.   Latin *appendix*, *-icis*, *appendēre*, hang to.   A supplement, subsidiary addition, usually bound as part of the book.   It follows the last chapter and precedes the index.

APPROXIMATE RHYME.   *See* NEAR RHYME.

APRON STAGE.   A term applied to that part of the stage which projects beyond the proscenium arch.   This Elizabethan platform stage served the purpose of an unlocalized 'platea', or place, and Shakespeare designed his plays for such a stage.

AQUATINT. Latin *aqua tincta*, dyed water; *tingĕre*, dye. A method of engraving on copper by use of a resinous solution and nitric acid. An aquatint resembles a drawing in water-colours, sepia, or Indian ink.

ARABESQUE. French *arabesque*, Arabian. A style of decoration derived from the Moors and Arabs, exhibiting fantastic patterns of lines, leaves, fruit or flowers (or an abstract from them).

ARABIC NUMERALS. Those commonly used for the text (1, 2, 3 . . .) as distinct from *roman* numerals composed of letters (i, ii, v, x . . .) used for prelims.

ARCADIA. Greek *Arkadía*, a mountainous district in the Peloponnese taken as an ideal rustic paradise. In pastoral verse, Arcadia is the home of shepherds and shepherdesses living in simple innocence. In *Eclogues*, Virgil, in the words *Arcadēs ambo*, 'Arcadians both', refers to Corydon and Thyrsis, young shepherds and poets. In 1504, Sannazzaro published *Arcadia*, a series of verse eclogues, which connected the pastorals of Theocritus and Virgil and those of Philip Sidney, Spenser and other Renaissance writers.

ARCHAISM. Greek *arkhaîos*, ancient. The use of an old or obsolete word, idiom or form in speech or in literary style. *Albeit, trow, wreak, yclept* are words once in common use, now archaic.

Coleridge uses many archaisms in *The Rime of the Ancient Mariner*:

> He holds him with his skinny hand,
> 'There was a ship,' quoth he.
> 'Hold off! unhand me, grey-beard loon!'
> Eftsoons his hand dropt he.

ARCHETYPE. Greek *archétupon*, pattern, model. The original pattern from which copies are made; a prototype. In his *Contributions to Analytical Psychology*, Jung, the psychologist, makes a distinction between collective consciousness (the acceptable dogmas and 'isms' of religion, race, and class), and those predetermined patterns or archetypes in the collective unconscious. These archetypes are inherited in the human mind from the typical experiences of our ancestors — birth, death, love, family life, struggle.

These experiences, to give unity to a diversity of effects, are expressed in myths, dreams, literature. Writers use archetypal themes, and archetypal images. In *The Form of Things Unknown*, Herbert Read refers to Vaughan's *Silex Scintillans* and Herbert's *Peace* and says:

> In these two related poems we have at least three archetypal images: The unwithering flower; the Rose or Crown Imperial; the Wise Old Man; and the transubstantiating bread, made from wheat which springs from the grave of the Prince of Peace.

See Maud Bodkin's *Archetypal Patterns in Poetry*.

ARCHIVE. Greek *arkheîon*, public building, residence of the chief magistrate. The place where public records or historical documents are kept. Also the records and documents stored there. Dating from the eighteenth century, archive is also a title-word for scientific or academic periodicals.

ARGOT. French, of unknown origin. Jargon, slang, originally that of thieves and vagabonds.

ARGUMENT. Latin *argūtāre*, frequentative of *arguĕre*, to prove. The summary of the subject-matter of a book. A brief outline of the plot of a literary work or of each part of it. Each book of Milton's *Paradise Lost* begins with an Argument in prose. The first one opens with these words:

> This first Book proposes first in brief the whole Subject, Man's disobedience, and the loss thereupon of Paradise wherein he was plac't: Then touches the prime cause of his fall, the Serpent, or rather Satan in the Serpent; who revolting from God, and drawing to his side many legions of Angels, was by command of God driven out of Heaven with all his Crew into the great Deep.

ARLECCHINO. *See* PANTOMIME.

ARMARIAN. Latin *armārium*, chest, safe, bookcase. In the Middle Ages the term referred to a library, particularly in a monastery, then to the monk responsible for the care of the books in the monastery library.

ARSIS. Greek *ársis*, raising, lifting. The unstressed part of a metrical foot in Greek and Latin prosody. In English prosody it is the stressed syllable.

ARTEFACT: ARTIFACT. Latin *ars, artis*, art, *facĕre, factum*, to make. A product of human workmanship; deliberately transforming materials already existing. The term is used frequently in archaeology to distinguish flint implements made by man from flints shaped by nature.

ART FOR ART'S SAKE. *See* AESTHETIC MOVEMENT.

ARTICLE. Latin *articulus*, a little joint; *artus*, a joint. A particular material object considered as separate from others of the same class. A separate portion or clause of a document setting forth a distinct point; for example, *The Thirty-nine Articles* in the Book of Common Prayer. A literary composition dealing with a particular topic, included in a newspaper, periodical, encyclopaedia, but self-contained and independent.

ASIDE. Old English *on*, and *sīde*. Words spoken in an undertone. In a theatrical production, words spoken by an actor which the other persons on the stage are supposed not to hear. This device was freely used in melodrama towards the end of the nineteenth century.

ASSIMILATION. Latin *assimilāre*, to liken. The action of making or becoming like or similar. The word is used in grammar to mean the changing of one letter into another identical or near in sound. Fowler gives these examples: 'as when the *d* of godsibb (related to God) becomes *s* in gossip, or when the dental of *in* (not) becomes the labial *m* before the labial *p* in *impius*, impious'.

ASSOCIATION. Latin *associāre*; *socius*, sharing, allied. The mental connexion between an object and ideas. In *Biographia Literaria*, Coleridge says:

> The general law of association, or more accurately the common condition under which all exciting causes act, and in which they may be generalized, according to Aristotle is this: Ideas by having been together acquire a power of recalling each other; or every partial representation awakes the total representation of which it had been a part.

Metaphors, similes, allusions, analogies, references are all used by poets to evoke association.

Falstaff says to Bardolph in *1 Henry IV*:

> I never see thy face but I think upon hell-fire, and Dives that lived in purple; for there he is in his robes, burning, burning. If thou wert any way given to virtue, I would swear by thy face: my oath should be 'By this fire, that's God's angel'.

ASSONANCE. Latin *assonāre*, to sound, to respond to; *ad*, to, *sonāre*, to sound. Correspondence in sound between two words as regards the stressed vowels but different consonants, or the same consonant sound but different vowels, thus forming an imperfect rhyme. An example of the first is *fate, take*; an example of the second is *stone, stain*.

Assonance is a common method of producing a musical effect in poetry. Keats uses it in his *Ode to Autumn*:

> Who hath not seen thee oft amid thy store?
>   Sometimes whoever seeks abroad may find
> Thee sitting careless on a granary floor,
>   Thy hair soft-lifted by the winnowing wind;
> Or on a half-reap'd furrow sound asleep,
>   Drows'd with the fume of poppies . . .

ASTERISK. Greek *asterískos*, diminutive of *astér*, a star. A figure of a star (*) used in printing and writing as a sign of reference to a footnote, or to indicate an omission or a defect in the manuscript.

ASYNDETON. Greek *asúndetos*, *-on*, unconnected; *a-*, not, *sún*, together, *déō*, I bind. A figure of speech in which conjunctions are omitted. The second line of this passage from *Hamlet* is an example:

> O, what a noble mind is here o'erthrown ·
> The courtier's, soldier's, scholar's, eye, tongue, sword;
> The expectancy and rose of the fair state,
> The glass of fashion and the mould of form,
> The observed of all observers, quite, quite down!

Also the absence of syntactical sequence in the construction of a sentence.

ATMOSPHERE. The general mood of a literary work. Atmosphere is presented by the setting, time, conditions under which the characters live. In *Macbeth*, the first appearance of the three witches establishes an atmosphere of danger and the foreboding of the supernatural, which runs through the play.

ATMOSPHERE OF THE MIND. Henry James invented this phrase, which is explained by Leon Edel in *The Psychological Novel*, 'Subjective-novel writers are trying to capture for the reader the atmosphere of the mind'. He then goes on to describe it in terms of the stream of consciousness.

ATTIC SALT. Latin *sal Atticus*, wit of Attica, or of its capital Athens. Refined, delicate, poignant wit.

In Sterne's *Tristram Shandy*, Mr. Shandy reprimands a servant with a witty retort and then:

> Triumph swam in my father's eyes at the repartee; the Attic salt brought tears into them; — and so Obadiah heard no more about them.

ATTITUDE. Latin from *aptus*, fit. The attitude of a writer to his subject determines the particular tone of his work: he may be melancholy, satirical, optimistic or enraged. In regard to certain forms of poetry, tone has been defined as 'the manner of reading compelled upon one'.

AUBADE. French *aube*, dawn, with suffix *-ade* as in serenade, morning song; literally, song to be sung at dawn. It is called an *alba* in troubadour verse of Provence, and *Tagelied* in German. One famous example occurs in *Cymbeline*:

> Hark, hark! the lark at heaven's gate sings,
> And Phoebus 'gins arise,
> His steeds to water at those springs
> On chalic'd flow'rs that lies;
> And winking Mary-buds begin
> To ope their golden eyes.
> With everything that pretty bin,
> My lady sweet, arise;
> Arise, arise!

The aubade is also a song sung in despair by departing lovers at dawn. It may be spoken, as in *Romeo and Juliet*, when the lovers must part upon their wedding night:

> *Juliet:* Wilt thou be gone? it is not yet near day:
> It was the nightingale and not the lark,
> That pierc'd the fearful hollow of thine ear.
> Nightly she sings on yon pomegranate tree:
> Believe me, love, it was the nightingale.
> *Romeo:* It was the lark, the herald of the morn,
> No nightingale: look, love, what envious streaks
> Do lace the severing clouds in yonder east:
> Night's candles are burnt out, and jocund day
> Stands tiptoe on the misty mountain tops.

AUDIENCE. Latin *audientia*, a hearing, audience; *audīre*, to hear The act of hearing. An assembly of listeners, and of readers. In *Paradise Lost*, Milton proclaims of his audience:

> Standing on earth, not rapt above the Pole,
> More safe I sing with mortal voice, unchang'd
> To hoarse or mute, though fall'n on evil days,

B

> On evil days though fall'n and evil tongues.
> In darkness, and with dangers compass'd round,
> And solitude; yet not alone, while thou
> Visit'st my slumbers nightly or when morn
> Purples the east: still govern thou my song,
> Urania, and fit audience find, though few.

Coleridge echoes this when he says:

> A poem is not necessarily obscure because it does not aim to
> be popular. It is enough if a work be perspicuous to those
> for whom it is written and
> > Fit audience find, though few.

AUDITORIUM. Latin *audiō*, hear. The part of a building in which the audience sit to hear speeches, lectures; the same part in a theatre or concert hall.

AUFKLÄRUNG. German, literally, enlightenment. The great revival of art and letters, and the liberation of the human spirit brought by the Renaissance in the fourteenth century and continued during the fifteenth and sixteenth centuries.

In Germany, the principal figures of the Aufklärung, during the eighteenth century, are Leibniz, the philosopher and mathematician, Kant, the founder of modern thought, and Lessing, the leading representative of the intellectual ideals of the movement. Lessing also stands at the end of their domination.

AUGUSTAN AGE. A great classical period in the literary life of any nation. It is named after the emperor Augustus (27 B.C. – A.D. 14), in whose reign Virgil, Horace, Ovid, Tibullus were famous. In England, the term is applied to the period of Pope and Addison, extended sometimes to bring in Dryden at the beginning and Johnson towards the end. Some writers limit the period to the reign of Queen Anne.

In 1774, Horace Walpole wrote hopefully to Horace Mann:

> The next Augustan age will dawn on the other side of the
> Atlantic. There will, perhaps, be a Thucydides at Boston,
> a Xenophon at New York, and, in time, a Virgil at Mexico,
> and a Newton at Peru.

AUNT EDNA. Aunt Edna first appeared in a preface by Terence Rattigan. In *Tynan on Theatre*, Kenneth Tynan tells us about her:

> I understand, though I cannot applaud, Rattigan's allegiance to
> a mythical, middle-class admirer called 'Aunt Edna', whom
> he holds to be the backbone of the theatre . . . she follows,
> never leads, intelligent taste.

AUTHORIZED VERSION. The Authorized Version of the English Bible was not authorized by any official pronouncement. It arose out of a conference convened by James I at Hampton Court in 1604 between the High Church and Low Church parties. On agreement, forty-seven scholars undertook the work of revision and retranslation, and the 'Authorized Version' appeared in 1611. It is in many ways the version of William Tyndale, who was the first to translate the New Testament into English from the Greek text (1525).

AUTOBIOGRAPHY. Greek *autobiographía*; *autós*, self, *bíos*, life, *gráphein*, to write. The art and practice of writing a continuous narrative of one's own life. Other personal records are diaries' journals, confessions, memoirs, letters. These, however, lack continuity and are written for private purposes. Of autobiography, Montaigne says: 'There is no description equal in difficulty to a description of oneself, and certainly none in profitableness'.

AVANT-GARDE. French, the vanguard or van of an army. In literature, this military metaphor is applied to new writing showing innovations in style and matter. 'The words suggest an attack by progressive elements on the bastions of some presumed-to-be-reactionary Establishment' (George MacBeth, *Radio Times*, 28th June 1965).

AXIOM. Greek *axíōma*, that which is thought fit and worthy. In philosophy and mathematics, a self-evident proposition which needs no proof or demonstration.

B

BABERY: BABEWYNNERY. Italian *babbuino*, baboon. The term used in the fourteenth century for illuminating with figures the margins of manuscripts. At that time, monkeys were popular in decorative art, hence the term.

BABU: BABOO. Hindi *bābū*. Originally used like the English *Mr.*, hence, a native Hindu gentleman, or a native official who speaks English.

BACKWARD RHYMES. *See* AMPHISBAENIC RHYMES.

BALANCED SENTENCE. A sentence in which one part corresponds to another in the form of its phrases and clauses and the position of its words. This example is from Johnson's *Thoughts on the late Transactions respecting Falkland's Islands*:

> By incommodious encampments and unwholesome stations, where courage is useless, and enterprise impracticable, fleets are silently dispeopled, and armies sluggishly melted away.

BALANCING OF SOUNDS. It has been said that the balancing of sounds and silences follows a more elastic system than conventional scansion admits. George Gascoigne recognized this when he wrote that though Chaucer's lines

> ... are not always of one selfe same number of Syllables, yet, beyng redde by one that hath understanding, the longest verse, and that which hath most Syllables in it, will fall (to the eare) correspondent unto that whiche hath fewest sillables in it: and like wise that whiche hath in it fewest syllables shalbe founde yet to consist of woordes that have suche naturall sounde, as may seeme equall in length to a verse which hath many moe sillables of lighter accentes.

BALLAD. Old French *ballade*, from Provençal *ballada*, from Low Latin *ballāre*, to dance. Originally a song accompanied by a dance. Later the name was applied to a narrative poem. This was anonymous, of folk origin, sung to their own accompaniment by the minstrels. Ballads, passed down by word of mouth, were direct and simple, with romantic, historical, or supernatural setting. Of these true medieval ballads, well-known examples are *Chevy Chase, Sir Patrick Spens, Clerk Saunders*.

In 1765, Bishop Percy published many old ballads in his *Reliques of Ancient Poetry*. Sir Walter Scott collected the Border ballads. Scott imitated the ballad form and produced *Lochinvar*; Coleridge showed his knowledge of the ballad in *The Rime of the Ancient Mariner*.

Other notable examples are Kipling's *Barrack-room Ballads*, Masefield's *Salt-water Ballads*, and W. S. Gilbert's *Bab Ballads*.

The term *ballad* was used in the late nineteenth century for a type of simple, sentimental song dealing with everyday life.

BALLAD METRE. A four-line stanza with alternating four-stress and three-stress lines rhyming *a b c b*, or sometimes *a b a b*. A refrain is not unusual.

> She hadna sail'd a league, a league,
> A league but barely three,
> Till grim, grim grew his countenance
> And gurly grew the sea.
>
> *The Daemon Lover*

BALLAD OPERA. In *The Oxford Companion to the Theatre*, Alfred Loewenberg says:

> An entirely novel contribution to the musical stage was Gay's *Beggar's Opera* (1728), a play with music arranged by John Christopher Pepusch (1667–1752). This was the first and best example of the ballad opera, a play of popular and often topical character with spoken dialogue and a large number of songs fitted to existing tunes. After a few years of unbroken success the new genre disappeared as suddenly as it had sprung up; but traces of it remained in the English theatre, in plays which contained a good deal of compiled music, as, for example, Sheridan's *The Duenna* (1775).

BALLADE. This verse form, derived from Old French poetry, consists of three stanzas of eight or ten lines concluding with an envoy of four or five lines. There must be three (or four) rhymes only throughout, in the same order in each stanza, and with the same line ending each stanza and the envoy. The envoy was often addressed to an important person and forms an invocation or dedication.

The seven-lined decasyllabic stanza, rhymed *a b a b b c c*, called Rhyme Royal, first appeared in English in Chaucer's *Compleynte unto Pite*. Shakespeare used it in *Lucrece*.

The ballade form is exemplified in Austin Dobson's *Ballade to Queen Elizabeth*. Here are the first stanza and the envoy:

> King Philip had vaunted his claims;
> He had sworn for a year he would sack us;

With an army of heathenish names
He was coming to fagot and stack us;
Like the thieves of the sea he would track us,
And shatter our ships on the main;
But we had bold Neptune to back us,—
And where are the galleons of Spain?
Envoy
GLORIANA! — the Don may attack us
Whenever his stomach be fain;
He must reach us before he can rack us, . . .
And where are the galleons of Spain?

BARBARISM. Greek *barbarismós*, impropriety of speech, speaking like a foreigner. The unjustified use of foreign expressions which are not in keeping with the classical standard of a language. Johnson said in *The Rambler*:

I have laboured to refine our language to grammatical purity, and to clear it from colloquial barbarisms, licentious idioms, and irregular combinations.

BARD. Gaelic and Irish *bàrd, bardh*. A Celtic tribal singer, minstrel, poet, and chronicler. The word is still used for a recognized singer at the Welsh musical festival, Eisteddfod. Now it is a synonym for poet: Shakespeare, *the Bard of Avon*.

BAROQUE. A word adapted from the Italian *barocco*, Portuguese *barroco*, Spanish *barrueco*, meaning a rough or imperfect pearl. It is applied to the vigorous and well-balanced ornamental style of architecture that succeeded the style of the Renaissance. Baroque reached its culmination in France and Italy in the first part of the eighteenth century. In mass gives sense of boundless energy. A baroque literary style is exuberant, characterized by excess of ornament. For example:

In that sweet soil it seems a holy quire
Founded to th' name of great Apollo's lyre;
Whose silver roof rings with the sprightly notes
Of sweet-lipp'd angel-imps, that swill their throats
In cream of morning Helicon.

Richard Crashaw, *Music's Duel*

BARSETSHIRE NOVELS. These novels of Anthony Trollope, depicting life in a fictitious English county, are: *The Warden, Barchester Towers, Doctor Thorne, Framley Parsonage, The Small House at Allington*, and *The Last Chronicle of Barset*.

BAS BLEU. French. A blue-stocking, a literary woman.

BASIC ENGLISH. A language formulated by C. K. Ogden and I. A. Richards, set out in book form in 1930. Its select vocabulary consists of 850 words, of which 600 are nouns (400 general, 200 pictured), 150 adjectives, and 100 'operators' (verbs, adverbs, prepositions, conjunctions). 'A week or two with the rules and the special records gives complete knowledge of the system for reading and writing.'

BASTARD TITLE. Greek loan-word *bastázō*, I carry; (by extension) applied to all sorts of things which differ in some way from the standard type; not genuine. Here, an abbreviated or short title preceding the full title-page. Now usually called the *half-title*.

BATHOS. Greek, *báthos*, depth, height, from *bathús*, deep. The descent from the sublime to the ridiculous in writing or speech, generally more sudden than anticlimax. The term bathos was first used in this sense by Pope in his title *On Bathos, or Of the Art of Sinking in Poetry*, a witty effusion inspired by *On the Sublime* by the Greek critic, Longinus.

This example appears in Pope's *The Rape of the Lock*:

> Not louder shrieks to pitying heaven are cast,
> When husbands, or when lapdogs, breathe their last.

BEACH-LA-MAR. Corruption from Portuguese *bicho do mar* (bêche-de-mer), sea-slug. 'Pidgin' English used in the Western Pacific. A three-masted, screw-driven steamer with two funnels is described 'thlee piecee bamboo, two piecee puff-puff, walk-along-inside, no can see'. A piano is called 'a big fellow box, you fight him he shout out'.

BEAD-ROLL. Old English *ġe-bed*, *bēd*, prayer. A roll of parchment on which prayers were inscribed to honour the dead. From the ninth century onwards, whenever an abbot died, such rolls were sent from monastery to monastery and new prayers were added. *Bede-roll* and *obituary roll* are other names used.

> Dan Chaucer, well of English undefiled,
> On Fame's eternal bead-roll worthy to be filed.
>
> Spenser, *The Faerie Queene*

BEAST EPIC. In the Middle Ages, stories in which human beings are satirized as beasts, birds, and fishes. These stories have their origin in the fables of Aesop in Greece, and those of Phaedrus in Rome.

BEATNIK. Adding *-nik* (as in *Sputnik*) to *Beat*, the *Beat* Generation. Young people using unconventional dress, manners, and behaviour as a way of social protest. Jack Kerouac's *On the Road* (1957) speaks for 'the *Beat* Generation'. Other writers on the movement are Allen Ginsberg, Kenneth Rexroth, and Lawrence Kipton. Lady Caroline Freud describes the vocabulary of Beatniks as 'an abbreviated version of already abbreviated Jazz talk'.

BELLES-LETTRES. French, literally 'fine letters'. The term has been applied to polite or elegant literature. Its meaning is restricted to literary studies, essays and treatises, as distinct from technical and scientific works.

BESTIARY. Medieval Latin *bestiārium*, menagerie, from Latin *bēstia*, beast. A medieval moralizing treatise on beasts. In these books, animals became symbols, not only of moral qualities, but of religious doctrines. Thus the unicorn with its one horn symbolized Christ (the one Saviour), or the gospel (the one way of salvation).

BESTSELLER. Properly, a book that sells in large numbers, i.e. at least twenty thousand copies in a hardcover edition and sometimes up to a million or more. The author of such a book. In *Five Hundred Years of Printing*, S. H. Steinberg says:

> Next to the Bible the outstanding examples of 'steady-sellers' are Homer and Horace among the ancients, Dante's *Divina Commedia* and Thomas à Kempis's *Imitation of Christ* among medieval books, Shakespeare's plays and Cervantes's *Don Quixote* among the writers of the European baroque.

BEZONIAN: BESONIO. Italian *bisogno*, 'need, want; also, a fresh needy souldier' (Florio). French *besoin*, need. Spanish *bisoño*, a raw recruit, a needy rascal.

In *2 Henry IV*, Pistol says to Shallow:

> Under which king, Bezonian? speak or die.

BIBELOT. French *bibelot*, small curio or artistic trinket. Also, an unusually small book.

BIBLICAL CRITICISM. *See* HIGHER CRITICISM.

BIBLIOCLASM. Greek *biblíon*, little book, *klásma* from *kláein*, to break. The destruction of books or of the Bible to further religious or ideological aims.

BIBLIOCLAST. Greek *biblíon*, book, *klástēs* from *kláein*, to break. A destroyer of books.

BIBLIOGNOST.   Greek *biblíon*, book, and *gnóstēs*, one who knows.
'One knowing in title-pages and colophons . . . and all the minutiae
of a book.'   Isaac D'Israeli, *Curiosities of Literature*

BIBLIOGONY.   Greek *biblíon*, book, and *gonía*, generation.   The
production of books.

BIBLIOGRAPHY.   Greek   *bibliographía*,   book-writing;   *biblíon*,
book, and *gráphein*, to write.   The writing of books; the systematic
description and history of books, their authorship, printing,
publication, editions; a book containing such details; a list of the
books of a particular author, printer, or country, or of those dealing
with any particular theme; the literature of a subject.

BIBLIOLATRY.   Greek *biblíon*, book and *latreía*, worship.   The
worship of books or of a book.   The worship of the Bible, which
takes the form of an exaggerated attachment to the literal word of
Holy Writ.

BIBLIOMANCY.   Greek *biblíon*, book, and *manteía*, divination.
Divination by opening a Bible at random, and taking the first
verse or verses to meet the eye as a prophecy of future happenings.

BIBLIOMANIA.   Greek *biblíon*, book, and *maniá*, madness.   A
passion for collecting and possessing books.

BIBLIOPHILE.   Greek *biblíon*, book, and *phílo-(s)*, loving.   A lover
of books; a book-fancier.

BIBLIPHOBIA.   Greek *biblíon*, book, and *phóbos*, dread.   Dread of,
or aversion to, books.

BIBLIOPOLE.   Greek *bibliopólēs*, from *biblíon*, book, and *pólēs*,
seller, merchant, dealer.   A dealer in books; a bookseller.

BIBLIOTAPH.   French *bibliotaphe* from Greek *biblíon*, book, and
táphos, tomb.   One who buries books by keeping them under lock
and key.

BIBLIOTHECA.   Greek *bibliothḗkē*, bookcase, library; from *biblíon*,
book, and *thḗkē*, repository.   A collection of books, or treatises; a
library; a bibliographer's catalogue.

BIBLUS: BYBLUS.   Latin *biblus*, Greek *bíblos*, papyrus.   The
papyrus, a reed from which paper was made.   The inner bark of
that plant.

BILDUNGSROMAN. German *Bildung*, formation, *Roman*, novel.
Bildungsroman is a novel portraying a young person growing up.
Examples are Charlotte Brontë's *Jane Eyre, David Copperfield* by
Charles Dickens, and Samuel Butler's *The Way of All Flesh.*
  Erziehungsroman (Erziehung, education, upbringing) may be used
with the same meaning as *Bildungsroman.*

BIOGRAPHY.   Greek *biographia*; *bios*, way of life, *graphia*, account.
A written account of a person's life.   Of Boswell's *Life of Johnson*,
Lord Macaulay said:

> This is assuredly a great, a very great work.   Homer is not more
> decidedly the first of heroic poets, Shakespeare is not more
> decidedly the first of dramatists, Demosthenes is not more
> decidedly the first of orators, than Boswell is the first of
> biographers.

Carlyle declared, 'No great man lives in vain.   The history of the
world is but the biography of great men.'

BLACK LETTER.   A term used to describe a type with angular
outlines which superseded the lighter roman type in the twelfth
century.   It is also known as Gothic, Old English, Fraktur.   Hitler
made an attempt to revive it in Germany as being more truly
'German', but since 1945 it has been far less common.

BLANK VERSE.   French *blanc*, white;   sense of 'left white', requiring something to be filled in.   Verse without rhyme, especially
the iambic pentameter or unrhymed heroic.   This is the regular
measure of English dramatic and epic poetry.   Blank verse was first
used by the Earl of Surrey in his translation of Books II and III
of the *Aeneid*.   In 'The Verse', added to *Paradise Lost* in 1668,
Milton defends the use of unrhymed verse:

> The measure is *English* Heroic Verse without Rime, as that of
> *Homer* in *Greek*, and of *Virgil* in *Latin*;   Rime being no
> necessary Adjunct or true Ornament of Poem or good Verse,
> in longer Works especially, but the Invention of a barbarous
> Age, to set off wretched matter and lame Meeter.

Here are the opening lines of *Paradise Lost*:

> Of Mans First Disobedience, and the Fruit
> Of that Forbidden Tree, whose mortal taste
> Brought Death into the World, and all our woe,
> With loss of *Eden*, till one greater Man
> Restore us, and regain the blissful Seat,
> Sing Heav'nly Muse . . .

BLEED.   A book was said to bleed if the edges were cut down so as to injure the print.   *Bleed* now means to run an illustration to the very edge of a page, leaving no margin.   The block of such an illustration, usually a half-tone, is known as a 'bleeding block'.

BLIND TOOLING.   Ornaments impressed on the covers of a book, but without gilding.   Called, also, *antique*.

BLOCK-BOOKS.   Books printed on one side of the leaf only, from engraved blocks of wood.   This work was executed in Germany and Flanders early in the fifteenth century.

BLOOMSBURY GROUP.   Virginia Woolf was the centre of this group of writers, most of whom lived in Bloomsbury, a then residential district in the borough of Holborn, very near to central London.   Early members were Leonard Woolf, Lytton Strachey, Clive Bell, Roger Fry, Duncan Grant, Maynard Keynes, and E. M. Forster.   After the First World War the circle was widened to include Christopher Isherwood and David Garnett.   The group was influenced by the ideas expressed in G. E. Moore's *Principia Ethica*.

BLUEPRINT.   A white photographic print on blue sensitized paper, made from a photographic negative or from a drawing on transparent paper.   At one time it was submitted as a rough proof of an illustration before the block was available, though nowadays most printers supply a 'block pull' on ordinary white paper.

BLUE-STOCKING.   A woman having or affecting literary tastes; a female literary pedant.   The origin of the term is to be found in the evening parties held around 1750 in the house of Mrs. Elizabeth Montagu.   The substitute for card-playing was conversation with literary men.   One of these men, Benjamin Stillingfleet, wore blue worsted stockings instead of those of black silk.   In view of this, Admiral Boscawen dubbed the coterie the 'Blue Stocking Society'.

BLURB.   A publisher's glowing descriptive notice of a book, usually printed on the jacket or half-title.   The term has been attributed to an American author, Gelett Burgess, also remembered for *The Purple Cow*:

> I never saw a Purple Cow,
> I never hope to see one;
> But I can tell you, anyhow,
> I'd rather see than be one!

BOANERGES.   Greek *boanergés*, Hebrew *b'nē regesh*, sons of
thunder.   A violent preacher.   The name given by Jesus Christ to
James and John (Mark iii. 17), because they wanted to bring down
fire from heaven to destroy the surly Samaritans (Luke ix. 54).

BOASTING POEM.   A poem in which the hero boasts of his
success in battle.   *Beowulf*, an Old English narrative, includes a
number of these poems.

BOLD FACE.   Any type which has a heavy, black face, **like this.**
Some headings are set in bold face.

BOMBAST.   Greek, *bómbux*, silkworm, silk; Latin *bombyx*, silkworm, something made of silk, any fine fibre, cotton; Old French
bombace, cotton.   Originally, cotton or any soft material used for
padding to produce clothes in the fashion of the sixteenth century.
The term came to mean a high-flown unnatural style, rather inflated
and insincere.

BOOK-MAKING.   'Bookmaking means that the publisher sees a
need for a certain book, or reckons that a work on such-and-such
a subject will sell, or simply finds an attractive set of illustrations
that need wrapping up in some kind of text.   He does the thinking;
the highly professional author then writes the book required.   At
best this system can produce a really useful book, just as the best
type of editing can greatly improve a novel, and we can only be grate-
ful when it does.   But it can also result in worthless rubbish—often
commercially worthless too—and if the practice spreads it is bound
to damage the initiative and originality on which both creative
writing and scholarship depend !   (*The Times Literary Supplement*,
27th May 1965).

BORACHIO.   Spanish *borracho*, a large leather bottle made of pig-
skin; hence a drunkard.   In *Much Ado About Nothing*, Borachio
thus plays upon his own name:

> Stand thee close then under this penthouse, for it drizzles
>   rain; and I will, like a true drunkard, utter all to thee.

As drunkard, the word is used by Congreve, Middleton, and
others.

BO-TREE.   The distortion, through Sinhalese, of Pali *bodhitaru*, the
perfect-knowledge tree.   The sacred tree of the Buddhists, under
which Gautama, the founder of Buddhism, meditated.

BOURGEOIS DRAMA. French *bourgeois,* citizen. A term describing realistic drama today, which presents aspects of middle-class life.

BOUSTROPHEDON. Greek from *boûs,* ox and *stroph-, stréphein,* to turn; as an ox turns in ploughing. An expression used to describe the early Greek way of writing, the first line written from left to right, the second from right to left and so on alternately.

BOUTS RIMÉS. French, rhymed ends. A set of rhyming words unattached to verses. From the eighteenth century this has been a form of verse-making, in which rhyming words are given from which impromptu verses are made.

In the *Spectator,* Addison says:

> The bouts-rimez were the favourites of the French nation for a whole age together. . . . They were a List of Words that rhyme to one another, drawn up by another Hand, and given to a Poet, who was to make a poem to the Rhymes in the same Order that they were placed upon the list.

BOWDLERIZE. From the name of Dr. Thomas Bowdler who published in 1818 an edition of Shakespeare intended for family reading. He expurgated everything which he considered indelicate or profane. The term now means to expurgate a text without very sound judgment.

BRACHYLOGY. Greek *brachylogía,* short speech. A condensed expression after the manner of the *Laconians* or Spartans. Concise, brief, laconic.

BRAGGADOCIO. Middle English *brag(g)en,* boast, sound loudly (of voice); from *brag,* with Italian suffix, vain, noisy, boasting. In *The Faerie Queene,* Spenser creates Braggadochio, the typical braggart, who speaks these words:

> When Braggadochio saide; 'Once I did sweare,
> When with one sword seven knightes I brought to end,
> Thenceforth in battaile never sword to beare,
> But it were that which noblest knight on earth doth weare.'

BRAILLE. Louis Braille of Paris developed an embossed-dot system which could easily be written with a simple instrument, and first published his type in 1829. This was used to print books for the blind, and some years later the Braille alphabet became one of the most widely used for the blind in the world.

BREVIARY. Latin *breviārium*, summary, from *brevis*, short. A book used by priests in the Roman Catholic Church, containing Divine Office for each day.

> It properly contains: Calendar; Psalter; Proprium de Tempore (collects and lessons); Proprium de Sanctis (collects for Saints' Days); Hours of the Virgin, burial services, i.e. Small Offices. It does not contain the Communion Service of Mass.
>
> G. A. Glaister, *Glossary of the Book*

BROADSIDE. A sheet of paper consisting of a single page printed on one side only; especially a popular ballad or tract so printed and sold in the streets. Also a 'vehicle for political agitation'.

Broadsides are also known as *broadsheets, single sheets, street-* or *stall-ballads*.

BROCHURE. French *brocher*, to stitch. A pamphlet or other short work which has its pages stitched, not bound. Now, usually a small pamphlet or tract irrespective of how it is bound.

BROKEN RHYME. This term is, in a way, a misnomer. A word is broken to produce the rhyme, as in *The Windhover* by Gerard Manley Hopkins.

> I caught this morning morning's minion, king-
>   dom of daylight's dauphin, dapple-dawn-drawn
>   Falcon, in his riding
> Of the rolling level underneath him steady air,
>   and striding
> High there, how he rung upon the rein of a wimpling wing
> In his ecstasy! then off, off forth on swing.

Hopkins did this to compel his verse to be read, as he wished, 'with the ears'.

BUCOLIC. Greek *boukolikós*; *boukólos*, a herdsman. Connected with herdsmen and shepherds; rustic, countrified. Virgil's pastoral poems are known as *Bucolics*; they deal with country life. Pope addressed John Gay as a 'divine bucoliast' in a letter dated 4th May 1714.

BULL. German dialect *bulle*; Anglo-Saxon *bulluc*. *John Bull* as the typical Englishman dates from John Arbuthnot's satirical pamphlet (1712) which was called 'Law is a Bottomless Pit, exemplified in the case of the Lord Strutt, John Bull, Nicholas Frog, and Lewis Baboon, who spent all they had in a Law-Suit'. The collection of his pamphlets was known as *History of John Bull*. Also (often *Irish* bull, origin unknown), an expression containing a ludicrous inconsistency unnoticed by the speaker. For example: This is the entrance out. *See* Maria and Richard Edgeworth's *Essay on Irish Bulls* (1802).

BUNKUM: BUNCOME. Empty clap-trap oratory, from *Buncombe*, the name of a county in North Carolina, U.S.A. The use of the word originated near the close of the debate on the 'Missouri Question' in the 16th Congress, when the member for this district rose to speak, and persevered in spite of impatient calls for the 'Question', declaring he was bound to *make a speech for Buncombe*.
(*Oxford English Dictionary*)

BURDEN: BOURDON. Late Latin *burdo*, drone bee, probably imitative of humming, buzzing; French *bourdon*, drone bee, base stop in an organ. The refrain or chorus of a song coming at the end of each verse, from Romanic *bourdon*, the 'drone' of a bagpipe.

BURLESQUE. French from Italian *burlesco* from *burla*, jest, mockery, ridicule. A burlesque is an imitation of a literary work designed to ridicule the speech, action, ideas. It presents ludicrous imitation, caricatured reproduction, parody, handling a lofty subject in a trivial way or a low subject with mock-heroic dignity.

The Knight of the Burning Pestle by Beaumont and Fletcher, printed in 1613, is at once a burlesque of knight-errantry and of Thomas Heywood's *The Four Prentices of London*.

The Rehearsal by George Villiers, Duke of Buckingham, 1672, is a burlesque of the heroic tragedies of the day.

Samuel Butler's *Hudibras* (1663–1678) is a burlesque of the hypocrisy and self-seeking of the Presbyterians and Independents.

Patience, an opera by Gilbert and Sullivan, produced in 1881, is a burlesque of the aesthetic movement.

In the Age of Reason, Dr. Johnson wrote this burlesque of the epigram:

> If a man that turnips cries
> Cry not when his father dies,
> 'Tis a proof that he would rather
> Have a turnip than a father.

BURLETTA. Italian *burletta*, joke, farce, vaudeville. A musical farce, popular in the eighteenth and nineteenth centuries in England. The music in these productions evaded the law which limited legitimate drama to patent theatres (established by letters patent, not licensed by the Lord Chamberlain). *Tom & Jerry, Life in London* by Pierce Egan was a successful burletta, produced at the Adelphi in 1821 and 1822.

BURNS STANZA. A six line stanza, $a\ a\ a^4\ b^2\ a^4\ b^2$, named after Robert Burns. This is from his *To a Mountain Daisy*:

> Wee modest crimson-tippèd flow'r,
> Thou's met me in an evil hour;
> For I maun crush amang the stoure
>   Thy slender stem:
> To spare thee now is past my pow'r
>   Thou bonnie gem.

The Burns stanza is a variant of the usual structure of the *tail-rhyme stanza*.

BUSKIN. Old French *broissequin*, Old Italian *borzacchino*, short leather half-boot. A thick-soled boot, the *cothurnus*, Greek *kóthornos*, worn by actors in ancient Greek and Roman tragedy. Hence *buskin* consequently became a symbol for acting in tragedy or writing in the lofty style suitable for tragedy.

'The buskin in poetrie is used for tragical matter.' is found in the Glossary in Spenser's *Shepheards Calender*.

> Som time let Gorgeous Tragedy
> In Scepter'd Pall com sweeping by,
> Presenting Thebs, or Pelops line,
> Or the tale of Troy divine.
> Or what (though rare) of later age,
> Ennnobled hath the Buskind stage.
>
> Milton, *Il Penseroso*

C

CACOETHES SCRIBENDI.   Latin, literally, the itch to write, used in the derogatory sense.

CACOPHONY.   Greek *kakós*, bad, *phōnĕ*, sound, tone.   Ugly sound, discord of sounds.   Cacophony may be used deliberately for effect as in these lines in Browning's *A Grammarian's Funeral*:

> Fancy the fabric
> Quite, ere you build, ere steel strike fire from quartz,
> Ere mortar dab brick.

CADENCE.   Latin *cadĕre*, to fall.   A falling, a fall of the voice, rise and fall of the voice in speaking.   The word is used by Milton in *Paradise Lost* of the sound of the wind:

> The sound of blustering winds, which all night long
> Had roused the sea, now with hoarse cadence lull
> Seafaring men o'erwatched.

Cadence is the rhythm in poetry and prose produced by the arrangement of stressed and unstressed syllables.   This is a fine example in Collins's *Ode to Evening*:

> And hamlets brown, and dim-discover'd spires,
> And hears their simple bell, and marks o'er all
> Thy dewy fingers draw
> The gradual dusky veil.

In music, cadence is a technical term for 'any melodic or harmonic progression which has come to possess a conventional association with the ending of a composition, a section, or a phrase'.   Percy A. Scholes.

CADMEAN VICTORY.   'A victory involving one's own ruin' (Liddell and Scott).   It is usually associated with Cadmus, who was the founder of Thebes.   *See also* PYRRHIC VICTORY.

CAESURA.   Latin *caedĕre, caesum*, to cut off.   The break or pause between words within a metrical foot; a pause in a line of verse generally near the middle.

> Whether the nymph | shall break Diana's law,
> Or some frail China jar | receive a flaw;
> Or stain her honour, | or her new brocade;

Forget her pray'rs, | or miss a masquerade;
Or lose her heart, | or necklace, | at a ball;
Or whether Heav'n has doom'd | that Shock must fall.

Pope, *The Rape of the Lock*

CALAMUS. Latin *calamus*, reed, reed-pen. A pen made of a reed sharpened and then split at the point. It was used by the ancients for writing on parchment or paper.

Hinc quam sit calamus saevior ense patet. From this it is clear how much more cruel the pen is than the sword.

Robert Burton, *Anatomy of Melancholy*

CALENDER. Greek *kúlindros*, roller. To impart to a paper-surface a glaze or polish by passing the sheets through a stack of cylinders or rollers, known as calenders.

CALLIGRAPHY. Greek *kállos*, beauty, and -graphy, Greek *gráphein*, to engrave, to draw, to write. Beautiful handwriting, penmanship. In *Glossary of the Book*, G. A. Glaister says:

From Roman times to the sixteenth century such scripts as half-uncial, Carolingian, humanistic, and their derivatives attained their finest forms in the service of religion, law, and commerce.

CALYPSO. Etymology unknown. An improvised ballad, chanted to an African rhythmic beat, composed and sung by West Indians at carnivals and public celebrations.

CAMBRIDGE SCHOOL OF CRITICISM OR CRITICS. *See* NEW CRITICISM.

CANCELLED FIGURES. Figures with diagonal strokes through them; found principally in mathematical textbooks: $\not{1}$ $\not{2}$ $\not{3}$ $\not{4}$ $\not{5}$.

CANCELLERESCA CORSIVA: CHANCERY CURSIVE. In the history of handwriting the finest period began in Italy in the fifteenth century. The lettering of scribes was based on Carolingian Minuscule and this slowly developed into Cursive writing. Pope Eugenius IV decreed that Papal Briefs should be engraved in the Cursive hand. It became known, hence, as *Cancelleresca Corsiva* or *Chancery Cursive*. Ultimately this became the everyday hand of educated people throughout Europe.

The revival of today has produced many writing masters, who acknowledge the skill of those early calligraphers, Bartholomew Dodington and Roger Ascham.

CANON. Greek *kanón*, straight rod or bar, carpenter's rule, rule or standard of excellence. Greek authors were known as *kanónes*, models of excellence. Books of the Bible established by the Christian Church: *Books of the Canon*. The works of an author which are accepted as genuine: *the Chaucer Canon, the Shakespeare Canon*. Also a list of saints canonized by the Roman Catholic Church.

CANSO. In Provençal verse, a love lyric.

CANTICA. Latin *cantō*, to sing. In Roman plays, the portions that were sung or recited to musical accompaniment.

CANTICLE. Latin *canticulum*, little song, diminutive of *cantus*, song. Little song, hymn or chant; one of the Prayer-Book hymns, as the *Nunc Dimittis, Benedicite, Te Deum, Magnificat*; plural *Canticles*, the Song of Solomon.

CANTING MARK. In heraldry, canting applied to crests meant a device on the shield which made a pun on the family name of the bearer. Thus Talbot of Cumberland had talbots (mastiffs) on his shield; Tuck had a stabbing sword or 'tuck'; bent bows were borne by Bowes; John Samon sealed with arms of 'Three salmon swimming'. Canting mark is a printer's device in which the design is based on a pun on the printer's name. Two famous examples are those used by Andrew Myllar of Edinburgh (a windmill) and John Day (a sunrise and the legend 'Arise for it is Day').

G. A. Glaister, *Glossary of the Book*

CANTO. Italian from Latin *cantus*, song. A singing or chant section of a poem. Then a chief division of a long poem. (Also called in Old English a *fit* or *fytte*.) Dante's *Divina Commedia*, Spenser's *The Faerie Queene*, and Byron's *Don Juan* are divided into cantos.

CANZONET. Italian *canzonetta*, diminutive of *canzone*, from Latin *cantiōnem*, from *canĕre*, to sing. A short, light song resembling a madrigal.

CAPA Y ESPADA. See CLOAK AND SWORD.

CAPTION. See HEADLINE.

CARICATURE. Italian *caricatura* from *caricare*, to load a cart (later, to load with exaggeration). First given its present meaning by Annibale Carraci as applied to his drawings, and to those of others, in Bologna in the sixteenth century. In literature, it refers to a character so exaggerated or distorted as to appear ridiculous yet recognizable.

CARMEN FIGURATUM. Latin, literally, a shaped poem. The verses of such a poem are written or printed to form a design on the page, as shown in George Herbert's *Easter Wings*:

> Lord, who createdst man in wealth and store,
> Though foolishly he lost the same,
> Decaying more and more,
> Till he became
> Most poore:
> With thee
> O let me rise
> As larks, harmoniously,
> And sing this day thy victories:
> Then shall the fall further the flight in me.
>
> My tender age in sorrow did beginne:
> And still with sicknesses and shame
> Thou didst so punish sinne,
> That I became
> Most thinne.
> With thee
> Let me combine,
> And feel this day thy victorie:
> For, if I imp* my wing on thine,
> Affliction shall advance the flight in me.

Wither, Quarles, Benlowes, Herrick, and Traherne all wrote pattern or shaped poems.

* imp: strengthen by grafting.

CAROL. Italian *carola*, originally a ring-dance. It may have been first a round dance, then a song accompanying the dance. It is known especially as a song of joy sung at Christmas-time to celebrate the Nativity. Wynkyn de Worde, a pupil of Caxton, printed in 1521 the first collection of Christmas carols that has remained with us.

CAROLINE. From Medieval Latin *Carolus*, Charles. A term applied to the writers of the period of Charles I (1625–1649). Caroline poets included Herrick, Herbert, Crashaw, Vaughan, and Carew, who wrote chiefly love poems and religious poems. The Cavalier poets, Richard Lovelace and Sir John Suckling, of the same period, wrote love lyrics and poems of battle.

CARPE DIEM. Latin, enjoy the day. This phrase was first used by Horace (65–8 B.C.).

CARTOON. Italian *cartone*, from *carta*, paper. A preparatory drawing on stout paper as a design for frescoes, tapestry, painting, mosaic. Any large comic or satirical drawing in a paper or periodical. An animated cartoon is a film made by photographing a succession of drawings.

CARTOUCHE. Italian *cartoccio*, from Latin *carta*, card. Any ornament in the form of a scroll, sometimes based on the shapes of rocks and shellwork, typical of rococo. It was used in architecture, monuments, ceramics, painting, book illustrations and book plates.

CAST OFF. To estimate the space taken in print by the typescript or manuscript.

CATACHRESIS. Greek *katákhrēsis*, misuse of a word, from *katá*, against, in opposition to, and *khrêsis*, use, employment. The use of a word in the wrong sense. *Aggravate* for *annoy*, *chronic* for *severe*, *shambles* for *muddle* are examples.

CATALECTIC. Greek *katalēktikós*, incomplete, stopping short; *katalégein*, to stop. Applied to a metrical line which lacks one syllable in the last foot, as in these lines from Shelley's *Music, When Soft Voices*:

> Music, | when soft | voices | die,
> Vibrates | in the | memor|y —

CATALOGUE RAISONNÉ. French, from Greek *katálogos*, counting up, enrolment, from *légein*, to choose. A descriptive catalogue of books, pictures, etc., arranged according to the different subjects, with brief explanatory notes given on each item.

CATASTROPHE. Greek *katastrophḗ*, overturning, overthrowing. The change which produces the final event of a play or narrative. The dénouement or falling action.

CATCH. Latin *captiāre* from *capĕre*, seize, take. In music, 'a round for three or more voices, in which each singer begins a line behind the preceding one, so arranged that the parts of the singers all harmonize'. H. C. Wyld.
In verse, the term *catch*, equivalent to the Greek *anákrousis*, is used for the extra unstressed syllable at the beginning of a line, when the

normal line has a stress on the first syllable. It occurs in early English stressed poetry such as *Piers Plowman*.

Edmund Gosse says the catch in the third line of the stanza below, from *On Vicissitude*, is 'perhaps the most delicate metrical effect Gray ever attained'.

> Néw-born flocks, in rustic dance,
> Frisking ply their feeble feet;
> Forgétful of their wintry trance,
> The birds his presence greet —

CATCH-WORD. This is a term used by early printers for the word at the bottom of each page set under the *last* word of the *last* line. The word was the first at the top of the following page.

CATECHESIS. Greek *katékhēsis*, oral instruction. Instruction by word of mouth. The Socratic method of instruction by skilful questioning.

CATHARSIS. Greek *kátharsis*, cleansing, purification; *kathaírō*, I cleanse; *katharós*, pure, clean. Purgation. Outlet to emotion afforded by art, especially by the drama. The term was used by Aristotle in *Poetics 6*:

> A tragedy is the imitation of an action that is serious, and also, as having magnitude, complete in itself . . . with incidents arousing pity and terror, with which to accomplish its purgation of these emotions.

CAUSERIE. French *causer*, to talk, converse. Informal talk, essay or article, especially on literary topics, often appearing as one of a series. Named after *Causeries du lundi* ('Monday talks') and weekly criticisms in *Le Globe* and *Le Constitutionnel* by Charles Augustin Sainte-Beuve, in the nineteenth century.

CEDILLA. Spanish *zedilla*, Italian *zediglia*, diminutive of *zeda* from Greek *zêta*, letter Z. A mark (ς) derived through the letter Z from the Arabic letter *sād*. It is written under the letter c (especially in French and Portuguese words) to show that it is sibilant.

CENSORSHIP. Latin *censūra*; *censēre*, to estimate or judge. The office, powers, of a censor. It is the censor's duty to inspect books, journals, plays, films to secure that they contain nothing immoral, libellous, heretical. Strict control of publications is enforced during wartime. In normal times censorship often produces bitter controversy. Milton makes a famous attack on censorship in *Areopagitica*:

> As good almost kill a man as kill a good book: who kills a man kills a reasonable creature, God's image; but he who destroys a good book, kills reason itself, kills the image of God, as it were in the eye. Many a man lives a burden to the earth; but a good book is the precious lifeblood of a master spirit, embalmed and treasured up on purpose to a life beyond life.

CENTO. Greek *kéntrōn*, patchwork; Latin *cento*, a garment of patchwork. A literary patchwork made up of bits from various writers.

CEROGRAPH. Greek *kērós*, Latin *cēra*, wax, Greek *gráphein*, to draw, to write. Literally, wax writing. An engraving, or writing, on wax spread on a sheet of copper, then treated with acid which eats away exposed lines in the copper, forming a plate from which impressions are taken. This process is used in making maps. A print is also called a *cerotype*.

CEROTYPE. *See* CEROGRAPH.

CHAIN VERSE. Verse in which the stanzas are linked by rhyme. A good example is the *villanelle*.

The term is also applied to verse in which the last line of each stanza is repeated as the first line of the next, so that the whole is linked together like a chain. An example is to be found in a well-known hymn of John Byrom (1692–1763):

> My spirit longs for Thee
> Within my troubled breast,
> Though I unworthy be
> Of so divine a guest:
>
> Of so divine a guest
> Unworthy though I be,
> Yet has my heart no rest,
> Unless it come from Thee.
>
> Unless it come from Thee,
> In vain I look around:
> In all that I can see
> No rest is to be found.
>
> No rest is to be found
> Save in Thy blessed love:
> O let my wish be crowned,
> And send it from above.

CHALCOGRAPHY.   Greek *khalkós*, copper, brass, and *gráphein*, to write or scratch.   The art of engraving on copper or brass.

CHAM.   An obsolete form of the word *Khan*, applied especially to the Khan of Tartary.   In *Much Ado About Nothing*, Benedick says of Beatrice:

> Fetch you a hair off the great Cham's beard;   do you any embassage to the Pigmies — rather than hold three words' conference with this harpy.

Smollet, in a letter to John Wilkes, 16th March 1759 (quoted in Boswell), says, 'That great Cham of literature, Samuel Johnson'.

CHANSONNIER.   Latin *cantō*, to sing.   A collection in manuscript of Provençal troubadour poems.

CHANSONS DE GESTE.   French, songs of deeds.   French verse-romances describing the exploits of historical heroes, mostly connected with Charlemagne and his followers.   Among the many surviving examples of the *Chansons de geste*, the *Chanson de Roland* is the most famous.   These romances, composed in the eleventh to the thirteenth centuries, were presented by *jongleurs*, minstrel-entertainers of the time.

CHANT ROYAL.   This verse form, rare in English, consists of five eleven-line stanzas rhyming *a b a b c c d d e d e*, and an envoy rhyming *d d e d e*.

CHAP-BOOK.   A small book, tract, or pamphlet, usually containing popular tales or ballads, such as *John Gilpin* and *Robinson Crusoe*, hawked in the sixteenth, seventeenth, and eighteenth centuries by chapmen.   Old English *cēapmann*, merchant, pedlar, from *cēap*, price, bargain.   Cf. German *Kaufmann*, merchant.

CHARACTER.   Greek *kharaktér*, stamp; *kharássein*, to engrave. The 'characters' were short prose sketches of different types of people moulded to a pattern.   This way of writing derived from the *Characters* of the Greek philosopher Theophrastus (*c.* 372–*c.* 287 B.C.), a pupil of Aristotle.   They served as a model to the seventeenth-century writers, Joseph Hall, Sir Thomas Overbury, and John Earle in his *Microcosmographie*.

CHARIVARI.   From fourteenth-century French and medieval Latin words, origin unknown, for mock music with pans, kettles, and tea-trays expressing popular disapproval.   Also the title of a satirical journal in Paris; hence the former sub-title of *Punch*.

CHARLATAN   Italian *ciarlatano, ciarlare,* to jabber, prate. An impostor. Empty pretender to knowledge or skill.

In *The Study of Poetry,* Matthew Arnold said, 'Charlatanism is for confusing or obliterating the distinctions between excellent and inferior, sound and unsound, true and untrue or only half-true . . . And in poetry, more than anywhere else, it is impermissible to confuse or obliterate them; For in poetry the distinction . . . is of paramount importance'.

CHARLEY: CHARLIE. French *Charles.* This name is identical with German *kerl,* fellow. The name given in earlier times to a night-watchman. The origin is unknown. The name may come from Charles I, who extended in 1640 the use of watchmen in London.

CHAUCERIAN STANZA.   *See* RHYME ROYAL.

CHAUVINISM.   French *chauvin,* jingo, exaggerated patriotism. Derived from Nicolas Chauvin of Rochefort, a veteran of the Grande Armée, who appeared in the *Soldat laboureur* of Scribe, and other popular French plays of the early nineteenth century. This form of patriotism was later ridiculed.

CHIAROSCURO.   Latin *clārus,* clear, bright, *obscūrus,* dark, obscure. Italian *chiaroscuro,* bright-dark. The effects of light and shade in nature; the treatment of light and shade in pictorial art; the use of contrast and of transitions in literature.

CHIASMUS.   Greek *khīasmós,* placing crosswise, from *khīázein,* to form the Greek letter *khî,* a letter shaped like our diagonal X. This is a figure of speech by which contrasted terms are arranged crosswise, the word order in the first phrase being reversed in the second.

Examples:

> I cannot dig, to beg I am ashamed.
>
> Destroying others, by himself destroy'd.

CHICHEVACHE.   From French *chiche face,* thin-face. The name of a monster said to feed only on patient wives, hence all skin and bone because her food was so scarce. Her husband, the Bycorne, grew fat on good and enduring husbands.

> O noble wyves, ful of heigh prudence,
> Let noon humilitie your tongues nayle . . .
> Lest Chichevache you swolwe in her entrayle.
>
> Chaucer, *Clerk's Tale*

CHINOISERIE. French, literally, Chinese curio. Chinese conduct, art, interests.

CHOLIAMBIC. Greek *khōliambos*, lame, halting iambic. A classical metre adopted from the Greek by Catullus and Martial; a limping iambic verse having always a spondee in the sixth and an iambus in the fifth foot. Also called *scazon*.

CHOPINE. Spanish *chapin*, from *chapa*, plate of metal. A kind of shoe raised by a cork sole or the like. It was worn about 1600 in Spain and Italy, and on the English stage Hamlet says to one of the Players: 'By'r lady, your ladyship is nearer to heaven than when I saw you last by the altitude of a chopine.' Speaking to a boy-actor, Hamlet implies that the boy has grown.

CHORIAMB: CHORIAMBUS. Greek *khoríambos* from *khorós*, a dance in a ring, a festive dance, and *íambos*, a metrical foot consisting of a short syllable followed by a long. A *choriambus* is a four-syllabled metrical foot with two stressed and two unstressed syllables (′ ◡ ◡ ′). Here are some lines from *Choriambics* by Rupert Brooke, in which he imitates this classical metre:

Ah! not | now, when desire | burns, and
the wind | calls, and the suns | of spring
Light-foot | dance in the woods, | whisper of life, |
woo me to way | faring:
Ah! not | now should you come, | now when the road |
beckons and good | friends call
Where are | songs to be sung | fights to be fought, |
yea! and the best | of all. . . .

In a choriambic line, the first foot is a trochee, the last foot an iamb.

CHORUS. Greek *chorós*, company of dancers or singers. In ancient Greece the chorus was a band of men who performed songs and dances at religious festivals. As the drama developed, the importance of the chorus diminished. In Aeschylus, the chorus takes part in the action of the play. Sophocles uses the chorus as a comment on the action. Euripides gives the chorus a lyrical quality. Elizabethan dramatists were guided in their use of the chorus by Roman plays. In *Henry V*, Shakespeare uses the Chorus as a commentator on the action, giving it the character of an individual. In modern plays choruses are little used, though T. S. Eliot presented multiple choruses in *Murder in the Cathedral*.

CHRESTOMATHY. Greek *khrēstomátheia*, from *khrēstós*, good, useful, and *math*, stem of *máthēma*, learning. A collection of choice passages, used in the study of a language and in the appreciation of literature.

CHRISTABEL METRE. The metre of *Christabel* by Coleridge is based on the importance in Old English poetry of the stressed syllable in each metrical foot, and the small importance of the number of unstressed syllables. Great variation of the number of syllables occurs in what is basically tetrameter.

> There is not wind enough to twirl
> The one red leaf, the last of its clan,
> That dances as often as dance it can,
> Hanging so light and hanging so high;
> On the topmost twig that looks up at the sky.

CHRONICLE. Greek *khroniká*, annals; *khrónos*, time. A detailed and continuous record of events in historical order. The *Chroniques* of Jean Froissart (*c.* 1337–1410) cover the period 1325–1400, dealing with the affairs of France, Flanders, Spain, Portugal, and England.

CHRONICLE PLAY. A dramatization of historical events taken from the chronicle histories of England, Scotland, and Ireland. An example is *Edward the Fourth* by Thomas Heywood.

CHRONOGRAM. Greek *khrónos*, time, *grámma*, something written, from *gráphein*, to write. An inscription in which certain letters, usually made conspicuous, stand also for Roman numerals, their numerical values placed together making a date which it is desired to record. An example is in the motto of a medal struck by Gustavus Adolphus in 1632: ChrIstVs DVX; ergo trIVMphVs. By placing the capital letters in the correct order we obtain MDCXVVVVII, i.e. MDCXXXII, or 1632.

CICERONIAN SENTENCE. Named after Cicero, the Roman orator (106–43 B.C.). From Thrasymachus onwards, prose-rhythm was a recognized branch of rhetoric. Cicero stated that prose should be metrical in character, though it should not be entirely metrical, since this would be poetry (*Orator*, 220). Rhythm, he said, should pervade the whole sentence, but is most important at the end or *clausula*, where the swell of the period sinks to rest.

Examples of these elaborate, dignified, cadenced sentences are found in Dr. Johnson's prose.

CIPHER. Old French *cyfre* from Arabic *çifr*, zero, originally an adjective, empty. A method of secret writing either by substitution or transposition of letters. Julius Caesar wrote *d* for *a*, *e* for *b*, and so on. This arrangement is found in the Jewish rabbis, and even in the sacred writers. In this passage from Swift's *Journal to Stella*, the cipher is solved by reading only every alternate letter:

> He gave me al bfadnuk lboinlpl dfaonr nfainfbtoy dpionufnad, which I sent him again by Mr. Lewis . . .

i.e. a bank-bill for fifty pound.

CIRCA: CIRCITER: CIRCUM. Latin, about, round about. Used with dates to indicate 'approximately', e.g. *circa* 1300; abbreviation *c.* or *circ.*

CIRCUIT EDGES. Flaps designed to overlap the edges of some Bibles and Prayer Books, especially those made for the pocket; also called *Ribbon edges*.

CIRCUMLOCUTION. Latin *circum*, about, *loquī*, *locūtus*, to speak. Roundabout and evasive speech. The use of many words where few would be clearer. A similar term is *periphrasis*, Greek, from *phrázein*, to speak.

CLARENDON TYPE. A thick-faced, condensed type. Formerly a general name for all **bold** types.

CLASSICAL. Latin *classis*, one of the six divisions of the Roman people. Then came to mean 'of the highest excellence', referring particularly to Greek and Roman authors. Pertaining to the ancient culture of Greece and Rome, especially the language and literature. The term is characterized by a sense of form, balance, proportion. It implies self-knowledge, self-control, an unfaltering sense of reality; also an adherence to externally imposed rules and canons. Though *classical* may be usefully opposed to the word *romantic*, yet they are not mutually exclusive. The works of many writers possess to some degree the qualities of both.

CLASSICISM. Adherence to classical principles and taste in literature and art. Scholarship in Greek and Latin. The use of Greek and Latin idiom in another language. Classicisms occur frequently in Milton's *Paradise Lost*:

> Now when ambrosial Night with Clouds exhal'd
> From that high mount of God, whence light & shade
> Spring both, the face of brightest Heav'n had changd
> To grateful Twilight (for Night comes not there
> In darker veile) and roseat Dews dispos'd
> All but the unsleeping eyes of God to rest,

Wide over all the Plain, and wider farr
Then all this globous Earth in Plain outspred
(Such are the Courts of God) Th' Angelic throng
Disperst in Bands and Files their Camp extend
By living Streams among the Trees of Life,
Pavilions numberless . . .

CLERIHEW.   A short, witty, or nonsensical verse, usually in four
lines, purporting to give point to the character of some notable
person.   It was first used by Edmund Clerihew Bentley.   G. K.
Chesterton wrote about him:

> It was he (Bentley) who invented that severe and stately form of
> free verse known by his own second name as 'The Clerihew'
> or 'Biography for Beginners', which dates from our days at
> school, when he sat listening to a chemical exposition, with
> his rather bored air and a blank sheet of blotting-paper
> before him.   On this he wrote, inspired by the limpid spirit
> of song, the unadorned lines:

> > Sir Humphry Davy
> > Abominated gravy.
> > He lived in the odium
> > Of having discovered sodium.

CLICHÉ.   French *clicher*, to stereotype.   A trite or hackneyed
phrase, used without thought in contexts where it is no longer apt.
Examples are: 'tender mercies', 'acid test', 'leave no stone
unturned', 'to get down to brass tacks', 'to be made the recipient
of '.   Eric Partridge's *Dictionary of Clichés* is a useful collection.
   ' Life is so full of clichés that some of us would be very hard up for
ordinary conversation if by any chance we forgot all the clichés that
we use so frequently.'   The Rev. W. Hutchinson, quoted in the
Sunday Telegraph, 16th August 1964.

CLIMATE OF OPINION.   A phrase applied to ideas, thought and
expression which are in harmony with the Spirit of the Age.

CLIMAX.   Greek *klîmax*, a ladder; *klînein*, to slope, slant.   The
arrangement of a series of ideas or expressions in ascending order
of importance or emphasis; the last term of the arrangement; a
culmination.   For example: 'Some books are to be tasted, others
to be swallowed, and some few to be chewed and digested.'   Bacon,
Of Studies.

CLOAK AND DAGGER.   This term is applied to exciting plays of
espionage, showing the dangers and deceptions of spying today.

CLOAK AND SWORD. The comedies dealing with love and intrigue among the aristocracy. They were written in the sixteenth and seventeenth centuries by Spanish playwrights such as Lope de Vega and Calderón de la Barca. The Spanish term is *capa y espada*.

CLOAK WITHOUT DAGGER. In Graham Greene's *Ministry of Fear* someone cries, 'The world has been remade by William Le Queux'. Spy-fiction had suddenly grown from the thriller. Then, at the time of the Vassall Tribunal, we were reading new tales of foreign agents operating hidden radio transmitters in cellars in the suburbs. We moved from Somerset Maugham's *Ashenden* to Eric Ambler, from Michael Innes's *The Secret Vanguard* to the post-war sensation in spy-fiction, the James Bond novels by Ian Fleming. With a copious mixture of sex and sadism this author appeals, as he said, to 'intelligent uninhibited adolescents of all ages'. Len Deighton's *The Ipcress File* may follow the success of Fleming's *Dr. No* and *Goldfinger*.

CLOG ALMANAC. Middle English *klogge*, block of wood. This old kind of calendar, formerly used in England, was made by notching the figures of dates on the four edges of a square piece of wood. This was sometimes called a runic staff.

CLOOTIE. From dialect *cloot*, cloven hoof, from Old Norse *klō*, claw. A name for the Devil.

> O thou! whatever title suit thee,
> Auld Hornie, Satan, Nick or Clootie.
>
> Burns, *Address to the Deil*

CLOSED COUPLET. One that is grammatically or logically complete. Each line has a logical pause at the end, as in this closed couplet by Pope in *An Essay on Man*:

> Hope springs eternal in the human breast;
> Man never is, but always to be blessed.

CLOSET DRAMA. A play which has been read rather than performed, as *Otho the Great* by Keats. Also a play, which, written for the theatre, has been accepted as a dramatic poem, as Shelley's *The Cenci*.

CLOUD-CUCKOO-LAND. *See* NEPHELOCOCCYGIA.

COATED PAPER. Paper whose surface has been treated with clay or a pigment and an adhesive mixture, or other suitable material, to improve the quality of the surface for printing.

COCK-AND-BULL STORY. A long, vague, rambling story. Similarly, the French *coq-à-l'âne*, a loosely connected, extravagant tale. In his *Anatomy of Melancholy*, Robert Burton says:

> Some mens whole delight is . . . to talk of a
> cock and a bull over a pot.

COCKAIGNE: COCKAYNE. Middle English *cokaygn(e)* from Old French (*pais de*) *cocaigne* (modern *cocagne*), literally, land of cakes, from Middle Low German *Kokenje*, sweet cake. An imaginary land of luxury and idleness. It may be a nickname for the 'Fortunate Isles', which the ancient Greeks and Romans believed lay west of the Pillars of Hercules in the Atlantic Ocean.

COCKNEY SCHOOL. This was a nickname bestowed by *Blackwood's Magazine* on Leigh Hunt, Keats, Hazlitt, and their friends. Shelley was later added to the 'school', as some say, because of one ill-sounding rhyme — *time*, *name*. Faults of taste and diction are to be found in Leigh Hunt, the main target. This is how Lockhart made his scurrilous attack:

> They are by far the vilest vermin that ever dared to creep upon
> the hem of the majestic garment of the English muse. They
> have not one idea that is worthy of the name of English in
> the whole circle of their minds. . . . And yet with what an
> ineffable air of satisfaction these fellows speak of themselves
> as likely to go down to posterity among the great authors of
> England! It is almost a pity to destroy so excellent a joke.
> Unless the salt of the nickname they have got preserve them,
> they cannot possibly last twenty years in the recollection even
> of the Cockneys.

CODA. Latin *cauda*, tail. The tail-piece, occasionally added to a sonnet, giving it sixteen lines or more instead of the orthodox fourteen. These lines follow the fourteenth line of Milton's sonnet *On the new forcers of Conscience under the Long Parliament*:

> That so the Parliament
> May with their wholsom and preventive Shears
> Clip your Phylacteries, though bauk your Ears,
>   And succour our just Fears
> When they shall read this clearly in your charge
> *New Presbyter* is but *Old Priest* writ Large.

CODEX. Latin, earlier *caudex*, tree-trunk, wooden tablet, book. Originally, wooden tablets coated with wax for writing on. Hence when parchment and paper were substituted for wood and made into a book, the term *codex* was still used. Manuscript volume.

COFFEE-TABLE BOOK. The term applied to the large glossy art-book or similar volume displayed on social occasions as a status symbol.

COIN. Latin *cuneus*, wedge. Old French *coi(g)n*, wedge, stamping-die. To invent, put into use, a new word or expression. In *The English Language*, Ernest Weekley says:

> No work, except Shakespeare, has had so much influence on the phraseology of English as the Authorized Version of the Bible, at one time familiar to all households. This Version, however, owes much to earlier translations, especially those of Tyndale (1525, 1530–1531) and Coverdale (1535). To Tyndale we owe *long-suffering*, *peacemaker*, *stumbling-block*, the *fatted calf* and *filthy lucre*, while his *scapegoat*, if, as is now believed, it is a mistranslation, is one of those lucky accidents that have enriched the language. Coverdale gave us *loving-kindness*, *tender mercy*, the *valley of the shadow of death* and the *avenger of blood*.
>
> Of Shakespeare it may be said without fear of exaggeration that his contribution to our phraseology is ten times greater than that of any writer to any language in the history of the world ... From *Hamlet* come such phrases as *this too too solid flesh*; *mind's eye*; *the primrose path*; *there's the rub*; *to speak daggers*; *hoist with his own petard*; *to cudgel one's brains*; *ministering angel*; *towering passion*; and many other expressions which form an integral part even of colloquial English.
>
> Milton coined *pandemonium*, *anarch*, and *moon-struck*; *human face divine*; *fallen on evil days*.
>
> Individual writers have made small contributions, from Bunyan's *Vanity Fair* and *Slough of Despond* down to Keats's *magic casements* and Tennyson's *rift within the lute* ... Scott introduced into literature a number of picturesque dialect words, such as *raid* and *weird*, *gruesome*, *glamour*, and *stalwart*. . . . To Carlyle we owe *self-help*, *the dismal science*, *the unspeakable Turk*, *swansong*, *bolt from the blue*.

COLLAGE. French *collage*, sticking, pasting things on. Collage is the technique of applying pieces of newspaper and other materials to a canvas or panel as part of the picture. *Papiers déchirés*, 'tattered papers', invented by Picasso, consisted of twisted paper shapes stuck to the picture. In literature, submerged quotations from other writers, allusions and foreign expressions are made a part of some poems to create wider horizons and give an effect of surprise. Collage is found in the work of Joyce, Eliot, and Pound. Here is an example in the closing lines of T. S. Eliot's *The Waste Land*:

> I sat upon the shore
> Fishing, with the arid plain behind me
> Shall I at least set my lands in order?
> London Bridge is falling down falling down
> falling down
> *Poi s' ascose nel foco che gli affina*
> *Quando fiam uti chelidon* — O swallow swallow
> *Le Prince d'Aquitaine à la tour abolie*
> These fragments I have shored against my ruins
> Why then Ile fit you. Hieronymo's mad againe.
> Datta. Dayadhvam. Damyata.
> Shantih shantih shantih

COLLATE. Latin *collātum*, from *conferre*, to bring together. To bring together in order to compare. To examine critically a text or manuscript and compare one copy with another. To scrutinize and place in order the sheets of a book; to check the order of the sheets by the signatures. Collate also means to appoint a clergyman to a benefice.

COLLINS, WILLIAM. A pompous, conceited young clergyman in Jane Austen's *Pride and Prejudice*. The solemn letter of thanks he sent to Mr. Bennet (Chapter 23, the text is not given) after his stay has applied his name colloquially to such letters, which are also called 'roofers'.

COLLOQUIAL. Latin *colloquium*, from *colloqui*, to speak together. Pertaining to words peculiar to the vocabulary of everyday talk.

COLLOTYPE. Greek *kólla*, glue; *túpos*, a blow, mark of a blow, impress. Photographic print made directly from colloid film; a form of gelatine process in book illustration and advertising. 'It is a planograph photographic method of printing which uses a film of light-hardened gelatine adhering to a glass support (instead of a stone or plate). No screen is used. It depends on the reticulative property of bichromated light-hardened gelatine for its tone gradations.' John C. Tarr, *Printing To-day*.

COLOPHON. Greek *kolophón*, the summit, finish, and finishing stroke. The tail-piece in old books, often ornamental, giving the name of the printer, often the title, and usually the date of printing. This information is now placed on the title-page or verso.

COLPORTEUR. Latin *collum*, neck, *portāre*, carry. A book-hawker, especially one employed by a Society to distribute Bibles and religious tracts.

COLUMBINE. Adapted from the Italian proper name *Colombina* which means dove-like. A character in Italian comedy, she was the daughter of Pantaloon and mistress of Harlequin. She now plays a part in English pantomime.

COMBINATION PLATE. A plate on which line work and half-tone are combined and etched for both line and halftone depth. Separate negatives are made for the line work and the halftone, and then combined on metal before printing.

COMÉDIE LARMOYANTE. French, tearful comedy. The Sentimental Comedy of the eighteenth century led, in France, to the *comédie larmoyante*, established by the pathetic plays of Nivelle de la Chaussée, and then replaced by the *drame bourgeois*.

COMEDY. French *comédie*; Greco-Latin *cōmoedia*, from *kômos*, revel, and *aeidein*, to sing. Drama dealing with humorous, familiar events and the behaviour of ordinary people, speaking the language of everyday life. Its purpose is to amuse, and the treatment of character often has touches of exaggeration and caricature. Comedy can have a serious purpose as in the humorous satire of Aristophanes, and in the presentation by Chekhov of the universal predicament of sensitive, struggling people.

COMEDY OF HUMOURS. A term applied especially to the type of comic drama written by Ben Jonson and John Fletcher, where ‘humour’ is a personification of some individual passion or tendency.

COMEDY OF INTRIGUE. This form of comedy, which sub-ordinates character to plot, originated in Spain, and was practised in England by Mrs. Aphra Behn. Her most popular plays were *The Rover*, 1677–1681, and *The City Heiress*, 1682.

COMEDY OF MANNERS. This originated in France with Molière's *Les Précieuses ridicules* in 1658, and Molière himself defined it when he said ‘correction of social absurdities must at all times be the matter of true comedy’. The Comedy of Manners flourished in Restoration England, and gave us the plays of Congreve and Etherege.

COMEDY OF MORALS. A comedy presenting the correction of abuse by the lash of ridicule. The greatest exemplar is Molière's *Tartuffe* (1664), a play 'which could not be written or understood outside its own country'.

COMIC RELIEF. A comic, diverting element in a serious literary work, especially in a play, which relieves the tension, and also, by contrast, heightens the significance of the tragic theme. An example is the drunken porter's speech in *Macbeth*.

COMMEDIA DELL'ARTE. Italian, improvised comedy of the sixteenth and seventeenth centuries. In the history of Italian drama, this improvised drama was performed by professional actors. This drama developed in the sixteenth century from the popular character comedy, itself a kind of popular farce connected with Atella, a town of the Osci in Campania. The companies presented typed characters. Masks and traditional costumes were worn by the old men and the clowns. This form of Italian drama is said to have been invented by Francesco Cherea, who was a favourite actor of Pope Leo X.

The Neapolitan troupe of Peppino de Filippo, which has been claimed as the last indigenous survival of *commedia dell'arte*, appeared in *The Metamorphosis of a Wandering Minstrel*, at the Aldwych Theatre, London, in April 1964.

COMMEDIA ERUDITA. 'Learned comedy'. Following the elegance of plot of Roman New Comedy, writers such as Aretino, Ariosto, and Machiavelli established wit and sharp satire in the drama of the Renaissance. Machiavelli's *La Mandragola* written between 1513 and 1520 is a fine example of such a comedy.

COMMON MEASURE. The quatrain of the ballad stanza $a^4 b^3 c^4 b^3$, but retains the exact rhymes and the strict iambic metre found in the hymnal; therefore it is also called *hymnal stanza*. The hymnal stanza sometimes rhymes *a b a b*.

COMMONPLACE BOOK. A book in which quotations in prose and verse, remarks and ideas are entered for further use.

COMMON RHYTHM. Metrical form in which stressed and unstressed syllables alternate. Also known as *running rhythm*.

COMMUNICATION. Latin *commūnicāre*, to share with others, to have in common. Cleanth Brooks maintains that the poet is not a communicator; that the full aesthetic experience of the poem is of the first importance, not the ideas expressed. In *Principles of Literary Criticism*, I. A. Richards said, 'The arts are the supreme form of the communicative activity'. F. R. Leavis claims that the poet's 'capacity for experiencing and his power of communicating are indistinguishable; not merely because we should not know of the one without the other, but because his power of making words express what he feels is indistinguishable from his awareness of what he feels '.

COMMUS. Greek. In ancient drama, dialogue in lyrical form sung by the chorus to express deep emotion. The actors sometimes joined the chorus to increase the effect.

COMPENSATION. Latin *compensāre*, to weigh together, from *pensāre*, from *pendēre*, to weigh. The method of putting right omissions in a line of metrical verse. These omissions usually consist of one or more unstressed syllables. An omitted syllable may be compensated for in the following line, but it is usually added to another foot in the same line or replaced by a pause. Each word in the first line of this stanza by Tennyson is stressed, and followed by a pause:

> Break, break, break,
>> On thy cold grey stones, O sea!
> And I would that my tongue could utter
>> The thoughts that arise in me.

COMPLAINT. Low Latin *complangĕre*: *com-*, intensive, *planĕgre*, bewail. A lyric which expresses the grief or distress of the poet.

> Accept, thou shrine of my dead Saint,
> Instead of dirges this complaint;
> And for sweet flowers to crown thy hearse,
> Receive a strew of weeping verse
> From thy griev'd friend, whom thou might'st see
> Quite melted into tears for thee.
>> Henry King, *The Exequy*

Sometimes, a complaint may have a humorous touch, as in 'The Complaint of Chaucer to His Empty Purse':

> To you, my purse, and to non other wight
> Compleyne I, for ye be my lady dere!
> I am so sorry, now that ye be light.

COMPOSITOR. Latin *com-*, together, *pōnĕre*, to place. One who sets type, makes it into pages, and locks the pages into correct position in a chase.

COMPOUND ADJECTIVES. In *The English Language*, Ernest Weekley says:

> The formation of compound adjectives in which the first element is instrumental dates from the modern period, and

the most picturesque examples of this type are often individual creations, e.g. *blood-stained* (Shakespeare), *cloud-capped* (Shakespeare), *dew-besprinkled* (Gay), *ivy-mantled* (Gray), *sunlit* (Shelley), *moonlit* (Tennyson). The freedom of the English language appears in the conversion of phrases into adjectives in a *matter-of-fact* man, an *up-to-date* idea, a *go-ahead* firm.

Colloquial English is rather impatient of compounds, and commonly substitutes *-er* for the second element, e.g. *diner* for *dining-car*, *fiver* for *five-pound note*. So also *dynamo* for *dynamo-electric machine*, *movies* for *moving pictures*, *nighty*, *undies*, etc.

CONCEIT. Latin *concipĕre*, *conceptum*, from *con-*, and *capĕre*, to take. A fanciful image or startling comparison. In *On Metaphysical Poetry*, James Smith says, ‘The elements of the conceit must be such that they can enter into a solid union and, at the same time, maintain their separate and warring identity’. The conceit was frequently used in Elizabethan poetry, and became a feature characteristic of Donne and other Metaphysical poets of the seventeenth century. A famous example is in *A Valediction Forbidding Mourning*, where Donne speaks of his soul and that of his mistress:

> If they be two, they are two so
> As stiff twin compasses are two;
> Thy soul, the fix’d foot, makes no show
> To move, but doth, if th’other do.

> And though it in the centre sit,
> Yet when the other far doth roam,
> It leans and hearkens after it,
> And grows erect as that comes home.

CONCORDANCE. Latin *concordāre*, to be of one mind, to agree together. An alphabetical arrangement of the chief words used in a book, or by an author, with citations of the passages concerned; a concordance of the Bible, of the works of Shakespeare.

CONCRETE. Latin *concrētus*; *con*, together, *crēscĕre*, to grow. A way of suggesting the immediate experience of realities; dealing with actual things or events; real, specific, particular.

CONFESSIONAL LITERATURE. Latin *confitērī*, to confess; *fatērī*, to admit. A form of autobiography in which the author describes parts of his life normally withheld. Examples are *Confessions* by St. Augustine of Hippo, Rousseau's *Confessions*, De

Quincey's *Confessions of an English Opium-Eater*, and George Moore's *Confessions of a Young Man.*

CONFIDANT: CONFIDANTE. Latin *confīdĕre*, to have complete trust. Also known as *raisonneur*. A character in drama or fiction to whom others confide their secrets. The device of the confidant in drama has been common from classical Greek plays. It was ridiculed in the eighteenth century. Sheridan has this stage direction in *The Critic*:

> Enter Tilburina, stark mad in white satin, and her confidante, stark mad in white linen.

CONFLICT. Latin *conflictus*, from *conflīgĕre*, to strike together. In literature, the struggle between two forces or between characters. Conflict may take place within one character; in *Julius Caesar*, Brutus is 'with himself at war'; between two characters, such as Iago and Othello; or between groups in society, as is shown in *Waiting for Lefty* by Clifford Odets.

CONNOTATION. Latin *connotāre*, to mark together. Denotation is the accepted meaning of a word. Connotation is the implication of something more than the accepted or primary meaning; it refers to the qualities, attributes, and characteristics implied or suggested by the word. From its plain meaning and its sound the word may have associations, images, echoes, impressions. Poetry in particular makes full use of connotation, and creates wider ripples of meaning in the mind of the responsive reader.

In *Modern English Usage*, H. W. Fowler says:

> *Ugly* connotes ugliness or violation of standards of beauty, repellent effect on the observer, etc. The sum of the common attributes is the word's *connotation* or connotative meaning.
> *Ugly* denotes Socrates, Wilkes, the black country, cowardice, and all other things to which the connotation of *ugly* applies. The whole of the objects taken together are the word's *denotation* or denotative meaning.

CONSISTENCY. Latin *consistĕre*, to stand firm. The quality of congruity in the action and in the tone of a literary work. A logical sequence in the development of the characters.

CONSONANCE. Latin *consonāre*, to sound with, to harmonize. Agreement or unison of sounds; recurrence of same or similar sounds in words. It is the pairing of words in which the vowels differ but the final consonants of the stressed syllables agree. This is shown in these lines from J. C. Ransom's *Judith of Bethulia*:

The heathen are all perished. The victory was furnished,
We smote them hiding in our vineyards, barns, annexes,
And now their white bones clutter the holes of foxes,
And the chieftain's head, with grinning sockets, and varnished —
Is it hung on the sky with a hideous epitaphy?
No, the woman keeps the trophy.

This device has also been called *consonantal assonance, consonantal rhyme, half rhyme, oblique rhyme,* and *suspended rhyme.*

CONSONANTAL ASSONANCE. *See* CONSONANCE.

CONSONANTAL DISSONANCE. Latin *dissonāre,* to disagree in sound. A harsh combination of sounds. The 'rhyming' of vowel sounds related but not identical, in words with close resemblance in consonants, but lacking in harmony. Such dissonance is frequent in the poetry of Wilfred Owen, Gerard Manley Hopkins, and Dylan Thomas.

The last words in these two lines from Wilfred Owen's *Strange Meeting* show this effect:

To miss the march of the retreating world
Into vain citadels that are not walled.

CONSONANTAL RHYME. *See* CONSONANCE.

CONTE. French *conte,* story, tale. Short story, as a form of literary composition. The *contes* of Guy de Maupassant reveal a master of the short story.

CONTENT. Latin *continēre,* to contain. The content of a poem, as opposed to form, consists of thought, feeling, attitude, and intention. It is conveyed by the words and their arrangement. The rhythm produced welds the poem together, and gives it a significance beyond any prose rendering. It is only by a close scrutiny of all the qualities of the words (meaning, sound, associations), and also of the ordering of the rhythm, that the poem can be understood, and its value estimated.

CONTEXT. Latin *contextus,* from *contexĕre,* to weave together. Those parts of a work of literature which precede and follow a given word, phrase or passage. Such words or phrases, to be properly understood or judged, should be read in their context.

CONTRAPUNTAL. The adjective of Counterpoint. The term derives from the Latin expression *punctus contra punctum,* point against point or note against note. Percy A. Scholes says:

A single 'part' or 'voice' added to another is called 'a counter-point' to that other, but the more common use of the word is that of the combination of simultaneous 'parts' or 'voices', each of significance in itself and the whole resulting in a coherent texture. In this sense Counterpoint is the same as *Polyphony*.

CONTRAST. Late Latin *contrāstāre*, to stand against. The juxta-position of images or thoughts to show striking differences. Con-trast is shown in these lines from Shakespeare's Sonnet 35:

> Roses have thorns, and silver fountains mud;
> Clouds and eclipses stain both moon and sun,
> And loathsome canker lives in sweetest bud.
> All men make faults.

CONVENTION. Latin *conventiōn-(em)*, an agreement, compact. In *Convention and Revolt in Poetry*, John Livingston Lowes says:

> Convention, so far as art is concerned, represents concurrence in certain accepted methods of communication. And the fundamental conventions of every art grow out of the nature of its medium. Conventions beget conventions, to be sure, and their ramifications and permutations are endless.

> Let me quote a part of Goethe's famous answer to those enquiring spirits who kept asking what idea he sought to embody in *Faust*:

>> 'It wasn't on the whole, my way, as a poet, to strive after the embodiment of something abstract. I received within myself impressions — impressions of a hundred sorts, sensuous, lively, lovely, many-hued — as an alert imagina-tive energy presented them. And I had as a poet nothing else to do but mould and fashion within me such observa-tions and impressions, and through a vivid representation to bring it about that others should receive the same impression, when what I had written was read or heard.'

> There we have it again in a nutshell: the phantasmagoria of the concrete world; the poet's mind like a sensitized film, alive to impressions; the impulse to give to these impressions form, and to communicate.

COPY. Latin *cōpia*, abundance, plenty, opportunity, means; in phrase *dare cōpiam legendi*, to give means of reading. Any single book or set of books. The manuscript, reprint, or proof from which the compositor sets the type.

COPYRIGHT. The exclusive right given by law for a term of years to reproduce a literary, dramatic, musical, or artistic work; also to perform, translate, film or record such a work. In Britain, the copyright on an author's work generally ceases fifty years after his death.

CORANTO: COURANT. French *courant*, runner. A pamphlet containing foreign news taken from foreign papers, issued between 1621 and 1641. One of the first forms of journalism in England, the corantos were followed by the 'newsbook'.

CORRECTNESS. This was the literary ideal of Alexander Pope and his contemporaries in the Augustan Age. In *Epistle to Mr. Pope Epistle II from Oxford*, Edward Young addresses Pope in these lines:

> Excuse no fault; though beautiful, 'twill harm;
> One fault shocks more than twenty beauties charm.
> Our age demands correctness; Addison
> And you this commendable hurt have done.
> Now writers find, as once Achilles found,
> The whole is mortal, if a part's unsound.

This is the interpretation of the word given by Leslie Stephen, 'the quality which is gained by incessant labour, guided by quick feeling, and always under the strict supervision of common sense'.

CORRELATIVE VERSES. These are verses taking the form of abbreviated sentences. In this example, George Wither ends an epitaph on Lady Scott with this couplet:

> The poor, the world, the heavens, and the grave,
> Her alms, her praise, her soul, her body have —

This means 'the poor have her alms, the world has her praise, the heavens have her soul, and the grave has her body'.

And, in *Paradise Lost*, even Milton writes these correlative verses:

> Air, water, earth,
> By fowl, fish, beast, was flown, was swum, was walked.

CORRIGENDUM: (pl.) CORRIGENDA. Latin *corrigĕre*, to correct. That which requires correction. Also, a slip inserted into a book by the publisher containing a correction or corrections to the text, which have come to light after the book has gone to press.

COTERIE. French, association of country people, from Old French, *cotier*, cot-dweller. A group of people associated by common interests. A select circle in society.

COTHURNUS.   Greek *kóthornos*, buskin worn in tragic drama.   A thick-soled laced boot worn by actors in ancient tragedy.   Also the dignified spirit of such drama.

COUNTERPLOT.   *See* SUBPLOT.

COUNTERPOINT RHYTHM.   Gerard Manley Hopkins explains that Counterpoint Rhythm is

> . . . the superinducing or mounting of a new rhythm upon the old; and since the new or mounted rhythm is actually heard and at the same time the mind naturally supplies the natural or standard foregoing rhythm, for we do not forget what the rhythm is that by rights we should be hearing, two rhythms are in some manner running at once and we have something answerable to counterpoint in music, which is two or more strains of tune going on together, and this is Counterpoint Rhythm.   Of this kind of verse Milton is the great master and the choruses of *Samson Agonistes* are written throughout in it.

This is counterpoint: '*Home* to his mother's house *private* returned' and '*But to vanquish* by wisdom hellish wiles'.
                                                                Paradise Regained

COUP DE THÉÂTRE.   An unexpected and sensational turn in a play.

COUPLET.   French diminutive of *couple*, from Latin *cōpula*, a band, bond.   A couplet consists of two consecutive lines of verse rhyming together, usually in the same metre.   A closed couplet is one that is logically and grammatically complete.

COURTESY BOOK.   A book, popular in the Renaissance, outlining behaviour.   The most famous book of this kind is *Il Cortegiano* (1528) by the Italian humanist, Baldassare Castiglione.   Here all the qualities of the ideal courtier, as soldier, sportsman, scholar, are presented.   The work had a marked influence in England on the writings of Surrey, Philip Sidney and Spenser.

COURTLY LOVE.   The tradition of courtly love was that knights should serve and revere some noble lady.   The idea arose in Provence in the eleventh century.   Courtly love was not a part of marriage, and therefore it was secret, adulterous, and faithful.   The

lover observed a kind of medieval veneration for his lady as we see
in the Squyer in Chaucer's *Prologue*

> was of evene lengthe,
> And wonderly delivere, and greet of strengthe.
> And he hadde been somtyme in chivachye,
> In Flaundres, in Artoys, and Picardye,
> And born him wel, as of so litel space,
> In hope to stonden in his lady grace.

COWLEYAN ODE. An ode in the grand manner, in which the
stanzas are irregular in the pattern of the rhyme, and in the length
and number of the lines. Abraham Cowley invented this metrical
form, which came to perfection in Dryden's *Song for St. Cecilia's
Day*, Wordsworth's *Ode on Intimations of Immortality*, and Tennyson's *Ode on the Death of the Duke of Wellington*. Here is the first
stanza of Cowley's ode *Life and Fame*:

> Oh Life, thou Nothing's younger Brother!
>   So like, that one might take one for the other!
>   What's Some Body, or No Body?
> In all the Cobwebs of the Schoolmens Trade,
> We no such nice Distinction woven see,
>   As 'tis To be, or Not to be.
> Dream of a Shadow! a Reflection made
> From the false Glories of the gay reflected Bow,
>   Is a more solid thing than thou.
> Vain weak-built Isthmus, which dost proudly rise
>   Up betwixt two Eternities;
>   Yet canst nor Wave nor Wind sustain,
> But broken and o'erwhelm'd, the endless Oceans meet again.

CRADLE BOOKS: INCUNABULA. Latin *incūnābula*, swaddling-
clothes; infancy; origin, beginning; from *in*, in, *cūnābula*,
diminutive of *cūnae*, a cradle. Early books produced in the infancy
of the art of printing, especially those printed before 1500.

CRAFT CYCLE. *See* LITURGICAL DRAMA.

CREDO. Latin, literally, I believe. The first word of the Apostles'
and Nicene Creeds in Latin. Hence a name for either of these
creeds.

CRISIS. Greek *krísis*, decision, from *krínein*, to judge. The
decisive moment in a play or story when a situation is dangerous
and a decision must be made. Several crises may occur, leading to
a climax. In *Hamlet* a crisis comes during the play scene. Claudius

sees his own crime presented before him. This brings the climax; he rises, shouts for lights, and runs out, deeply disturbed.

CRITERION: (pl.) CRITERIA. Greek *kritĕrion*, a means of judging; *kritĕs*, a judge. A standard by which something is judged. A test of truth or validity.

CRITICAL APPARATUS. In *Principles of Literary Criticism*, I. A. Richards says:

> The qualifications of a good critic are three. He must be an adept at experiencing, without eccentricities, the state of mind relevant to the work of art he is judging. Secondly, he must be able to distinguish experiences from one another as regards their less superficial features. Thirdly, he must be a sound judge of values.
> There are certain broad features in which all agree a poem of Swinburne is unlike a poem of Hardy. The use of words by the two poets is different. Their methods are dissimilar, and the proper approach for a reader differs correspondingly. An attempt to read them in the same way is unfair to one o the poets, or to both, and leads inevitably to defects in criticism which a little reflection would remove. It is absurd to read Pope as though he were Shelley, but the essential differences cannot be clearly marked out unless such an outline of the general form of a poetic experience has been provided.

CRITICISM. Greek *kritikós*, able to discern and decide. These are valuable comments on criticism:

> Read not to contradict and confute, nor to believe and take for granted, nor to find talk and discourse, but to weigh and consider.   Francis Bacon, *Of Studies*

> They wholly mistake the nature of criticism who think its business is principally to find fault. Criticism, as it was first instituted by Aristotle, was meant a standard of judging well; the chiefest part of which is, to observe those excellencies which should delight a reasonable reader.
>   Dryden, *Prefaces and other Essays*

> I am bound by my own definition of criticism: a disinterested endeavour to learn and propagate the best that is known and thought in the world.
>   Matthew Arnold, *Functions of Criticism at the Present Time*

> We must grant the artist his subject, his idea, his *donné*: our criticism is applied only to what he makes of it.
>   Henry James, *The Art of Fiction*

CRITICISM OF LIFE. Matthew Arnold said in *Essays in Criticism, Second Series*: *Wordsworth*:

> It is important, therefore, to hold fast to this: that poetry is at bottom a criticism of life; that the greatness of a poet lies in his powerful and beautiful application of ideas to life, — to the question: How to live. Morals are often treated in a narrow and false fashion. . . . We find attraction at times even in a poetry of revolt against them. . . . Or we find attractions in a poetry indifferent to them; in a poetry where the contents may be what they will, but where the form is studied and exquisite. We delude ourselves in either case; and the best cure for our delusion is to let our minds rest upon that great and inexhaustible word *life*, until we learn to enter into its meaning. A poetry of revolt against moral ideas is a poetry of revolt against *life*; a poetry of indifference to moral ideas is a poetry of indifference towards *life*.

CRITIQUE. Greek *kritikós*; *krīnein*, to judge. An essay or article in criticism of a literary work.

CROCODILE'S TEARS. Greek *krokódīlos*, lizard. In the *Oxford Companion to English Literature*, Paul Harvey says:

> The crocodile was fabulously said to weep, either to allure a man for the purpose of devouring him, or while devouring him. Whence many allusions in literature. Sir John Mandeville (xxviii) says, 'In that contre . . . ben gret plentee of Cokadrilles. Theise serpents sleu men, and thei eten them wepynge.' Sir J. Hawkins' Voyage in Hakluyt, iii, has this passage: 'In this river we saw many Crocodils . . . His nature is ever when hee would have his prey, to cry and sob like a Christian body, to provoke them to come to him, and hee snatcheth at them.'

CROSSED RHYME: INTERLACED RHYME. This occurs in a lengthy rhymed couplet; the words in the middle of each line rhyme, thus breaking the couplet into four alternating rhyming short lines:

> Laurel is green for a season, and love is sweet for a day;
> But love grows bitter with treason, and laurel outlives not May.
>   Swinburne, *Hymn to Proserpine*

CROSS-REFERENCE. A note at the end of an entry in a book or catalogue referring the reader to some other author or book on the same subject as the entry itself. For example: Scotland. *See also* Great Britain.

CROWN OF SONNETS. A lyrical poem consisting of seven sonnets which are interlinked. The last line of each stanza is also the first line of the next stanza. The last line of the seventh sonnet is also the first line of the first sonnet. An example is Donne's *La Corona*. The opening and closing line of the poem is:

> Deign at my hands this crown of prayer and praise.

CUBISM. Greek *kúbos*, cube. A style in art in which objects are so presented as to give the effect of a collection of geometrical figures and shapes. Cubism has its roots, as R. G. Haggar says in *Dictionary of Art Terms*, 'in the planimetric analysis of Cézanne's later pictures and the doctrine of treating "nature by the cylinder, the sphere, the cone" which he advanced in a letter to the young painter Émile Bernard in 1904'.

CULTURE. Latin *cultūra, colĕre*, to cultivate, to worship. In the Preface to *Culture and Anarchy*, Matthew Arnold says, 'Culture being a pursuit of our total perfection by means of getting to know, on all the matters which most concern us, the best which has been thought and said in the world.'

In *Literature and Dogma* he defines the term again, 'Culture, the acquainting ourselves with the best that has been known and said in the world, and thus with the history of the human spirit.'

CURIOSA FELICITAS. Latin, literally, painstaking good fortune. In *Principle in Art*, Coventry Patmore said, '*curiosa felicitas* . . . means the careful luck of him who tries many words, and has the wit to know when memory, or the necessity of metre or rhyme, has supplied him unexpectedly with those which are perhaps even better than he know how to desire'.

CURTAIN-RAISER. Usually a one-act play given at the beginning of a programme before the main play.

CURTAL SONNET. Latin *curtus*, shortened. Gerard Manley Hopkins designed what he called a curtal sonnet, a shortened version of the sonnet. The sextet rhymes *a b c a b c*, the quatrain rhymes *d b c d c* (or as a variant *d c b d c*), the sonnet ending with a short single line or tail.

His poem *Pied Beauty* shows the pattern:

> Glory be to God for dappled things —
> 　　For skies of couple-colour as a brinded cow;
> 　　　　For rose-moles all in stipple upon trout that swim;
> Fresh-firecoal chestnut-falls, finches' wings;
> 　　Landscape plotted and pieced — fold, fallow, and plough;

And áll trádes, their gear and tackle and trim.

All things counter, original, spare, strange;
 Whatever is fickle, freckled (who knows how?)
  With swift, slow; sweet, sour; adazzle, dim;
He fathers-forth whose beauty is past change:
    Praise him.

CUT. An engraved block or plate; an impression made from this, an illustration; a woodcut.

CYNEGETICI. Greek *kunēgetikoí.* Poets writing about the chase.

D

DACTYL. Greek *dáktulos*, a finger. A metrical foot consisting of three syllables, one long or stressed syllable followed by two short or unstressed syllables / ‿‿, like the joints of a finger.

For example, two lines from *The Tempest*:

Mérrily, | mérrily | shàll I live | nów
Únder thè | blossòm thàt | hàngs òn thè | bóugh.

DADAISM. French *dada*, hobby-horse; *être sur son dada*, to ride one's hobby-horse. A disruptive, nihilistic movement in art and literature started in Zürich, about 1916, by Tristan Tzara, Hugo Ball, Hans Arp. It was the expression of a spirit of revolt rising out of the horrors of the war, and sought through terms of derision to destroy all sense of tradition in the arts, all values of conduct. Joán Miró, Marcel Duchamp, Max Ernst were among its exponents. Kurt Schwitters created the *Merzbild* — pictures made out of leftovers — and stated, 'Anything the artist spits is Art'. In a cabaret, Hugo Ball, in fantastic clothes, read his poem, which began:

> Gadji beri bimba
> glandridi lauli lonni cadori

and ended in equal darkness.

Dadaism moved between phantasy and destruction. Its influence spread from Paris to London and New York, then somewhere in the 1920s it merged with Surrealism.

DAGUERREOTYPE. A method of making and fixing a photographic image on a silver or silvered copperplate exposed to iodine or bromine vapour. It was invented in 1833 by Louis Daguerre, and was the forerunner of modern photography.

DEAD METAPHOR. This term is used in two different senses. First in the sense of metaphors like *a baker's dozen*, which are no longer part of the current language. The more usual sense is that of words which start off as metaphors, but which are no longer regarded as such, and have come to be accepted as a second literal meaning: e.g. *broadcast* (in connexion with radio).

DÉBAT. French, debate. A kind of medieval fabliau taking the form of a discussion between two persons or between two birds or animals. *Débats* are included in these collections of French literature, *Barbazan, Méon, Le Grand d'Aussy.*

DEBATE. Latin *dē*, and *bātuĕre*, to beat. A discussion, controversy, public argument.

DECADENCE. Latin *dēcadĕre*, to fall, to decay. A decline in values, or the decline of the quality of an art or literature after a period of greatness. This is shown in the state of English drama after Shakespeare, and in the literary movement of the nineties in France.

DECASYLLABIC. Greek *déka*, ten. A line of verse composed of ten syllables. Milton's *Paradise Lost* is a fine example of the variety this line can achieve:

> Sing, Heavenly Muse, that, on the secret top
> Of Oreb, or of Sinai, didst inspire
> That shepherd who first taught the chosen seed
> In the beginning how the heavens and earth
> Rose out of Chaos.

DECKLE. The feathery edge formed upon paper in the process of manufacture. It is sometimes left on the printed sheet for artistic effect.

DECORUM. Latin *decōrus*, becoming. What is appropriate in behaviour; propriety of conduct. Particular usage required by politeness or decency.

> Dulce et decorum est pro patria mori.
> To die for fatherland is a sweet thing and becoming.
>
> Horace, *Odes*

DEDUCTION. Latin *dēdūcĕre*, to lead down. A form of reasoning from the general to the particular; basing the truth of a statement upon its being a case of a wider statement known or admitted to be true. 'I shall die because I know that all human beings do so, and I am a human being.'

DEFINITIVE EDITION: TEXT. Latin *dēfīnītīvus*, explanatory, definitive, from *fīnis*, end. The author's own, final, chosen text; with anonymous work it is the best contemporary text.

DEISM. Paul Harvey states that deism or 'natural religion' is the belief in a Supreme Being as the source of finite existence, with rejection of revelation and the supernatural doctrines of Christianity.

In England, the chief Deists who held this belief were Lord Herbert of Cherbury (1583–1648), Charles Blount (1654–1693),

John Toland (1670–1722), Matthew Tindal (1657–1733), Thomas
Chubb (1679–1747), and the third Earl of Shaftesbury (1671–1713).

DELPHIN CLASSICS. A set of sixty-four Greek and Latin
classics edited in France from 1674 to 1730 by thirty-nine scholars,
under the direction of Montausier, Mme Anne Dacier, Bossuet,
and Huet for the use of the Grand Dauphin, son of Louis XIV.

DENOTATION. Latin *dēnotāre*, to set a mark on, to point out,
specify, designate. The meaning of a term excluding the feelings
of the writer; the literal and factual meaning of a word. In logic,
the aggregate of objects that may be included under a word,
compared with *connotation* (q.v.).

DÉNOUEMENT. French, literally, untying (of plot). French
nouer is Latin *nōdāre*, from *nōdus*, knot. The issue of a play or
narrative regarded as the unravelling of the complications of the plot.

DERIVATIVE. Latin *dērīvāre*, to turn or draw off (liquid), to
disperse; *dē*, down, from, *rīvus*, a river. Not original, derived or
taken from something else. A word formed from another word.

DEROGATORY. Latin *dērogāre*, to repeal part of a law. Tending
to detract from, to impair. Disparagement or discredit to a person
or thing.

DESCRIPTION. Latin *dēscrībĕre*, to write down, copy. In a
literary work, description presents the chief qualities of time and
place, and creates the setting of the story. Sir Walter Scott,
writing on Jane Austen, said:

> The Big Bow-Wow strain I can do myself like any now going;
> but the exquisite touch which renders ordinary common-
> place things and characters interesting, from the truth of the
> description and the sentiment, is denied to me.

DETECTIVE STORY. Latin *dētegĕre*, *dētect-(um)*, to uncover. A
narrative in which a crime, often involving murder, is solved by a
detective. In 1841, *The Murders in the Rue Morgue*, by Edgar
Allan Poe, introduced the first fictional detective, Auguste Dupin.
In England, this form of story starts with *The Moonstone* (1868) by
Wilkie Collins. In 1887 begins the classic period with Conan
Doyle's *Study in Scarlet* and Sherlock Holmes. Then other writers
sprang up: G. K. Chesterton introduced Father Brown; Agatha
Christie created the Belgian detective Hercule Poirot; Dorothy
Sayers made intellectual puzzles for Lord Peter Wimsey. America
had many exponents, including Ellery Queen and Erle Stanley

Gardner, whose sturdy lawyer Perry Mason wins every case with speed of action and adroit court-room manœuvres.

DEUS EX MACHINA. Latin, god from the machine. In the ancient Greek drama, when a god was introduced to deal with a difficult situation, he was brought on to the stage by some mechanical device. Euripides uses this method in many of his plays. This expedient, however, was criticized. In the *Poetics,* Aristotle maintained that the resolving of the plot should develop naturally from the action itself. *Deus ex machina* has been extended to imply an unexpected event in a play or novel which clears up a difficulty. In contrast the term *diabolus* (devil) *ex machina* is used.

DEUTERAGONIST. Greek *deuteragōnistḗs,* an actor taking the second part in a drama; *deúteros,* second, *agōnistḗs,* actor. A person of next importance to the protagonist in drama. Aeschylus is generally regarded as the real founder of Greek tragedy. He introduced a second actor, the deuteragonist, where there had before been only one actor and the chorus. This made possible true dialogue and dramatic action.

DEVIL'S ADVOCATE. Greek *diábolos,* slanderer, from *diabállein,* to slander. Latin *advocātus,* called in. In *Modern English Usage,* H. W. Fowler says:

> Devil's advocate is very dangerous to those who like a picturesque phrase but dislike the trouble of ascertaining its sense. In the following example, for instance, the not unnatural blunder is made of supposing that it means a whitewasher, or one who pleads for a person who either is or is supposed to be wicked: 'Because the devil's advocate always starts with the advantage of possessing a bad case, Talleyrand's defender calls forth all our chivalrous sympathy.' The real devil's advocate, on the contrary, is one who, when the right of a person to canonization as a saint is being examined, puts the devil's claim to the ownership of him by collecting and presenting all the sins that he has ever commited; far from being the whitewasher of the wicked, the devil's advocate is the blackener of the good.

DIACRITIC. Greek *diakritikós,* from *diakrínein,* to separate, distinguish. A mark or sign under or above a letter used to distinguish its various values or sounds, e.g. ç, å, é, ö.

DIAERESIS. Greek *diaíresis*; *diá,* apart, *hairéein,* to take. A mark (¨) placed over the second of two vowels indicating that they are not one sound, as *naïve, aërated.* American English uses the diaeresis in words such as *preëminent*, *coöperate*, where the normal English usage is a hyphen.

DIALECT. Greek *diálektos*, from *dialégesthai*, to discourse. The language of a particular district or class. Much of the poetry of Burns is not written in the standard literary language. William Barnes wrote poems in the dialect of Dorset. Tennyson's *Northern Farmer* is a good example. George Eliot's tales of provincial life and Hardy's Wessex novels naturally introduce dialect in conversation. The strange forms and idioms hold our attention, for dialect has not the 'veil of familiarity'.

> Zoo up I clomb upon the thatch,
> An clapp'd en on; an' slided
> Right down ageän, an ran drough hatch,
> Behind the hedge, an' hided.
> The vier that wer clear avore,
> Begun to spweil their fun, min;
> The smoke all roll'd toward the door,
> For I'd a stopp'd the tun, min.
>
> Barnes, *What Dick an' I did*

DIALECTIC. Greek *dialektiké*, the art of logical discussion. The testing of truth by logical and analytical argument. A systematic line of deductive reasoning.

DIALOGUE. Greek *diálogos*, a conversation; *dialégesthai*, to discourse. A conversation between several people. A literary work in the form of a conversation; when joined to action the dialogue becomes a drama. The Greek philosophers adopted dialogue as the best way to instruct their pupils. Question and answer was the method used by Socrates. Plato's form of dialogue survives in the works of Herodas. Lucian's *Dialogues of the Dead* was borrowed by the French eighteenth-century writers Fontenelle and Fénelon in their *Dialogues des morts*. Landor used the method in his *Imaginary Conversations* and Oscar Wilde in *The Critic as Artist*.

The recent use of the word *dialogue* denotes an exchange of views and ideas between people or parties of different opinions, e.g. Roman Catholics and Protestants.

DIARY. Latin *diārium*, a daily allowance (of food and other things). A daily record of events. The two most famous diaries in English are those of Samuel Pepys and John Evelyn, both of the seventeenth century. These are documents of extraordinary interest, throwing light on the author's character, and on contemporary, everyday life.

DIATRIBE. Greek *diatribé*, a wearing away of time, study, discourse. A wordy attack upon some person or work. A bitter and violent criticism. Examples of the *diatribe* in Greek, characteristic of the Cynic and Stoic schools, are found in the works of Epictetus and Teles.

DIBRACH. Adaptation of Latin *dibrachys*, of two short syllables. In Greek and Latin prosody, a foot consisting of two short, unstressed syllables. A pyrrhic, represented by ◡ ◡.

DICTION. Latin *dīcĕre*, *dictum*, to say. The selection and arrangement of words in speech and writing. Dryden early used the word 'diction' when he said, 'There appears in every part of Horace's diction, or (to speak English) in all his expressions, a kind of noble and bold purity.'

DIDACTIC. Greek *didaktikós*, from *didáskein*, to teach. Intended to teach. Having the manner or purpose of a teacher. Many literary works are didactic. Hesiod's *Works and Days* is a practical treatise on farming. *De Rerum Naturā* of Lucretius is an exposition of the theories of Epicurus. Virgil's *Georgics* gives detailed advice on agriculture. Bagehot said it was not the purpose of poetry 'to chill you with didactic icebergs'. It may be argued that much of our greatest literature is in part didactic: Spenser's *Faerie Queene* is a vindication of the Protestant faith; Milton wrote *Paradise Lost* to 'justify the ways of God to men'; Bunyan's purpose in *The Pilgrim's Progress* is to lead men into the way of salvation.

There are degrees of didacticism. We may turn from George Eliot the 'interpreter of philosophical ideas' to Cowper who 'recommended private tuition at home'. Dryden speaks clearly when he says 'Delight is the chief if not the only end of poesy; instruction can be admitted but in the second place; for poesy only instructs as it delights.'

DIES IRAE. 'Day of wrath', the opening words of the greatest among medieval Latin hymns, ascribed to Thomas of Celano (*fl. c.* 1225), an early disciple of St. Francis of Assisi.

DIMETER. Greek *dímetros*, having two measures, from *di*, two, and *métron*, a measure. A verse consisting of two measures, a measure being a metrical foot. Iambic dimeter is exemplified in these lines from Dryden's *Alexander's Feast*:

> With ráv|ish'd Ears
> The Món|arch héars,
> Assúmes | the Gód,
> Affécts | to nód,
> And seéms | to shake | the Sphéres.

DIPHTHONG. Greek *diphthoggos*, having two sounds, from *di-*, twice, *phthóggos*, sound, voice. The combination of two vowel-sounds pronounced in one syllable (au, ou). The term is often misused for the *ae* ligature, as in *Caesar*, which is, of course, not a diphthong, but a simple vowel. The term is a phonetic one, and may be represented in writing by a single symbol, as in *cow*.

DIPODY. In the case of iambs, trochees, and anapaests, the Greeks regarded the unit as consisting of two feet, a dipody. An iambic trimeter accordingly consists of six iambs or three dipodies; this form is the metre of Greek tragic dialogue.

DIRECT SPEECH: *ORATIO RECTA*. The actual words used by a speaker. This is opposed to indirect speech, or *oratio obliqua*, in which the spoken words are changed into reported speech.

DIRGE. Latin *dīrige*, imperative of *dīrigĕre*, to direct; the first word of the opening Latin antiphon in the Matins part of the Office of the Dead, *Dirige Domine*. A song sung at burial, or in commemoration of the dead. Originally chanted in Roman funeral processions. The Greek threnody, *thrēnōidía; thrênos*, a lament, *ōidĕ*, a song, was also a song of lamentation. Later, the term is used for lyrics of mourning, such as *Fidele's Dirge* in Shakespeare's *Cymbeline*:

> Fear no more the heat o' the sun,
>   Nor the furious winter's rages;
> Thou thy worldly task hast done,
>   Home art gone, and ta'en thy wages.
> Golden lads and girls all must,
>   As chimney-sweepers, come to dust.

DIRTY PROOF. A proof returned to the printers which contains many corrections and additions.

DISCORDIA CONCORS. This phrase of the bringing together by the Metaphysicals of things which disagree was used by Johnson in his *Life of Cowley*:

> Wit, abstracted from its effects upon the hearer, may be more rigorously and philosophically considered as a kind of *discordia concors*, a combination of dissimilar images or discovery of occult resemblances in things apparently unlike. Of wit thus defined they (Donne and the other Metaphysicals) have more than enough.

DISSOCIATION OF SENSIBILITY. In his essay 'The Metaphysical Poets', T. S. Eliot says:

> The poets of the seventeenth century, the successors of the dramatists of the sixteenth, possessed a mechanism of sensibility which could devour any kind of experience. . . . In the seventeenth century a dissociation of sensibility set in, from which we have never recovered; and this dissociation, as is natural, was aggravated by the influence of the two most powerful poets of the century, Milton and Dryden. Each of these men performed certain poetic functions so magnificently well that the magnitude of the effect concealed the absence of others. The language went on and in some respects improved; the best verse of Collins, Gray, Johnson, and even Goldsmith satisfies some of our fastidious demands better than that of Donne or Marvell or King. But while the language became more refined, the feeling became more crude. The feeling, the sensibility, expressed in the *Country Churchyard* (to say nothing of Tennyson and Browning) is cruder than that in the *Coy Mistress*.

DISSONANCE. Latin *dissonāre*, to disagree in sound. A discord. A combination of harsh-sounding words which is sometimes effective.

> For how to the heart's cheering
> The down-dugged ground-hugged grey
> Hovers off, the jay-blue heavens appearing
> Of pied and peeled May!
> Blue-beating and hoary-glow height . . .
>
> Gerard Manley Hopkins, *The Wreck of the Deutschland*

DISTANCE. Latin *distāre*, to stand apart. Distance and objectivity is the detached, impartial attitude of the artist, showing facts without obvious colouring due to individual tastes and views.

DISTICH. Greek *distikhon*, from *di*, twice, two, double and *stikhos*, a line. A pair of verse lines making complete sense; a couplet; term *distich* is often used for the couplet employed in classical elegiacs, introduced by Ennius and perfected by Tibullus, Propertius, and Ovid.

DISTRIBUTED STRESS. The effect produced when it is hard to determine which of two consecutive syllables takes the stress. The stress or accent seems to hover over both syllables, so it is called *hovering accent.* In the following lines from *Paradise Lost*, Milton uses distributed stress to create a sad, fading sound:

So farewell hope, and, with hope, farewell fear. . . .
Now came still Evening on, and Twilight gray.

DITHYRAMB. Greek *dīthúrambos*, dithyramb; a Greek choral lyric originally connected with the worship of Dionysus, sung by a 'circular choir' probably of fifty singers. 'The name, of uncertain origin, is perhaps connected with *thríambos*, the Latin *triumphus*.' (J. M. Edmunds.) Any wild chant or song, in tone and structure suggesting the dithyramb.

DIVERBIUM. Latin *dīverbium*, the dialogue of a comedy. Roman comedies comprised spoken dialogue and portions that were declaimed and sung. The spoken dialogue was called *dīverbium*. All other portions are usually called *cantica*.

DIVERTISSEMENT. French. A short ballet given between longer pieces. A diversion; a light work of literature.

DOG-LATIN. Mongrel, unidiomatic Latin. In *English Humorists*, Thackeray says:

> 'Nescio quid est materia cum me,' Sterne writes to one of his friends (in dog-Latin, and very sad dog-Latin too); 'sed sum fatigatus et ægrotus de meâ uxore plus quam unquam:' which means, I am sorry to say, 'I don't know what is the matter with me: but I am more tired and sick of my wife than ever.'

DOGGEREL. Probably from Latin *doga*, cask-stave. Compare this with sixteenth-century dudgeon verse. Dudgeon was a kind of wood used for knife-handles. The word was usually applied contemptuously, the wooden handle being contrasted with ivory, metal and other fine materials. Doggerel is a rather vague term of abuse applied to trivial, jingling or irregular measures in burlesque verse. Chaucer used it for 'undistinguished or unpoetic verse or rhyme of any kind.' In his *Prologue to Melibeus* he says:

> No more of this for Goddes dignitee,
> Quod oure hoste, for thou makest me
> So wery of thy veray lewednesse,
> That al so wisly God my soule blesse,
> Min eres aken of thy drafty speche.
> Now swiche a rime the devil I beteche;
> This may wel be rime dogerel, quod he.

Skelton's immense vivacity gives his doggerel immediate interest.
Here is an example from his *Doctors of the Vintrie*:

> A little rag of rhetoric,
> A less lump of logic,
> A piece or a patch of philosophy,
> Then forthwith by and by
> They tumble so in theology,
> Drowned in dregs of divinity,
> That they judge themselves to be
> Doctors of the chair in the Vintrie
> At the Three Cranes . . .

DOLCE STIL NUOVO. Italian, literally, sweet new style. Dante
uses this phrase in the 'Purgatorio' of the *Divine Comedy*. He was
influenced by his predecessor, Guido Guinizelli, 'il padre mio',
finding in his poetry a new belief that man's love for woman had its
source in God. In his great epic poem, Dante himself presents this
combination of earthly and divine love.

DOMESTIC TRAGEDY. Latin *domesticus*, of the house and home.
In the eighteenth century an effort was made to adapt the formula
of classical tragedy to the domestic life of the time, resulting in
such plays as *The London Merchant* by George Lillo and *La
Brouette du vinaigrier* by Louis Mercier. The term has also been
applied to what may be called the Elizabethan domestic tragedy,
including such plays as *Arden of Feversham* (which has been
attributed to Shakespeare) and *A Woman Kilde with Kindnesse* by
Thomas Heywood.

DORIC. Greek *Dōrikós*, derived from Doris, a small country in
Greece, the home of the Dorians. The first pastoral poets, Theocritus, Bion and Moschus, wrote in the Doric dialect of Greek, and
in *Lycidas* Milton uses 'Doric lay' for pastoral poem:

> With eager thought warbling his Doric lay.

The word has come to mean 'unrefined', 'rustic', as opposed to
'Attic'. It is used of a 'broad' dialect, as that of the North of
England, and Scotland.

DOUBLE-DECKER NOVELS. In the Victorian Age the plain and
direct purpose of the novel was considered to be to amuse by a
succession of scenes painted from nature, and by a thread of
emotional narrative. This view of the novel with its emphasis on
'what happened next' encouraged serial publication. When the
final issue was in two parts the name 'double-decker' novel was
used. A 'three-decker' was a serial novel with a final issue in
three parts.

DOUBLE ENTENDRE. French of the seventeenth century, superseded now by (mot) à double entente. An ambiguous word or phrase with two meanings, one usually absurd or indecent.

DOUBLE RHYME. When the stressed rhyming syllable is followed by one or more unstressed syllables the rhyme is double or feminine. These rhymes are found most often in humorous verse, as shown in these lines from John Byrom's *Epigram on the Feuds between Handel and Bononcini*:

> Some say, that Signor Bononcini,
> Compar'd to Handel's a mere ninny;
> Others aver, to him, that Handel
> Is scarcely fit to hold a candle.

DRAMA. Greek *drâma*, a deed, action on the stage, from *drân*, to do, act. Latin *dramatis personae*, characters of the play. Stage-play. The composition and presentation of plays.

> The stage but echoes back the public voice.
> The drama's laws the drama's patrons give,
> For we that live to please, must please to live.

Samuel Johnson, *Prologue at the Opening of Drury Lane*, 1747

DRAMATIC IRONY. This is the device of putting into a speaker's mouth words which have for the audience a meaning not intended by the speaker. Sophocles used dramatic irony with great effect in *Oedipus Tyrannus*. Shakespeare presents it strikingly in *Troilus and Cressida*, and in *Macbeth* when the drunken porter jestingly talks of being the porter at Hell's gate.

There is a second type of dramatic irony, where words spoken by a person later recoil upon him. After the murder of Duncan, Lady Macbeth says to her husband, 'A little water clears us of this deed'; yet in the sleep-walking scene she says that all the waters of the ocean will not remove the stain of blood from her hand.

In Galsworthy's *Strife*, Roberts contends that anyone can 'stand up to nature' if only he has the will. The death of his wife from weakness and starvation brings it home to him that he is wrong.

DRAMATIC LYRIC. Browning's *Dramatic Lyrics* appeared in 1842. He achieved great success in this poetic form in which a single character, in his speech, reveals his own personality and a particular dramatic situation. Here is the opening stanza of *Soliloquy of the Spanish Cloister*:

> Gr-r-r — there go, my heart's abhorrence!
> Water your damned flower-pots, do!
> If hate killed men, Brother Lawrence,
> God's blood, would not mine kill you!

What? your myrtle-bush wants trimming?
Oh, that rose has prior claims —
Need its leaden vase filled brimming?
Hell dry you up with its flames!

Other examples of the dramatic lyric are: Tennyson, *Tithonus*, *St. Simeon Stylites*; Yeats, *A Last Confession*; John Heath-Stubbs, *Stone-Age Woman*.

DRAMATIC MONOLOGUE: MONODRAMA. A poem in the form of a monologue, which reveals a dramatic situation and the characters of other people besides the speaker. Examples are Browning's *Mr. Sludge 'The Medium'*, and *My Last Duchess*.

DRAMATIC RULES, NEO-CLASSIC PERIOD. Boileau's *Art poétique* (1674), did much to establish immutable rules for dramatic writing, based on the unities, during the Augustan period. Dryden, Pope in his *Essay on Criticism*, and later George Farquhar, criticized rules which had been formalized by academic writers. In *The Rambler*, Johnson made a balanced judgment:

It ought to be the first endeavour of a writer to distinguish nature from custom; or that which is established because it is right, from that which is right only because it is established; that he may neither violate essential principles by a desire of novelty, nor debar himself from the attainment of beauties within his view, by a needless fear of breaking rules which no literary dictator had authority to enact.

DRAMATURGE. Greek *drāmatourgós*, a maker of plays. A dramatist.

DRAMATURGY. From Greek *drāmatourgós*, a maker of plays. The art of composing dramas, and of producing them on the stage.

DREAM ALLEGORY. Greek *allēgoría*, from *állos*, other, *agoreúein*, to speak, from *agorá*, place of assembly. A type of medieval verse-romance put into the form of a dream. Some of the conventions were established by *Roman de la Rose*, written in the thirteenth century by Guillaume de Lorris and completed some years later by Jean de Meung. *Romaunt of the Rose*, attributed to Chaucer, was a translation of this allegorical love poem, and introduces a number of allegorical personages to us: the God of Love, Gladness, Courtesy, and others. Chaucer wrote other dream allegories: *The Book of the Duchesse*, *The Hous of Fame*, *The Parlement of Foules*. William Langland used the same form for *Piers Plowman*.

DROLL: DROLL-HUMOURS. French *drôle*, probably from Dutch *drollig*, odd. The ordinance of 2nd September 1642 forbade stage plays. To evade this during the Commonwealth, farces or comic scenes were adapted from earlier plays, or invented by the actors, and performed at fairs or taverns. These *drolls* included short scenes with Falstaff, Bottom the Weaver, and the grave-diggers from *Hamlet*.

DRY-POINT. A process of engraving upon copper plate with a hard steel needle by which fine lines are drawn without acid. Also an engraving so produced.

DUODECIMO. Latin *duodecimus*, the twelfth. Abbreviation 12mo or 12°. The size of a book (about 5 × 7½ inches) composed of sheets folded so as to make twelve leaves, twenty-four pages.

DUOLOGUE. Irregularly formed from Greek *dúo*, two, Greek *lógos*, discourse. A dramatic piece with two actors. A conversation between two people.

DUPLE METRE. Latin *duplus*, double, twofold. When the metrical pattern is in feet of two syllables, the rhythm of the line is duple. Herrick's *Upon his departure hence* is an example:

> Thus I
> Passe by,
> And die:
> As One,
> Unknown,
> And gon.

E

ECCLESIASTICAL DRAMA. *See* Liturgical Drama.

ECHO VERSE. A device in verse by which one line repeats the concluding syllables of the preceding line, with a change in meaning. Here is an example, *A Gentle Echo on Woman* by Jonathan Swift:

> *Shepherd:* Echo, I ween, will in the woods reply,
>> And quaintly answer questions: shall I try?
>>> Echo: Try.
>> What must we do our passion to express?
>>> Press.
>> How shall I please her, who ne'er loved before?
>>> Be Fore.
>> What most moves women when we them address?
>>> A dress.
>> Say, what can keep her chaste whom I adore?
>>> A door.

ECHOIC. Greek *ēkhṓ*, a sound. Of the nature of an echo, a repetition of sounds. Many echoic words are found in everyday speech: *crash, gargle, twitter*. In *The English Language*, Ernest Weekley quotes a Spanish professor who asks:

> How could one improve on *splash, smash, ooze, shriek, slush, glide, squeak, coo*? Who could think of anything more *sloppy* than *slop*? Is not the word *sweet* a kiss in itself, and what could suggest a more peremptory obstacle than *stop*?

More expressive than ordinary words they play effective part in poetry:

> Double, double toil and trouble
> Fire burn, and cauldron bubble.   *Macbeth*

> The mellow lin-lan-lone of evening bells.
>> Tennyson, *Far-far-away*

> Strong gongs groaning as the guns boom far,
> Don John of Austria is going to the war,
> Stiff flags straining in the night-blasts cold
> In the gloom black-purple, in the glint old-gold,
> Torchlight crimson on the copper kettle-drums,
> Then the tuckets, then the trumpets, then the
>> cannon, and he comes.
>> G. K. Chesterton, *Lepanto*

ECLECTIC. Greek *eklektikós*, *eklégō*, pick out. In ancient use, it defined those philosophers 'who selected such doctrines as pleased them in every school' (Liddell and Scott). It applies to the person who borrows freely from various sources, without being exclusive in taste or opinion.

ECLOGUE. Greek *eklogē*, selection; *eklégō*, pick out. A short poem in the pastoral tradition and in the form of a dialogue between shepherds, as in Virgil's *Eclogues* and *Bucolics*. In the Renaissance it applied to any verse on pastoral themes such as Alexander Barclay's *Eclogues* in 1515, and Spenser's *The Shepheards Calender*. In the eighteenth century the term referred only to the form. In such modern poems as Frost's *Build Soil*, Allen Tate's *Eclogue of the Liberal and the Poet*, MacNeice's *Eclogue from Iceland*, and *Age of Anxiety* by Auden, the eclogue has become a political and social pastoral.

EDITIŌ PRINCEPS. Latin. First or earliest printed edition of a book. Often of great value to critical scholars, as being a record of readings of manuscripts long since lost.

EDITION. Latin *ēditus*; *ēděre*, to give out. A first edition is the book as it is originally published. A new impression, if it involves either no changes in the text or illustrations or only minor corrections, is called a new printing. A thorough revision, resulting in a markedly different book, is called a new edition. The term edition applies also to a version of a text by a particular editor, as Verity's edition of *King Lear*.

EDWARDIAN AGE. The early years of the twentieth century, the reign of Edward VII (1901–1910). An age of criticism and reaction, as seen in the works of Bernard Shaw and H. G. Wells. Also a period of great prosperity, stability, and assurance.

EGLOGUE. *See* ECLOGUE.

EGO. Latin *ego*, I. Introduced in the eighteenth century to connote the 'conscious, thinking subject', and borrowed by the Freudian school of psychoanalysis in the nineteenth.

EGOTISTICAL SUBLIME. Latin *ego*, I. The phrase means an exalted degree of self-centredness which Keats saw in Wordsworth.

> As to the poetical Character itself (I mean that sort of which, if I am anything, I am a Member — that sort distinguished from the Wordsworthian or egotistical sublime, which is a thing per se and stands alone) it is not itself — it has no self.

It is everything and nothing — it has no character — it enjoys light and shade; it lives in gusts, be it foul or fair, high or low, rich or poor, mean or elevated. It has as much delight in conceiving an Iago as an Imogen.

Keats: letter to Richard Woodhouse, 27th October 1818

See John Jones's *The Egotistical Sublime: a History of Wordsworth's Imagination.*

EINFÜHLUNG. See EMPATHY.

EISTEDDFOD. Welsh word meaning 'session', from *eistedd*, to sit. A congress of Welsh bards held annually. Its purpose is to promote the use of the Welsh language, both spoken and literary.

ELECTROTYPE. Greek *ĕlektron*, amber. A facsimile plate of another plate made by taking an impression in wax, depositing on the wax a thin sheet of copper by electrolysis, and backing the copper sheet with type metal. Exact copies can then be printed in very large numbers. The use of 'electros', as they are called, has made possible the large-scale printing of newspapers.

ELEGANCE. Latin *ēlegant(em)*, from *ēligĕre*, to pick out; hence originally daintiness, fastidiousness. A highly wrought, refined, and artificial way of writing.

ELEGANCY. A tastefully correct, delicate, or dignified word displacing a more ordinary word, such as *abode* for *home*, *assemblage* for *collection*, *emporium* for *shop*.

ELEGANT VARIATION. Latin *ēligĕre*, to pick out, hence originally daintiness, fastidiousness. In *Modern English Usage*, H. W. Fowler says:

It is the second-rate writers, those intent rather on expressing themselves prettily than on conveying their meaning clearly, and still more those whose notions of style are based on a few misleading rules of thumb, that are chiefly open to the allurements of elegant variation. . . . The fatal influence is the advice given to young writers never to use the same word twice in a sentence — or within twenty lines or other limit:
Were I an artist I could *paint* the Golf Links at Gaya and call it 'A Yorkshire Moor'; I could *depict* a water-way in Eastern Bengal and call it 'The Bure near Wroxham'; I could *portray* a piece of the Punjab and call it 'A Stretch of Essex'.

We should remember that not all variation is mere elegant variation.

ELEGIAC.   Greek *élegos*, a lament.   In Greek and Latin verse the metre consisted of alternate dactylic hexameters and dactylic pentameters.   The elegiac (or heroic) quatrain in English verse is iambic pentameter rhyming alternately, as in Gray's *Elegy*:
> Here rests his head upon the lap of Earth
> A youth to fortune and to fame unknown.
> Fair Science frown'd not on his humble birth,
> And Melancholy mark'd him for her own.

ELEGY.   Greek *elegeía*; *élegos*, mournful poem.   A song of lamentation over someone dead.   It is a personal, reflective poem.   The great English elegies are Milton's *Lycidas*, on the death of Edward King; Gray's *Elegy written in a Country Churchyard*; Shelley's *Adonais*, commemorating John Keats; Tennyson's *In Memoriam* written in memory of Arthur H. Hallam; and Matthew Arnold's *Thyrsis* to commemorate Arthur Hugh Clough.

ELEVATION.   Latin *ēlevātiōn-(em)*, a lifting, raising.   The rise in dignity which comes to certain words.   Dr. Johnson described *clever*, *fun*, and *gambler* as rather low words.   Pierce Egan indicates many words in his *Life in London; or the Day and Night Scenes of Jerry Hawthorn and his elegant friend Corinthian Tom* as low, by setting them in italics.

In his book on *The English Language* (1912), Logan Pearsall Smith spoke of 'words like *rowdy*, *bogus*, *boom* and *rollocking*, at which we boggle'.   Today they have become accepted, as have those mentioned by Dr. Johnson above.

ELISION.   Latin *ēlīdĕre*, to strike out.   The dropping out or suppressing of a vowel or syllable in pronunciation, or, less frequently, of a passage in a book.   The omission of an unstressed syllable so that the line may conform to the metrical scheme as shown in this line:
> What was th'impediment that broke this off?

The elision of two vowels at the end of one word and the beginning of the next is called *synalepha*, from Greek *sunaloiphĕ*, contraction of two syllables.

In *Essays and Studies*, Swinburne says 'elision is a necessity, not a luxury, of metre'.

ELIZABETHAN.   A term applied to the persons and writers of the reign of Elizabeth I (1558–1603) and of the first Stuart, James I (1603–1625).

ELLIPSIS.   Greek *élleipsis*; *elleípein*, to fall short, deficiency.   The omission in a sentence of one or more words, which would be needed to express the sense completely.

> Yet to imagine
> An Antony, were nature's piece 'gainst fancy,
> Condemning shadows quite.   *Antony and Cleopatra*

> What! all my pretty chickens and their dam
> At one fell swoop?   *Macbeth*

ELOCUTION. Latin *ēlocūtiō-(nem)*, a speaking aloud. The effective use of voice and gesture in public speaking.

EMBATERION. Greek. A marching song.

EMBLEM-BOOK. A book containing pictures whose symbolic meaning is expressed in words. This form of expression was first used by Alciati, of Milan, whose *Emblematum Libellus* appeared in 1522. His English followers were Quarles and Wither. *Emblems* by Quarles was published in 1635, containing quaint engravings. Wither produced religious exercises, including *Heleluiah* in 1641, and a rhomboidal dirge in *Faire-Virtue*, 1622. Here is the first stanza:

> *Ah me!*
> Am I the Swaine,
> That late from sorrow free,
> Did all the cares on earth disdaine?
> And still untoucht, as at some safer Games,
> Play'd with the burning coals of Love & Beauties flames?
> Was't I, could dive & sound each passions secret depth at will;
> And, from those huge overwhelmings, rise, by help of Reason still?
> And am I now, oh heavens! for trying this in vaine,
> So sunk, that I shall never rise againe?
> Then let Dispaire, set Sorrows string,
> For *Strains* that dolefulst be,
> And I will sing,
> *Ah me.*

EMBRYONIC RHYME. *See* NEAR RHYME.

EMENDATION. Latin *ēmendāre*, to correct, to emend; from *menda*, a fault. The removal of errors from the text of a book.

EMOTIVE LANGUAGE. Latin *emovēre*, to stir. Language tending to excite emotion in regard to its subject. It is opposed to referential language which is intended for reference, as in the study of science. C. K. Ogden and I. A. Richards in *The Meaning of Meaning* make a clear distinction between emotive and referential language.

EMPATHY. Greek *empátheia*, affection, passion. The power of projecting one's personality into (and so fully comprehending) the object of contemplation (*Concise Oxford Dictionary*).

Keats wrote in his letter of 22nd November 1817 to Benjamin Bailey:

> The Setting Sun will always set me to rights, or if a Sparrow come before my Window, I take part in its existence and pick about the gravel.

EMPHASIS. Greek from *emphaínein*, from *en* and *phaínein*, to show. The stress laid on words to indicate the special significance of the thing said. This may be done by various other methods: the use of contrast, repetition, inversion, antithesis, exclamation, climax, overstatement.

EMPIRICAL. Greek *empeirikós*, from *empeiría*, experience, from *peîra*, trial. Based on the results of trial or experiment only. Known by observation and experience, and not by theory. *Empiricism* is the system which regards experience as the only source of knowledge.

ENALLAGE. Greek *enallagé*, change. The substitution of one grammatical form for another, e.g. present for past tense, singular for plural, noun for verb. We can *toe* the line, *ditch* a car, be quickly *nettled*, and have a good *cry*.

> Eros,
> Wouldst thou be *window'd* in great Rome and see
> Thy master thus with pleach'd arms . . .
> *Antony and Cleopatra*

> But me no buts.   *Richard II*

> Why is this thus? What is the reason of this thusness?
> *Artemus Ward's Lecture*

The term only applies to words so used intentionally, for effect, and in the full knowledge of the fact that it is a breach of normal usage — not to the slipshod use of nouns as verbs and so on, which has become so common of late, e.g. *to loan, to signature.*

ENCHIRIDION. Greek *encheirídion*, a manual. A manual; a book to be carried in the hand.

ENCLOSED RHYME. This is the form *a b b a*, as in Tennyson's *In Memoriam*.

> Now fades the last long streak of snow,
>   Now burgeons every maze of quick
>   About the flowering squares, and thick
> By ashen roots the violets blow.

ENCOMIASTIC VERSE. Greek *egkômion*, a song of praise, from *kômos*, revelry. A Greek choral hymn praising some man, not a god; then a eulogy of the host at a banquet; then eulogies in general. First used by Simonides of Ceos; then by Pindar, praising the winners at the Games. Wordsworth glorifies a virtue in his *Ode to Duty*, and Tennyson in his *Ode on the Death of the Duke of Wellington* exclaims:

> The last great Englishman is low.

ENDPAPERS. In bookbinding this is pasting together white or coloured sheets for lining the insides of the covers. The endpapers, which are often illustrations or maps, are sewn or pasted on to the book. There are more than fifteen ways of constructing them.

END-RHYME. One which comes at the end of a line of verse. This type of rhyme is found in conventionally rhymed verse, as in these lines from Pope's *An Essay on Criticism*:

> A little learning is a dang'rous thing;
> Drink deep, or taste not the Pierian spring:
> There shallow draughts intoxicate the brain,
> And drinking largely sobers us again.

END-STOPPED LINE. Having a strong pause at the end of the line of verse. For example:

> His ransom there is none but I shall pay:
> I'll hale the Dauphin headlong from his throne:
> His crown shall be the ransom of my friend;
> Four of their lords I'll change for one of ours.
>
> *1 Henry VI*

> Soft is the strain when zephyr gently blows,
> And the smooth stream in smoother numbers flows;
> But when loud surges lash the sounding shore,
> The hoarse, rough verse should like the torrent roar.
>
> Pope, *An Essay on Criticism*

ENJAMBMENT: ENJAMBEMENT. French *enjambement*, from *enjamber*, to stride over, from *jambe*, leg. The continuation of the sentence beyond the second line of one couplet into the first line of the next. The following examples come from Pope's *January and May*:

> Th'assuming Wit, who deems himself so wise,
> As his mistaken patron to advise,
> Let him not dare to vent his dang'rous thought.

'Nay', (quoth the King), 'dear Madam, be not wroth:
I yield it up; but since I gave my oath,
That this much-injur'd Knight again should see;
It must be done — I am a King', said he,
'And one, whose faith has ever sacred been.'

In English poetry enjambed lines are also called *run-on* or *unstopped*.

ENTELECHY.   Greek *entelékheia, en télei ékhein,* to be in perfection. An Aristotelian term meaning the realization or complete expression of what was potential.   Used by later writers to signify whatever helps to develop perfection.   In Rabelais, *Entelechy* is the kingdom of the lady Quintessence.

ENTHYMEME.   Greek *enthúmēma,* a thought, argument.   A syllogism in which one premise is omitted, as 'rain is water and therefore rain is wet'; the major premise, 'water is wet', has been omitted.

ENTR'ACTE.   A performance, usually musical, in the interval between the acts of a play.

ENVELOPE STANZA.   This term is applied to a stanza which has enclosing rhymes.   A famous example is the stanza of Tennyson's *In Memoriam*:

> Our little systems have their day;
>   They have their day and cease to be:
>   They are but broken lights of thee,
> And thou, O Lord, art more than they.

ENVOY.   Old French *envoye, envoiier,* to send; *en voie,* on the way. The final section of a poem commending the poem to the reader or the person to whom it is dedicated.   Oscar Wilde ends 'With a Copy of *A House of Pomegranates*' with this Envoy:

> Go little book
> To him who, on a lute with horns of pearl,
> Sang of the white feet of the Golden Girl:
> And bid him look
> Into thy pages: it may hap that he
> May find that golden maidens dance thru thee.

EPANADIPLOSIS.   Greek *diplōsis,* a compounding of words.   A figure of speech in which a sentence begins and ends with the same word, as in this example from Sidney's *Arcadia*:

> The thoughts are but overflowings of the mind, and the tongue is but a servant of the thoughts.

EPANODOS. Greek *epánodos*, a repeating of words. The same word or phrase repeated at the beginning and middle, or the middle and the end of a sentence. A return to the regular thread of discourse after a digression. For example, a line from Sidney's *Arcadia*:

Hear you this soul-invading voice, and count it but a voice?

EPANORTHOSIS. Greek, literally, a setting straight again. This figure of speech is a kind of turning back on something said, in order to correct it, or to comment on it. In *The Shepheards Calender*, Spenser says:

I love thilke lasse (alas! why doe I love?)
And am forlorne, (alas! why am I lorne?)

ÉPATER LE BOURGEOIS. See PHILISTINE.

EPIC. Greek *epikós*, from *épos*, word, narrative, poem. Epic is usually held to be synonymous with heroic poem. In *Short Handbook of Literary Terms*, George Loane says:

Homer's *Iliad* and *Odyssey* have set a standard to all succeeding poets, and from them also Aristotle drew the famous 'rules' over which the critics have quarrelled much. It seems essential to the idea of an epic (i) that its action should be one, great, and entire; (ii) that its hero should be distinguished and more our concern; (iii) that the episodes should easily arise from the main fable, i.e. there should be no parts detachable without loss to the whole. Wordsworth and Coleridge agreed with the earlier critics that the agency of beings superior to man is a necessary part of the conception. Length is clearly essential. To succeed in such a poem requires a comprehensive intellect of the first order, and great industry, in addition to the sensibility which is characteristic of all poets.

Virgil's *Aeneid*, Dante's *Divina Commedia*, the *Mahābhārata* and *Rāmāyana* of Hindu literature, the *Chanson de Roland*, the *Poema del Cid*, Ariosto's *Orlando Furioso*, Tasso's *Gerusalemme Liberata*, Camoens's *Lusiado*, Milton's *Paradise Lost* and *Paradise Regained*, are famous epics.

EPIC NARRATIVE. In *The Anatomy of Poetry*, Marjorie Boulton says:

I would use this term to denote poems in the dignified, formal style associated with epic, or in some other highly ornamented style, telling a story of heroic action or suffering, but with one simple action and without the length and complexity of the true epic.

Examples: Chaucer, *The Prioresses Tale, The Clerk's Tale*; Shakespeare, *Venus and Adonis, The Rape of Lucrece*; Tennyson, *The Idylls of the King*; Matthew Arnold, *Sohrab and Rustum*; John Masefield, *The Everlasting Mercy*; C. Day Lewis, *Nabara*.

EPIGONES. Greek *epígonoi*, those born after. The less distinguished successors of a great generation. *The Scholar-Gipsy* and *Thyrsis* by Matthew Arnold may be called *epigones* of English pastoral poetry.

EPIGRAM. Greek *epígramma*, an inscription; *epí*, upon, *grámma*, a writing; *gráphein*, to write. Four meanings which have developed quite naturally. Originally an inscription, usually in verse, on a building, tomb, or coin. Then a short poem ending in a witty or ingenious turn of thought. Hence a pungent or antithetical saying. Lastly, a style marked by such sayings. Here is *Epigram ii, The Dead Poet* of Callimachus, translated by William Cory:

> They told me, Heraclitus, they told me you were dead;
> They brought me bitter news to hear and bitter tears to shed.
> I wept, as I remember'd how often you and I
> Had tired the sun with talking and sent him down the sky.

Coleridge's definition is an epigram itself:

> What is an epigram? A dwarfish whole:
> Its body brevity, and wit its soul.

Further examples:

> I would live to study and not study to live.
> > Francis Bacon, *Memorial of Access*

> I can resist everything except temptation.
> > Oscar Wilde, *Lady Windermere's Fan*

> Her whole life is an Epigram, smart, smooth and neatly pen'd,
> Platted quite neat to catch applause with a sliding noose at the end.
> > Blake, *Miscellaneous Poems and Fragments*

EPIGRAPH. Greek *epigraphḗ*; *epí*, upon, *gráphō*, write. An inscription on stone, statue, coin. A quotation placed before a book or chapter as a motto. The imprint on a title-page (now obsolete).

EPILOGUE. Greek *epílogos*, conclusion; *epí*, upon, *légein*, to speak. The peroration or final section of a speech. The conclusion of a literary work; the moral of a fable. A speech by one of the actors at the end of a play asking for the indulgence of the critics and the audience.

EPINIKION. Greek *nikē*, the victory ode.

EPIPHANY. Greek *epipháneia*, manifestation (in the New Testament applied to the 'appearing' of Christ). The appearance of some divine or superhuman being. The festival commemorating the manifestation of Christ to the Gentiles symbolized in the persons of the Magi; celebrated on the sixth of January. Hence 'Twelfth Night', which is the festival of the 'Three Kings'.

EPIRRHĒMA. The satiric speech on current affairs spoken in Greek comedy by the leader of the chorus after the *parábasis*.

EPISODE. Greek *epeisódion*, coming in besides, from *epí*, on, *eis*, into, *hodós*, way. An incidental event within a longer narrative. It is sometimes closely related to the plot.

Also, the sections into which a serialized work is divided are referred to as *episodes*.

EPISODIC. Greek *epeisódion*, coming in besides, from *epí*, on, *eis*, into, *hodós*, way. Of the nature of an episode. A literary work which has a number of episodes not closely connected with the central theme of the story.

EPISTEMOLOGY. Greek *epistēmē*, knowledge. The theory of the method of knowledge.

EPISTLE. Greek *epistolé*; *epí*, on the occasion of, *stéllein*, to send. A letter, especially one from an apostle, forming part of the canon of Scripture and ranking as literature, such as *The Epistle of Paul the Apostle to the Romans*.

It is also a verse letter, a form used by many English poets, including Donne, Johnson, Burns, Shelley, Byron, and Pope, whose *Epistle to Dr. Arbuthnot* begins:

> Shut, shut the door, good John! fatigu'd I said,
> Tye up the knocker, say I'm sick, I'm dead.
> The Dog-star rages! nay 'tis past a doubt,
> All Bedlam, or Parnassus, is let out:
> Fire in each eye, and papers in each hand
> They rave, recite, and madden round the land.

EPISTROPHE. Greek *epí*, upon, at, *strophé*, turning, from *stréphō*. A figure of speech in which each sentence or clause ends with the same word, as 'we were born to sorrow, pass our time in sorrow, end our days in sorrow' (*Oxford English Dictionary*).

EPITAPH. Greek *epitáphion*, a funeral oration, from *epí*, upon, over, and *táphos*, a tomb. Words inscribed on a tomb or monument in memory of the dead. 'Here rests one that never rested before.'

A poem or prose statement in memory of the dead, expressing respect and sometimes disrespect. An example is the Epitaph from Gray's *Elegy Written in a Country Churchyard*. Burns wrote this epitaph on a schoolmaster:

> Here lie Willie Michie's banes;
> O Satan, when ye tak him,
> Gie him the schoolin' of your weans,
> For clever deils he'll mak them!

Charles Lamb, when a little boy, walking in a churchyard with his sister, and reading the epitaphs, said to her, 'Mary, where are all the naughty people buried?'

EPITHALAMIUM. Greek *epithalámion*, a bridal song, from *thálamos*, bride-chamber. A song or poem in honour of a marriage. As a literary form it was brought to perfection by such poets as Sappho, Anacreon, Pindar, Theocritus, and Catullus. In English literature, the most famous examples are Spenser's *Epithalamion* and *Prothalamion*; the former was written in celebration of his marriage with Elizabeth Boyle in 1594. It is the most perfect of all his poems, and was printed with the *Amoretti*.

EPITHET. Greek *epítheton*, attributed, added; *epí*, on, *tithénai*, to place. An adjective expressing a quality or attribute considered characteristic of a person or thing. An appellation or descriptive term, as in Charles *the Bold* or Alphonse *the Avenger*.

> Ah, fair Zenocrate! — divine Zenocrate!
> Fair is too foul an epithet for thee.
>
> Marlowe, *Tamburlaine*

> The belching whale
> And humming water must o'erwhelm thy corpse,
> Lying with simple shells.
>
> Shakespeare, *Pericles*

EPITOME. Greek *epitomé*, an abridgement; from *epitémnein*, to cut short; *témnō*, cut. A brief summary or abstract of the chief points in a book. A condensed account. A thing that represents another in miniature, shown in these lines from Dryden's *Absalom and Achitophel*:

> A man so various, that he seem'd to be
> Not one, but all Mankind's Epitome.
> Stiff in Opinions, always in the wrong;
> Was Everything by starts, and Nothing long:
> But, in the course of one revolving Moon,
> Was Chymist, Fidler, States-man, and Buffoon.

EPIZEUXIS. Greek *epízeuxis*, a fastening together. A figure of speech by which a phrase or word is repeated with vehemence or emphasis, as in this line of Sir Philip Sidney:

The time is changed, my lute, the time is changed.

EPODE. Latin *epōdus*, from Greek *epōidós*, last portion of an ode, additional song. A lyric metre invented by Archilochus, in which a longer line is followed by a shorter. In Greek choruses it was chanted after the antistrophe. In Roman literature it refers to poems (e.g. the *Epodes* of Horace) written in that metre.

EPONYMOUS. Greek *epónymos*, giving the name to; *epí*, upon, to, *ónoma*, a name. Especially used of mythical characters from whose names the names of people, places, were reputed to be derived. An eponymous hero gives his name also to a play, as Hamlet does to *Hamlet*.

EPOPEE. French *épopée*, from Greek *epopoiía*, poem-making. Epic poem or poetry.

EPOS. Greek *épos*, word, song. Early unwritten epic poetry; epic poem.

EPYLLION. Greek *epúllion*, a scrap of poetry. A brief epic, such as the poem of Theocritus on Heracles as an infant, and that of Catullus on the marriage of Thetis and Peleus.

EQUIVALENCE. Late Latin *aequivalēre*, to be of equal value. In prosody, the use of a foot other than that normally required by the particular metre. In classical, quantitative verse one long syllable was considered equal to two short syllables. Therefore anapaests, dactyls, spondees, tribrachs, and amphibrachs could be substituted for one another. When an iamb was substituted for a trochee (just as a dactyl for an anapaest), the result was a *reversed* or *inverted* foot.

ÉQUIVOQUE. French, literally, a word or phrase used in a double sense; from Latin *aequivocus*, of equal voice or significance. A verbal ambiguity; a pun.

ERRATUM: (pl.) ERRATA. Latin *errāre*, go astray. Error in printing or writing; more often used in the plural (*errata*).

ERSE. Early Scottish *Erische*; Old Norse *Irskr*, Irish. The term is a variant of Irish Gaelic. Of Irish origin, it is the Gaelic language of Scotland.

ERZIEHUNGSROMAN. See *BILDUNGSROMAN.*

ESCAPISM. Old North French *escaper*, from Latin *ex* out, *cappā*, cloak. Greek *ekdũesthai*, to put off one's clothes, escape by leaving one's cloak in the hands of the pursuer, as in the story from *St. Mark*: 'And there followed him a certain young man, having a linen cloth cast about his naked body; and the young men laid hold on him: and he left the linen cloth, and fled from them naked'. The desire or tendency to escape from the realities of life into fantasy.

In some of their poetry Rossetti and Swinburne are escapists; so in early poetry are Tennyson, Yeats, and Bridges.

> Wherefore to-night so full of care,
> My soul, revolving hopeless strife,
> Pointing at hindrance, and the bare
> Painful escapes of fitful life?

Bridges, *Dejection*

ESEMPLASTIC POWER. Greek *plássein*, to mould; an irregular formation after German *Ineinsbildung*, forming into one. Moulding into unity. Making into one. Coleridge called the imagination the Esemplastic Power. J. C. Hare commented on this error, 'Nor I trust will Coleridge's word esemplastic ever become current'.

ESOTERIC. Greek *esōterikós*, inner; *ésō*, *eisō*, within. A word used by Lucian attributing to Aristotle the limitation of his own works to a few disciples. Intended for a select few, an inner circle of the initiated. Secret, mysterious. Opposite to *exoteric.*

ESPARTO. Spanish from Greek *spárton*, rope of the plant *spártos.* Kinds of coarse grass imported from Spain and North Africa for paper-making.

ESPERANTO. An artificial language designed for universal use. It was introduced in 1887 by Dr. L. L. Zamenhof of Warsaw, and named from French *espérer*, to hope, or from Spanish *esperanza*, hope.

ESSAY. Latin *exagium*, weighing, trial by weight. In the *Times Literary Supplement*, a critic recently said, 'The essay is not to be cornered in a definition. For what genius could find a common denominator for essays as contrary in tendency as Locke on the Human Understanding and Lamb on Roast Pig?' Montaigne first used the name in 1580 for his informal reflections on himself and mankind. Francis Bacon's *Essays* were 'counsels for the successful conduct of life, and the management of men'. Steele and Addison developed the essay to bring 'Philosophy out of closets and libraries, schools and colleges, to dwell in clubs and assemblies, at tea-tables, and in coffee-houses'.

Other great English essayists are Goldsmith, Hazlitt, and Macaulay. G. K. Chesterton, E. V. Lucas, and Hilaire Belloc stand out among twentieth-century essayists.

ESSENCE: EXISTENCE. Latin *essentia*, from *esse*, to be. In *Biographia Literaria*, Coleridge said:

> *Essence*, in its primary signification, means the principle of *individuation*, the inmost principle of the possibility of anything, as that particular thing. It is equivalent to the *idea* of a thing, whenever we use the word idea with philosophic precision. *Existence*, on the other hand, is distinguished from essence by superinduction of *reality*. Thus we speak of the essence, and essential properties of a circle; but we do not therefore assert that anything, which really exists, is mathematically circular.

ESSENTIALISM. Latin *essentia* from *esse*, to be. This maintains that man's essence, his absolute being, and not his mere existence, establishes his true value.

ETHIC DATIVE. In *Modern English Usage*, H. W. Fowler says:

> This, in which the word means emotional or expressive, is the name for a common Greek and Latin use in which a person no more than indirectly interested in the fact described in the sentence is introduced into it, usually by himself as the speaker, in the dative, which is accordingly most often that of the first personal pronoun.

In *Julius Caesar*, Casca says this of Caesar,

> He plucked *me* ope his doublet.

Here me='on my word of honour he did', or 'believe me or believe me not'. It introduces an element of feeling into the statement.

The ethic dative is obsolete in modern English. In *The Taming of the Shrew*, Petruchio's remark to Grumio, 'Villain, I say, knock me at this gate' has been replaced today by 'Knock at the gate, can't you?'

ETHNIC. Greek *éthnos*, a nation. Concerning a race. Also, pertaining to the Gentiles or the heathen.

ETYMOLOGY. Greek *etumología*, from *étumos*, true. The systematic tracing of the derivation, original form and meaning of words. The branch of the science of language concerned with this.

EULOGY. Greek *eulogía,* fair speaking, praise. A statement, oration, whether spoken or written, in praise of a person or action. High commendation.

In *Julius Caesar,* Mark Antony eulogizes Brutus:

> This was the noblest Roman of them all:
> All the conspirators, save only he,
> Did that they did in envy of great Caesar;
> He only, in a general honest thought
> And common good to all, made one of them.
> His life was gentle, and the elements
> So mix'd in him that Nature might stand up
> And say to all the world 'This was a man!'

EUPHEMISM. Greek *euphēmismós; euphēmízein,* to speak words of good omen; *eu-,* well, *phánai,* to speak. The substitution of a less distasteful word or phrase for a more truthful but more offensive one. Euphemism is often extended with circumlocution. Examples:

> 'He passed away peacefully' for 'he died'.
> 'Juvenile delinquents' for 'young hooligans'.
> Discord fell on the music of his soul; the sweet sounds and wandering lights departed from him; yet he wore no less a loving face, although he was broken-hearted.
>
> E. B. Browning, *On Cowper's Madness*

Livingstone tells of certain Africans who, in offering an ox as a present, would say, 'Here is a little piece of bread for you'.

EUPHONY. Greek *euphōnía,* sweetness of sound, or voice; *eu-,* well, *phōnē,* sound, voice. Pleasing sound; harmony. Sounds free from harshness.

This is a most euphonious passage from *Paradise Lost:*

> Thus with the year
> Seasons return, but not to me returns
> Day, or the sweet approach of ev'n or morn,
> Or sight of vernal bloom, or summer's rose,
> Or flocks, or herds, or human face divine.

EUPHUISM. Greek *euphuēs,* graceful. An artificial or affected style which takes its name from John Lyly's prose romance *Euphues* (1579). Its chief characteristics are the excessive use of antithesis, emphasized by alliteration; of involved sentence construction; and of allusions to mythological and historical personages, and to natural history:

> Do we not commonly see that in painted pots is hidden the deadliest poison? that in the greenest grass is the greatest serpent? in the clearest water the ugliest toad? How frantic

are those lovers which are carried away with the gay glistening of the fine face? the beauty whereof is parched with the summer's blaze, and chipped with the winter's blast, which is of so short continuance that it fadeth before one perceive it flourish, of so small profit that it poisoneth those that possess it, of so little value with the wise, that they account it a delicate bait with a deadly hook, a sweet panther with a devouring paunch, a sour poison in a silver pot.

EVEN STRESS: LEVEL STRESS. This is the stress which falls with equal emphasis on two syllables in a word which may be disyllabic or polysyllabic, as in *dáybréak*, *mánkínd*, *óvercóme*.

EVOCATIVE. Latin *ēvocāre*, to call out. Tending to call forth. Evocative language, therefore, calls forth images, associations, memories, feelings, reactions.

Evocative names of characters and places suggest some characteristic of the person or place in question. Examples are Shakespeare's Sir Oliver Martext, a vicar of *As You Like It*, Wycherley's Mr. Horner, of *The Country Wife* (a reference to the proverbial horns of the cuckold), and Thackeray's Lord Bareacres of *Vanity Fair*. For places Carlyle's 'village of Dumdrudge' (*Sartor Resartus*), suggesting that the people there are dumb drudges. The effectiveness of such names depends upon their subtlety. If they are too obvious they become a clumsy and cheap device (e.g. Mr. Sweater, the employer of cheap labour in *The Ragged-Trousered Philanthropists*).

EXCALIBUR. Old French *Escalibor*, a corrupt form of *Caliburnus*, the name used by Geoffrey of Monmouth, *c.* 1140. There is in Irish legend a sword *Caladbolg*, 'hard belly', i.e. voracious, the devourer. The name of King Arthur's sword which he drew out of the stone (Malory, I. iv), or the sword which he received from the Lady of the Lake (Malory, II. iii). Sir Bedivere threw Excalibur into the lake when King Arthur was dying.

EXCURSUS. Latin *excursiō*, a running out. A dissertation added to a work, in which some particular point is discussed at length.

EXEGESIS. Greek *exḗgēsis*, *exēgéesthai*, to explain; *ex*, out, *hēgéesthai*, to guide. An exposition, especially of the Scriptures. Also a classification of a difficult text.

EXEMPLI GRATIA. Latin, for example, for instance. Abbreviation e.g. or ex. gr.

EXEMPLUM. Latin *exemplum*, a pattern, a model. A short moralizing tale. The *Gesta Romanorum*, a collection of tales in Latin, contained exempla which were used by preachers in the Middle Ages. *The Pardoner's Tale* and *The Nun's Priest's Tale* in *The Canterbury Tales* are further examples. The exemplum was presumed to be true, and the moral was placed at the beginning, not at the end as in the parable.

EXHORTATION. Latin *exhortārī*, from *hortārī*, to encourage. A speech or formal discourse intended to urge strongly and earnestly a course of action. This example is taken from Tennyson's *Ulysses*:

> We are not now that strength which in old days
> Moved earth and heaven; that which we are, we are;
> One equal temper of heroic hearts,
> Made weak by time and fate, but strong in will
> To strive, to seek, to find, and not to yield.

EXISTENTIALISM. Latin *ex(s)istĕre*, from *sistĕre*, reduplicated form of *stāre*, to stand. Christian existentialism, influenced by Kierkegaard, stressed the idea 'that in God man may find freedom from tension'. The other form, by Jean-Paul Sartre and Martin Heidegger, states that 'man is alone in a godless universe'. Sartre himself says:

> Revolutionary man must be a contingent being, unjustifiable but free, entirely immersed in the society that oppresses him, but capable of transcending this society by his effort to change it. Idealism mystifies him in that it binds him by rights and values that are already given; it conceals from him his power to devise roads of his own. But materialism also mystifies him, by depriving him of his freedom. The revolutionary philosophy must be a philosophy of transcendence.

The movement is based on the assumption that reality as existence can be lived but can never become the object of thought.

EXODUS. Greek *éxodos*; *ex*, out, *hodós*, a way. The final scene in Greek tragedy, after the last *stasima*, songs of the chorus. Also the final scene in Greek comedy, in which the predominant note is rejoicing.

EXORDIUM. Latin *exōrdīrī*, to begin. The beginning of anything, especially the introductory part of a composition or discourse.

EXOSTRA. Greek. In ancient drama, this was a machine at the back of the stage showing the inside of a house. It was used in the plays of Aeschylus and of Sophocles. *In exostra* means open scene, before the eyes of everyone.

EXOTERIC. Greek *exōterikós*, outer; *éxō*, outside. Of a doctrine or school of thought, intelligible to outsiders other than disciples or initiates. The opposite of *esoteric*.

EXPLETIVE. Latin *explētīvus*, filling out. A word inserted merely to fill up a gap; a word which adds nothing to the sense. In literature, the most interesting expletive is 'to do' used as an auxiliary verb, for example, 'I don't think I shall go, though I might do.' It is common in Spenser, and in the Authorized Version of the Bible. Of the words *do* and *did*, Johnson says, in his *Life of Cowley*, '. . . they much degrade in present estimation the line that admits them'.

Another example is the use by uneducated people of the tags 'you know', 'sort of', when they have no real meaning. Swear words are also often referred to euphemistically (or humorously) as expletives.

EXPLICATION DE TEXTE. A detailed analysis of the content and style of a passage of verse or prose.

EXPOSITION. Latin *expositiōn-(em)*, a showing forth. Giving the necessary information about the characters and the situation at the beginning of a play or novel. Shakespeare does this with directness in *Richard III* and *Henry V*. In *Hamlet* and *Othello* he combines information with action. Ibsen revealed the past of his characters as the play developed.

EXPRESSIONISM. Latin *expressus* from *exprimĕre*, to imitate, copy. In *Dictionary of Art Terms*, R. G. Haggar says:

> This is a form of romantic art in which emotion or emotive elements, expressed through violent distortion and exaggeration, are taken to the point of excess. It is a characteristic of art which emerges and becomes dominant in times of spiritual and social stress, arising from *Angst*, the anguish of the times.

In modern literature any deliberate distortion of reality could be a form of expressionism.

Expressionism was inaugurated in German drama in 1912 by Reinhard Sorge's play *Der Bettler*, and developed in the plays of Georg Kaiser (1878–1945) and Walter Hasenclever (1890–1940).

EXPURGATE. *See* BOWDLERIZE.

EXTENSION. Latin *extendĕre*, to stretch out. In formal logic, the extension of a word is the aggregate of all the objects or concepts to which it may be applied.

EXTRAMETRICAL. *See* HYPERCATALECTIC.

EXTRAMETRICAL VERSE. *See* ACATALECTIC.

EXTRAVAGANZA. Italian *stravaganza*, influenced by extravagance. An extravagant or eccentric musical, dramatic, or literary production, or behaviour. The most prolific and most notorious writer of extravaganzas was J. R. Planché (1796–1880).

EYE RHYME. The term applied to the use for rhyming purposes of two words which, from the spelling, look as though they should rhyme, but which actually do not (e.g. *love* and *move*). A hymn by Samuel Longfellow has as its opening lines,

> O God, in whom we live and move,
> Thy love is law, thy law is love.

Another example is provided by the following lines from Yeats:

> Many times man lives and dies
> Between his two eternities.

Eye-rhyme is fairly common in English poetry, though it may sometimes be the result of a change in pronunciation since the poem was written.

F

FABIAN SOCIETY. Latin *Fabianus* (Quintus Fabius Maximus, surnamed *Cunctator* or 'the delayer', commander against Hannibal, 217 B.C.). A society of socialists founded in 1884 advocating a Fabian policy to wear out an opponent by cautious, dilatory action. Sidney Webb, Beatrice Webb, and G. B. Shaw are associated with it. The phrase 'inevitability of gradualism' is associated with them.

FABLE. Latin *fābula*, from *fārī*, to speak. A short narrative illustrating some moral truth. The word has several meanings; it is used for the plot of a play, the meaning of a poem, a story in which animals and birds play the parts of men and women. Animal fables are sometimes called *apologues*, and make satirical comment upon human life.

The Roman writer Phaedrus preserved Aesop's Fables. Other examples of this form are the *Fables* of La Fontaine, John Gay's *Fifty-one Fables in Verse* (1727), Kipling's *Just So Stories*, George Orwell's political satire *Animal Farm*.

FABLIAU. Low Latin *fābulellus*, diminutive of *fābula*, story. A short tale in verse, often in octosyllabic couplets, dealing with incidents of ordinary life from a comic and satirical point of view. This form was popular in France in the twelfth and thirteenth centuries. Chaucer's *The Miller's Tale* in *The Canterbury Tales* is an example of the *fabliau*.

FAÇADE. Italian *facciata*, the front of a building; *faccia*, the face. The exterior front of a building. The appearance presented to the world, especially if there is little behind it.

FACETIAE. Latin *facētus*, urbane, witty. Pleasantries, witticisms. A bookseller's term for books of humorous or obscene character.

FACSIMILE. Latin *fac*, imperative of *facĕre*, to make, and *simile*, neuter of *similis*, like. An exact copy, especially of handwriting or picture or printed work.

FAIRY TALES. Stories of mythical beings, such as fairies, gnomes, pixies, elves, or goblins. Such tales are found in the folklore of many countries and were handed down by word of mouth. In 1697, Charles Perrault, in France, compiled one of the first printed collections, which contains 'The Sleeping Beauty', 'Red Riding Hood', 'Puss in Boots' and 'Cinderella'. The brothers Grimm began to publish their famous collection of German fairy tales in 1812. Hans Christian Andersen first issued his fairy tales in 1835. Home-made fairy tales were composed by Ruskin, Thackeray, Charles Kingsley, Jean Ingelow, and Oscar Wilde. Drayton's *Nymphidia* may be called fairy verse, a style followed by Lewis Carroll's *Hunting of the Snark* (1876) and Alfred Noyes's *Flower of Old Japan* (1903) and *Forest of Wild Thyme* (1905).

FALLACY. Latin *fallācia*, from *fallĕre*, to deceive. A fallacy in logic is an argument which violates the laws of correct demonstration. It is a flaw in syllogism.

FALLING ACTION. The part of a play which follows the climax.

FALLING RHYTHM. One in which the stress falls on the first syllable of the metrical foot, as in this stanza by Suckling:

> Why so | pále and | wán, fond | lóver,
> Prýthee, | why so | pále?
> Will, when | looking | wéll can't | móve her,
> Looking | ill pre|váil?
> Prýthee, | why so | pále?

FALSE MASQUE. *See* ANTI-MASQUE.

FANCY. Contraction of *fantasy, phantasy*. Greek *phantasĭā*, used in Late Greek, of spectral apparition. The faculty of calling up things not present, of inventing images. In *Biographia Literaria*, Coleridge says:

> The fancy brings together images which have no connection natural or moral, but are yoked together by the poet by means of some accidental coincidence.

See also IMAGINATION.

FANTASY. Greek *phantasía*, a making visible, from *phainein*, to show. The capacity for making images, especially when fanciful, whimsical or visionary. A world of fantasy is created in *The Faerie Queene*, and in *Comus*, from which these lines are taken:

> What might this be? A thousand fantasies
> Begin to throng into my memory,
> Of calling shapes, and beckoning shadows dire,
> And airy tongues, that syllable men's names
> On sands, and shores, and desert wildernesses.

FARCE. Vulgar Latin *farsa*, from *farcīre*, to stuff viands. Originally a farce was an impromptu interlude 'stuffed in' between the parts of a more serious play. A form of drama with extravagant, boisterous comic action. A ludicrous comedy. There are farcical scenes in *A Midsummer-Night's Dream* and *Twelfth Night*.

FEMININE CAESURA. Latin *caedĕre*, *caesum*, to cut off. A caesura coming after an unstressed syllable:

> To err is human, | to forgive, divine.

FEMININE ENDING. An extra unstressed syllable at the end of a line of verse. In blank verse, it is the unstressed eleventh syllable, overhanging after the final stressed tenth syllable.

> And I be pléased to gíve ten thóusand dúcats
> To have it ban'd.   *The Merchant of Venice*

This is sometimes a *light* or *weak ending*. When the final syllable in a line of verse is stressed, it is a *masculine ending*.

FEMININE RHYME. When the stressed syllable is followed by an unstressed, the rhyme is *feminine* or *double*, as in Pope's couplet from *An Essay on Man*:

> What can ennoble sots, or slaves, or cowards?
> Alas! not all the blood of all the Howards.

FESCENNINE VERSES. From *Fescennia* in Etruria, famous for scurrilous verse dialogues.

FESTSCHRIFT: (pl.) **FESTSCHRIFTEN.** German *Fest*, feast, celebration, *Schrift*, from *schreiben*, to write. A symposium in honour of an eminent scholar or writer, written and published on the occasion of his retirement or birthday. An example is the tribute to Sir Lewis Namier, edited by Richard Pares and A. J. P. Taylor and entitled *Essays presented to Sir Lewis Namier* (1956).

FEUILLETON. French *feuilleton*, leaflet, from *feuille*, leaf.
The ruled-off portion at the foot of newspapers (especially French ones). This portion is devoted to a serial story, literary criticism, humorous article.

FICTION. Latin *fictiōnem*, from *fingĕre*, to shape, fashion. Any imagined or invented narrative; literature consisting of such narrative, usually in prose.

FIGURATIVE. Latin *figura*, form, shape, from *fingĕre*, to fashion. This term is equivalent to metaphorical, and opposed to literal.

Figurative language includes metaphor, simile, personification, and metonymy. A great part of language is figurative, as it is based on images or pictures of things seen and actions experienced.

Many words losing the literal sense come to be used figuratively, as when we say 'to grasp an idea'. Conversely, some figurative meanings in course of time come to be accepted as additional literal ones: e.g. broadcast.

FIGURES OF SPEECH. Any of the devices of figurative language, ranging from expression of the imagination to deviation from ordinary usage for the sake of ornament.

FIN DE SIÈCLE. French, end of the century. Characteristic of the end of the nineteenth century, meaning decadent, cynical, disillusioned. In the novel *À Rebours* by Huysmans, des Esseintes in his abnormal behaviour typifies the decadent. The phrase *fin de siècle* is applied to the writers of the 1890s; representative figures are Oscar Wilde, Ernest Dowson, John Davidson, together with artists such as Aubrey Beardsley and other contributors to *The Yellow Book.*

'FINGERING.' This term, which determines the phrasing, is used in music. In his *Anthology of Canadian Verse*, Ralph Gustafson states that the Canadian 'phrasing' is not the American, and is certainly not the English. F. R. Scott's *Old Song* gives the Canadian 'fingering' plain:

> a quiet calling
> of no mind
> out of long aeons
> when dust was blind
> and ice hid sound
>
> only a moving
> with no note
> granite lips
> a stone throat

So does A. J. M. Smith's *The Lonely Land*:

> This is a beauty
> of dissonance,
> this resonance
> of stony strand
> this smoky cry
> curled over a black pine.

FIVE TOWNS, THE. In the novels of Arnold Bennett these are Burslem, Hanley, Longton, Stoke-upon-Trent and Tunstall, now making together the county borough of Stoke-on-Trent. The five towns are represented in the novels by Bursley, Hanbridge, Longshaw, Knype, and Turnhill.

FLASH-BACK. A scene of the past shown momentarily in a film, by way of explanation or comment. It may also be inserted into a play, story, or novel.

FLAT CHARACTERS. In *Aspects of the Novel*, E. M. Forster divides characters into flat and round:

> Flat characters were called 'humours' in the seventeenth century, and are sometimes called types, and sometimes caricatures. In their purest form, they are constructed round a single idea or quality: when there is more than one factor in them, we get the beginning of the curve towards the round. The really flat character can be expressed in one sentence such as 'I never will desert Mr. Micawber.' There is Mrs. Micawber — she says she won't desert Mr. Micawber; she doesn't, and there she is.

FLESHLY SCHOOL OF POETRY, THE. The title of an article in the *Contemporary Review* of October 1871, in which Robert Buchanan, under the pseudonym of Robert Maitland, gave this name to the Pre-Raphaelite group of poets. He made an especial attack upon D. G. Rossetti, who wrote a controlled reply with the title 'The Stealthy School of Criticism'.

FLEURONS: FLOWERS. A kind of printer's ornament originally copied from the stamping irons (*petits fers*) used by early bookbinders.

FLIBBERTIGIBBET. In the *Oxford Companion to English Literature*, Paul Harvey says:

> Probably in its original form 'flibbergib', which Latimer uses in a sermon for a chattering or gossiping person. Harsnet in his *Popish Impostures* (1603) gives 'Fliberdigibbet' as the name of a devil of fiend. And Shakespeare in *King Lear* III. iv. has 'Flibbertigibbet', 'the foul fiend' who walks at night, 'gives the web and the pin, squints the eye, and makes the hare-lip'. Scott in *Kenilworth* gives the nickname 'Flibbertigibbet' to Dickie Sludge.

FOLIO. Latin, ablative of *folium*, leaf. A leaf of paper folded in half, across its longer dimension, from a standard size; volume made of such sheets; largest-sized volume. A page number of a printed book. Leaf of paper numbered only on the front. A page, or two opposite pages, of a ledger used for both sides of an account. A unit for estimating the length of a document, in Britain 72 words, or 90 words for an Act of Parliament.

All Shakespeare's completed plays (excepting *Pericles*) were first collected in 1623 and published in a folio edition. The reference is actually to the size of the page, but in effect it means the early collected editions of his plays appearing in 1632, 1663, 1664 and 1685.

FOLKLORE.   Old English *folc*, Middle English *fōlk*, people. The beliefs, tales, legends, songs, sayings of a people handed down by word of mouth. It includes the traditional customs, ceremonies and ways of life; and the study of them. The term was first introduced by W. J. Thoms in the *Athenaeum* in 1846.

FOLK PLAYS.   This name applies to the dramatic entertainments given at village festivals, not by minstrels, but by the villagers themselves. These plays were given at times of celebration such as Harvest Home or Christmas. From primitive festivals came the themes of symbolic death and resurrection, later to include the stories of legendary figures. St. George, the patron saint of England, was replaced after 1596 by the Seven Champions of Christendom. Song and dance provided part of the action. A well-known survival is the Morris Dance. Folk drama later changed to the Mumming Play, which was given between Christmas and Twelfth Night, or on the Monday after Epiphany, known as Plough Monday.

FOLKSONG.   After German, *Volkslied*. Traditional song and melody, current among the common people, and usually of unknown origin.

FOLK TALE.   Old English *folc*, Middle English *fōlk*, people. A popular story handed down by oral tradition or written form from much earlier days. This term covers a wide range of material from myths to fairy-tales. In more modern times we have the stories of Hans Andersen, preceded by the 'Kinder- und Hausmärchen' of Jacob and Wilhelm Grimm.

FOOT.   German *Fuss*, from Latin *pes*, Greek *poús*, foot. A unit in the scansion of verse, containing in English poetry one strong stress or accent. The most commonly used feet are as follows:

Iambus	∪ ⁄	despaír
Trochee	⁄ ∪	dáilў
Anapaest	∪ ∪ ⁄	serĕnadé
Dactyl	⁄ ∪ ∪	trémŭloŭs

Occasional feet are:

Spondee	／ ／
Pyrrhic	∪ ∪
Amphibrach	∪ ／ ∪

FOOTNOTE. An explanatory note or citation set at the foot of a page or table, and usually referred to in the text or table by a superior number or by one of the reference marks.

FORE-EDGE. The front or outer edge of a book. *Fore-edge painting* is the decoration of the front and sometimes of the top edge of a book with coloured design.

FORESHADOWING. *See* ATMOSPHERE.

FOREWORD. Introductory remarks to a book, especially written by a person other than the author of the book in which it appears.

FORM. Latin *forma*, shape. There is a definite sense in which literature is form. We recognize the significance of form in the work of the potter when he converts a lump of wet clay into a vase. We commonly admire the shape of the vase and not the substance out of which it is made, though shape and substance are one. It is somewhat similar with poetry. When the poet has cast his thought into the physical form of a sonnet or an ode, we are aware that this 'shape' has given a greater significance to the theme.

FORMAT. The general style of a book, including such details as size of page, and type, margins and dimensions.

FORME. An assemblage of type or plates, locked up and ready for press, comprising the pages that are printed at one time — usually 8, 16, 32 or 64.

FOUL PROOF. The marked proof from which corrections have been made by the printer. Not synonymous with *dirty proof*.

FOUNDRY PROOF. A proof pulled from type after it has been locked up. Each page is surrounded by a black border made by the bearers. Ordinarily foundry proof is not submitted to the author, but is checked by the publisher.

FOUNT. A fount of type is the complete set of type characters of any one style and size. It includes roman capitals, small capitals, and lower case, italic capitals and lower case, bold capitals and lower case, punctuation marks, reference marks, figures, fractions, accented letters and spaces.

FOUR-COLOUR PROCESS PLATES. An amplification of the three-colour process, the fourth plate being usually printed in black. The addition of this plate allows many more shades of brown and grey to be obtained. This improves the detail in the subject.

FOURTEENERS. *See* HEPTAMETER.

FOXED. Foxmarks are brown stains which appear on the leaves of books and on engravings. They are caused by damp acting on the chemicals used in bleaching the rags of which the paper is made. A book so marked is said to be *foxy* or *foxed*.

FRAME STORY. A story within a story; a narrative which unfolds itself within the frame of another. Examples are Boccaccio's *Decameron* and Chaucer's *Canterbury Tales*.

FREE ASSOCIATION. In psychology, an unconstrained sequence of ideas or of words. One object or idea recalls another with which it is in some way connected. By repetition a sequence of association is formed, the final thought or image having no readily recognizable connection with the first. This process of free association is effective in the *stream of consciousness* and the *interior monologue*.

FREE VERSE. A kind of verse with no regular scansion, no observing of the strict laws of form. The irregularity may give some force to the thought and expression. In an address on 17th May 1935, Robert Frost said, 'Writing free verse is like playing tennis with the net down'.

FREYTAG'S PYRAMID. In 1863 Gustav Freytag published *Die Technik des Dramas*. Here he described the structure of the well-made play, drawing attention to the rising action, climax, and falling action. The pyramid, or diagrammatic plot, is shown below.

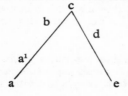

a. Introduction
a¹. Inciting moment
b. Rising action
c. Climax
d. Falling action
e. Catastrophe.

FRONTISPIECE. Medieval Latin *frontispicium*, façade of a building, from *frons*, front, *specĕre*, to see, behold. In architecture, the principal façade of a building. An illustration at the beginning of a book, facing the title-page.

FULL RHYME. *See* PERFECT RHYME.

FUNAMBULISM. From Latin *fūnambulus*, from *fūnis*, rope, *ambulāre*, to walk. In *The Tightrope Walkers*, Giorgio Melchiori says:

> I have preferred to use tentatively the word 'Funambulism' to describe the style of our time. I think it is as good a term as any to express the sense of danger — or should we say with Auden, anxiety — and precariousness so vividly reflected both in the form and in the content of the artistic and literary works of the first half of this century. It seems to convey the achievement of the true artist in our age, who, like the successful acrobat, succeeds in keeping step by step, moment by moment, his balance, while being aware of the void or the turmoil round him. It is of course a balance which has nothing to do with the permanent and pre-established one found in ages of stability and faith.

FUSTIAN. Old French *fustaigne*, Italian *fustagno*, from modern Greek *phoústani*, named after Fostat, a suburb of Cairo, where the material was made. Coarse, twilled, short-napped cotton cloth, usually dyed a dark colour; resembles velveteen. Also comes to mean turgid, bombastic speech or writing. Pope makes reference to a writer in these lines from *Epistle to Dr. Arbuthnot*:

> And he, whose fustian's so sublimely bad,
> It is not poetry, but prose run mad.

G

GABERLUNZIE. French *gaban*, cloak; *lunzie*, diminutive of *laine*, wool; coarse woollen gown. A mendicant, one of the king's bedesmen, who were licensed beggars. 'The Gaberlunzie Man', a ballad in Percy's *Reliques*, is attributed to King James V of Scotland.

GALLEY or SLIP PROOF. Old French *galie*, used of a tray to hold type. An impression taken from composed type before the matter is made up into pages. This is usually about eighteen inches long. In this form, corrections can be made more cheaply than when the type is set in pages. 'Page-on-galley' proofs consist of two or three pages set on a galley.

GALLIAMBIC. The metre of the vigorous *Attis* of Catullus. It was imitated by Tennyson in *Boadicea* and by George Meredith in *Phaethon*. It may be named after Galli or priests of Cybele, who used a similar metre in their songs.

GALLICISM. French *gallicisme*. The actual French words or expressions (like *arrière-pensée*, *savoir-faire*) used within the context of a sentence in another language, are not Gallicisms. In *Modern English Usage*, H. W. Fowler distinguished several kinds of Gallicisms:

1. One form consists in taking a French word and giving it an English termination or dropping an accent or the like, as in *actuality*, *banality*, and *redaction*.
2. Another in giving to an existent English word a sense that belongs to it only in French or to its French form only, as in *intrigue* (v.t., = interest, perplex), *impayable* (= priceless for absurdity, impudence), *arrive* (= attain success etc.).
3. Another in giving vogue to a word that has had little currency in English, but is common in French, such as *veritable* and *envisage*.
4. Another in substituting a French form or word that happens to be English also, but in another sense, for the really corresponding English, as when *brave* is used for *honest* or *worthy*.
5. Another in translating a French word or phrase, as in *jump* or *leap to the eyes, gilded youth, castle in Spain, on the carpet*.

GATHERING. A printed sheet folded into pages is called a signature. The signatures are gathered, by hand or by machine, in their proper sequence. This process of gathering is preparatory to binding.

GAZETTE. Italian *gazzetta*, a Venetian coin; the name comes from the name of the coin paid for the paper. A news-sheet; a periodical publication giving an account of current events, appointments, legal notices, despatches. A *gazetteer* is an alphabetical list of place-names giving statistical and other information.

GENIUS. Latin from *gignĕre*, to beget; *genius*, the spirit or deity watching over each person from birth. Originally, this was a spirit guarding a person or place, then two opposed spirits directing human action for good or evil. Also a person having great influence upon another. Later it was applied to the prevailing tendency or guiding principle of a nation or of an age. Genïus is also extraordinary intellectual and imaginative and creative power.

In his *Life of Cowley*, Dr. Johnson said, 'The true Genius is a mind of large general powers, accidentally determined to some particular direction.' Miguel de Unamuno wrote in *Essays and Soliloquies*, 'There is a certain characteristic common to all those whom we call geniuses. Each of them has a consciousness of being a man apart.'

GENIUS LOCI. Latin, literally, the genius of the place. The presiding spirit of a place. Shelley expresses the idea in *Adonais*:

> Pass, till the spirit of the spot shall lead
> Thy footsteps to a slope of green access
> Where, like an infant's smile, over the dead
> A light of laughing flowers along the grass is spread.

GENRE. French, from Latin *gener-*, stem of *genus*, birth. Kind, style. A literary type, such as epic, lyric, tragedy, comedy. From the fifteenth century to the eighteenth, the various *genres* showed marked differences which were accepted by the writers of the time. Today, less concern is shown in these distinctions.

Genre painting deals with subjects taken from ordinary daily life. We may say, by analogy, that writing which deals with everyday life is in the *genre* category.

GENTEELISM. Latin *gentīlis*, belonging to the same *gens* or clan, well-bred. French *gentil*, elegant. Graceful in manners or in form. Now used only with mocking reference to a standard of false refinement. Shown also in the choice of another word for the more natural one, such as *serviette* for *napkin*.

GENUS IRRITABILE VATUM.   Latin, literally, the irritable race of poets.   The writers, bards or poets, who are irritable because of poverty or frustration.

GEORGIAN POETRY.   An anthology of contemporary verse so entitled because it was initiated in the reign of George V, though some of the poems included had been written before he came to the throne.   A group consisting of Rupert Brooke, John Drinkwater, W. W. Gibson, Edward Marsh (the editor), Harold Monro, Walter de la Mare, John Masefield, Robert Graves, James Elroy Flecker, and Arundel del Ré, brought out the first volume in 1912.

In retrospect, *Georgian Poetry* has come to represent a period of no great literary value, a mere interim before the appearance of Pound, Eliot, and Yeats.

George Sampson, in *The Concise Cambridge History of English Literature,* says:

> . . . it will be seen that *Georgian Poetry* was not all of one kind, that it would range from the calculated sentiment of Chesterton to the simple sincerity of de la Mare, from the winsome warblings of Davies to the more subtle rhythm of Lawrence. It would not appear that Marsh or Monro had any conscious critical aim; their avowed intention was simply to introduce to a wider public the poetry being written at the time, and in this they were successful, the volumes being deservedly popular.

GEORGIC.   Greek *geōrgiká, geōrgós,* husbandman;   *gê,* earth, *érgon,* work.   A poem about husbandry and rustic life.   One book of the *Georgics,* Virgil's poem on husbandry.

GEST: GESTE.   Latin *gesta,* things done, exploits.   A medieval tale of romance and adventure.   One of the most famous collection of tales in Latin was the *Gesta Romanorum,* first printed in the fifteenth century.

GESTALT PHILOSOPHY.   German *Gestalt,* form, figure, shape; the manner of literary composition.   Herbert Read says, 'Coleridge contends that in both prose and poetry there is a characteristic *construction,* what we should now (and what Schelling even then did) call a *Gestalt.*'

GHAZAL: GAZEL.   Arabian *ghazal,* love-song, from *ghazila,* to court.   Oriental verse-form, usually twelve lines, on an erotic or mystical theme.

GHOST-WORDS.   A term used by W. W. Skeat to stand for words which have no real existence, 'coinages due to the blunders of printers or scribes, or to the perfervid imaginations of ignorant or blundering editors'.

In *Morte d'Arthur*, Malory wrote:

Pleaseth it yow to see the estures of this castel.

Estures, which means 'apartments', was printed by Caxton *eftures*, and this is a ghost-word.

GHOST-WRITER. One who does another person's literary work for him, often without acknowledgement in the book, although, occasionally, some such expression as 'Edited by' or 'As told to' appears on the title-page. Such a book is said to be 'ghosted'.

GIBBERISH. Perhaps imitative. Unintelligible speech; meaningless sounds; inarticulate chatter. Smollet uses the word, 'He repeated some gibberish, which by the sound seemed to be Irish.'

GLEE. Anglo-Saxon *glīw, glēo*, minstrelsy, merriment. A part-song for three or more voices, often without accompaniment. Its great period was from about 1750 to about 1830, although choirs of 'glee-singers' still persist in the United States.

GLOSS. Greek *glôssa*, (foreign) tongue, an obscure or foreign word. Originally a word or phrase inserted between lines or in the margin to explain a difficult word or phrase in the text. A commentary, an explanation such as those marginal glosses provided by Coleridge himself to his *Rime of the Ancient Mariner*.

GLOSSARY. Greek *glôssa*, (foreign) tongue, an obscure or foreign word. A collection of glosses, explanations of abstruse, unfamiliar words. A glossary is often appended to a technical or scientific work, or any work in which a specialist vocabulary is used.

GNOMIC VERSE. Greek *gnōmikós*, based on gnomes; aphoristic. A form of early Greek poetry, usually written in elegiacs characterized by gnomes, or aphorisms. Phocýlidês is the best-known gnomic writer. This style of verse continued till the time of *Beowulf*. Here is *A Small City on a Rock* by Phocýlidês (who always mentioned his name in each of his poems), translated by Sir Maurice Bowra:

> This also said Phocýlidês:
> A tiny rock-built citadel
> Is finer far, if ordered well,
> Than all your frantic Ninevehs.

GNOSTIC. Greek *gnōstikós*, pertaining to knowledge. Member of the heretical Christian sect of the second century A.D., who claimed special spiritual knowledge as to how the soul in man became detached from the divine world and how it later returned there. Such religion was mystic, and allied to Manichaeism.

GOBBLEDYGOOK: PUDDER. Pompous, high-flown, official jargon. *Gobbledygook* (originally American) is the imitation of the noise of a turkey-cock. *Pudder* is taken from a prayer by King Lear where it means 'commotion':

> Let the great gods,
> That keep this dreadful pudder o'er our heads,
> Find out their enemies now.

GOLDEN AGE. Greek and Roman poets thought that this was the first and the best age of the world, when man lived in a state of happiness, culture, and prosperity. The reign of Saturn was so mild and beneficent that this was called the Golden Age, the *Saturnia regna* of Roman poets.

GOLIARDIC VERSE. Old French *goliard*, from Latin *gula*, glutton. Satirical Latin verse of the twelfth and thirteenth centuries in France, Germany, and England, attributed to the Goliards, educated buffoons. They were supposed to take their name from Golias, who was satirized in Latin poems as exhibiting the vices laid upon monks. A collection of Goliardic verse is the *Carmina Burana* from the Benedictine monastery of Benedictbeuern in Bavaria.

GONGORISM. An affected and intricate poetic style introduced into Spanish literature by the poet Don Luis de Góngora y Argote (1561-1627). His *Polifemo*, *Soledades*, and *Pyramo y Thisbe* are overlaid with 'stilted metaphors, grotesque Latinisms, and pompous phraseology', so much so that this new style was called Gongorism, or *estilo culto*. It was akin to Euphuism in England and Marinism in Italy.

GOTHIC. Greek *Góthos*, Goth. The word Gothic lost the slur of 'barbarous', a derivative from the hordes of the Goths. It applied to the architectural style prevalent in Western Europe in the twelfth to the sixteenth centuries.

Gothic Novels included *The Castle of Otranto* by Horace Walpole, *The Mysteries of Udolpho* by Ann Radcliffe, *The Monk* by Matthew Gregory Lewis.

In the eighteenth century the word was used in the sense of 'barbarous, uncouth, uncultured'.

GOTHIC TYPE. A name now generally given to bold sanserif and grotesque types.

GRAIL, THE HOLY. Medieval Latin, *sanctus gradalis*, perhaps from Latin *crātēr*, a cup. In medieval legend the word *Grail* meant the cup used by our Saviour at the Last Supper, in which Joseph of Arimathea received Christ's blood at the Cross.

The Grail cycle has two distinct legends. One is the early history of the Holy Grail. The other is the quest by Perceval, a knight of the Round Table, for certain talismans.

GRAINING. 'The process of preparing the surface of a lithographic stone or plate by oscillating, in a plate-graining machine, a number of glass or porcelain marbles with sand, glass or pumice powder.' J. C. Tarr, *Printing Today*.

GRAND GUIGNOL. French *Guignol*, perhaps from *Chignolo Po* in Italy, the native place of the Italian who introduced puppets at Lyons about the end of the eighteenth century. One puppet character became popular, was brought from Lyons to Paris, and gave his name to a theatre, the Grand Guignol (Great Punch). Here short pieces, dealing with the horrific and the gruesome, are played successively, by real actors. The term *Grand Guignol* is now applied to any play of this kind.

GRANGERIZE: GRANGERISM. 'To illustrate a book by the addition of prints, engravings, etc., especially such as have been cut out of other books. In 1769 James Granger (1723–1776) published a "Biographical History of England", with blank pages for the reception of engraved portraits or other pictorial illustrations of the text. The filling up of the "Granger" became a favourite hobby, and afterwards other books were treated in the same manner.' (*Oxford English Dictionary*)

GRAVEYARD SCHOOL. The imitators of Robert Blair and Edward Young. In 1743, Blair published his poem *The Grave*, in which he dwells upon death, the solitude of the tomb, and the agonies of bereavement. His contemporary, Young, published in 1742–1745 a long poem *Night Thoughts on Life, Death, and Immortality*. These poems enjoyed considerable popularity for a time.

GRAVURE. Short for *photogravure*. Engraving by means of photography; a print thus produced.

GREEK CALENDS. A humorous expression for 'never'. The Greeks had no Calends, which were the first day of each month in the Roman calendar. The Latin word, *kalendae*, means called out, or proclaimed publicly.

GREEK TRAGEDY: STRUCTURE OF.   A Greek tragedy contained the following parts:

(a) *Prologos*, the prologue, the part before the entrance of the
chorus, setting forth in monologue or dialogue the subject of
the drama.

(b) *Parodos*, the song accompanying the entrance of the chorus.

(c) *Epeisodia*, the episodes, scenes in which one or more actors
took part, with the chorus.

(d) *Stasima*, songs of the chorus, now 'standing in one place',
and expressing emotions rising from the drama.

(e) *Exodos*, the last *stasimon* or final scene.

Paul Harvey, *The Oxford Companion to Classical Literature*

GROTESQUE.   Greek *kruptĕ*, vault, *krúptō*, hide; Italian *grottesca*,
antique work, perhaps because *grotta* was used of mural paintings
found in excavated buildings.   Decorative painting or sculpture
which is monstrous in appearance, combining animal and human
forms with foliage and scrollwork.   Grotesques are a feature of
Pompeian decoration.   In architecture, a style which is distorted
and bizarre.   Applied to literature, *grotesque* means a style
fantastically extravagant and incongruous.

Wordsworth, Tennyson, and Browning; or, Pure, Ornate, and
Gro. sque Art in English Poetry.

Title of Essay, National Review, November 1864

In printing, grotesque is a form of sanserif type.

GROUP, THE.   'The writers who are usually regarded as being
central to the Group are Peter Redgrove, Peter Porter, Martin Bell,
Edward Lucie-Smith, George MacBeth and David Wevill. All of
these came into the Group at different times between 1955 and 1959,
and at my invitation as the then chairman.   Many similar invitations
have been made since, by the present chairman, Edward Lucie-
Smith . . . the Group is neither a literary movement nor a new
fashion in literature, and . . . its poets have never needed to shelter
under any kind of doctrine.   It would be far more accurate to refer
to the Group as a seminar in creative writing — practical criticism
applied to the work of its various participants. . . .'   An extract from
Philip Hobsbaum's letter to the *Spectator* of 9th October 1964.)

GRUB STREET.   In his Dictionary, Johnson says:

Originally the name of a street near Moorfields in London,
much inhabited by writers of small histories, dictionaries, and
temporary poems, whence any mean production is called
grubstreet.

The name of the street was changed in the nineteenth century to Milton Street (Cripplegate). Today the term Grub Street is applied to any form of literary hack-work.

GRUNDY, MRS.   A symbol of social convention and 'the British idea of propriety' in its more intolerant aspects.   The character is referred to in *Speed the Plough*, a play written by Thomas Morton in 1798.   Actually she never appears at all, though everyone seems to stand in awe of her and of what she will say.   The play is included in *Five Eighteenth-Century Comedies*, edited by Allardyce Nicoll. The remark, 'What will Mrs. Grundy say?' explains Herbert Spencer's comment in *Essays on Education*, 'The tyranny of Mrs. Grundy is worse than any other tyranny we suffer under.'

GUIGNOL.   *See* GRAND GUIGNOL.

GYMNOSOPHIST.   Greek *gumnosophistĕs*; *gumnós*, naked, *sophistĕs*, a wise man.   Name given by Greeks, in the time of Alexander the Great, to members of an Indian sect, who lived naked and devoted themselves to meditation.

H

HACK WRITER. Old French *haquenée,* an ambling horse or mare. In early use for horses kept for hire, whence hack, hackney-carriage. 'Hack' referred to the overworked horse, then to the person employed to do dull work. The common literary drudge is known as a hack writer.

HAGIOGRAPHY. Greek *hagio,* saint(ly), sacred(ly), *hagiógrapha (biblía),* (books) sacredly written. The writing or the study of the lives of saints. 'Because of the excesses and credulity of many hagiographers the word is sometimes used in a depreciatory sense' (Donald Attwater, *The Penguin Dictionary of Saints*). *Hagiology* is a similar term.

HAIKU: HOKKU. Writing of this Japanese poem, Babette Deutsch says, in *Poetry Handbook*:

> It is in three lines, of five, seven and five syllables respectively, which presents a clear picture so as at once to arouse emotion and suggest a spiritual insight. The strict rules governing the form cannot be followed in translation, especially since Japanese is unstressed. This version of a haiku by the sixteenth-century poet Moritake may hint at the structure:

> > The falling flower
> > I saw drift back to the branch
> > Was a butterfly.

> The poem refers to the Buddhist proverb that 'the fallen flower never returns to the branch; the broken mirror never again reflects'.

HAIR-LINE. The finest line that can be engraved or etched on a printing plate.

HALF-RHYME. *See* NEAR RHYME.

HALF-TITLE. The title, together sometimes with a blurb, printed on the leaf preceding the full title-page. Called also a *bastard title.*

HALF-TONE. A relief photo-engraving. The negative for this has been made by photographing the original through a screen, so that the light and dark tones of the original are reproduced by dots varying in size but uniformly placed.

HALIEUTICI.   Greek *halieutikós*, from *halieutēs*, fisher, from *háls*, salt sea. Poets of the sea.

HALLEL.   A hymn of praise consisting of Psalms 113–118, each being headed with 'Hallelujah'.   They were embodied in the Jewish liturgy for the great festivals: the Passover, Pentecost, Dedication, and Tabernacles.

HAMARTIA.   Greek *hamartía*, error, sin.   An error in judgment, caused by ignorance or sudden weakness.   Aristotle says this, in *Poetics*, when discussing the tragic hero: 'He should be a man, not pre-eminently virtuous and just, whose misfortune is brought upon him, not by vice and wickedness, but by some personal error.'

HANDBOOK: HANDLIST.   A short manual, treatise, guide-book, which gives a list of titles, subjects, etc., for handy reference.

HAPLOGRAPHY.   Greek *haplóos*, simple.   A copyist's error which consists of writing only once a letter or letters which should be written twice, as *tillate* for *titillate*.

HARANGUE.   Low Latin *harenga*, originally, speech made in a ring of people.   A speech made to a crowd in a loud and declamatory way to rouse their emotions.   In *Julius Caesar*, Antony's speech over Caesar's dead body is a striking example of the *harangue*.

   Today *harangue* usually has a derogatory meaning, that of rabble-rousing or demagogy.

HARLEQUIN.   From the Italian *arlecchino*, originally a character in Italian comedy, a mixture of childlike ignorance, wit, and grace, always in love, always in trouble, easily despairing, easily consoled; in English pantomime a mute character supposed to be invisible to the clown and the pantaloon, the rival of the clown in the affections of Columbine.   The Italian word is possibly the same as the old French *Hellequin*, *Hennequin*, one of a troop of demon horsemen riding by night.   (*Oxford English Dictionary*)

HARMONY.   Greek *harmonía*, from *harmózein*, to fit together.   Due proportion of the parts of a work of art to each other in relation to the whole.   A composition in which the elements are brought together in such a way as to display their essential unity.

> Untwisting all the chains that ty
> The hidden soul of harmony.
>
> Milton, *L'Allegro*

> Until, the breath of this corporeal frame
> And even the motion of our human blood
> Almost suspended, we are laid asleep
> In body, and become a living soul:
> While with an eye made quiet by the power
> Of harmony, and the deep power of joy,
> We see into the life of things.
>
> Wordsworth, *Lines composed a few miles above Tintern Abbey*

HEAD CLAUSE. This term is sometimes used by the more academic type of grammarian (especially some of the Continental ones) to denote the clause on which a subordinate clause depends. It is not synonymous with *main clause*. It may be a main clause or another subordinate clause.

HEADLESS LINE. *See* ACATALECTIC.

HEADLINE. The (running) headline at the top of the page of a book, which is sometimes omitted, gives the title of the book or chapter or the contents of the page.

HEAD RHYME. *See* ALLITERATION.

HEAD-WORD. In typography, a word forming a heading.

HEBRAISM. This term was used in a special sense by Matthew Arnold, who emphasized the strictness of conscience in Hebraism when contrasting it with Hellenism. In *Culture and Anarchy*, he says:

> The final aim of both Hellenism and Hebraism, as of all great spiritual disciplines, is no doubt the same: man's perfection or salvation. The very language which they both of them use in schooling us to reach this aim is often identical. . . . The uppermost idea with Hellenism is to see things as they really are; the uppermost idea with Hebraism is conduct and obedience. Nothing can do away with this ineffaceable difference. The Greek quarrel with the body and its desires is, that they hinder right thinking, the Hebrew quarrel with them is, that they hinder right acting. . . . The governing idea of Hellenism is *spontaneity of consciousness*; that of Hebraism, *strictness of conscience*.

HEDONISM. Greek *hēdoně*, pleasure. The doctrine in which pleasure is regarded as the chief good. This was, in some ways, the doctrine of the Cyrenaic school of philosophy, founded by Aristippus in the fifth century B.C.

HEIGHT-TO-PAPER. The standard height of type and printing plates in letterpress printing. In Great Britain, the Commonwealth, and the United States it is 0.918 inches; on the Continent (the Didot scale) mainly 0.928 inches.

HELLENISM. Greek *Hellēnikós*, Greek. The Greek spirit. A term applied to the civilization, language, art, and literature which is Greek in its character. The attitude to life based upon intellect and the appreciation of beauty, seen in Shelley, Keats, Landor, Pater. Matthew Arnold says, in *Culture and Anarchy*:

> To get rid of one's ignorance, to see things as they are, and by seeing them as they are to see them in their beauty, is the simple and attractive ideal with Hellenism holds out before human nature.

See also HEBRAISM.

HEMISTICH. Greek *hēmi*, half, *stíkhos*, line of verse. A half-line of verse.

HENDECASYLLABIC. Greek *hendekasúllabos*, having eleven syllables. A line of verse of eleven syllables. The term usually refers to the classical pentameter line, generally in Catullus and Martial, in which the first and last feet are spondees, the second foot a dactyl, the third and fourth trochaic. In *Milton. Hendecasyllabics*, Tennyson imitated it in lines beginning:

> Look, I come to the test, a tiny poem
> All composed in a metre of Catullus,
> All in quantity, careful of my motion,
> Like the skater on ice that hardly bears him.

HENDIADYS. Greek *hén dià duoîn*, one thing by means of two. A figure of speech by which a single complex idea (such as that normally contained in a noun and an adjective) is expressed by two words joined by 'and', as 'pour libation from bowls and from gold' for 'from golden bowls'. Fowler gives as another example of hendiadys, 'try and do better' for 'try to do better'. This is a passage from the *Psalms*:

> Such as sit in darkness and in the shadow of death, being fast bound in misery and iron.

The idea of the last three words, 'misery and iron', is not two but one: the iron shackles *are* the misery.

There is a single complex idea in the words 'show and gaze' in this line from *Macbeth*:

> Live to be the show and gaze o' the time.

HEPTAMETER.   Greek *heptá*, seven.   A line of verse consisting of seven metrical feet, illustrated in these lines from Macaulay's *Virginia*:

> And none | will grieve | when I | go forth, |
>   or smile | when I | return,
> Or sit | beside | the old | man's bed, | or weep |
>   upon | his urn.

The seven-foot line is also called the *septenary*, as it follows the pattern of Latin verse, *septenarii*.   Here are some lines from Arthur Golding's translation of Ovid's *Metamorphoses*:

> More cheerful than the winter's sun or summer's shadow cold,
> More seemly and more comely than the plane-tree to behold,
> Of value more than apples be although they were of gold . . .

The *septenary* is also known as the *fourteener*, the 'long lines' con sisting of seven iambic feet.   In four and three feet it is Ballad Metre.

HEPTASTICH.   Greek *heptá*, seven, *stikhos*, line of verse.   A stanza of seven lines.

HEROIC COUPLET.   A rhyming couplet, in iambic pentameter, so called because it was used for epic or heroic poetry.   In English, Dryden first showed mastery of the heroic couplet, a verse form perfected by Pope, and used effectively by Johnson, Goldsmith, and Crabbe.

> Eye Nature's walks, shoot folly as it flies,
> And catch the manners living as they rise.
> Laugh where we must, be candid where we can;
> But vindicate the ways of God to man.
> Say first, of God above or man below,
> What can we reason but from what we know?
>
> Pope, *An Essay on Man*

HEROIC DRAMA.   A type of play in rhymed couplets popular in England from 1664 to 1678.   It was influenced by the French classical forms, and took the theme of 'love and honour' from the Golden Age of Spain.   Heroic drama found its greatest exponents in Dryden, Howard, and Otway.   It was satirized by Buckingham in *The Rehearsal* (1672), and later by Sheridan in *The Critic* (1779).

HEROIC LINE.   Iambic pentameter, so called because it is used for heroic or epic poetry in English.   A quatrain in iambic pentameter is called the *heroic stanza*.

HEROIC POEM. A narrative poem that celebrates, as does the epic, the adventures of the heroes of history or legend. A good example is *Beowulf*, a long poem of historical events of the sixth century.

HEROIC VERSE. The verse used in epic poetry. In Greek and Latin poetry this is the hexameter; in English, the iambic pentameter; in French poetry, the Alexandrine consisting of twelve syllables. This fine example is from *Paradise Lost*:

> So spake the Sovran voice, and Clouds began
> To darken all the Hill, and smoak to rowl
> In duskie wreathes, reluctant flames, the signe
> Of wrauth awak't: nor with less dread the loud
> Ethereal Trumpet from on high gan blow:
> At which command the Powers Militant,
> That stood for Heav'n, in mighty Quadrate joyn'd
> Of Union irresistible, mov'd on
> In silence thir bright Legions, to the sound
> Of instrumental Harmonie that breath'd
> Heroic Ardor to advent'rous deeds
> Under thir God-like Leaders, in the Cause
> Of God and his *Messiah*. On they move
> Indissolubly firm. . . .

HETERODOX. Greek *heteródoxos*, having different opinions. Having beliefs or opinions differing from those generally taught and accepted as sound. Verging towards heresy; unorthodox.

HEXAMETER. Greek *héx*, six, *métros* from *métron*, measure. A line of six metrical feet. The dactylic hexameter, the oldest known form of Greek verse, was the metre of epic poems including those of Homer. The first four feet were either dactyls or spondees, the fifth was a dactyl, and the sixth a spondee.

An example is the opening line of Virgil's *Aeneid*:

$$\text{Ā́rmă vĭrūmquĕ cănō, Trṓiǣ quī prīmŭs ăb ṓris}$$

HEXASTICH. Greek *héx*, six, *stíkhos*, line of verse. A stanza of six lines.

HIATUS. Latin *hiātus*, opening, gap, from *hiāre*, to gape, to cause a hiatus. A pause or break between vowels coming together without an intervening consonant in successive words or syllables, as in *co-ordinate*.

HIERATIC. Greek *hierātikós*, priestly, devoted to sacred purposes; *hieráomai*, to be a priest. Appropriate to or used by the priestly class. Applied to a style of ancient Egyptian writing consisting of abridged forms of hieroglyphics, and to a style of conventional religious art.

HIEROGLYPH.   Greek *hierogluphikón*; *hierós*, sacred, *glúphein*, to carve.   A sacred character, a figure of a tree, an animal, standing for a word or sound, forming part of a way of writing on ancient Egyptian monuments or records.   It was extended to the picture-writing of other races.

HIERONYM.   Greek *hierós*, sacred, *ónoma*, name.   A sacred name used as a pseudonym.

HIGH COMEDY.   In *Theatre Language*, W. P. Bowman and R. H. Ball say that High Comedy is subtle and articulate, giving rise to thoughtful laughter;   and add that Drawing Room Comedy, Comedy of Manners, and High Comedy are sometimes inter-changeable.

In *The Idea of Comedy and the Uses of the Comic Spirit*, George Meredith wrote:

> The laughter of comedy is impersonal and of unrivalled politeness, nearer a smile — often no more than a smile.   It laughs through the mind, for the mind directs it. . . . The test of true comedy is that it shall awaken thoughtful laughter.

HIGHER CRITICISM.   The growth of biblical studies in the nineteenth century led to a classification into two separate depart-ments, which have been named (1) Lower or textual Criticism, and (2) Higher Criticism.   The field of Lower Criticism was to find out the original autograph readings of the Old and New Testaments. Higher Criticism examines internal evidence to find when and by whom the book was written, and to establish its place in literary history.

HINDSIGHT.   Presumably this term is formed by analogy with *foresight*.   It means the ability to see, in retrospect, the significance of past events in a way which could not be apparent at the time. In *Saint Joan*, Shaw makes the medieval clerics speak of Joan's religious ideas as Protestantism, and to say that if the authority of the Catholic Church were to be undermined, it would lead to religious wars.   This is really Shaw's hindsight; he is speaking *ex post facto*, 'after the deed has been done'.

HISTORIC PRESENT.   The use of the present tense in the narration of past events.   In *Hamlet*, the player in this way describes the fight between Pyrrhus and Priam:

> Anon he finds him
> Striking too short at Greeks; his antique sword,

Rebellious to his arm, lies where it falls,
Repugnant to command. Unequal match'd,
Pyrrhus at Priam drives, in rage strikes wide;
But with the whiff and wind of his fell sword
Th' unnerved father falls.

In newspaper headlines the historic present is used in reference
to something that has already taken place: e.g. Man Bites Dog.

HISTORICAL LINGUISTICS. *See* LINGUISTICS.

HISTORICAL NOVEL. A narrative based upon history to
represent an imaginative reconstruction of events, such as is found
in the novels of Sir Walter Scott, e.g. *Ivanhoe, Kenilworth, The
Heart of Midlothian.* Later examples are Bulwer Lytton's *The
Last Days of Pompeii* and Harrison Ainsworth's *Tower of London.*
How prominent must the historical element be to justify the
classification as a historical novel? We may ask whether the
following (which all have historical events as their setting) are
historical novels: Thackeray's *Esmond*, Dickens's *Barnaby Rudge*
and *A Tale of Two Cities*, Stevenson's *Kidnapped*.

HISTORICAL RHYME. A rhyme which was a perfectly good one
(irrespective of spelling) at the time when the work in question was
written, but which is no longer so owing to a change in the pronunciation of one of the words. An example is provided by the
following couplet from Pope's *Essay on Criticism*:

> Good nature and good sense must ever join;
> To err is human, to forgive, divine.

In Pope's day *join* was pronounced as *jine*.

HISTORY PLAY. *See* CHRONICLE PLAY.

HOKKU. *See* HAIKU.

HOLD. Old English (*ġe*)*heald, -hāld*, holding, protection. In
music this is a pause; a note or rest is prolonged. In poetry it is
the dwelling upon a syllable. In *Poetry Handbook*, Babette Deutsch
quotes a line of Kipling's to illustrate its use:

> Thûs | saïd thĕ | Lôrd | in thĕ |
> Vaūlt ă|bōve thĕ | Cherŭ|bim,∧

'The pauses on the first and fourth syllables may be interpreted as
rests, but are more easily read as *holds*.'

HOLOGRAPH. Greek *hólos*, whole, *gráphein*, to write. A document
wholly in the handwriting of the person in whose name it appears.

Many holographs of literary works reveal the creative process. The holograph of *Finnegans Wake* by James Joyce, now in the British Museum, is of immense importance to the scholar.

HOMERIC EPITHET.   Homer joined certain adjectives and nouns to make compound adjectives which are called *Homeric epithets*: wine-dark sea, rosy-fingered dawn, swift-footed Achilles.   Such combinations are regarded as Homeric epithets only when they are applied to stock nouns, with which they are frequently found in association.   *Swift-footed* would not be a Homeric epithet if it were applied to someone other than Achilles.

HOMERIC OR EPIC SIMILE.   An extended simile in which the second of two objects compared is described at length.   It is often used in epic poetry.   This passage is from *Paradise Lost*:

> Thus Satan talking to his nearest mate
> With head uplift above the wave, and eyes
> That sparkling blazed; his other parts besides
> Prone on the flood, extended long and large
> Lay floating many a rood, in bulk as huge
> As whom the fables name of monstrous size,
> Titanian, or Earth-born, that warred on Jove,
> Briareos or Typhon, whom the den
> By ancient Tarsus held, or that sea-beast
> Leviathan, which God of all his works
> Created hugest that swim the ocean stream:
> Him haply slumbering on the Norway foam
> The pilot of some small night-foundered skiff,
> Deeming some island, oft, as seamen tell,
> With fixëd anchor in his scaly rind
> Moors by his side under the lee, while night
> Invests the sea, and wishëd morn delays:
> So stretched out huge in length the Arch-Fiend lay
> Chained on the burning lake . . .

In a letter bewailing the labour of translating Homer, Cowper has this parody of the Homeric simile:

> As when an ass, being harnessed with ropes to a sand-cart, drags with hanging ears his heavy burden, neither filling the long-echoing streets with his harmonious bray, nor, throwing up his heels behind, frolicsome and airy, as asses less engaged are wont to do: so I . . .

There are several well-known examples in Matthew Arnold's *Sohrab and Rustum*.

HOMILETIC.   Greek *homīlētikós*, from *homīléein*, to converse with, from *hómīlos*, crowd.   Pertaining to sermons.   *Homiletics* is the art of preaching.

HOMILY.   Greek *homīlía*, converse, discourse; *homoû*, together, *ílē*, crowd.   A sermon explaining a part of the Bible and offering some guidance.   A tedious moralizing discourse.   *Books of Homilies*, published in 1547 and 1563, were appointed to be read in parish churches.

> O most gentle pulpiter! what tedious homily of love have you wearied your parishioners withal, and never cried 'Have patience, good people'!   *As You Like It*

HOMME MOYEN SENSUEL.   French, literally, the average sensitive reader.

HOMOGRAPH.   Greek *hómos*, like, same, *gráphein*, to write.   A word written the same as another but pronounced differently, as *tear* (the verb, or the noun corresponding to it, and a drop of water from the eye); *wound* (injury in the form of a cut, and the past tense of the verb *to wind*).

HOMONYM.   Greek *homṓnumon*, having the same name.   Applied to words both written and pronounced the same, but having different meanings and derived differently, e.g. *seal*, the animal, and *seal*, a stamp or device for making an impression.

HOMOPHONE.   Greek *homóphōn*, thing having the same sound.   Applied to written symbols or characters expressing the same sound, as *C* and *K*; and to words pronounced the same, but written differently, as *key — quay; pane — pain; hare — hair; tear* (the drop of water) — *tier*.

HORATIAN ODE.   An ode in which each stanza follows the same metrical pattern, so called after the Roman poet Horace.   His *Odes*, showing incomparable grace and economy, are universally recognized.   Here are stanzas from *An Horatian Ode upon Cromwell's Return from Ireland* by Andrew Marvell:

> So restless Cromwell could not cease
> In the inglorious arts of peace,
>   But through adventurous war
>   Urged his active star;
>
> And, like the three-forked lightning, first
> Breaking the clouds where it was nurst,
>   Did thorough his own side
>   His fiery way divide.

HORNBOOK. A single leaf of paper containing the alphabet, Roman numerals, and the Lord's Prayer protected by a thin piece of translucent horn, and mounted on wood with a projecting handle. It was used for teaching children to read. The term is used by Thomas Dekker in *The Guls Hornebooke*, his satirical book of manners, published in 1609. Shakespeare uses it in *Love's Labour's Lost*:

> Yes, yes, he teaches boyes the Horne-booke.

HOVERING ACCENT. *See* DISTRIBUTED STRESS

HOWLER. Latin *ululāre*, to howl, *ulula*, screech-owl. (Colloquial) a glaring blunder, often in an examination. In connexion with the name of Malchas, the servant of the High Priest, Ernest Weekley gives this 'genuine' howler:

> A schoolboy asked to explain certain Biblical phrases, thus elucidated 'First the blade, then the ear' (Mark iv. 28) — 'These words were said by St. Peter, as he silently approached the high priest's servant'.

HUBRIS: HYBRIS. Greek *húbris*, insolence, pride. The insolent pride in the Greek tragic hero leads him to ignore the warning of the gods and invites disaster.

HUDIBRASTIC VERSE. Octosyllabic couplets after the manner of Samuel Butler's burlesque-heroic poem, *Hudibras*:

> He'd undertake to prove by force
> Of Argument, a Man's no Horse.
> He'd move a Buzard is no Fowl,
> And that a *Lord* may be an *Owl*,
> A Calf an *Alderman*, a Goose a *Justice*,
> And Rooks *Committee-men*, and *Trustees*;
> He'd run in Debt by Disputation,
> And pay with Ratiocination.
> All this by Syllogism, true
> In mood and Figure, he would do.

HUMANISM. Latin *hūmānitās; hūmānus; homo*, man, human being. This is devotion to human interests. The word comes to us from the humanists of the Renaissance, who were devoted to the works of classical poets, philosophers, and historians. Humanism is an attitude of mind, a system of thought, which concentrates especially upon the activities of man, rather than upon the external world of nature, or upon religious ideals.

This word has been used in several different senses since the Renaissance. At the present time there is a humanist school of thought within the Unitarian Church. It has not many adherents in this country, but is stronger in the United States. Here we have still a different form of humanism, within the Christian tradition, and forming a sort of left wing of a Christian denomination.

HUMOUR. Latin (*h*)*umōrem*, moisture. In *Richter*, Carlyle says:
>The essence of humour is sensibility; warm, tender fellow-feeling with all forms of existence. Nay, we may say that unless seasoned and purified by humour, sensibility is apt to run wild.

He goes on to quote Schiller:
>The last perfection of our faculties is that their activity, without ceasing to be sure and earnest, becomes *sport*. True humour is sensibility, in the most catholic and deepest sense; but it is this *sport* of sensibility; wholesome and perfect therefore; as it were, the playful teasing fondness of a mother to her child.

George Eliot wrote, 'Humour is thinking in jest while feeling in earnest,' and Leslie Stephen, in *Hours in a Library*, maintained it was 'the faculty which always keeps us in mind of the absurdity which is the shadow of sublimity'.

Addison sought in the style of Dryden for a definition, but gave instead an ingenious genealogy. Truth, he says, in the *Spectator*, was founder of the family, and father of Good Sense. His son was Wit, who married Mirth, and Humour was their child.

HUMOURS. Latin (*h*)*umōr-em*, moisture. In ancient and medieval physiology, the four fluids of the body (*cardinal humours:* blood, phlegm, choler, and melancholy, formerly held to determine the physical and mental qualities of human beings). Ben Jonson says in *Everyman out of his Humour*:
>The choler, melancholy, phlegm and blood . . .
>Receive the name of humours. Now thus far
>It may by metaphor apply itself
>Unto the general disposition:
>As when some one peculiar quality
>Doth so possess a man that it doth draw
>All his effects, his spirits, and his powers,
>In their confluxions, all to run one way,
>This may be truly said to be a humour.

HUPOKRITÉS. Greek, literally, an actor on the Greek stage. And so a hypocrite is one who pretends to be other than he is; a dissembler, a pretender.

HYBRID. Latin *hybrida*, offspring of tame sow and wild boar, from Greek *húbris*, insolence. In *Modern English Usage*, H. W. Fowler defines hybrid derivates as words formed from a stem or word belonging to one language by applying to it a suffix or prefix belonging to another. He lists the following words as hybrids: *amoral* (Greek + Latin); *bi-daily* (Latin + English); *cablegram* (English + Greek); *floatation* (English + Latin); *gullible* (English + Latin); *sendee* (English + French).

HYBRIS. *See* HUBRIS.

HYMN. Greek *húmnos*, a song praising gods or heroes. In a religious service, a song of praise to God, sometimes distinguished from psalm and anthem. A song of praise in honour of any exalted person, as Ben Jonson's *Hymn to Cynthia* and Akenside's *Hymn to the Naiads*.

HYMNAL STANZA. A four-line stanza written in iambics with a strict rhyming pattern *a b c b* or *a b a b*. This is also known as *common measure*. This form of stanza is used by Isaac Watts:

> When I survey the wondrous Cross,
> On which the Prince of Glory died,
> My richest gain I count but loss
> And pour contempt on all my pride.

HYPALLAGE. Greek *hupallássein*, to exchange. The transference of an epithet from its appropriate noun to another to which it does not properly belong; also called *transferred epithet*. It is a common poetic device:

> And with Sansfoy's dead dowry you endew.
>
> Spenser, The Fairie Queene

> The murmurous haunt of flies on summer eves.
>
> Keats, Ode to a Nightingale

Many examples appear in ordinary speech, as in 'a restless night', 'the condemned cell', 'a happy morning'.

HYPERBATON. Greek *huperbaínein*, to go over; *hupér*, beyond, *baínein*, to go. A figure of speech in which words are transposed from their normal order, as in these lines from *Othello*:

> Yet I'll not shed her blood,
> Nor scar that whiter skin of hers than snow.

HYPERBOLE. Greek *huperbolḗ*, overshooting; from *huperbállein*, to throw beyond, to exceed; *hupér*, over, *bállein*, to throw. Exaggeration, for the purpose of emphasis:

> If thou prate of mountains let them throw
> Millions of acres on us, till our ground,
> Singeing his pate against the burning zone,
> Make Ossa like a wart.   *Hamlet*

My vegetable love should grow
Vaster than empires, and more slow,
An hundred years should go to praise
Thine eyes, and on thy forehead gaze.

Marvell, To His Coy Mistress

HYPERCATALECTIC. Greek *huperkatálēktos,* beyond the last metrical foot. Having an extra syllable at the end of the metrical line. Such lines are also described as *hypermetrical* or *extrametrical.*

His wish | and best | advan|tage, us | asund|er.

Paradise Lost

HYPERMETRIC SYLLABLE. *See* HYPERCATALECTIC.

HYPOCORISM. Greek *hupokoristikós,* from *hupokorízomai,* play the child. A pet-name, such as Bill for William. *Hypocoristic language* is that which makes use of endearing, familiar terms, using abbreviations for the full name. In the field of literature, examples are Will Shakespeare, Dick Steele, Sam Johnson, and Jack Squire (for Sir John Squire).

HYSTERON PROTERON. Greek, literally, later earlier. A figure of speech in which what should logically come last comes first; putting the cart before the horse in speech. It may be done to achieve a rhetorical or a humorous effect. Here, in *Much Ado About Nothing,* Dogberry speaks:

> Write down that they hope they serve God: and write God first; for God defend but God should go before such villains! Masters, it is proved already that you are little better than false knaves, and it will go near to be thought so shortly.

I

IAMB: IAMBUS. Greek *iambos*, from *iáptein*, to assail; this metre was used in early Greek satires. A metrical foot of two syllables, an unstressed followed by a stressed syllable, ◡ —. It is the normal foot of English verse. The following quatrain is in iambic metre:

> Stand close around, ye Stygian set,
>   With Dirce in one boat convey'd!
> Or Charon, seeing, may forget
>   That he is old and she a shade.
>
> Landor, Dirce

-IANA. *See* -ANA.

IBIDEM. Latin *ibīdem*, in the same place, in that very place. In the same book, chapter, passage. Abbreviations: ibid., ib.

ICHTHUS. Greek, literally, fish. In early Christian days the word was used as a symbol of Christ because it was composed of the initials of these words: Iesous CHristos THeou Uios Soter, Jesus Christ, son of God, Saviour.

ICON. Greek *eikōn*, image; *eikō*, be like. An image or statue, represented in the Eastern Church by paintings and mosaic, of a sacred personage, and itself regarded as sacred. *The Eikon Basilike, the Pourtraicture of His Sacred Majestie in His Solitudes and Sufferings* is a book by Dr. John Gauden, attributed to Charles I himself, published shortly after his execution. The book was immediately popular; parliament replied in the form of Milton's *Eikonoklastes* in 1649. *Eikon Basilike* means royal image; *Eikonoklastes* means image-breaker.

ICONOCLAST. Late Greek *eikonoklástēs*, from *eikōn*, image, *kláein*, to break. One who assails established or cherished beliefs.

ICTUS. Latin *ictus*, blow, from *īcěre*, strike. Rhythmical or metrical stress. The metrical stress placed on certain syllables in a line of verse, usually represented (′). Gerard Manley Hopkins marks the ictus in his *Spring and Fall*, sometimes in an unexpected place:

> Márgarét are you grievíng
> Over Goldengrove unleaving?

> Leaves, like the things of man, you
> With your fresh thoughts care for, can you?
>
> Ah! as the heart grows older
> It will come to such sights colder
> By and by, nor spare a sigh
> Though worlds of wanwood leafmeal lie.

IDEAL SPECTATOR. Latin *spectāre*, to look. The ideal spectator acts in all parts of his life as a looker-on preserving an exact neutrality throughout. Addison, in many ways the ideal spectator, says in one of his essays:

> Thus I live in the world rather as a Spectator of mankind than as one of the species, by which means I have made myself a speculative statesman, soldier, merchant, and artisan, without ever meddling with any practical part in life. I am very well versed in the theory of a husband, or a father, and can discern the errors in the economy, business, and diversions of others, better than those who are engaged in them; as standers-by discover blots, which are apt to escape those who are in the game.

IDEM. Latin *īdem*, the same. The same word, name, title. Abbreviation: id.

IDENTICAL RHYME. Latin *īdem*, the same. This term stands for the repetition of the same word in the rhyming position, so used for emphasis, as in these lines from *The Ancient Mariner*:

> Then all averred, I had killed the bird
> That brought the fog and mist.
> 'Twas right, said they, such birds to slay,
> That bring the fog and mist.

Identical rhyme also applies to the rhyming of two words sounding the same, spelled differently, and having different meanings. An example occurs in Chaucer's *Prologue* to the *Canterbury Tales* as he describes the pilgrims on their way:

> The hooly blisful martir for to seke,
> That hem hath holpen when that they were seeke.

IDEOGRAPH. Greek *idéa*, form idea, *gráphein*, to write. A written symbol, e.g. in Chinese, which represents a picture of the thing itself or stands for the idea without giving the sounds which make up the name.

ID EST. Latin, that is. That is to say. Abbreviation: i.e.

IDIOM.   Greek *idiōma*, a peculiarity in language; from *idió-omai*, make one's own.   A special way of expression, use or grouping of words peculiar to language.   For example: 'Follow events at close *hand*'; 'Is to a great *measure* true'; '*Rise* to the occasion'.

IDOLA TRIBUS, SPECUS, FORI, THEATRI.   Latin, literally, idols (that is false images of the mind, spoiling knowledge) of the tribe, cave, market, theatre.   This is Francis Bacon's classification of the fallacies of human beings in his *Novum Organum*, a philosophical treatise in Latin.

IDYLL.   Greek *eidúllion*, a little picture.   An idealized story of happy innocence, in a pastoral form, often in verse.   The *Idylls* of the Greek poet Theocritus were the first examples of pastoral poetry, imitated by Virgil and others.   There is no pastoral element in Tennyson's *Idylls of the King*, and the style is the decorative-heroic.   But contact with medieval feeling in these separate poems reminds us frequently of the classical idylls.

   Here is the use of the word *idyllic* in Wells's *The History of Mr. Polly*: 'Mr. Polly sat up, after an interval of an indeterminate length, among the ruins of an idyllic afternoon.'

ILK.   Old English *ilca*, Middle English *ilke*, same; probably from pronominal *i-* and *-līc*, like.   In Scottish, means 'same', *of that ilk* implies of the same place or name; e.g. *Campbell of that ilk*, Campbell of Campbell.   Used mistakenly as meaning 'of the same kind'.

ILLUMINATI.   From Latin *illūmināre*, to throw into light.   There háve been four societies so called: (1) The Alombrados of Spain in the sixteenth century; (2) the Guérinets of France in the seventeenth century; (3) the Mystics of Belgium in the eighteenth century; (4) the order of the Illuminati of Germany founded at Ingolstadt in Bavaria in 1776 by Professor Adam Weishaupt, and having for its object the establishment of a religion consistent with 'sound reason'.

   The name is often satirically applied to persons claiming special enlightenment on any subject.

ILLUSION.   Latin from *illūdĕre*, to mock, deceive, from *lūdĕre*, to play.   An impression which is other than true of what is perceived. A theatre audience experiences an illusion of reality by a process called by Coleridge 'a willing suspension of disbelief'.

ILLUSIONS OF THE FIRST TIME.   The effective actor should give the impression of spontaneity.   In each performance he should make it appear that these are his first reactions to the dramatic situation.

ILLUSTRATE. Latin *illustrāre*, to make light, to make known, to explain. To make clear a statement by giving specific examples. To furnish a book with figures and pictures of the things dealt with.

IMAGERY. Latin *imāgō*, image; *imitārī*, to imitate. A distinguishable part of a poem is imagery. Not only is the poet a maker of verbal music, he is also a maker of pictures in words. He does not here present the symbol of a thing, but he describes and makes us see and hear the thing itself. For example, Shakespeare is not content to say that it is winter, the word 'winter' standing as the symbol of the season, but he writes:

> When icicles hang by the wall,
>   And Dick the shepherd blows his nail,
> And Tom bears logs into the hall,
>   And milk comes frozen home in pail,
> When blood is nipp'd, and ways be foul,
> Then nightly sings the staring owl:
>   'Tu-who;
> Tu-whit, Tu-who' — A merry note,
> While greasy Joan doth keel the pot.

Here we see the typical sights of winter; we feel the cold, we hear the sounds of winter itself; in fact we experience the physical sensations of winter, through the power of our imagination, which is fed by the pictures Shakespeare gives us.

Another pleasure in the pictorial quality of poetry is that of recognition. We often find that a poet's imagery fills out and completes our own partial knowledge of things by that flash of recognition, which both instructs and delights; familiar objects are revealed in a new light, and the unfamiliar suddenly becomes real. In this passage from Keats:

> St. Agnes' Eve — Ah, bitter chill it was!
> The owl, for all his feathers, was a-cold;
> The hare limp'd trembling through the frozen grass
> And silent was the flock in woolly fold

so vivid is the picture in the third line with those two words 'limp'd' and 'trembling' that we seem to take part in the very sensations of the hare. Without such imagery, poetry might easily become abstract; instead, we have that poetic skill which gives to airy nothings 'a local habitation and a name'.

IMAGINATION. Latin *imāginātiō-(nem)*, imagination, fancy. The mental faculty of forming images of external objects which are not

present to the five senses.   Shakespeare expresses the meaning and
the power of imagination in this passage from *A Midsummer-Night's
Dream*:

> Lovers and madmen have such seething brains,
> Such shaping fantasies, that apprehend
> More than cool reason ever comprehends.
> The lunatic, the lover, and the poet
> Are of imagination all compact:
> One sees more devils than vast hell can hold,
> That is the madman; the lover, all as frantic,
> Sees Helen's beauty in a brow of Egypt;
> The poet's eye, in a fine frenzy rolling,
> Doth glance from heaven to earth, from earth to heaven;
> And as imagination bodies forth
> The forms of things unknown, the poet's pen
> Turns them to shapes, and gives to airy nothing
> A local habitation and a name.
> Such tricks hath strong imagination,
> That, if it would but apprehend some joy,
> It comprehends some bringer of that joy;
> Or in the night, imagining some fear,
> How easy is a bush supposed a bear!

Writing of imagination, Coleridge said in *Biographia Literaria*:

> This power . . . reveals itself in the balance or reconcilement of
> opposite or discordant qualities: of sameness, with difference;
> of the general, with the concrete; the idea with the image;
> the individual with the representative; the sense of novelty
> and freshness with old and familiar objects; a more than
> usual state of emotion with more than usual order; judgment
> ever awake and steady self-possession with enthusiasm and
> feeling profound or vehement . . .

In a letter to Benjamin Bailey, 22nd November 1817, Keats
wrote:

> I am certain of nothing but the holiness of the heart's affections,
> and the truth of imagination.   What the imagination seizes
> as beauty must be truth — whether it existed before or
> not. . . . The imagination may be compared to Adam's dream
> — he awoke and found it truth.

IMAGISM.   Latin *imāgināri*, to imagine, to picture to oneself.   A
kind of poetry which flourished in England and America at the
beginning of the twentieth century.   It was a revolt against excessive
romanticism.   The leading Imagists were T. E. Hulme, Ezra
Pound, Amy Lowell, Hilda Doolittle, Harriet Monroe, J. G.

Fletcher, Richard Aldington. T. S. Eliot was influenced by some of these poets.

Hulme maintained that the chief aim was to achieve accurate description, and to prove that beauty might be found in small commonplace things.

This is the beginning of an imagist poem by William Carlos Williams:

The Yachts

contend in a sea which the land partly encloses
shielding them from the too-heavy blows
of an ungoverned ocean which when it chooses

tortures the biggest hulls, the best man knows
to pit against its beatings, and sink them pitilessly.
Mothlike in mists, scintillant in the minute

brilliance of cloudless days, with broad bellying sails
they glide to the wind tossing green water
from their sharp prows while over them the crew crawls . . .

IMITATION. Latin *imitārī*, to imitate, copy. In *Poetics*, Aristotle said:

> A tragedy is the imitation of an action that is serious and also, as having magnitude, complete in itself . . . with incidents arousing pity and terror, wherewith to accomplish its purgation of such emotions.

He also said that literature was an imitation of life, of things 'as they are, as they are thought to be, as they ought to be'.

In *An Essay on Criticism*, Pope proclaims the value of imitating the ancients:

> Those RULES of old discovered not devis'd,
> Are Nature still, but Nature methodiz'd;
> Nature, like liberty, is but restrain'd
> By the same laws which first herself ordain'd.
>   Hear how learn'd Greece her useful rules indites,
> When to repress, and when indulge our flights:
> High on Parnassus' top her sons she show'd,
> And pointed out those arduous paths they trod;
> Held from afar, aloft, th' immortal prize,
> And urg'd the rest by equal steps to rise.

IMPARISYLLABIC. Latin *impār*, uneven, unequal; *syllaba*, a syllable. Unequal in syllables. A name given to those Greek and Latin nouns which have not the same number of syllables in all the cases, as nominative *dens*, tooth, genitive *dentis*.

IMPASTO. Italian *impastare*, to paste, to mix colours like paste.
The laying on of colour thickly.

IMPERFECT RHYME. *See* NEAR RHYME.

IMPERSONAL CONSTRUCTION. This is used to express an
action without naming the actor or actors, as when Milton says, in
Paradise Lost:

> Forthwith on all sides to his aide was run
> By Angels many and strong, who interpos'd
> Defence . . .

In *Childe Harold*, Byron has:

> Ah! then and there was hurrying to and fro,
> And gathering tears, and tremblings of distress,
> And cheeks all pale, which but an hour ago
> Blush'd at the praise of their own loveliness.

IMPRESSION. *See* EDITION.

IMPRESSIONISM. Latin *praestāre*, to offer. A way of writing
which does not deal with reality objectively, but gives the impressions formed by the author. The term comes from a doctrine
started in France in the first half of the nineteenth century, that 'a
picture should record the immediate sensuous impressions made
upon the painter when he looks at the objects which he is representing, and should not be a conventional representation of extraneous
facts which may be known from sources other than direct visual
experience'.

Lord Alfred Douglas, Oscar Wilde, and Arthur Symons produced
verse showing the influence of the French impressionists Verlaine,
Mallarmé, Corbière, Laforgue. Wilde's poem *Le Jardin* shows the
impressionistic technique:

> The lily's withered chalice falls,
>   Around its rod of dusty gold,
>   And from the beech-trees on the wold
> The last wood-pigeon coos and calls.
>
> The gaudy leonine sunflower
>   Hangs black and barren on its stalk,
>   And down the windy garden walk
> The dead leaves scatter, — hour by hour.
>
> Pale privet-petals white as milk
>   Are blown into a snowy mass;
>   The roses lie upon the grass
> Like little shreds of crimson silk.

IMPRESSIONISTIC CRITICISM. In the preface to *Studies in the History of the Renaissance*, Walter Pater speaks about the relationship between our impressions and criticism:

> Our education becomes complete in proportion as our susceptibility to these impressions increases in depth and variety. And the function of the aesthetic critic is to distinguish, analyse, and separate from its adjuncts, the virtue by which a picture, a landscape, a fair personality in life or in a book, produces this special impression of beauty or pleasure, to indicate what the source of that impression is, and under what conditions it is experienced.

Pater's own description of 'La Gioconda' by Leonardo da Vinci is a fine example of the sensibilities displayed in impressionistic criticism:

> She is older than the rocks among which she sits; like the vampire, she has been dead many times, and learned the secrets of the grave; and has been a diver in deep seas, and keeps their fallen day about her; and trafficked for strange webs with Eastern merchants; and, as Leda, was the mother of Helen of Troy, and, as Saint Anne, the mother of Mary; and all this has been to her but as the sound of lyres and flutes, and lives only in the delicacy with which it has moulded the changing lineaments, and tinged the eyelids and the hands.

IMPRIMATUR. Modern Latin *imprimatur*, let it be printed; from Latin *imprimĕre*, to impress, imprint. Official licence to print, now usually of works sanctioned by the Roman Catholic Church. Its official interpretation is:

> The *Nihil obstat* [q.v.] and *Imprimatur* are a declaration that a book or pamphlet is considered to be free from doctrinal or moral error. It is not implied that those who have granted the *Nihil obstat* and *Imprimatur* agree with the contents, opinions or statements expressed.

IMPRINT. Old French *empreinter*, from *empreindre*, to imprint, impress, stamp. That which is imprinted; an impression; *printers'*, *publishers' imprint*, name, place, date, printed on title-page or at the end of the book. In Britain, this latter is a legal requirement (see the Newspapers, Printers, and Reading Rooms Repeal Act, 1869).

IMPROPRIETY OF DICTION. Latin *improprietāt-(em)* improper. The incorrectness and unfitness in the use of words. Samuel Johnson said, 'Every language has likewise its improprieties and absurdities.'

INCANTATION. Latin *incantātiōnem*, from *incantāre*, to be-
witch with spells, enchant. The magic sound of words, used by the
poet as a form of spell. One does not need to understand the
meaning or the associations of the words in this passage from
Paradise Lost to be moved by the incantation:

> Not that faire field
> Of Enna, where Proserpin gathring flours
> Her self a fairer Floure by gloomie Dis
> Was gather'd, which cost Ceres all that pain
> To seek her through the world; nor that sweet Grove
> Of Daphne by Orontes, and th' inspir'd
> Castalian Spring might with this Paradise
> Of Eden strive.

In *The Forms of Things Unknown*, Herbert Read says of Ariel's
Song from *The Tempest*:

> It is an incantation, a dirge celebrating death and mortality,
> comparable to that earliest poetry that has survived from
> remote antiquity, the Egyptian Book of the Dead:

> > Full fathom five thy father lies;
> > Of his bones are coral made:
> > Those are pearls that were his eyes:
> > Nothing of him that doth fade,
> > But doth suffer a sea-change
> > Into something rich and strange.
> > Sea-nymphs hourly ring his knell:
> > > Ding-dong.
> > Hark! now I hear them, — ding-dong, bell.

INCONGRUITY. Latin *incongru-(us)*, inconsistent, unsuitable.
Something that is inconsistent, inappropriate. Incongruity is one
of the elements of humour, and is found also in dramatic irony, in
bathos, and the mock-heroic, where the incongruity is between the
subject and the manner in which it is treated.

INCREMENTAL REPETITION. Latin *incrēmentum*, from *in-
crēscĕre*, from *crēscĕre*, to grow. This refers to a structural device
of the ballad consisting of the repetition of certain parts of each
stanza to emphasize changes in the story. The method of question
and answer is fairly common, shown in this passage from the
medieval ballad *Edward, Edward*:

> 'Why does your brand sae drop wi' blude,
>   Edward, Edward?
> Why does your brand sae drop wi' blude,
>   And why sae sad gang ye, O?'

'O I hae kill'd my hawk sae gude,
    Mither, mither;
O I hae kill'd my hawk sae gude,
    And I had nae mair but he, O.'

'Your hawk's blude was never sae red,
    Edward, Edward;
Your hawk's blude was never sae red,
    My dear son, I tell thee, O.'

'O I hae kill'd my red-roan steed,
    Mither, mither;
O I hae kill'd my red-roan steed,
    That erst was sae fair and free, O.'

INCUNABULA. Latin *incūnābula*, swaddling-clothes, infancy, earliest stage; *in*, in, *cūnābula*, diminutive of *cūnae*, a cradle. Books printed in the early period of the printing art, before the year 1500. The origin, the early stages of anything.

INDENTION. Medieval Latin *indentāre*, to give a serrated edge to. Setting in from the margin; for example, the first line of a paragraph is usually indented. In hanging indention (as here), often used in the glossary and similar alphabetical lists, the first line begins flush and the subsequent lines are set in.

INDEX: (pl.) INDEXES, INDICES. Latin *index*, forefinger, mark, list, informer; *indicāre*, to show. Alphabetical list, usually at the end of the book, of subjects treated, with references.

INDEX EXPURGATORIUS. A list of passages to be expunged in books otherwise permitted by the Roman Catholic Church to be read.

INDEX LIBRORUM PROHIBITORUM. A list of books forbidden to Roman Catholics, or to be read only in expurgated editions. Commonly referred to as 'the Index'.

INDIRECT SPEECH: ORATIO OBLIQUA. This is the changing of spoken words into reported speech.

INDUCTION. Latin *indūcěre*, to lead or bring in. The method of reasoning from particular, or individual, cases to general conclusions. The introduction of facts to support a conclusion or principle. I make an induction if I argue, from the fact that all the Mulligans I have known are Irish, that Mulligan is an Irish name.

Induction is also an archaic word for preamble, prologue, introduction. In Shakespeare's *The Taming of the Shrew*, the opening scene is marked 'Induction', and is followed by Act I, Scene i.

INFERIOR LETTERS OR FIGURES. Small letters or figures, ranged below the line, as subscripts in mathematical and chemical material, for example, H_2O. In manuscript or proof an inferior character is indicated beneath a caret, as ⌄ or ⌄. Similar figures ranged above the line are termed *superior figures*.

INFLECTION: INFLEXION. Latin *inflectĕre*, to bend, to curve. A change in the form of a word to express different grammatical functions. The change is usually an addition to the stem of the word including declension, conjugation, and comparison. In English, the noun usually has one inflection, the addition of 's' to form the plural. Latin is a highly inflected language.

INITIAL INCIDENT. In drama, this is the incident in which the conflict, forming the plot, is started.

INKHORN TERM. Latin *encaustum*, from Greek *égkauston*, the purple ink used by the later Roman emperors for signature; from *égkaustos* (of colours), burnt in. Inkhorn, a horn vessel formerly used for holding and carrying ink. 'With a writer's inkhorn by his side.' *Ezekiel*. In Elizabethan times it was a phrase applied with distaste to affectedly learned, pedantic words conveyed into English from other languages. Thomas Wilson wrote in his *Arte of Rhetorique* (1553):

> Among all other lessons this should first be learned, that we never affect any straunge ynkhorne termes, but to speake as is commonly received.

IN MEDIAS RES. Latin. Into the thick of it. Into the midst of affairs.

INNUENDO. Latin *innuendō*, by nodding at; *innuĕre*, to nod to. Insinuation. The way of suggesting instead of stating openly what is meant. For example: 'Honesty is the best policy but advertising also pays.'

IN PRINCIPIO. Latin, literally, in the beginning. These are the first words of the Book of Genesis and of St. John's Gospel as it appears in the Vulgate. This name is given to the first fourteen verses of St. John, thought to possess especial virtues. In the *Prologue* to the *Canterbury Tales*, Chaucer says of the Friar:

> He was the beste begger in al his house,
> For though a widdewe hadde but oo schoo,
> So plesaunt was his *In principio*,
> Yet wolde he have a ferthing or he wente.

INSCAPE AND INSTRESS. W. H. Gardner says, in *Gerard Manley Hopkins*:

> As a name for that 'individually-distinctive' form (made up of various sense-data) which constitutes the rich and revealing 'one-ness' of the natural object, Hopkins coined the word *inscape*; and for that energy of being by which all things are upheld, for that natural (but ultimately supernatural) stress which determines an *inscape* and keeps it in being — for that he coined the name *instress*.
> It was not until 1868 that the terms *inscape* and *instress* began to appear frequently, and in a distracting variety of contexts.

INSINUATION. *See* INNUENDO.

INSPIRATION. Latin *inspīrātiōnem*, from *inspīrāre*, to breathe into. A term used in theology to denote a divine influence, as St. Paul said, 'All scripture is given by inspiration of God.' A divine influence was thought also to visit poets. In *Fasti*, Ovid wrote, 'A god has his abode within our breast; when he rouses us, the glow of inspiration warms us; this holy rapture springs from the seeds of the divine mind sown in man.' In *Reason in Church Government*, Milton maintained that the poet needed the help of the 'eternal Spirit . . . who sends out his seraphim with the hallowed fire of his altar'. Robert Burns says, in *Epistle to J. Lapraik*:

> Gie me ae spark o' nature's fire —
> That's a' the learning I desire.

INSTRESS. *See* INSCAPE AND INSTRESS.

INTAGLIO. Italian *intagliato*; *tagliare*, cut, from Late Latin *tāleāre*, from *tālea*, a cutting. Engraved, incised design. A printing plate in which the image to be printed is engraved or cut into the surface of the plate, and from which, in printing, the ink is lifted and transferred to the paper. *Intaglio* is the opposite of *relief*. Photogravure is a modern development of intaglio printing.

INTENSION. Latin *intensiōn-(em)*, a stretching out, straining. In formal logic, all the qualities or attributes comprised in a general term or general notion.

INTENTION. *See* MEANING, FOUR KINDS OF.

INTENTIONAL FALLACY. Latin *fallācia*, from *fallĕre*, to deceive. In *An Essay on Criticism*, Alexander Pope discources on the foundation of true criticism; the causes preventing it; and the causes producing it. He tells the critic how to regard the poet's intention:

> Whoever thinks a faultless piece to see,
> Thinks what ne'er was, nor is, nor e'er shall be.
> In every work regard the writer's End,
> Since none can compass more than they intend.

Many critics today hold a different view. To them it is a mistake to judge a literary work by the author's failure or success in achieving his intention. Intentional means not 'deliberate', but 'relating to the intention of the writer', i.e. the fallacy of accepting the writer's intention as the criterion of criticism.

INTERIOR MONOLOGUE. *See* STREAM OF CONSCIOUSNESS.

INTERLACED RHYME. *See* CROSSED RHYME.

INTERLEAF. An extra leaf, which is usually blank, inserted between the regular leaves of a book.

INTERLUDE. Medieval Latin *interlūdium*, from *lūdus*, play. A short comic play, of the kind popular in the fifteenth and sixteenth centuries. Interludes were performed at Court, in the halls of the nobles, and in colleges, often in the intervals of banquets and entertainments. They succeeded Miracle or Morality Plays. John Heywood established Interludes with *The Foure Ps* in 1569.

INTERMEZZI (INTERMEDII). In *The Oxford Companion to the Theatre*, Phyllis Hartnoll says:

> Interpolations of a light, often comic, character performed between the acts of serious drama or opera in Italy in the late fifteenth and early sixteenth centuries. They usually dealt with mythological subjects, and could be given as independent entertainments for guests at royal or noble festivals, on the lines of the English 'disguising' and dumb-show, or the French *momeries* and *entremets* and the Spanish *entremeses*.

INTERNAL NECESSITY. *See* POETRY AND PROSE.

INTERNAL RHYME: MIDDLE RHYME. This is rhyme falling in the middle as well as at the end of the same metrical line, as in Shelley's *The Cloud*:

> I am the daughter of Earth and Water,
>   And the nursling of the Sky;
> I pass through the pores of the ocean and shores;
>   I change, but I cannot die.
> For after the rain when with never a stain
>   The pavilion of Heaven is bare,
> And the winds and sunbeams with their convex gleams
>   Build up the blue dome of air,
> I silently laugh at my own cenotaph,
>   And out of the caverns of rain,
> Like a child from the womb, like a ghost from the tomb,
>   I arise and unbuild it again.

INTERPOLATION. Latin *interpolāre*, to furbish up, to alter. The insertion of spurious matter in a manuscript or book.

'INTIMACY' WITH NATURE. In his *Anthology of Canadian Verse*, Ralph Gustafson uses this phrase. He says, 'There are no Aphrodites in Canadian poetry — the seafoam is too cold. The Furies have to be imported. The Laurentian Shield is the intruder. There are no places for yearlong thought in a green shade.'

> And yet the marvels we have seen remain.
> We think of the eagles, of the fawns at the river bend,
> The storms, the sudden sun, the clouds sheered downwards.
>   Douglas Le Pan, *Canoe-trip*

INTONATION. Latin *intonāre*, to sound, from *tonus*, tone. Reciting in a singing voice. In Church Music it is the opening phrase of plain-song melody.

INTRIGUE. Latin *intrīcāre*, to entangle, from *trīcae* (pl.) tricks. Underhand plotting. The term is applied to plays which have intricate plots. *Love for Love* and *The Way of the World* by Congreve are known as *comedies of intrigue*.

INTRODUCTION. Latin *intrōdūcĕre*, from *dūcĕre*, to lead. An essay, sometimes a poem, which prepares the way for a literary work. Dr. Johnson says:

> There are two things which I am confident I can do very well: one is an introduction to any literary work, stating what it is to contain, and how it should be executed in the most perfect

manner; the other is a conclusion, showing from various causes why the execution has not been equal to what the author promised to himself and to the public.

INTUITIVE. Medieval Latin *intuitiōn-(em)*, from *intuērī*, to look upon, from *tuērī*, to behold. Perceived or known by immediate instinctive sense, not by the process of conscious reasoning.

INVECTIVE. Late Latin *invectiva (orātiō)*, abusive (speech). A violent attack in words; abusive oratory. Dunbar, Skelton, and Pope are renowned for their personal invective. A famous example occurs in Swinburne's *A Letter to Ralph Waldo Emerson*:

> A foul mouth is so ill-matched with a white beard that I would gladly believe the newspaper-scribes alone responsible for the bestial utterances which they declare to have dropped from a teacher whom such disciples as these exhibit to our disgust and compassion as performing on their obscene platform the last tricks of tongue now possible to a gap-toothed and hoary-headed ape, carried at first into notice on the shoulder of Carlyle, and who now in his dotage spits and chatters from a dirtier perch of his own finding and fouling.

INVENTION. Latin *invenīre*, to come upon, discover, from *venīre*, to come. Dr. Johnson said in his *Life of Pope*:

> Invention is the faculty by which new trains of events are formed and new scenes of imagery displayed ... and by which extrinsic and adventitious embellishments and illustrations are connected with a known subject.

In the Preface to the 1815 Edition of the *Lyrical Ballads*, Wordsworth said:

> The powers requisite for the production of poetry are . . . fifthly, invention, by which characters are composed out of materials supplied by observation, whether of the poet's own heart and mind, or of external life and nature; and such incidents and situations produced as are most impressive to the imagination, and most fitted to do justice to the characters, sentiments and passions which the poet undertakes to illustrate.

INVERSION. Latin *invertĕre*, to turn in. The reversal of the normal order of words in a sentence. Inversion is often used in poetry for the sake of the metre, as in this line in Tennyson's *Morte d'Arthur*:

> So spake he, clouded with his own conceit.

INVERTED ACCENT, FOOT, STRESS. *See* SUBSTITUTION.

INVOCATION. Latin *vocāre*, to call. The appeal for divine help often to Calliope, the muse of epic poetry, made by the poet at the beginning of an epic poem. This appeal became a literary convention. A famous invocation is made at the beginning of *Paradise Lost*. Here Milton appeals to Urania, the muse of astronomy, not the muse of poetry:

> Sing, Heavenly Muse, that on the secret top
> Of Oreb, or of Sinai, didst inspire
> That Shepherd, who first taught the chosen seed,
> In the beginning how the Heavens and Earth
> Rose out of chaos; or if Sion Hill
> Delight thee more, and Siloa's brook that flowed
> Fast by the oracle of God, I thence
> Invoke thy aid to my adventurous song,
> That with no middle flight intends to soar
> Above the Aonian mount.

IONIC. A classical metrical foot of four syllables, of which the first two are long and the last two are short. This is called the *greater Ionic*. If the first two are short and the last two long it is called the *lesser Ionic*. The Ionic metre is used by Horace in his Odes.

IRISH DRAMATIC MOVEMENT. In *The Oxford Companion to the Theatre*, Una Ellis-Fermor says:

> The history of Irish drama may be said to begin with the Irish Literary Movement at the end of the nineteenth century.
> The Irish Dramatic Movement, begun by W. B. Yeats and Lady Gregory in 1899, offered from the beginning plays by native dramatists upon native subjects; after their union with the Fays' company in 1901 the players were Irish too. After 1904 Miss Horniman's help resulted in the procuring of the now famous Abbey Theatre and the setting up of the Abbey Theatre company. The theatre differed from others in being wholly or mainly national in its repertory. After 1904 the Ulster Theatre formed an important part of the movement; its aims and methods, though independent, were fundamentally akin.

IRONY. Greek *eirōneia*, simulated ignorance. The use of words, with humorous or satirical intention, so that the meaning is the direct opposite of what is actually said. Irony implies also the simulated adoption of another's point of view for the purpose of ridicule and sarcasm.

Irony developed from the element of concealment or simulation. From *eirōneía* came the name *eírōn*, a dissembler, a stock character of Greek comedy. Being undersized, he resorted to various forms of deception to overcome *alazon*, the braggart captain.

Socrates, in discussion, adopted another person's viewpoint in order finally to ridicule him and reveal his weaknesses. This was known as *Socratic irony*.

Swift is the greatest master in English of sustained irony. F. R. Leavis, in his masterly analysis of this prose writer in *Determinations*, says:

> Swift's irony is essentially a matter of surprise and negation; its function is to defeat habit, to intimidate and to demoralize. What he assumes in the *Argument Against Abolishing Christianity* is not so much a common acceptance of Christianity as that the reader will be ashamed to have to recognize how fundamentally unchristian his actual assumptions, motives and attitudes are. And in general the implication is that it would shame people if they were made to recognize themselves unequivocally. If one had to justify this irony according to the conventional notion of satire, then its satiric efficacy would be to make comfortable non-recognition, the unconsciousness of habit, impossible.

Another example is Defoe's *The Shortest Way with Dissenters*, where the writer pretends to advocate what he actually disapproves of. (Defoe was himself a Dissenter.) *See also* DRAMATIC IRONY.

IRREGULAR ODE. *See* COWLEYAN ODE.

ISSUE. 'Some special form of the book, in which, for the most part, the original printed sheets are used, but which differs from the earlier or normal form by the addition of new matter, because it is printed on different paper, or because its contents are differently arranged.' (K. A. Mallaber, *A Primer of Bibliography*)

ITALIAN SONNET. *See* SONNET.

ITALIC TYPE. A species of printing type introduced by Aldus Manutius of Venice, in which the letters slope to the right. It was first used in an edition of Virgil in 1501, and dedicated to Italy.

IVORY TOWER. These two quotations from *The Decline and Fall of the Romantic Ideal* by F. L. Lucas explain to us this phrase:

> I have dwelt on Proust, because he is a fascinating case, and because such an example can, I think, bring out more clearly than ever the dangers of all literature that turns from

life, all literature that loses health of mind. For the Ivory Tower in this world, like Virgil's Ivory Gate in the world below, is, I believe, in the long run, the haunt of dreams that lie and of visions that betray.

The revolt of Aucassin may indeed be stimulating at first; but I doubt if either Bohemia or Ivory Towers are healthy for poets in the end. Ivory Towers have Ivory Gates, through which false and vain dreams come. Such a life divides the poet from his hearers; it divides him against himself.

J

JABBERWOCKY. This term is derived from a poem in Lewis Carroll's *Through the Looking-Glass*. Alice found a poem (printed backwards) all in some language she didn't know. It was a Looking-glass book. She held it up to a glass and read *Jabberwocky*. The poem began:

> 'Twas brillig, and the slithy toves
> Did gyre and gimble in the wabe:
> All mimsy were the borogroves,
> And the mome raths outgrabe.

Later in the story, Humpty Dumpty, who said he could explain all the poems that ever were invented, began to clarify this poem, and said to Alice, '*Brillig* means four o'clock in the afternoon — the time when you begin *broiling* things for dinner. . . . To *gyre* is to go round and round like a gyroscope. To *gimble* is to make holes like a gimlet.'

JACOBEAN. Greek *Iákōbos*, Latin *Jacobus*, Jacob. Belonging to the reign of James I (1603–1625). The term is applied to the drama of the period, to architecture, to furniture.

JARGON. Old French *jargon*, warbling of birds, chatter, talk. Unintelligible words; barbarisms or debased language. A way of speech full of unfamiliar terms; the vocabulary of a science, profession, or art.

In his *Art of Writing* is Quiller-Couch's well-known essay on Jargon.

JEREMIAD. A doleful complaint, in allusion to the *Lamentations of Jeremiah* in the Old Testament. This remark by Arthur Helps: 'I could sit down, and mourn, and, utter doleful Jeremiads without end' seems to echo Jeremiah: 'Is it nothing to you, all ye that pass by? Behold, and see if there be any sorrow like unto my sorrow.'

JEST-BOOKS. Collections of merry tales no longer serving a purely moral end, but rather aiming to entertain and divert. The *exempla* were the models and immediate parents of the jest-books, which were popular in the sixteenth century. *A Hundred Merry Tales*, which appeared in 1526, is one of the earliest jest-books in English. *Joe Miller's Jest-book* by John Mottley was published in 1739. The name comes from Joseph Miller (1684–1738), who was an actor and a well-known wit. *Shakespeare Jest-Books* by W. Carew Hazlitt was published in 1864.

JEU D'ESPRIT. French, literally, play of the mind. A witticism or a short passage distinguished by wit and pungency.

JOE MILLER. An oft-repeated jest or joke. The reference is to Joseph Miller (1684–1738), an actor in the Drury Lane company and a wit. In *Eōthen*, Kinglake says, 'It is a very old piece of fun, no doubt quite an oriental Joe Miller.'

JOHANNES FACTOTUM. Latin, literally, 'John Do-everything', a Jack of all trades. Similar phrases, *Dominus Factotum, Magister Factotum*, and the Italian *fa il tutto* are also found in the sixteenth century.

In the *Groatsworth of Wit* (1592), Robert Greene made his famous attack on Shakespeare:

> For there is an upstart crow, beautified with our feathers . . . and being an absolute *Johannes fac totum*, is in his own conceite the only Shake-scene in a countrey.

JOHNSONESE. A balanced, weighty, formal style of writing, full of Latinized constructions. It is named after Dr. Johnson. This passage is from *The Rambler*:

> It is natural to imagine upon the same principle, that no writer has a more easy task than the historian. The philosopher has the works of omniscience to examine, and is therefore engaged in disquisitions to which finite intellects are utterly unequal. The poet trusts to his invention, and is not only in danger of those inconsistencies, to which every one is exposed by departure from truth, but may be censured as well for the deficiencies of his matter, as for the irregularity of disposition, or impropriety of ornament. But the happy historian has no other labour than of gathering what tradition pours down before him, or records treasure for his use. He has only the actions and designs of men like himself to conceive and to relate, and is not blamed for the inconsistency of statesmen, the injustice of tyrants, or the cowardice of commanders.

JONGLEUR. French variant of *jingleur*, juggler. An itinerant minstrel.

JOURNAL. Latin *diurnālis*, from *diurnus*, from *dies*, day. A diary, magazine, daily newspaper or periodical. The recorded transactions of any society. Among the most noted journals in the eighteenth century are those of Daniel Defoe, James Boswell, and in modern times those of André Gide.

JOURNALESE. Latin *diurnālis*, from *diurnus*, from *dies*, day. A style considered characteristic of newspaper writing; striving after effect; marked by clichés or hackneyed phrases; the use of circumlocution and other clumsiness.

JOURNEYMAN. French *journée, jour*, a day; Latin *diurnus*, daily, lasting a day. One whose apprenticeship is completed, and is qualified to work at his craft or trade for daily wages. A hired workman.

JUNIUS. The name used by the author of a number of letters which appeared in the *Public Advertiser* from 1769 to 1771. These letters attacked leading figures of the day including Lord North, Lord Mansfield, the Duke of Grafton, the Duke of Bedford. Junius supported the Whigs, and came actively to the help of John Wilkes. His identity has never been established. Junius may have been Sir Philip Francis or Lord Temple.

JUVENILIA. Latin *juvenīlis*, from *juvenis*, young. Early works produced in the author's or artist's youth. Byron was under nineteen years of age when he published his 'Hours of Idleness', which was at first named 'Juvenilia'.

K

KABUKI. C. W. Bickmore says, in the *Oxford Companion to the Theatre*:

> The present-day Japanese theatre takes three distinct although related forms, the *Nō* or lyrical drama, *Ningyō-shibai* or marionettes, and *Kabuki*, the popular theatre. . . . The *Kabuki* scenery is elaborate and complete to the last detail. The costumes are fitted to the part; rich brocaded silks in historical subjects, plain where the scenes are drawn from common life. The performers are not masked. Female parts are taken exclusively by male actors who specialize in these roles.

KAILYARD SCHOOL. *Kailyard* means kitchen-garden. The name 'Kailyard School' was given to those writing of Scottish peasant life in an artificial and sentimental way. It comes from the motto 'There grows a bonnie brier bush in our kailyard', used in *Beside the Bonnie Brier Bush*, a novel by Ian McLaren (1850-1907).

KATHARSIS. *See* CATHARSIS.

KELLS, THE BOOK OF. This copy of the Four Gospels in Latin is a manuscript of Christian Celtic art produced in the Monastery at Kells, Ireland, in the eighth century. The manuscript is perhaps the most beautiful illuminated book of the Middle Ages. It is now permanently displayed in the Library at Trinity College, Dublin.

KENNING. Old English *cennan*, from *cunnan*, to know (how to do), to be able. A standard stock phrase used in Norse and Anglo-Saxon poetry, such as 'the earth-walker' for traveller, 'the game of blades' for battle, 'the helmet of night' for darkness. It is equivalent to such a stock phrase as 'the wine-dark sea' of Greek epics.

KEY NOVEL. *See* ROMAN À CLEF *and* SCHLÜSSELROMAN.

KING'S ENGLISH. Now, of course, the Queen's English, as it was in Victorian times. Correct, standard English. It is also taken to mean 'the linguistic currency of the realm'.

KITCHEN-SINK DRAMA. The name for this kind of social drama may have come from the kitchen-sink in Arnold Wesker's play, *The Kitchen*, and the attic tank in *Look Back in Anger* by

John Osborne. The paintings of John Bratby, member of the English Realist School, possibly contributed also. *A Taste of Honey* by Shelagh Delaney is another play in the same style.

Allardyce Nicoll, in *The Theatre and Dramatic Theory*, says:

> Kitchen-sink themes so far from being new, were old-fashioned many decades ago: Gorki trenchantly explored this area, and many of the early 'repertory' playwrights built much of their work on the use of 'working-class' material.

KOMMOI: KOMMOS (singular). Greek. In ancient drama these were songs alternating between the chorus and a character taking part in the scene.

KÜNSTLERROMAN. German *Künstler*, artist; *Roman*, novel, romance. A novel which shows an artist growing up from childhood.

L

LABEL NAMES. This term was invented by William Archer to describe the names in plays of men and women chosen to fit their special character, as Sneer, Mrs. Candour, Sir Benjamin Backbite. *See also* EVOCATIVE NAMES.

LACUNA. Latin, *lacūna*, a ditch; a pool. In a metaphorical sense, a gap, a deficiency. A hiatus, a blank or defect in a manuscript or book.

LAID PAPER. Paper with a ribbed finish of parallel lines which can be seen when the paper is held to the light.

LAKE POETS. The misleading name given to the three poets Wordsworth, Coleridge, and Southey, who at the beginning of the nineteenth century lived among the lakes of Cumberland. 'Lake School' first appears in this sense in the *Edinburgh Review*, August 1817. Wordsworth and Coleridge had a good deal of poetic theory in common. Southey highly disapproved of this poetic theory. 'The term arose', says Coleridge, in *Coleorton Letters*, 'from our not hating or envying one another.' The term was seized upon by Byron, who despised their poetry. 'I hate and abhor', he wrote to Murray, 'that puddle of water-worms whom you have taken into your troop . . . pond-poets.' Later he says, 'the Lakers, who whine about nature because they live in Cumberland'.

LAMENT. Latin *lāmentāre*, late formation from *lāmentum*, wailing, moaning, weeping. A conventional form of mourning. A dirge, an elegy composed and sung or played on the occasion of some death or calamity. The *Lamentations of Jeremiah*, the *Lament of David over Saul and Jonathan* are among the most famous. Anglo-Saxon literature includes *The Wanderer*, *Deor's Lament*. Burns wrote *Lament for Culloden* and *Lament for Flodden*.

LAMPOON. Old French *lampon*, from *lampons*, let us guzzle, used as a refrain of scurrilous songs. A virulent or scurrilous piece of satire either in prose or verse. Lampoons, which are personal attacks, appeared widely in the seventeenth and eighteenth centuries, and were later checked by libel laws. In these lines from his *Epistle to Dr. Arbuthnot*, Pope lampoons Lord Hervey:

> Amphibious thing! that acting either part,
> The trifling head, or the corrupted heart,

159

Fop at the toilet, flatt'rer at the board,
Now trips a Lady, and now struts a Lord.
Eve's tempter thus the Rabbins have exprest,
A Cherub's face, a reptile all the rest,
Beauty that shocks you, parts that none will trust,
Wit that can creep, and pride that licks the dust.

LANGUAGE OF POETRY. In 1742 Gray wrote in a letter to Richard West:

> The language of the age is never the language of poetry, except among the French, whose verse, where the thought or image does not support it, differs in nothing from prose. Our poetry, on the contrary, has a language peculiar to itself, to which almost everyone that has written has added something.

In his *Preface to Lyrical Ballads*, 1800, Wordsworth said, 'Is there then, it will be asked, no essential difference between the language of prose and metrical composition? I answer that there neither is nor can be any essential difference.'

LARGE-PAPER EDITION. Books printed on a paper of extra large size with wide margins, the letterpress being the same as in the small-paper copies.

LATINISM. Latin *Latīnus*, pertaining to Latium, part of Italy where this dialect was spoken. An idiom peculiar to Latin introduced into the style of another language.

In *Explorations in Shakespeare's Language*, Hilda Hulme says:

> King Henry, attacking the town of Harfleur, calls on his men to 'bend vp euery Spirit':

> Stiffen the sinewes, commune vp the blood,
> Disguise faire Nature with hard-fauour'd Rage . . .

Cooper's *Thesaurus* shows a Latin verb *Communio* with the sense 'To fortifie: to make strong: to fense on all partes'. It may be argued, therefore, that Shakespeare's audience would have no difficulty with the simple root formation 'commune' of this passage.

Later editors have corrected 'commune' to 'summon' to avoid this Latinism.

LAUREATE. *See* POET LAUREATE.

LAY. Old French *lai*, perhaps from Teutonic, Old High German *leich*, melody. A short lyric or narrative poem which is intended to be sung. During the latter part of the twelfth century, lays, dealing with legend or romantic adventure, were sung by minstrels in France. Some, known as 'Breton lays', had an influence on narrative poems in England in the fourteenth century. The prologue of Chaucer's *Franklin's Tale* begins with these words:

> Thise olde gentle Britouns in hir dayes
> Of diverse aventures maden layes,
> Rymeyed in hir firste Briton tonge;
> Which layes with hir instrumentz they songe.

The term applies to verse narrative to be recited without music, such as Scott's *Lay of the Last Minstrel*, Macaulay's *Lays of Ancient Rome*, and Aytoun's *Lays of the Scottish Cavaliers*.

LEAF. Each separate sheet of paper in a book. Each leaf consists of two pages.

LECTIONARY. Ecclesiastical Latin *lectiōnārium*; *legĕre, lectum,* to read. A book containing portions of Scripture to be read at divine service.

LEFT BOOK CLUB, THE. A series of books published by Victor Gollancz between 1936 and 1947, which dealt with various aspects of Socialism and Fabianism, and contemporary events in Spain, Germany, China, etc. Many distinguished authors wrote for the Left Book Club, among them Victor Gollancz himself, John Strachey, George Orwell, Arthur Koestler, and G. D. H. Cole.
A rival Right Book Club was established by Foyle's to promote the opposite viewpoint, but never really caught the public imagination to the extent of the Left Book Club.

LEGEND. Medieval Latin *legenda,* to be read, from *legĕre,* to read. Originally it was an account of a saint's life which was read aloud as a duty. *The Golden Legend,* a compilation of the lives of saints, was a version of the 'Legenda Aurea' of Jacobus de Voragine (1230–1298) Archbishop of Genoa. It was published by Caxton in 1483. Later the legend was extended to include stories of other kinds, generally of a marvellous character. Then the legend became a traditional, popular tale with a basis of fact, but including imaginative material. Chaucer's *Legend of Good Women* is in praise of women, and narrates nine stories of good women, including the historical figure Cleopatra, and Philomela from mythology.

LEGITIMATE DRAMA. This is sometimes abbreviated to 'the legit'. Phyllis Hartnoll says, in *The Oxford Companion to the Theatre*:

> The term arose in the eighteenth century during the struggle of the Patent Theatres — Covent Garden and Drury Lane —

against the upstart and illegitimate playhouses springing up all over London. It covered in general those five-act plays (including Shakespeare) which had little or no singing, dancing, and spectacle, and depended entirely on acting. In the nineteenth century the term was used . . . as a defence against the encroachments of farce, musical comedy, and revue.

LEITMOTIV: LEITMOTIF. German *leiten*, to lead, and *Motiv*, a motive. Percy A. Scholes says that Wagner used short orchestral phrases ('Leading Motives') characterizing the personalities of the drama and recurring again and again to underline the thought or emotion behind the dramatic position at the moment: the whole score of a scene thus became fluid. *Leitmotiv* is used frequently in films.

LEONINE RHYME. A kind of Latin verse much used in the Middle Ages in which the last word rhymes with that preceding the caesura; for instance:

> Ni fallat *fatum*, Scoti, quocunque *locatum*
> Invenient *lapidem*, regnare tenentur *ibidem*;
> Gloria *factorum* conceditur *honorum*.

These verses are so called from the inventor Leoninus, a canon of the church of St. Victor, in Paris, in the twelfth century.

Although the term is sometimes limited to hexameters, or alternate hexameters and pentameters, as used by Leoninus, it can be extended to lines of seven metrical feet as in Tennyson's *Revenge*:

> Spanish ships of war at sea! we have sighted fifty-three!
> Then sware Lord Thomas Howard: 'Fore God I am no coward;
> But I cannot meet them here, for my ships are out of gear,
> And the half my men are sick. I must fly, but follow quick.

LETTERPRESS. Contents of an illustrated book other than the illustrations; printed matter relating to illustrations. Printing from a raised surface, such as type, as distinguished from printing by planographic or intaglio methods.

LETTERS. Latin *littera*, letter of the alphabet, handwriting. Literary culture, literature, learning. The term is used in the following phrases: *art and letters; a man of letters; the profession of letters*.

LETTER-SPACING. In typesetting the putting of thin spaces between the letters in a word to increase the length of the word or to make the white space between the letters appear uniform.

LEVEL STRESS. *See* EVEN STRESS, DISTRIBUTED STRESS.

LEXICOGRAPHER. Greek *léxis*, a word, *légein*, to speak. Dr. Johnson, the great lexicographer, defines that word: 'a writer of dictionaries, a harmless drudge'.

LEXICOGRAPHY. Greek *léxis*, a word, *légein*, to speak. The art of compiling a dictionary.

LEXICON. Greek *lexicón*, a dictionary; *léxis*, a word, *légein*, to speak. A word-book or dictionary, especially of Greek, Hebrew, Syriac or Arabic.

> Two men wrote a lexicon, Liddell and Scott;
> Some parts were clever, but some parts were not.
> Hear, all ye learned, and read me this riddle,
> How the wrong part wrote Scott, and the right
>   part wrote Liddell.
>
> *On Henry Liddell and Robert Scott, co-authors*
> *of the Greek Lexicon,* 1843

LIBRETTO. Italian diminutive of *libro*, Latin *liber*, a book. The book or words of an opera, oratorio, or long musical work. Lorenzo da Ponte was the librettist of Mozart's *Le Nozze di Figaro, Don Giovanni*, and *Così fan tutte*. Wagner was his own librettist. Hugo von Hofmannsthal collaborated with Richard Strauss in stage works including *Elektra, Der Rosenkavalier, Ariadne auf Naxos*.

LIGATURE. Latin *ligāre*, to bind. A character of two or more letters joined together and cast in one piece, as ff, ffi, ffl, fi, fl, æ, œ.

LIGHT ENDING. *See* FEMININE ENDING.

LIGHT FACE. Ordinary type as distinguished from **bold type.** This book is set in light-face type.

LIGHT RHYME. This occurs where the final rhyming syllable of a word is unstressed. This is frequent in the old ballads.

LIGHT STRESS. A stress, in verse, on a word which is not normally stressed in speech, as in this line in Wordsworth's *Ode on Intimations of Immortality*:

> That thére hath páss'd awáy a glóry fròm the éarth.

where the word 'from' is stressed.

LIGHT VERSE. Verse written to entertain. It usually deals with 'the everyday social life of its period or the experiences of the poet as an ordinary human being'. Light verse includes parodies, limericks, epigrams, and lyrics in French fixed forms, such as the

triolet, ballade, and the rondeau. Nonsense verse is represented by
nursery rhymes, and the poems of Lewis Carroll and Edward Lear.

> How many miles to Babylon?
> Threescore miles and ten.
> Can I get there by candle-light?
> Yes, and back again.
> If your heels are nimble and light,
> You may get there by candle-light.
>
> *Songs for the Nursery*

LIGNE DONNÉE.   French, literally, given line.   Stephen Spender,
in *The Making of a Poem,* has this to say:

> Paul Valéry speaks of the *ligne donnée* of the poem.   One line
> is given to the poet by God or by nature, the rest he has to
> discover for himself.

LILLIBULLERO.   A meaningless seventeenth-century song refrain
against the Irish soldiers of James II.

LIMERICK.   In *The Universal English Dictionary*, H. C. Wyld says:

> . . . so called (not by Lear) on account of refrain 'Won't you
> come up, come up, won't you come up to Limerick?', which
> is said to have been sung or recited after each verse, but
> which is now never heard.

Nonsense verse set out in a facetious jingle.   The first instances
occur in *Anecdotes and Adventures of Fifteen Young Ladies* and the
History of Sixteen Wonderful Old Women in 1820.   The limerick
was popularized by Edward Lear in his *Book of Nonsense* and *More
Nonsense*.   He declared that the following lines from *Anecdotes and
Adventures of Fifteen Gentlemen* showed 'a form of verse lending
itself to limitless variety for Rhymes and Pictures':

> There was an old man of Tobago,
> Who lived on rice, gruel, and sago;
> Till, much to his bliss,
> His physician said this —
> To a leg, Sir, of mutton you may go.

Limericks have been composed on many different subjects, ranging
from unusual place-names to the doctrine of philosophy.   This
modern limerick deals briefly with Relativity:

> There was a young lady named Bright
> Who would travel much faster than light.
> She started one day
> In the relative way,
> And came back the previous night.

LIMITED EDITION. An edition confined to a specific number of copies. It is not to be reprinted in the same form. Copies of a limited edition are usually numbered.

LINEATION. Latin *lineāre*, to reduce to a line. The action of marking with lines or drawing lines. A division into lines of verse.

LINE BLOCK. A letterpress printing plate. It is photo-mechanically engraved, consisting of solid areas and lines, reproduced from a black-and-white drawing without any intermediate or continuous tones. In a line engraving all lines are reproduced as they appear in the drawing.

LINE DRAWING. A drawing made with a pen, pencil, brush or special crayon in such a way that it can be reproduced by the line-etching process.

LINGO. Latin *lingua*, tongue, speech, language. A term applied in a derogatory way to a foreign language; the vocabulary of a special subject or class of people.

LINGUA FRANCA. Italian, literally, Frankish tongue. A mixed Italian jargon used in the Levant. Any mixed language or stock of ideas, serving as a medium of expression between different peoples.

LINGUISTIC. Latin *lingua*, tongue. Pertaining to the study of languages. Linguistics is the science of languages.

LINKED RHYME. A device found in early Welsh verse. Such rhyme is formed by linking a final syllable in one line to the first sound of the next. Gerard Manley Hopkins makes use of it in *The Wreck of the 'Deutschland'*:

> She drove in the dark to leeward,
> She struck — not a reef or a rock
> But the combs of a smother of sand: night drew her
> Dead to the Kentish Knock . . .

Here he joins the sound of *her* in the third line to the initial letter D in *dead* in the following line to make a rhyme with *leeward*, first line.

LINOCUT. Latin *līnum*, flax, *oleum*, oil. Design cut in relief by hand on a block of linoleum and mounted on a wood base to the height of type. A print obtained from this.

LINOTYPE. A composing machine that automatically produces complete lines of words, 'line o' type', in one piece from individual matrices assembled by the operator of a keyboard. This is a substitute for type-setting; much used in printing newspapers. The lines of type so produced are termed 'slugs'.

LITANY. Greek *litaneía*, from *litaneúein*, to pray, from *litē̂*, supplication. Series of petitions recited by the clergy in church services or processions, with responses repeated by the congregation.

LITERAL. Latin *litterālis*, from *littera*, letter of the alphabet. Pertaining to a letter of the alphabet. Based on what is actually written or expressed. Giving an exact rendering word for word. Taking words in their usual or primary sense, thus apt to miss the real spirit and meaning. Hence unimaginative, matter-of-fact.

In printing, a literal is the misprint of a letter.

LITERATI. Latin *litterātus*, learned. Men of letters; the learned class.

LITERATIM. Latin, 'literally'. Letter for letter; textually.

LITERATURE. Latin *litterālis*, from *littera*, letter. Writings in verse or prose of acknowledged excellence whose value lies in their intense, personal expression of life. Much has been written about literature.

> A true classic is an author who has enriched the human mind, augmented its treasure, and made it advance a step.
> Charles Augustin Sainte-Beuve

> Literature flourishes best when it is half a trade and half an art.
> William Ralph Inge

> Writing is not literature unless it gives to the reader a pleasure which arises not only from the things said, but from the way in which they are said. Stopford A. Brooke

> The difference between literature and journalism is that journalism is unreadable, and literature is not read.
> Oscar Wilde

LITHOGRAPHY. Greek *líthos*, stone; *gráphein*, to write. The art or process of making designs on prepared stone and taking impressions or prints from this. Aloysius Senefelder (1771–1834), of Bavaria, was the inventor of lithography. Today, metal is used instead of stone.

LITOTES. Greek *lītós*, plain, meagre. An ironically moderate form of speech. Sometimes a rhetorical understatement in which a negative is substituted for the positive remark. 'A citizen of no mean city' for 'a great city'. 'I praise you not' certainly says 'I blame you'.

LITTÉRATEUR. Latin *littera*, a letter. A literary man, a writer of literary works.

LITTLE MAGAZINE. This is a literary magazine, small in format and usually un-commercial. It features experimental writing, and attracts a small numbers of readers.

LITURGICAL DRAMA. Greek *leitourgía*, public worship. It applies especially to the service of the Holy Eucharist or Mass.

In the ninth century, the celebration of the Mass was dramatized, enhanced by ritual and antiphonal singing, which soon took on a dialogue form. It was, in fact, one of the sources of modern drama.

Liturgical drama developed in different ways. The services of Christmas and Easter gave scope for the dramatization of parts of the life of Christ, and led to the Mystery Play.

A wandering scholar, Hilarius, pupil of Abelard, wrote plays of the lives of saints. This form, still within the Church, became the Miracle Play.

From local folk-plays came a further influence. Plays now showed the struggle between Good and Evil; biblical figures gave place to personified abstractions; the action was simple and didactic. These Morality Plays belong mainly to the fifteenth century. The most famous were *Ane Pleasant Satyre of the Three Estaits*, *Everyman*, and *Lusty Juventus*.

LIVING NEWSPAPER. This was a stage production which made use of the devices of the cinema. It presented problems of modern social life in a series of short, quick-moving scenes, each putting forward methods of dealing with those problems. The living newspaper was first evolved by the Federal Theatre in the United States. During the Second World War, it was used in England for a form of education in the armed forces.

Among well-known living newspapers were *Triple-A Ploughed Under* and *One Third of a Nation*.

L.M. The abbreviation for LONG MEASURE (q.v.).

LOCAL COLOUR. Writing in which the scene set in a particular locality plays an unusually important part. The use of local colour in the English novel developed in the nineteenth century. The Brontës set their novels in Yorkshire; George Eliot placed hers in Warwickshire. Other examples are the 'Barsetshire' novels of Trollope, the 'Wessex' novels of Hardy, Mary Webb's Shropshire novels, Arnold Bennett's Five Towns' series.

LOCO CITATO. Latin. In the place cited. Abbreviation: loc. cit. or l.c.

LOGAOEDIC.   Greek *logaoidikós*, discourse and song (somewhere in rhythm between prose and verse).   In Greek and Latin prosody, a metre composed of dactyls combined with trochees, or anapaests with iambs.

LOGIC.   Greek *logikẽ* (*tékhnẽ*), logic art, the art of reasoning, from *lógos*, word, reason.   The science of reasoning, and of the laws according to which pure reasoning should be conducted.   The chain of argument correct or incorrect.

> He was in logic a great critic,
> Profoundly skill'd in analytic.
> He could distinguish, and divide
> A hair 'twixt south and south-west side.
> On either which he would dispute,
> Confute, change hands, and still confute.
>   Samuel Butler, *Hudibras*

LOGICAL POSITIVISM.   This is the name given by Blumberg and Feigl (1931) to the philosophical movement emanating from the 'Vienna Circle', marked by 'logical', 'scientific' empiricism. Prominent members included Rudolf Carnap, Friedrich Waismann, Ludwig Wittgenstein, A. J. Ayer.

LOGICAL STRESS.   In poetry, the emphasis required by the metre is the *metrical stress*.   When this is reinforced by the particular emphasis demanded by the meaning this is called the *logical* or *rhetorical stress*.   It is also known as *sense stress*.   This is shown in a line from Langland's *Piers Plowman*:

> In a sómer séson when sóft was the sónne.

LOGION.   Greek *lógos*, a saying.   A saying of Jesus Christ preserved elsewhere than in the Gospels.

LOGODAEDALUS.   Greek *logodaidalía*, *lógos*, word, *daidállein*, to form, shape a thing skilfully.   One who is cunning in playing with words.   Coleridge said in his *Aids to Reflections*, 'For one instance of mere logomachy, I could bring ten instances of logodaedaly or verbal legerdemain.'

LOGOGRAPHY.   Greek *lógos*, word, and *gráphein*, to write.   A method of printing with several letters, or a word, cast together on the same body.   Examples are *Mr.*, *Stop*, *Road*.

LOGOGRIPH.   Greek *lógos*, word, *gríphos*, riddle.   A kind of anagrammatic word-puzzle.

LOGOMACHY. Greek *logomakhía*, a fight about words; *lógos*, word, *mákhē*, contest. A dispute about words, turning on verbal points. Examples appear in Swift's *Tale of a Tub*, where the author satirizes the hair-splitting practised by religious sects over the precise significance of words in the scriptures. Also in the disputes of the Big-Endians and the Little-Endians in *Gulliver's Travels*.

LOGOPOEIA. Greek, literally, the making of words. Poetry regarded as the handling of words with full consideration of all their qualities: meaning, sound, associations, allusions.

In *A.B.C. of Reading*, Ezra Pound said:

> Language is a means of communication. To charge language with meaning to the utmost possible degree, we have the three chief means:
>
> (i)   throwing the object (fixed or moving) on to the visual imagination (phanopoeia).
>
> (ii) inducing emotional correlations by the sound and rhythm of the speech (melopoeia).
>
> (iii) inducing both of the effects by stimulating the associations (intellectual or emotional) that have remained in the receiver's consciousness in relation to the actual words or word groups employed (logopoeia).

LOGORRHOEA. Greek *lógos*, a word, and *rhoía*, a flow, flowing. An excessive flow of words; verbosity, prolixity.

LOGOS: POIEMA. In *An Experiment in Criticism*, C. S. Lewis says:

> A work of literary art can be considered in two lights. It both *means* and *is*. It is both *Logos* (something said) and *Poiema* (something made). As Logos it tells a story, or expresses an emotion, or exhorts or pleads or describes or rebukes or excites laughter. As Poiema, by its aural beauties and also by the balance and contrast and the unified multiplicity of its successive parts, it is an *objet d'art*, a thing shaped so as to give great satisfaction. From this point of view, and perhaps from this only, the old parallel between painting and poetry is helpful.

LOGOTYPE. Greek *lógos*, word, from *légō*, speak, and *túpos*, blow, impress, from *túptō*, strike. A type cast in one piece containing a word or two or more letters occurring frequently in combination such as *th*, *sh*. It is distinguished from ligature, which is a single character.

LOG-ROLLING. The practice whereby authors give favourable reviews to, or otherwise recommend, each other's books, on the understanding that the favour will be reciprocated. The metaphor is presumably from lumbering. Synonymous with *back-scratching*.

LONG MEASURE. A hymnal stanza, rhyming *a b a b* or *a b c b*, in which all four lines are iambic tetrameter. Abbreviated to L.M.

LONGUER. French, literally, length, slowness. A lengthy, wearisome passage of writing.

LOOSE SENTENCE. A sentence in which the main clause comes first, followed by subordinate units. A sentence which is grammatically complete at one or more points before its end.

LOW COMEDY. In a play, dialogue and incidents designed to make the audience laugh. Often, low comedy consists of farce, slapstick, and stupidities. From the time of medieval drama, the character of Vice by practical jokes developed into the clown. The clown, a figure in Elizabethan tragedies, gave relief from the main theme.

LOWER CRITICISM. *See* HIGHER CRITICISM.

LUCIDITY. Latin *lūcidus*, from *lūx*, *luc-*, light. Expressing meaning with clearness, and without ambiguity.

LXX. *See* SEPTUAGINT.

LYRIC. Greek *lurikós*, singing to the lyre; a lyric poet. Originally a song intended to be sung and accompanied on the lyre. The meaning has been enlarged to include any short poem directly expressing the poet's own thoughts and emotions. Examples are the love songs of Burns, and Shelley's shorter poems. The ballad, ode, elegy, and sonnet are special forms of the lyric

M

MACARONIC VERSE. Italian *maccaroni*, earlier form of *maccheroni*, etymology unknown. A burlesque verse containing Latin or other foreign words, and vernacular words with Latin terminations. Also applied to any form of verse in which two or more languages are jumbled together; at first written mainly for humorous effect, later to display learning. An Italian, Teophilo Folengo (1496–1544), was the chief writer of macaronic verse. This macaronic verse is from *Polka* by G. A. à Beckett:

> Qui nunc dancere vult modo,
> Wants to dance in the fashion, oh!
> Discere debet ought to know
> Kickere floor cum heel and toe.
> One, two, three,
> Come hop with me,
> Whirligig, twirligig, rapidee.

MACHINERY. In the preface to *The Rape of the Lock*, Pope says, 'Machinery is a term invented by the critics to signify that part which the deities, angels or demons are made to act in a poem.' As it is derived from the mechanical means used by the Greeks introducing a deity on the stage, it belongs properly to tragedy. However, it is applied chiefly to the epic because Homer had many deities in the action of the *Iliad*. So supernatural figures were called 'machines'. In his *Essay on Satire*, the Earl of Mulgrave says, 'Milton's heavenly machines are many, and his human persons are but two.' George Loane, in his *Handbook of Literary Terms*, comments on Pope's sylphs in *The Rape of the Lock* as a 'happy travesty of the epic machinery'.

Eliphaz the Temanite tells Job of a machine in a vision, 'Fear came upon me, and trembling, which made all my bones to shake. Then a spirit passed before my face; the hair of my flesh stood up. It stood still, but I could not discern the form thereof. An image was before mine eyes, there was silence, and I heard a voice saying, Shall mortal man be more just than God?'

MACROCOSM. Medieval Latin *macrócosmus*, from Greek *makrós*, great, *kósmos*, world. The 'great world' or universe as distinguished from the 'little world' or microcosm.

MACRON. Greek *makrón*, long. The name of the straight line — , or symbol, placed, in quantitative verse, over a vowel to show that it is 'long'. The time taken by a long syllable in such verse is two *morae*.

MADRIGAL.   Greek *mándra*, fold; thus originally a 'pastoral song'. A form of unaccompanied part-song designed for several voices. The madrigal may be a pastoral, satirical, or love song.   Found in Italy from the late thirteenth century, it flourished in England at the end of the sixteenth century.   Thomas Morley, who edited *The Triumphs of Oriana*, madrigals in praise of Queen Elizabeth, Thomas Weelkes and John Wilbye were some of the renowned English madrigal composers.   The *madrigal proper* shows the full resources of contrapuntal choral composition.

> Faustina hath the fairer face,
> And Phillida the feater grace;
> Both have mine eye enriched.
> This sings full sweetly with her voice,
> Her fingers make as sweet a noise;
> Both have mine ear bewitched.
> Ay me! sith Fates have so provided,
> My heart, alas! must be divided.
>
> Anonymous, from *Airs and Madrigals*, 1598

MAGAZINE.   Arabic *makhāzin*, plural of *makhzan*, storehouse.   A periodical publication containing articles on various subjects by different writers.

MAGICAL EFFECT.   In *The Anatomy of Poetry*, Marjorie Boulton says:

> Magic makes great use of repetitions; we are all familiar with stories in which something has to be done or said three or seven times; religious rituals, which are more or less akin to primitive magic, depending on the degree of intellectual development, make great use of repetition with prayers for the various occasions of life, prayer-wheels, rosaries, and repeated observances; and repetition plays a great part in the more primitive, emotional parts of our lives.

> Thrice tosse these Oaken ashes in the ayre,
> Thrice sit thou mute in this inchanted chayre;
> And thrice three times tye vp this true loues knot,
> And murmur soft, shee will, or shee will not.
>
> Thomas Campion, *The Third Booke of Ayres*

MAGNUM OPUS: (pl.) *MAGNA OPERA*.   Latin, a great work. An author's most important book.

MAJUSCULE. Latin *mājuscula,* somewhat greater; *mājor,* greater, larger. In printing, a large letter, whether capital or uncial.

MALAPROPISM. The ridiculous misuse of words in speech or writing caused by the replacing of one word for another, similar in sound but different in meaning. This kind of mistake is made frequently by Dogberry in *Much Ado About Nothing*; He says, 'Comparisons are odorous', and later, to the busy Leonato, 'It shall be suffigance.' But it is from Mrs. Malaprop in Sheridan's *The Rivals,* produced in 1775, that the term derives. Here she is misapplying long words:

> If I reprehend any thing in this world, it is the use of my oracular tongue, and a nice derangement of epitaphs!

MALEDICTION. Latin *maledictiōnem,* from *maledīcĕre,* to curse. The utterance of a curse; reviling; slander.

MANICHAEISM. From Late Greek *Manikhaîos,* from the name of the founder of the sect. A religious system founded by Mani (or Manichaeus), a Persian of Ecbatana, who lived in the third century after Christ. It is a dualistic theology representing Satan as coeternal with God, and the principal elements as darkness and light, body and soul. It is essentially ascetic, and was widely accepted, up to the fifth century, from China to southern France.

> And (wonder beyond wonder) here was harbour'd safe,
> flourishing and multiplying, that sect of all sects
> abominable, persecuted and defamed,
> who with their Eastern chaffering and insidious talk
> had ferreted thru' Europe to find peace on earth
> with Raymond of Toulouse,— those ancient Manichees.
>
> Robert Bridges, *The Testament of Beauty*

MANNERISM. The use of a distinctive manner in literature or art. Examples are Lamb's Elizabethan style, Macaulay's use of antithesis, Carlyle's eruptive, angular expression.

MANUSCRIPT. Medieval Latin *manūscriptus; manū,* by hand, *scriptus, scrībĕre,* write. A book or document written by hand, not printed. The author's copy for the printer. Abbreviation: MS. (singular); MSS. (plural). The term *typescript* is correctly applied to a typewritten MS.

MÄRCHEN. German, literally, folk tale, fairy story.

MARGINALIA. From Latin *marginālis,* marginal. Marginal notes, references or decorations. Sometimes marginalia can be valuable, as the notes and comments made by Coleridge.

MARINISM. A style of writing named after Giovanni Battista Marino (1569–1625), a Neapolitan poet. His long poem, *Adone*, reveals far-fetched conceits, flamboyance, and bad taste. This *seicento* school of poetry had some influence upon Herbert and Crashaw.

MARIVAUDAGE. Writing marked by an elaborate and subtle analysis of sentiment in the style of the eighteenth-century French author Pierre de Marivaux. His famous romance *La Vie de Marianne* shows his affected, 'precious' style, and with his best comedy *Le Jeu de l'amour et du hasard* fixes the term *Marivaudage*.

MARTIN MARPRELATE. This is the name assumed by the author of a number of anonymous pamphlets (seven are extant) issued in 1588–1589 from a secret press, containing attacks in a railing rollicking style on the bishops and defending the Presbyterian system of discipline. They were occasioned by the decree issued in 1586 by Archbishop Whitgift and the Star Chamber, with the object of checking the flow of Puritan pamphlets, requiring the previous approval of the ecclesiastical authorities to every publication.

Paul Harvey continues, in *The Oxford Companion to English Literature*, to say, 'The importance of the Marprelate tracts lies in the fact that they are the best prose satires of the Elizabethan age. ... They called forth replies from such noted writers as Lyly and Nash, and Gabriel and Richard Harvey were presently involved in the controversy. But the replies show less literary ability than the original tracts.

The suspected authors of these, a Welshman named Penry and a clergyman named Udall, were arrested. The latter died in prison, the former was executed. Their collaborator, Job Throckmorton, probably the real author, denied his complicity at the trial of Penry, and escaped punishment.'

MASCULINE ENDING. This occurs when a line of verse concludes on a stressed syllable, as in these lines by Ben Jonson on *Fancy*:

And Fancy, I tell you, has dreams that have wings,
And dreams that have honey, and dreams that have stings.

MASCULINE RHYME. This is a rhyme limited to a single stressed syllable, as here used by Edward Lear:

There was an old man in a Marsh,
Whose manners were futile and harsh.

MASKED COMEDY. *See* COMMEDIA DELL' ARTE.

MASQUE. French *masque*, Spanish *máscara*, Italian *maschera*, of doubtful origin. An elaborate, semi-dramatic, courtly form of entertainment introduced from Italy to England during the first half of the sixteenth century. The earliest masques consisted only of music, dancing, mime and spectacle, and did not present any consecutive story. The masque flourished in the reign of James I, when poets like Ben Jonson, Samuel Daniel, and William Browne wrote the songs and dialogue, Henry Lawes composed the music, and the elaborate stage machinery was designed by the great theatrical architect, Inigo Jones. Masques were generally of allegorical or abstract significance, with only slight dramatic interest. They were highly picturesque and inventive. Ben Jonson's *Masque of Christmas* has such figures as Minced-Pie and Baby-Cake.

There is a masque in *The Tempest*, and another in *Henry VIII*. Milton's *Comus* is not really characteristic, its success depending upon the poetry. This form of entertainment came to an end during the Civil War (1642–1648). *See also* ANTI-MASQUE.

MATIN: MATINS. Latin *mātūtīnus*, belonging to the morning. One of the seven canonical hours of the Roman Catholic Church, properly a midnight office, sometimes recited at daybreak. The public morning prayer in the Church of England. A morning song of birds.

MATRIX. Latin from *māter*, mother. A brass or phosphor-bronz mould in which type is cast or shaped. A papier-mâché mould taken from a type-forme and used in the preparation of stereos and electros.

MAUNDY. Latin *mandātum*, command. Originally the word was applied to the washing of the feet of the poor by men of noble birth on the day before Good Friday. At the service, the antiphon was taken from the discourse which followed the washing of the Apostles' feet by Our Lord:

> If I then, *your* Lord and Master, have washed your feet; ye also ought to wash one another's feet. For I have given you an example, that ye should do as I have done to you. Verily, verily, I say unto you, The servant is not greater than his lord; neither he that is sent greater than he that sent him. If ye know these things, happy are ye if ye do them . . .
> A new commandment I give unto you, That ye love one another; as I have loved you, that ye also love one another.
> *The Gospel of St. John*

MAXIM. Latin *maxima*, greatest. A general truth which is drawn from experience. It is also a rule of conduct; a precept.

> Success is getting what you want;
> happiness is wanting what you get.

> If you dwell with a lame man, you
> will learn to limp.
>
> Plutarch, *Moralia: De Liberis Educandis*

MAXIMUM SCENE TECHNIQUE. The novelist Dorothy Richardson was an early exponent of the stream of consciousness method in her works under the title *Pilgrimage*. Phyllis Bentley called this method the Maximum Scene Technique.

MAZARINADE. A song against Cardinal Mazarin, ruler of France during the minority of Louis XIV.

MEANING. Two types of meaning, emotive and cognitive (or referential) are usually distinguished. The emotive meaning of the word *philosopher* induces respect and admiration; its cognitive meaning is a process of thought that leads to a man who seeks and expresses truth.

MEANING, FOUR KINDS OF. In *Practical Criticism*, I. A. Richards, discussing the meaning of a communication, says:

> It is plain that most human utterances and nearly all articulate speech can be profitably regarded from four points of view. Four aspects can be easily distinguished. Let us call them *Sense*, *Feeling*, *Tone*, and *Intention*.
>
> (1) *Sense*. We speak *to say something*, and when we listen we expect something to be said.
>
> (2) *Feeling*. But we also, as a rule, have some feelings *about these items*, about the state of affairs we are referring to. We have an attitude towards it, some special direction, bias, or accentuation of interest towards it, some personal flavour or colouring of feeling; and we use language to *express* these feelings, this nuance of interest.
>
> (3) *Tone*. Furthermore, the speaker has ordinarily *an attitude to his listener*. He chooses or arranges his words differently as his audience varies, in automatic or deliberate *recognition of his relation to them*. The tone of his utterance reflects his awareness of this relation, his sense of how he stands towards those he is addressing.
>
> (4) *Intention*. Finally, apart from what he says (Sense), his attitude to what he is talking about (Feeling), and his attitude to his listener (Tone), there is the speaker's

intention, his aim, *conscious or unconscious*, the effect he is endeavouring to promote. Ordinarily he speaks for a purpose, and his purpose modifies his speech. The understanding of it is part of the whole business of apprehending his meaning. Unless we know what he is trying to do, we can hardly estimate the measure of his success.

MEANING, FOUR LEVELS OF. Dante explained to Can Grande della Scala how *The Divine Comedy* should be read. The reader should be aware of four levels of meaning: '(i) the literal or historical (actually occurs); (ii) the moral meaning; (iii) the allegorical; (iv) the anagogical (the meaning stating an eternal truth).'

MEDIEVAL DRAMA. In the ninth century, separate little scenes were added to the processional chants during church services. These were performed in Latin by the priests 'for the strengthening of faith in the unlearned vulgar and in neophytes'.

MEIOSIS. Greek *meiōsis*, lessening. The use of understatement to give the impression that a thing is less in size and importance than it really is. Often applied in the negative form illustrated under *litotes* (q.v.). It is commonly used in colloquial English. 'That was *some* opera.' 'The royal procession was *rather* good.'

MELIC POETRY. Greek *mélos*, song. Poetry, especially Greek strophic odes, intended to be sung. This poetry, which flourished between the seventh and the fifth centuries B.C., was to be found in the work of Sappho and Pindar.

MELODRAMA. French *mélodrame*, from Greek *mélos*, song. This was originally a stage play with songs and music interspersed. Now it denotes sensational, gruesome plays with touches of bathos, and sometimes a happy ending. Famous examples are: *Maria Marten; or, the Murder in the Red Barn* and *Mazeppa; or, the Wild Horse of Tartary.*

MELOPOEIA. Greek *melopoiós*, maker of songs. The art of composing melodies. That part of dramatic art concerned with music.

MEMOIR. French, from Latin *memoria*, memory. A biographical sketch. A record of events drawn from personal knowledge. A record of researches on any subject.

MEMORABILIA.   Latin *memorābilis*, worthy to be mentioned, memorable. Things noteworthy and memorable.

MENOLOGY.   Greek *mēnológion*, account of the month. A calendar, especially of the Greek church, with biographies of the saints and martyrs.

MESOSTICH.   Greek *mésos*, middle, *stíkhos*, row, line of poetry. A composition, usually in verse, when the middle letters in successive lines form a word when put together.

MESSAGE.   *See* MORAL.

MESSENGER.   Latin *mittĕre*, to send.   In Greek tragedy, action taking place off-stage is reported by a Messenger or Herald.   In the *Persians* of Aeschylus, the Messenger's long speech describes the defeat of Xerxes and the retreat of his army.   In Euripides' *Medea*, the Messenger arrives to announce that the princess is dead, and her death is described at length in vivid detail.   Action which was not depicted on the stage was most realistically described.

The best-known example in English literature is in *Samson Agonistes* (which is, of course, modelled on a Greek tragedy). Samson's death is reported by a messenger:

> *Messenger:* Ah *Manoa* I refrain, too suddenly
> To utter what will come at last too soon;
> Lest evil tidings with too rude irruption
> Hitting thy aged ear should pierce too deep.
> *Manoa:* Suspense in news is torture, speak them out.
> *Messenger:* Then take the worst in brief, *Samson* is dead.

METAPHOR.   Greek *metaphorá*, transference; *metá*, over, *phérein*, to carry.   The application of a name or a descriptive term to an object to which it is not literally applicable. An implied comparison. It is based on the idea of the similarity in dissimilars. 'Metaphor is a great excellence in style', said Johnson, 'when used with propriety, for it gives you two ideas for one; conveys the meaning more luminously, and generally with a perception of delight.'

Santayana said, in *Life of Reason*:

> There's no poetry in identifying things that look alike.   But the most opposite things may become miraculously equivalent if they arouse the same visible quality of emotion.   Even the sound and rhythm of words, in a sensitive language, have some congruity with the nature of the things signified.

A metaphor is a shift, a carrying over of a word from its normal use to a new one.   In a sense metaphor, the shift of the .word, is occasioned and justified by a similarity or analogy between the object it is usually applied to and the new object. In an emotive metaphor the shift occurs through some similarity between the feelings the new situation and the normal situation arouse. The same word may, in different contexts, be either a sense or an emotive metaphor. If you call a man a swine, for example, it may be because his features resemble those of a pig, but it may be because you have towards him something of the feeling you conventionally have towards pigs, or because you propose, if possible, to excite those feelings. Both metaphorical shifts may be combined simultaneously, and they often are.

I. A. Richards, *Practical Criticism*

Here are examples of the metaphor:
Boys and girls tumbling in the street, and playing, were *moving jewels.*

Thomas Traherne, *Centuries of Meditation*

The Indian Summer of the heart.
John Greenleaf Whittier, *Memories*

A child said What is grass? fetching it to
one with full hands; . . .
And now it seems to me the beautiful uncut
hair of graves.

Walt Whitman, *Song of Myself*

See also MIXED METAPHOR *and* DEAD METAPHOR.

METAPHYSICAL CONCEIT. *See* CONCEIT.

METAPHYSICAL POETRY. Ernest Weekley says, in *Etymological Dictionary of Modern English*:

The term metaphysics was applied to thirteen books of Aristotle which follow the books dealing with physics. These were called *tà metà tà phusiká*, the (works) after the physics, which came to be wrongly interpreted as the works beyond, or transcending physics.

Metaphysics is that branch of philosophy concerned with the ultimate nature of existence. Dryden criticized Donne's poetry, saying, 'he affects the Metaphysics not only in his Satires, but in his amorous verses, where Nature only should reign'. This led to the term Metaphysical being applied not only to Donne but also to Cowley, Crashaw, Marvell. Dr. Johnson reaffirmed the title in his *Lives*, 'About the beginning of the seventeenth century appeared a race of writers that may be termed the metaphysical poets.'

Metaphysical poetry is characterized by passionate thought, the succession of concentrated images, the exercise of elaborate ingenuity, and 'wit'.

METATHESIS. Greek *metáthesis*, transposition; *metá*, in exchange, *tithénai*, to place.

In *Modern English Usage*, H. W. Fowler says:

The interchange of position between sounds or letters in a word, as the *s* and *p* in *clasp* (earlier *clapse*), the *r* and *i* in *third* (earlier *thridde*), the *u* and *r* in *curly* (earlier *crulle*).

With lokkes crulle as they were leyd in presse.
Chaucer, *The Prologue*

METONOMY. Greek *metōnumía*, expressing change, name-change. The substitution of the name of an attribute of a thing for the name of the thing itself, as *crown* for *king*, *city* for *inhabitants*, *Shakespeare* for *Shakespeare's plays*.

METRE. Greek *métron*, measure. Formerly called measure, it is any form of poetic rhythm, determined by the type and number of feet in a line or in a passage of verse. Analysis of the metre is called *scansion*.

METRICAL ACCENT. *See* ACCENT.

METRICAL FOOT. *See* FOOT.

METRICAL ROMANCE. A story of adventure told in verse. Thomas Warton refers to 'the old metrical romances' in his *History of English Poetry* (1774–1781). Effective metrical romances are *The Knight's Tale* in the *Canterbury Tales*; Scott's *Marmion, The Lord of the Isles*; *The Giaour* and *The Corsair* by Byron.

MICROCOSM. Greek *mīkrós*, little, *kósmos*, world. The 'little world' of human nature; man viewed by ancient philosophers as an epitome of the 'great world', the macrocosm. On this subject, Henry Hallam says, 'The doctrine of a constant analogy between universal nature, or the macrocosm, and that of man, or the microcosm.' (*Oxford English Dictionary*)

MIDDLE COMEDY. The Old or Aristophanic Comedy in Greece was followed about 400 B.C. by Middle Comedy. Political satire now gives place to parody, myths are ridiculed, and literature and philosophy criticized. Antiphanes and Alexis were the chief poets of the Middle Comedy.

MIDDLE ENGLISH. This followed Old English during the period from 1100 to 1500. The transition was gradual, but changes can be seen in the entry for 1137, dealing with Stephen's reign, in the *Anglo-Saxon Chronicle*.

MIDDLE RHYME. This is rhyme occurring in the middle as well as at the end of the same metrical line.

MILES GLORIOSUS. 'The Braggart Soldier', a comedy by the Roman dramatist Plautus (*c.* 254–184 B.C.). The braggart captain, *miles gloriosus*, was a stock character in Roman comedy. He is the prototype of Ralph Roister Doister in Nicholas Udall's play, of Bobadill in Ben Jonson's *Everyman in his Humour*, and of other braggarts of the Elizabethan stage.

MILTONIC SONNET. A form, introduced by Milton, which observes the definite octave rhyme scheme of the Petrarchan sonnet *a b b a, a b b a*. Milton did not retain the pause after the octave and varied the rhyme scheme of the sestet. Here is his sonnet *On the late Massacre in Piedmont*:

> Avenge, O Lord, thy slaughtered saints, whose bones
> Lie scattered on the Alpine mountains cold;
> Ev'n them who kept thy truth so pure of old,
> When all our fathers worshipped stocks and stones,
> Forget not: in thy book record their groans,
> Who were thy sheep, and in their ancient fold
> Slain by the bloody Piedmontese, that rolled
> Mother with infant down the rocks. Their moans
> The vales redoubled to the hills, and they
> To Heav'n. Their martyred blood and ashes sow
> O'er all th' Italian fields, where still doth sway
> The triple Tyrant; that from these may grow
> A hundredfold, who, having learnt thy way,
> Early may fly the Babylonian woe.

MIME. Greek *mîmos*, a mimic. A kind of simple farcical drama among the Greeks and Romans. It originated in Sicily and southern Italy about the fifth century B.C. The actors wore grotesque masks, burlesqued gods and legendary heroes, and sometimes, by mimicry, presented events of ordinary life. Coarse dialogue was included in performances of this kind, which survived into the Middle Ages.

MIMESIS. Greek *mîmos*, an imitator. In the *Poetics*, Aristotle states that tragedy is, by skilful selection and presentation, an imitation of the action of life.

Shakespeare shows *mimesis*, 'the purpose of playing', in Hamlet's speech to the players:

> Anything so done is from the purpose of playing, whose end, both at the first and now, was and is, to hold, as 'twere, the mirror up to nature; to show virtue her own feature, scorn her own image, and the very age and body of the time his form and pressure. . . .
> I have thought some of nature's journeymen had made men, and not made them well, they imitated humanity so abominably.

MINIATURE. Italian *miniatúra*, miniature; from Latin *miniāre*, to paint in red lead or vermilion; Latin *minium*, native cinnabar, red lead. A coloured initial letter or small coloured picture in an illuminated manuscript. A small highly finished portrait, usually painted on ivory or vellum. A reduced image; something on a small scale.

MINNESINGER. German *Minne*, love. German lyrical poets in the Middle Ages who sang chiefly of love. They bear close resemblance to the French *troubadours*. One of the most celebrated of the minnesingers was Walther von der Vogelweide.

MINSTREL. Latin *ministeriālis*; *minister*, attendant. A professional musical entertainer of the Middle Ages, either attached to some great household, or wandering from place to place. He sang, played the harp, recited poetry, acted the buffoon. Known also as a *gleeman*, *jongleur*. Later, the term was applied to the itinerant singer or musician, to a troupe with blackened faces presenting negro songs.

MINUSCULE. Latin *minusculus*, rather small, diminutive of *minor*, smaller. Of a kind of cursive script developed in the seventh century; small or lower-case letter.

MIRACLE PLAY. *See* LITURGICAL DRAMA.

MISCELLANY. Latin *miscellāneus*; *miscēre*, to mix. A medley. A collection of writings in one volume.

In 1557, Richard Tottel published his 'Songes and Sonettes written by the ryght honorable Lorde Henry Howard late Earle of Surrey, and other'. This, known as *Tottel's Miscellany*, was followed by *The Paradise of Dainty Devices* (1576), Clement Robinson's *Handefull of Pleasant Delites*, and *The Gorgeous Gallery of Gallant Inventions* in 1578.

MISE EN SCÈNE. French, scenery and properties of an acted play;
stage setting; hence, the surroundings of an event.

MIXED METAPHOR. This arises from insensitiveness to the
literal meaning of words and phrases. The two elements in a mixed
metaphor are disparate, as in these examples:

> She is a budding star who already sings with a master hand.

> The tooth of time, which already has dried so many tears, will
> also let the grass grow over these wounds.

> I smell a rat in the air: I shall nip it in the bud.

MNEMONIC IRRELEVANCES. Greek *mnēmonikós*, from *mnēmōn*,
mindful, *mnâsthai*, to remember. Latin *in*, not, *relevāre*, to raise
up, to relieve. These are, as I. A. Richards says in *Practical
Criticism*:

> . . . misleading effects of the reader's being reminded of some
> personal scene or adventure, erratic associations, the inter-
> ference of emotional reverberations from a past which may
> have nothing to do with the poem. Relevance is not an easy
> notion to define or to apply, though some instances of
> irrelevant intrusions are among the simplest of all accidents
> to diagnose.

MOCK EPIC. Old French *mocquer*, to deride. A literary work
which burlesques the epic style or manner. A fine example in
Pope's *The Rape of the Lock* is the description of the game of
cards, which begins:

> Behold, four Kings in majesty rever'd,
> With hoary whiskers and a forky beard;
> And four fair Queens whose hands sustain a flow'r,
> Th' expressive emblem of their softer pow'r;
> Four Knaves in garbs succinct, a trusty band,
> Caps on their heads, and halberts in their hand;
> And particolour'd troops, a shining train,
> Draw forth to combat on the velvet plain.
> The skilful Nymph reviews her force with care:
> Let Spades be trumps! she said, and trumps they were.

The form is not merely burlesque. Pope's *Dunciad*, a mock epic,
is a serious satirical poem.

MOCK HEROIC. Old French *mocquer*, to deride, to jeer. The style
of a poem imitating in a burlesque manner the heroic style. Pope's

The Rape of the Lock is the finest example in English. Here are the opening lines:

> What dire offence from am'rous causes springs,
> What mighty contests rise from trivial things,
> I sing — This verse to CARYL, Muse! is due:
> This, ev'n Belinda may vouchsafe to view:
> Slight is the subject, but not so the praise,
> If She inspire, and He approve my lays.

MODULATION. Latin *modulātiōn-(em)*, rhythmical measure. In music, the change of key in the course of a passage. The inflexion or varying of the voice in speech. In poetry, the variation of the metrical pattern. In lyrical poetry, ordering of the rhythm adds emotive power, conveying the poet's experience.

MOLOSSUS. Greek *Molossós*, of or pertaining to Molossia, a a country in Epirus. A metrical foot of three long syllables.

MONAD. Greek *monád-(os)*, *monás*, unit, from *mónos*, alone, single. A primary individual organism. In the philosophy of Leibniz, it is one of the elements, or simple unities into which every compound can be resolved. He called God 'the supreme monad and perfect exemplar of the human soul', and embodied his system in *Monadologie* (1714).

MONODRAMA. A poem in the form of a dramatic monologue revealing a situation, a setting, and the characters of others besides the narrator. Browning called it a *dramatic lyric*, and used the form most successfully in *My Last Duchess* and *Mr. Sludge, The 'Medium'*.

MONODY. Greek *monōidós*, singing alone; *aeídō*, sing. An ode sung by a single actor in Greek tragedy. A poem mourning someone's death. In 1645, Milton added this brief introduction to his elegy *Lycidas*:

> In this Monody the Author bewails a learned Friend, unfortunately drown'd in his Passage from *Chester* on the *Irish* Seas, 1637. And by occasion foretels the ruine of our corrupted Clergy then in their height.

MONOGRAPH. Greek *mónos*, single, *gráphein*, to write. A separate treatise on one particular subject.

MONOLOGUE. Greek *monólogos*, speaking alone. A form of dramatic composition for one performer only. In a play, a long speech by a single actor in the presence of others. Cf. *soliloquy* (q.v.), in which the presence of others is not necessary, and where the speaker's words are not usually intended for others' hearing.

MONOMETER. Greek *mónos*, alone, single. A line of verse composed of one foot, iambic or trochaic. It is also called *monopody*. Herrick's *Upon his departure hence* is an example:

> I'm made
> A shade,
> And laid
> I'th grave,
> There have
> My Cave . . .

MONOPODY. *See* MONOMETER.

MONOPOLYLOGUE. Entertainment in which a sole performer plays many parts.

MONOSTICH. Greek, *monóstikhos*, one metrical line. A poem consisting of but one metrical line.

MONOSYLLABLES. Words of one syllable are characteristic of the English language. Henry Bradley, the philologist, remarks, in *The Making of English*, that in very few other languages can whole pages be written in monosyllables. He contrasts the phrase 'of two good men' with its Latin equivalent *duorum bonorum virorum*. However, such words lack the polysyllabic splendour of Greek and Latin. In *Britannia*, William Camden said they were fit only for expressing the first conceits of the mind. Lord Shaftesbury never wrote more than nine consecutive monosyllabic words, and Dryden calls them 'the dead weight of our mother tongue'. Pope, in *An Essay on Criticism*, condemns writers who let 'ten low words oft creep in one dull line' — the expression of his condemnation being an example.

But monosyllables can be skilfully used, as in Ben Jonson's praise of Shakespeare:

> He was not of an age, but for all time

and in Michael Drayton's sonnet:

> Since there's no help come let us kiss and part,
> Nay, I have done: you get no more of me,
> And I am glad, yea glad with all my heart,
> That thus so cleanly, I myself can free,
> Shake hands for ever, cancel all your vows,
> And when we meet at any time again,
> Be it not seen in either of our brows,
> That we one jot of former love retain;

> Now at the last gasp of Love's latest breath,
> When his pulse failing, Passion speechless lies,
> When faith is kneeling by his bed of death,
> And Innocence is closing up his eyes,
> Now if thou wouldst, when all have given him over,
> From death to life, thou might'st him yet recover.

MONTAGE. French *monter*, to mount. The process of making a consecutive whole of the separate shots taken when filming by selecting, cutting, and piecing together.

MOOD. Old English *mōd*, mind, heart; courage, pride. In a literary work the disposition of mind or feeling; the general tone. In *To his Coy Mistress*, Andrew Marvell's changes of mood show the alliance of levity and seriousness.

MORA. Latin *mora*, delay. A unit of metrical time equal to a short syllable in quantitative verse. It is represented by a symbol (◡) which is called a *breve* placed over a letter.

MORAL. Latin *mōrālis*, coined by Cicero from *mōr-*, stem of *mōs*, manner, custom, in order to represent Greek *ēthikós*, ethic. The moral teaching which may be derived from a literary work by implication or direct statement. Sometimes (as in many of Aesop's Fables) it is just worldly wisdom.

> His fall was destined to a barren strand,
> A petty fortress, and a dubious hand;
> He left the name, at which the world grew pale,
> To point a moral, or adorn a tale.
> <div align="right">Samuel Johnson, <i>Vanity of Human Wishes</i></div>

> 'Tut, tut, child!' said the Duchess.
> 'Everything's got a moral, if you can only find it.'
> <div align="right">Lewis Carroll, <i>Alice's Adventures in Wonderland</i></div>

MORALITY PLAY. *See* LITURGICAL DRAMA.

MOTIF. Low Latin *mōtīvus*, Latin *movēre*, *mōtum*, to move. A particular idea or dominant element running through a work of art, forming part of the main theme. Examples are the one-legged sailor in Joyce's *Ulysses*, the striking clocks in Virginia Woolf's *Mrs. Dalloway*.

MOTION. The name given to puppet-shows in the sixteenth and seventeenth centuries. In *The Winter's Tale*, Autolycus says:

> I know this man well: he hath been since an ape-bearer; then a process-server, a bailiff; then he compassed a motion of

the Prodigal Son, and married a tinker's wife within a mile
where my land and living lies.

Speed, in *Two Gentlemen of Verona*, exclaims:

> O excellent motion! O exceeding puppet! Now will he
> interpret to her.

MOTIVATE. Latin *movēre*, to move. To supply a motive which
determines the actions of a character in fiction. It is usually a
combination of circumstance and temperament, and should
realistically account for these actions.

MOT JUSTE: MOT PROPRE. French *mot*, word, saying. The
precise expression to convey the meaning intended. The phrase is
usually associated with Flaubert, who strove always to find the right
word. Max Beerbohm called the search for this exact word 'the
Holy Grail of the Nineties'.

MOVEMENT. Late Latin *movimentum*, from *movēre*, to move, set
in motion. A trend towards new development. 'Movement' may
describe a far-reaching change as the Romantic Revival, or denote
the work of a few artists, as Analytical Cubism.

MOVEMENT, THE. In *The Modern Writer and his World*, G. S.
Fraser says:

> Then, in 1953, with the death of Dylan Thomas, a powerful
> but evil influence, clarity and good sense, it is suggested,
> returned to English poetry with the group of poets who are
> usually lumped together as 'the Movement' . . . Robert
> Conquest's anthology, *New Lines*, in 1956 brought together
> 'the Movement' (the label was not his, but the invention
> earlier of some journalist* on the *Spectator*).

The poets who appeared in the anthology were Robert Conquest,
Elizabeth Jennings, Kingsley Amis, John Holloway, Thom Gunn,
Philip Larkin, John Wain, Donald Davie.

MUMBO-JUMBO. A West African bugbear or bugaboo used by
husbands to terrify their wives. It is described as Mandingo by
Mungo Park (1771–1806). The term is used in English to signify
an object of senseless veneration.

> Mumbo-Jumbo is dead in the jungle.
>
> N. Vachel Lindsay, *The Congo*

MUMMERY. Old French *momer*, from *momon*, mask. The light
touches, during religious celebration in the Middle Ages, often

* J. D. Scott, 'In the Movement', *Spectator*, 1st October 1954.

appeared as mumming. This meant wearing masks and odd
costumes when dancing in dumb show. The term was used later
for theatrical performances, in which dancers wore masks and
performed in 'antic style'. Mummery may refer to acting itself.

'MUSCULATURE'. A term from music, which has been applied
by critics to a quality found in some Canadian poets. It is found
everywhere in E. J. Pratt and in Earle Birney.

> From stone to bronze, from bronze to steel
> Along the road-dust of the sun,
> Two revolutions of the wheel
> From Java to Geneva run.
>
> E. J. Pratt, *From Stone to Steel*

> He invented a rainbow but lightning struck it
> shattered it into the lake-lap of a mountain
> so big his mind slowed when he looked at it
> Yet he built a shack on the shore
> learned to roast porcupine belly and
> wore the quills on his hatband.
>
> Earle Birney, *Bushed*

MUSES. Greek *Moûsa*, from root *men-*, *mon-*, think, remember. In
Greek mythology the daughters of Zeus and Mnemosyne were nine
Muses. They were conceived as minor goddesses, inspirers of
poetry, music, drama. The following lines are based on an epigram
written by George Wither:

> The acts of ages past doth Clio write,
> The tragedy's Melpomene's delight,
> Thalía is with comedies contented,
> Euterpe first the lyric song invented,
> Terpsichore doth lead the choric dance,
> Sweet Erato sings lovers' dalliance,
> Calliope on epic verses dwells,
> The secrets of the stars Urania tells,
> Polyhymnia decks with words sublime the hymn,
> And great Apollo shares with all of them.

Poets, traditionally, appealed for help to a particular Muse.
Homer begins the *Iliad* by calling on the Muse for inspiration.
Milton, in the seventh book of *Paradise Lost*, invokes the Muse
Urania:

> Descend from Heav'n *Urania*, by that name
> If rightly thou art call'd, whose Voice divine
> Following, above th' *Olympian* Hill I soare,
> Above the flight of *Pegasean* wing.

Writers use the notion of the Muse without calling before us a classical figure, as in the Chorus of *Henry V*:

> O! for a Muse of fire, that would ascend
> The brightest heaven of invention . . .

MUSICAL COMEDY. Phyllis Hartnoll says, in *The Oxford Companion to the Theatre*:

> It is a popular type of light entertainment, which derives from a fusion of burlesque and light opera, taking from the latter the tradition of a sketchy plot, songs arising from it, and concerted finales for each act. Burlesque provided topicality and an intermission of speciality sketches. The first English musical comedy was *In Town*, 1892. Outstanding successes since then have been *The Merry Widow, Showboat, Oklahoma!* and *Carousel*.

MYSTERY PLAY. *See* LITURGICAL DRAMA.

MYSTICISM. Latin *mysticus*, from Greek *mustikós*, of, pertaining to, a *mústēs*, an initiate to the mysteries. The mystic is defined in *The Oxford English Dictionary* as 'one who seeks by contemplation and self-surrender to obtain union with or absorption into the Deity, or who believes in spiritual apprehension of truths inaccessible to the understanding'. In *Creative Intuition in Art and Poetry*, Jacques Maritain draws a distinction between poetic experience and mystical experience. They are distinct in nature:

> . . . poetic experience is concerned with the created world and the enigmatic and innumerable relations of beings with each other; mystical experience with the principle of things in its own incomprehensible and supramundane unity . . . mystical experience tends towards silence, and terminates in an immanent fruition of the absolute.

Mystical experience finds expression in the works of Donne, Crashaw, Vaughan, Herbert, Traherne, Blake, and Wordsworth, who came to regard Nature as the source of his religion, 'the visible embodiment of God', shown in *Tintern Abbey*:

> Nor less, I trust,
> To them I may have owed another gift,
> Of aspect more sublime; that blessed mood,
> In which the burthen of the mystery,
> In which the heavy and the weary weight
> Of all this unintelligible world,
> Is lightened: — that serene and blessed mood,
> In which the affections gently lead us on, —

Until, the breath of this corporeal frame
And even the motion of our human blood
Almost suspended, we are laid asleep
In body, and become a living soul.

MYTH.   Greek *mûthos*, fable.   A traditional story or legend offering
an explanation of religious or supernatural phenomena such as the
gods, heroes, the many forces of nature.
   H. J. Rose says in *The Oxford Classical Dictionary*:

   . . . the myth often appeals to the emotions rather than the
   reason and, indeed, in its most typical forms seems to date
   from an age when rational explanations were not generally
   called for.   For example, it was commonly said that the
   gorge of the Peneus had been created by Poseidon clearing
   the mountain-chain which formerly closed in Thessaly on
   that side.   To Herodotus himself, this was merely a
   picturesque way of saying that the gorge had been formed
   by an earthquake, a solution very like the 'cataclysmic' school
   of geological theory once popular in modern Europe.   But
   it seems far more probable that the originator of the story
   had a vivid mental picture of the gorge, which to his eye
   suggested a great cut, being hewn out by a gigantic and
   powerful being, and that, finding the picture satisfactory to
   his imagination, he was not troubled with any question as
   to its probability.

MYTHOGRAPHY.   Greek *mûthos*, word, speech, tale, legend;
gráphein, to draw, write.   The expression or representation of
myths in literature, painting, or sculpture.

MYTHOLOGY.   Greek *muthología*, study of legends.   G. S. Fraser
says 'Mythology preserves the memory of ancient rituals, it is
concerned with the regular repetitive activities of many people,
under a very deep emotional compulsion, whereas history is what
a few people happened to do *once*'.

MYTHOPOESIS.   Greek *muthopoiós*, myth-making.   Myth-making
or relating to the making of myths.   This activity need not belong
only to Greek and Roman poets; Blake was a *mythopoet*.

N

NARRATIVE VERSE. Latin *narrāre*, to relate. Verse which tells a story. Notable examples in English are *The Canterbury Tales*, *The Giaour* by Byron, Matthew Arnold's *Sohrab and Rustum*.

NATURALISM. Latin *nātūrālis*, by birth, in accordance with nature. In art or literature, an attempt to achieve complete fidelity to nature by giving no idealized picture of life. Émile Zola was the chief figure in the French school of naturalistic fiction. After *Thérèse Raquin* in 1867, Zola studied the sordid, more animal side of human life. In his essay, *Le Roman expérimental*, he said that the novelist should be like the scientist, scrutinizing his subject with dispassionate minuteness.

Thomas Hardy did not accept Naturalism. He said:

> The recent school of novel writers forget in their insistence on life, and nothing but life, in a plain slice, that a story must be worth the telling, that a good deal of life is not worth any such thing, and that they must not occupy the reader's time with what he can get at first hand anywhere around him.

NATURE. Latin *nātūra*, from *nāscī*, *nāt-*, to be born. In his poetry Wordsworth is 'communicating a new order of experience for which Nature serves as a point of departure'. There was no such 'experience' in English poetry before his time. Earlier writers saw Nature through the eyes of the Greek and Latin poets or fitted it into an ordered universe. Pope described the classical rules as 'nature methodized'.

These passages show the marked change:

> All Nature is but Art, unknown to thee;
> All Chance, Direction, which thou canst not see;
> All Discord, Harmony not understood;
> All partial Evil, universal Good:
> And, spite of Pride, in erring Reason's spite,
> One truth is clear, WHATEVER IS, IS RIGHT.
>
> Pope, *An Essay on Man*

> For I have learned
> To look on nature, not as in the hour
> Of thoughtless youth; but hearing oftentimes
> The still, sad music of humanity,
> Nor harsh nor grating, though of ample power
> To chasten and subdue. And I have felt

A presence that disturbs me with the joy
Of elevated thoughts; a sense sublime
Of something far more deeply interfused,
Whose dwelling is the light of setting suns,
And the round ocean and the living air,
And the blue sky, and in the mind of man:
A motion and a spirit, that impels
All thinking things, all objects of all thought,
And rolls through all things.

Wordsworth, *Lines written a few miles above Tintern Abbey*

NEAR RHYME.   Rhymes which are not true or exact are known as near or imperfect rhymes.

Lo! thy dread empire, Chaos! is restor'd;
Light dies before thy uncreating word.

Pope, *The Dunciad*

These substitute rhymes have also been called *approximate, embryonic, half, imperfect, oblique, paraphones,* and *slant rhyme.*

NEGATIVE CAPABILITY.   This expression is used by Keats, in his letter of 22nd December 1817, to his brothers George and Tom. He says:

I had not a dispute, but a disquisition, with Dilke upon various subjects; several things dove-tailed in my mind, and at once it struck me what quality went to form a man of achievement, especially in literature, and which Shakespeare possessed so enormously — I mean *negative capability,* that is, when a man is capable of being in uncertainties, mysteries, doubts, without any irritable reaching after fact and reason. Coleridge, for instance, would let go by a fine isolated verisimilitude caught from the penetralium of Mystery, from being incapable of remaining content with half-knowledge. This pursued through volumes would perhaps take us no farther than this; that with a great Poet the sense of Beauty overcomes every other consideration, or rather obliterates all consideration.

NEMESIS.   Greek *némesis,* retribution; *némein,* to deal out, dispense.   The Greek goddess of vengeance; retributive justice. Applied to the principle of tragic poetic justice, when evil brings about its own downfall.

NEO-CLASSIC.   Greek *néos,* new.   A revival of the style and outlook of Greek and Roman classical writers.   In English literature, the term applies to writers of the seventeenth and eighteenth centuries such as Dryden, Pope, Swift, Addison, and Johnson.

NEOLOGISM. French *néologisme*, new-coined word. The coining or using of new words. The tendency to adopt new views in theology.

NEO-PLATONISM. 'A school and system of philosophy, arising in Alexandria in the third century A.D., combining some of the doctrines of Greek philosophy, including those of Plato, with the mystical religious ideas of the East.' (H. C. Wyld, *Universal English Dictionary*)

NEPHELOCOCCYGIA. Greek *nephélē*, cloud, *kókkux*, cuckoo. Cloud-cuckoo-land. In the *Birds* of Aristophanes, an imaginary city built in the clouds by the cuckoo. An ideal realm.

NEUTRAL STYLE. In *Metaphysical Poets*, Herbert Grierson wrote:

> The Metaphysicals are masters of the neutral style, a diction equally appropriate, according as it may be used, to prose or verse.

NEW COMEDY. Greek comedy of the third and fourth centuries B.C. first prevalent about 336. This was pure comedy of manners. It used stock characters and conventional turns of plot. The scene represented a street, where the love intrigues were enacted. The most eminent writers were Menander, Philemon, and Diphilus of Sinope. Their work became the model for Roman comedy, which flourished in the hands of Plautus and Terence.

NEW CRITICISM. *Principles of Literary Criticism* and *Practical Criticism* by I. A. Richards started this movement in literary criticism in the 1920s. It was continued by F. R. Leavis, who said in *Revaluation*:

> No treatment of poetry is worth much that does not keep very close to the concrete: there lies the problem of method. The only acceptable solution, it seemed to me, lay in the extension and adaptation of the method appropriate in dealing with individual poets as such. In dealing with individual poets the rule of the critic is, or should (I think) be, to work as much as possible in terms of particular analysis — analysis of poems or passages, and to say nothing that cannot be related immediately to judgments about producible texts.

This movement started in Cambridge, and is known as the Cambridge School of Criticism or Critics.

'New Criticism' in America owes much to Richards, Leavis, and

Empson. There, the major critical figures are Cleanth Brooks, Robert Penn Warren, Yvor Winters, R. P. Blackmur, Austin Warren, Wayne Booth, R. S. Crane, Allen Tate, Rosemond Tuve.

NEWSBOOKS: DIURNALLS. Latin *diurnālis*, from *dies*, day. In the evolution of the newspaper, these were the successors of the 'corantos'. They consisted first of one printed sheet (eight pages), later of two, contained domestic and general news, during the period 1641-1665.

NEWSLETTERS. A term applied to the records of parliamentary and court news, which were sent in manuscript twice a week to subscribers all over the kingdom from the London office of Henry Muddiman in the second half of the seventeenth century. In many provincial newspapers today the 'London Letter' still appears.

NIHIL OBSTAT. Latin, nothing hinders. When appearing on the verso of the title-page of a Roman Catholic book, indicates that it has received the approval of a Catholic censor as being free of doctrinal or moral error. *See also* IMPRIMATUR.

NINE WORTHIES. Caxton in the Preface to Malory's *Morte d'Arthur* lists the Nine Worthies of the World: Hector of Troy, Alexander the Great, Julius Caesar are three Paynims; Joshua, David, and Judas Maccabaeus are three Jews; Arthur, Charlemagne, and Godfrey of Bouillon are three Christian men. The list of worthies in Shakespeare's *Love's Labour's Lost* is not quite the same, for it includes Pompey and Hercules. Dryden mentions them in *The Flower and the Leaf*:

> Nine worthies were they called, of different rites —
> Three Jews, three pagans, and three Christian knights.

NOBEL PRIZES. These were established under the will of the Swedish scientist, Alfred Bernhard Nobel (1833-1896). Five annual prizes are awarded for eminence in literature, the most important discoveries in physics, chemistry, and physiology respectively, and for the greatest service to promote international peace. (Ironically, as regards the latter, Nobel was the inventor of dynamite!)

NOBLE SAVAGE. This phrase first appeared in English in *The Conquest of Granada* by Dryden:

> I am as free as nature first made man,
> Ere the base laws of servitude began
> When wild in woods the noble savage ran.

The belief that primitive man is essentially noble formed part of the concept of Romanticism. It is found in the writings of Rousseau, and was used by Montaigne and prominently by Chateaubriand.

NOH or NŌ PLAYS. 'These plays', says Paul Harvey in *The Oxford Companion to English Literature*, 'are a form of traditional, ceremonial, or ritualistic drama peculiar to Japan, symbolical and spiritual in character. It was evolved from religious rites of Shinto worship, was perfected in the fifteenth century and flourished during the Tokugawa period (1652–1868). It has since been revived. The plays are short (one or two acts), in prose and verse, and a chorus contributes poetical comments. They were formerly acted as a rule only at the Shogun's court, five or six in succession, presenting a complete life drama, beginning with a play of the divine age, then a battle piece, a "play of women", a psychological piece (dealing with the sins and struggles of mortals), a morality, and finally a congratulatory piece, praising the lords and the reign. The text was helped out by symbolic gestures and chanting. About two hundred Noh Plays are extant . . . In various respects the Noh Plays are comparable with the early Greek drama.'

NOM-DE-PLUME. Pen-name. A name assumed by a writer, as *Peter Pindar*, the *nom-de-plume* of Dr. John Wolcot. This is an English coinage of a French expression which does not exist in the French language itself, where the term is *nom de guerre*.

NOMINALISM. Latin *nōminālis*; *nōmen*, *nōminis*, name. The view of those schoolmen who regarded universals or abstract terms as mere names without corresponding reality. William of Ockham (1280–1349), the father of this school, condemned the doctrine of Realism without accepting the extravagances of Nominalism.

NOMINATIVE ABSOLUTE. When a noun or pronoun, instead of being subject or object to a finite verb, is subject to a participle, the phrase so formed, not firmly attached to the rest of the sentence, is called a nominative absolute. For example: 'He failing in his promise, I will withdraw mine.'

In Old English, the absolute case was the dative; in Latin it is the ablative. If an absolute participle has no noun for its subject, it is known as the unrelated participle. For example: 'Going to London, the road was crowded.'

NON SEQUITUR: NON SEQ. Latin, literally, it does not follow. A false argument, conclusion; a flaw in logic.

NONCE-WORD. A word invented for a special occasion and only used once. Nonce-words appear in Lewis Carroll's 'Jabberwocky', and in *Finnegans Wake* by James Joyce. Nonce comes from the Middle English *for then ōnes*, for the once, for the occasion.

NONSENSE VERSE. A form of light verse in which the sound and movement are more important than the sense. The two masters of this entertaining absurdity are Lewis Carroll and Edward Lear.

> 'Twas brillig, and the slithy toves
>> Did gyre and gimble in the wabe;
> All mimsy were the borogroves
>> And the mome raths outgrabe.
>>> Lewis Carroll, *Jabberwocky*

> When awful darkness and silence reign
> Over the great Gromboolian plain,
>> Through the long, long wintry nights
> When the angry breakers roar
> As they beat on the rocky shore; —
> When Storm-clouds brood on the towering heights
>> Of the Hills of the Chankly Bore.
>>> Edward Lear, *The Dong with the Luminous Nose*

NORM: POINT OF SANITY. In his lecture 'On Style', Quiller-Couch said:

> Although Style is so curiously personal and individual, and although men are so variously built that no two in the world carry away the same impressions from a show, there is always a norm somewhere; in literature and art, as in morality. Yes, even in man's most terrific, most potent inventions — when, for example, in *Hamlet* or in *Lear* Shakespeare seems to be breaking up the solid earth under our feet — there is always some point and standard of sanity — a Kent or an Horatio — to which all enormities and passionate errors may be referred; to which the agitated mind of the spectator settles back as upon its centre of gravity, its pivot of repose.

NOSTALGIA. Greek *nóstos*, return home, *álgos*, pain. Homesickness; sentimental longing for days of the past.

NOUMENON. Greek *nooúmenon*, from *noeîn*, to perceive. The object of pure reason. In Kantian philosophy: an object of intellectual intuition without the help of the senses. Kant introduced it in contrast to phenomenon.

NOVEL. Latin *novellus*, diminutive of *novus*, new. Italian *novella*, new things. It was first applied to such tales as those of Boccaccio. A fictitious prose narrative dealing with human beings and their actions over a period of time, and displaying varieties of human character in relation to life. In England, the novel established itself in the eighteenth century with Samuel Richardson's *Pamela* (1740), written in the epistolary form.

NOVEL OF THE SOIL. A story of man's struggle against nature. This form of the novel has developed during the twentieth century. Examples are *Tobacco Road* and *God's Little Acre* by Erskine Caldwell; *Grapes of Wrath* by John Steinbeck; *The Battle Ground* by Ellen Glasgow.

NOVELETTE. From Latin *novellus*, feminine *novella*; *novus*, new. A short novel, especially one without literary quality.

NOVELLA. Italian *novèlla*, a short story. A short prose narrative. The term was applied to such works as Boccaccio's *Decameron*. The plural is novelle.

NUMBERS. Latin *numerus*, quantity, measure. Metrical periods, or feet, or verse. Drayton says, in *Elegies upon Sundry Occasions*:

In Musickes Numbers my Voyce rose and fell.

> Will no one tell me what she sings? —
> Perhaps the plaintive numbers flow
> For old, unhappy, far-off things
> And battles long ago . . .
>
> Wordsworth, *The Solitary Reaper*

NURSERY RHYMES. Brief verses, often embodying traditional songs and tales, which are for the delight of young children.

The rhyme 'A was an apple-pie' was well known in the reign of Charles II. In 1671 John Eachard, a divine, quoted it in *Some Observations upon the Answer to an Enquiry into the Grounds and Occasions of the Contempt of the Clergy:* 'And why not, Repent rarely, evenly, prettily, elegantly, neatly, tightly? And also why not A Apple-pasty, B bak'd it, C cut it, D divided it, E eat it, F fought for it, G got it, etc. I had not time Sir, to look any further into their way of Preaching.'

O

OBITER DICTA. Latin, literally, things said by the way.

A legal term meaning an observation by a judge on a legal question suggested by a case before him, but not arising in such a manner as to require decision. It is not, therefore, binding as a precedent.

OBJECTIVE CORRELATIVE. T. S. Eliot says:

> The only way of expressing emotion in the form of art is by finding an 'objective correlative'; in other words, a set of objects, a situation, a chain of events which shall be the formula for that *particular* emotion; such that, when the external facts, which must terminate in sensory experience, are given, the emotion is immediately evoked.

Further in this essay on *Hamlet*, Eliot explains that the emotions which dominate the hero are not justified by the facts in the play:

> Hamlet's bafflement at the absence of objective equivalent to his feelings is a prolongation of the bafflement of his creator in the face of his artistic problem.

OBJECTIVITY. Reality as it is apart from the thoughts and feelings of the writer. The dealing with outward things. Treating events or phenomena as external rather than as affected by the reflections or feelings of the observer. A good deal of the writing of Fielding, Smollett, Dickens, and Trollope is objective.

OBLIGATORY SCENE. (French *scène à faire.*) In a play, this is an episode, foreseen by the audience in the development of the plot, which the dramatist is obliged to write. In *Macbeth*, after the brutal murder of Duncan, Malcolm and Donalbain, his two sons, are left in silence alone in their horror and perplexity. The audience anticipates the scene.

OBLIQUE RHYME. *See* NEAR RHYME.

OCCASIONAL VERSE. Poetry written for a special occasion. Some occasional verse is remembered because of its intrinsic literary value. Among the most famous are *Horatian Ode upon Cromwell's Return from Ireland*, by Andrew Marvell, *On the Late Massacre in Piedmont*, by Milton, Tennyson's *Ode on the Death of the Duke of Wellington*, and *The Wreck of the Deutschland*, by Gerard Manley Hopkins.

OCTASTICH. Greek *októ*, eight, *stíkhos,* line of verse. A group of eight lines of verse.

OCTATEUCH. Greek *octáteuchus,* containing eight books. The first eight books of the Old Testament; the Pentateuch together with Joshua, Judges, and Ruth.

OCTAVE. Latin *octo*, eight. A group of eight lines of verse, more specifically the first eight lines of the Petrarchan sonnet. A stanza of eight lines, specifically *Ottava Rima,* rhyming *a b a b a b c c.*

OCTAVO. From Latin *in octavo,* from *octāvus,* eighth. The size of a book in which the sheets are so folded that each leaf is one-eighth the size of a whole sheet. Abbreviated to 8vo.

OCTET. Latin *octo,* eight. A composition for eight voices. Eight singers who perform together. A group of eight lines of verse. Eight heroics, the first six rhyming alternately, the last two in succession, are known as *ottava rima.* Byron's *Don Juan* is a fine example.

OCTOMETER. Greek *októ,* eight, *métros* from *métron,* measure. A line of eight metrical feet. There are few poems in this measure. Here are some lines from Tennyson's *Locksley Hall*:

Cursèd | be the | social | wants that | sin a | gainst the | strength of | youth |
Cursèd | be the | social | lies that | warp us | from the | living | truth. |

OCTOSYLLABIC VERSE. Verse consisting of eight-syllable lines.

ODE. Greek *ōidé,* for *aoidé,* from *aeídein,* to sing. A poem meant to be sung. A lyric poem often addressed to a person or an abstraction, usually of exalted style and feeling. *The Progress of Poesy* by Gray is based on Pindar's Greek Choral Ode. Marvell's *Horatian Ode upon Cromwell's Return from Ireland* bears resemblance to many of the so-called 'odes', carmina, of Horace. The irregular ode by Wordsworth on *Intimations of Immortality* is in reality an extended and sustained lyric.

OFFSET PROCESS. A method of printing in which ink is first transferred from a zinc or aluminium plate to a uniform rubber surface and then to the paper. The rubber surface has no relief, it permits the use of rough paper for line or halftone designs, and results in a softer and more diffused effect.

OGHAM: OGAM. Modern Irish *ogham*, supposed to have been invented by a legendary *Ogma*. An ancient British and Irish form of writing having twenty letters. Also an obscure way of speaking, used by the ancient Irish.

OLD COMEDY. Greek comedy of the fifth century B.C. performed at the festivals of Dionysus. It was a curious blend of religious ceremony, serious satire and criticism, wit and buffoonery. The works of Crates and Eupolis, writers of Old Comedy, have been lost; the plays of Aristophanes have survived.

The artificial comedy in Restoration England was later called Old Comedy. It was disarming at its best, indecent at its worst, but always witty and detached from reality. It has been called 'the sublimation of the trivial'; it vanished from the English stage in 1767, to be revived under Sheridan 'with much wit and less indelicacy'.

OLD ENGLISH. English was originally the dialect of the Angles, extending to all the dialects whether Anglian or Saxon. Old English or Anglo-Saxon is the English language from the beginnings, placed A.D. 700, till the end of the period, about 1100. The writers of the time spoke of their language as *Englisc*.

OMNIBUS. Ablative plural of Latin *omnis*, all. A volume containing several works, usually reprints, frequently by a single author, published at a low price to be within the reach of all.

ONE-ACT PLAY. This form of play, usually farcical, served in the nineteenth century to prepare the audience for the main five-act play of the evening. It was diverting and experimental. In the early part of the twentieth century Strindberg, Shaw and O'Neill wrote a number of such plays.

ONOMATOPOEIA. Greek *onomatopoiia*, from *ónoma*, name and *poieîn*, to make. The formation of words from sounds which seem to suggest and reinforce the meaning. This accounts for words like *murmur, cuckoo, buzzing, twitter*. When applied to the choice of words in poetry, whereby the sound is made 'an echo to the sense', onomatopoeia has a real value. The most obvious examples are those in which the sense to be echoed is itself a sound, as in these lines from Tennyson's *Morte d'Arthur*:

> The bare black cliff clang'd round him, as he based
> His feet on juts of slippery crag that rang
> Sharp-smitten with the dint of armed heels

and these lines from *Paradise Lost*:

> Fountains and yee, that warble, as ye flow,
> Melodious murmurs, warbling tune his praise.

also:

> Anyone lived in a pretty how town
> (with up so floating many bells down)
> spring summer autumn winter
> he sang his didn't he danced his did
>
> e. e. cummings

ONTOLOGY. Greek *ón, óntos,* present participle of *eînai,* to be, *lógos,* discourse. The science or study of being. That part of metaphysics which relates to the being and essence of things.

O.P. Out of print. A book is said to be 'o.p.' when the stock has been exhausted and there is no present intention of reprinting it.

OPEN COUPLET. A couplet of which the second line is run-on and depends upon the first line of the following couplet to complete its meaning, as in the first of these couplets from Milton's *L'Allegro*:

> When the merry bells ring round,
> And the jocund rebecks sound
> To many a youth and many a maid
> Dancing in the chequered shade.

OPERA. Latin *opus, oper-,* work, labour. A drama set to music — entirely or partially, but in such a degree that the musical part is an essential and not an incidental element. 'Musical plays' and the like are not covered by the term.

OPÉRA BOUFFE. French *bouffe,* comic. An opera of farcical character. An operatic extravaganza.

OPERE CITATO. Latin, in the work cited. Abbreviated to op. cit.

OPISTHOGRAPHIC. Greek *opisthógraphos,* written on the back of. A term applied to early printed and block-books, printed on both sides of the leaf.

OPTICAL CENTRE. That point on a printed page which the eye seems naturally to seek as the centre. This point is slightly above the actual centre of the page, being approximately three-eighths of the distance from the top.

ORATIO OBLIQUA. *See* INDIRECT SPEECH.

ORATIO RECTA. *See* DIRECT SPEECH.

ORATION. Latin *orāre*, to pray. A formal speech delivered on a special occasion. In English literature, perhaps the most famous oration is Mark Antony's speech to the crowd in *Julius Caesar*.

> Friends, Romans, countrymen, lend me your ears;
> I come to bury Caesar, not to praise him.
> The evil that men do lives after them;
> The good is oft interred with their bones;
> So let it be with Caesar . . .

ORGANIC FORM. Greek *órganon*, instrument, cognate with *érgon*, work. The work is said to grow from its conception in the thought, feeling, and complete personality of the writer, as opposed to a work which, governed by mechanical form, is fitted arbitrarily into a preconceived mould. *Ode to a Nightingale* by Keats is a good example of the organic form.

OROTUND. Coinage from Latin *ōre rotundō*, with round mouth (Horace, *Ars Poetica*, 323). Pompous, imposing, pretentious. In *The English Language*, Ernest Weekley says, 'The orotund style is still employed by those who say *sufficient* instead of *enough*, prefer things to *transpire* rather than to *happen*, call a *farewell speech* a *valedictory address*'.

ORTHODOX. Greek *orthódoxos*, having right opinions. Correct in opinion or doctrine, especially in religious matters. The term is contrasted with *heterodox*. One of the ancient divisions of the Greek Church, which recognizes the headship of the Patriarch of Constantinople.

ORTHOEPY. Greek *orthós*, straight, right; *épos*, word. The science of correct pronunciation. In his essay 'Changes in the Language since Shakespeare's Time', W. Murison says:

> If a chapter from the Authorized Version or a scene from one of Shakespeare's plays were read to us with the contemporary pronunciation, the ear would be considerably puzzled to recognize certain of the words. For, while the spelling has remained tolerably constant, many of the sounds have changed a great deal . . .
> The vowel sound in *sea, meat, heat, treat, deal* was in the eighteenth century identical with the vowel sound in *day, name*; it is now the same as in *meet, feel, see.*

Till about 1820, *balcóny* was almost the only stress.   Cowper in *John Gilpin* has

> At Edmonton his loving wife
> From the balcony spied;

and Byron, in *Beppo*, rhymes *balcony* with *Giorgione*.

ORTHOGRAPHY.   Greek *orthográphein*, to write correctly.   Correct or conventional spelling.   In his essay 'Changes in the Language since Shakespeare's Time', W. Murison says:

> In spite of the changes in the pronunciation of English since the close of the sixteenth century, the spelling has altered little.   In the early years of the seventeenth century, the same volume, sometimes the same page, has such differences as the following: *beene, bene, bin*; *detter, debter*; *guests, ghestes*; *yles, isles*; *vitaile, victuals*; *hautie, haughtie*; *he, hee*; *least, lest.*   But it began to be felt more convenient to keep one spelling for a word; and, by the end of the eighteenth century our orthographical system was practically in its present shape. . . . Johnson spent much time and trouble in adjusting what he calls our 'unsettled and fortuitous' orthography.   He successfully anticipated the orthography that triumphed, for, with a few exceptions like *chymist, domestick, dutchess, translatour*, his spellings are ours.

OTTAVA RIMA.   A stanza consisting of eight iambic pentameter lines, rhyming *a b a b a b c c*.   Byron used it in *Don Juan*:

> His suite consisted of three servants and
> A tutor, the licentiate Pedrillo,
> Who several languages did understand,
> But now lay sick and speechless on his pillow,
> And, rocking in his hammock, long'd for land,
> His headache being increased by every billow;
> And the waves oozing through the port-hole made
> His berth a little damp, and him afraid.

OUTRIDES.   Gerard Manley Hopkins defines these as 'slack syllables added to a foot and not counting in the nominal scanning'.

OVERTONES.   In music this means the constituents (harmonics and partials) of a musical note, giving it pure tones.

In poetry, overtones are the associations of a word giving it the widest meaning.   Words are constantly being enriched by associations.   Sieges and sorties, battlements and scaling-ladders are all closely connected with the word 'castle'.   Gold and precious stones, mule-trains, the Spanish Main, pirates, old maps, have each added another association to the word 'treasure'.

OXFORD MOVEMENT. The Oxford or Tractarian Movement was a revival of the Anglican High Church which began with a sermon preached in 1833 at Oxford by John Keble. The principal leaders of the movement, besides Keble, were Newman, Pusey, and R. H. Froude. In 1864, appeared Newman's *Apologia pro Vita sua* in answer to Charles Kingsley's attack upon him.

OXYMORON. Greek *oxúmōros*, pointedly foolish, sharp-dull; *oxús*, sharp, *mōrós*, foolish. The combining in one expression of two words or phrases of opposite meaning, for effect. Here are examples of this form of concise paradox:

> Alas! that love, whose view is muffled still
> Should, without eyes, see pathways to his will . . .
> Here's much to do with hate, but more with love:
> Why then, O brawling love! O loving hate!
> O any thing! of nothing first create.
> O heavy lightness! serious vanity!
> Mis-shapen chaos of well-seeming forms!
> Feather of lead, bright smoke, cold fire, sick health!
> Still-waking sleep, that is not what it is!
> This love feel I, that feel no love in this!
> Dost thou not laugh?
> *Romeo and Juliet*

> But fare thee well, most foul, most fair! farewell,
> Thou pure impiety and impious purity!
> *Much Ado About Nothing*

> The shackles of an old love straiten'd him,
> His honour rooted in dishonour stood,
> And faith unfaithful kept him falsely true.
> Tennyson, *Lancelot and Elaine*

PAEAN. A Greek choral song of joy or praise, deriving its name from the invocation 'Iō Paián' addressed to Apollo, which formed a refrain. Perhaps originally it was a song of healing or incantation. A paean was composed by Sophocles to Asclepius, and one by Socrates to Apollo.

PAEON. Greek *paión*, Attic form of *paián*, hymn to Apollo. A metrical foot of four syllables, one long and three short; it is called a first, second, third or fourth paeon according to the position of the long syllable. In the grouped phrase 'dapple-dawn-drawn Falcon', Gerard Manley Hopkins used the first paeon:

> I caught this morning morning's minion, king-
>   dom of daylight's dauphin, dapple-dawn-drawn Fal-
>   con, in his riding
> Of the rolling level underneath him steady air, and
>   striding
>
> The Windhover

PAGEANT. Anglo-Latin *pāgina*, from Greco-Latin *pēgma*, a movable scaffold for theatrical use, from *pangere*, to fasten. In medieval times, the movable stage or platform upon which the processional religious play was performed. This stage on wheels had two apartments, the lower one used as a dressing-room, the upper one, open to the audience, used as the stage. The performance itself was called a pageant. Later, the term was applied to any imposing outdoor procession or spectacular performance.

PALAEOGRAPHY. Greek *palaiós*, ancient, and *gráphein*, to write. The art of deciphering ancient writing, inscriptions, and manuscripts.

PALILOGY. Greek *palillogía*, speaking over again. The repetition of a word or phrase for the sake of emphasis, as in this sentence from Sir Philip Sidney's *Arcadia*:

> O no, he can not be good, that knows not why he is good, but stands so far good, as his fortune may keep him unassailed.

PALIMPSEST. Greek *palímpsēston*; *pálin*, again, and *psáiō*, I rub smooth, I efface. A parchment or other writing material from which the original writing has been effaced and other matter written in its place. This was of frequent occurrence in the early Middle

Ages because of the cost of parchment. Valuable ancient works have been lost in this way, but sometimes the earlier writing has been visible as well as the more recent.

PALINDROME. Greek *palindromos*, running back again; *pálin*, again, *drom-* run. A word, sentence, or verse which reads the same backwards as forwards. Examples are: 'Madam, I'm Adam' and 'Able was I ere I saw Elba'. In 1706, John Phillips wrote this line:

Lewd did I live & evil I did dwel.

Among more up-to-date palindromes are:

A man, a plan, a canal—Panama!

Stop, Syrian, I start at rats in airy spots.

Desserts I desire not, so long no lost one rise distressed.

Name tarts, no, medieval slave. I demonstrate man.

But Ragusa store, babe, rots a sugar tub.

Eureka! Till I pull up ill I take rue.

Now stop, Major-general, are negro jam pots won.

Stiff, O Dairyman, in a myriad of fits.

(*The Times Educational Supplement*, 18th September 1964)

PALINODE. Greek *palinōidía*, singing over again, a recantation. A poem in which the author retracts something said in a former poem. During the Renaissance, the writing of palinodes was fairly common. In *The Legend of Good Women*, a famous palinode, Chaucer atones for the reflections on the fidelity of women contained in his poems *Romaunt of the Rose* and *Troylus and Cryseyde*.

PALLADIAN. Andrea Palladio, an Italian architect in the sixteenth century, imitated the ancient Roman style 'without regard to classical principles'. He gave his name to the Palladian school of architecture, which was extremely popular in England at the end of the seventeenth century and during the first half of the eighteenth century.

PAMPHLET. Possibly from a Latin poem *Pamphilus, seu de Amore*, very popular in the Middle Ages. A small treatise with fewer pages than would make a book, always unbound, with or without paper covers.

PANDEMONIUM. Greek *pân*, all, *daímōn*, divinity, tutelary genius. The word was coined by Milton, and appears in the first book of *Paradise Lost*:

Mean while the winged Haralds by command
Of Sovran power, with awful Ceremony
And Trumpets sound throughout the Host proclaim

A solemn Councel forthwith to be held
At *Pandæmonium,* the high Capital
Of Satan and his Peers.

PANEGYRIC. Greek *panēgurikós,* from *panéguris,* general assembly;
pan, all, *agorá,* assembly. A eulogy. A formal speech or piece of
writing praising some person, thing, or achievement. A panegyric
is often expressed in exaggerated terms.

PANEM ET CIRCENSES. Juvenal, the Roman satirical poet, said
the decadent Roman populace cared only about 'bread and circuses':

> nam qui dabat olim
> Imperium fasces legiones omnia, nunc se
> Continet atque duas tantum res anxius optat,
> Panem et circenses.

> And those who once, with unresisted sway,
> Gave armies, empires, every thing away,
> For two poor claims have long renounced the whole,
> And only ask — the Circus and the Dole.
>   (William Gifford's translation)

PANJANDRUM. ' "And there were present the Picninnies, and the
Joblillies, and the Garyulies, and the Grand Panjandrum himself,
with the little round button at top", part of the farrago of nonsense
composed by Samuel Foote to test the memory of Charles Macklin,
who asserted that he could repeat anything after once hearing it.
Hence "Panjandrum" is used as a mock title for an imaginary
personage of much power, or a personage of great pretensions.'
(Oxford English Dictionary)

PANORAMIC METHOD. From Greek *hórāma,* sight, from *horáō,*
I see. The *panoramic* or *pictorial method* in prose fiction means
description which is given directly by the author. Fielding, Scott,
George Eliot, and Thackeray all used this method in their novels.

PANTALOON. Adapted from the Italian *pantalone,* 'a kind of mask
on the Italian stage, representing the Venetian', of whom *Pantalone*
was a nickname, supposed to be derived from *San Pantaleone,*
formerly a favourite saint of the Venetians. The Venetian character
in Italian comedy was represented as a lean and foolish old man,
wearing slippers, pantaloons, and spectacles. In modern pantomime he is represented as a foolish and vicious old man, the butt of
the clown's jokes, and his abettor in his tricks. *(Oxford English
Dictionary)*

PANTHEISM. Greek *pân*, all; *theós*, a god. A doctrine that the whole universe is God, so that every part of the universe is a manifestation of God. The worship of all the pagan gods of whatever cult or race, as under the Roman Empire. In poetry it presents a belief that all life on earth is divine.

PANTOMIME. Greek *pantómimos*, all mimic; French *pantomime*, actor in a dumb show. This name was first given to a Roman actor in a dumb show. The art of dumb acting became popular in many parts of Europe. Pantomime later denoted not the performer but the piece performed, a kind of harlequinade. In England, this entertainment, founded on a version of the *Commedia dell' Arte*, was introduced by Arlecchino in the reign of James I. In the eighteenth century, the production became lavish in costume, with many changes of scene.

Pantomime still survives in the spectacular Christmas entertainments based on familiar fairy stories, with lively music, singing, dancing, and the broad comedy of clowns.

PANTOUM. French from Malayan *pantun*, a Malayan verse form. A series of quatrains rhyming *a b a b*. The second and fourth lines of each quatrain become the first and third in the next. The second and fourth lines of the last stanza must repeat the first and third lines of the first stanza reversed. Thus the last and the first line of the poem are the same.

PAPYRUS. Greek *pápūros*. The paper reed, a tall sedge, once common in Egypt. Its pith prepared as writing material by the Egyptians; a manuscript written on papyrus.

PARABASIS. Greek *parábasis*, a going, digression. In ancient Greek comedy, a part sung by the chorus, addressed to the audience on behalf of the poet. It was unconnected with the action of the drama, and consisted of an invocation to a god, followed by a witty, satiric speech on current affairs.

PARABLE. Greek *parabolé*, comparison, putting beside; from *parabállein*, to throw beside. A short, simple story setting forth a moral lesson. The Prodigal Son and the Good Samaritan, parables of Christ, are, perhaps, the most famous examples.

PARACHRONISM. Greek *khrónos*, time. Chronological error in placing an event at a date later than it really happened.

PARADOX. Greek *parádoxos*, contrary to received opinion or expectation. A statement which, though it seems to be self-contradictory, contains a basis of truth. A statement conflicting with received opinion or belief. A paradox often provokes the reader to consider the particular point afresh, as when Shakespeare says, 'Cowards die many times before their deaths'; and Wordsworth, 'The child is father of the man'.

In this stanza from *Rabbi Ben Ezra*, Browning uses the idea of paradox throughout:

> For thence, — a paradox
> Which comforts while it mocks, —
> Shall life succeed in that it seems to fail:
> What I aspired to be,
> And was not, comforts me.
> A brute I might have been, but would
> not sink i' the scale.

PARAGOGE. Greek *paragōgḗ*, a leading past, addition to the end of a syllable. The addition of an extra, or expletive, syllable or letter to the end of a word, to give emphasis or modify the meaning, as in *withouten, lovéd*.

PARALLELISM. Greek *parállēlos*, beside one another. The similarity of construction or meaning of phrases placed side by side. This is a persistent rhetorical device, found in the Psalms of David and the English Prayer Book. Here is an example from Pope's *An Essay on Man*:

> All Nature is but art, unknown to thee;
> All chance, direction, which thou canst not see;
> All discord, harmony not understood;
> All partial evil, universal good;
> And, spite of pride, in erring reason's spite,
> One truth is clear, Whatever is, is right.

See SYNONYMOUS PARALLELISM *and* ANTITHETICAL PARALLELISM.

PARAPHRASE. Greek *paráphrasis*, literally, beside phrase, beside speech; *pará*, beside, *phrásis*, speech. Rendering of the sense of a passage in other words; a free rendering of any work in verse or prose.

PARARHYME. Greek, literally, near rhyme. In this type of rhyme the vowel sounds of the accented syllables of the rhyming words are different, but the consonant sounds before and after the vowels are the same. Wilfred Owen made frequent use of pararhyme. These are the opening lines of *Strange Meeting*:

> It seemed that out of battle I escaped
> Down some profound dull tunnel, long since scooped
> Through granites which titanic wars had groined.
> Yet also there encumbered sleepers groaned.

PARCHMENT. French *parchemin*, from *Pergamum*, city of Mysia in Asia Minor, now Bergamo, where it was first adopted in the second century B.C. as a substitute for papyrus. It is the skin, especially of sheep or goats, prepared for use in writing or painting. Parchment was originally much the same as vellum.

PARENTHESIS. Greek, from *parentithénai*, to put in beside. A word, phrase, clause, inserted into a sentence which is grammatically complete without the insertion. A parenthesis is usually marked off by brackets, dashes, or commas. The term is used figuratively for an interlude, or interval.

PARISYLLABIC. Latin *pārisyllaba*, equal-syllabled. A name given to those Greek and Latin nouns which have the same number of syllables in the nominative as in the oblique cases of the singular, as nominative *collis*, genitive *collis*.

PARLANCE. Late Latin *parabolāre*, talk. A way of speaking; characteristic speech; as in *common, legal, military, vulgar parlance*.

PARNASSIAN SCHOOL. The name given to a group of French romantic poets of the latter half of the nineteenth century. It came from the title, 'Le Parnasse Contemporain', of three collections of their poems published in 1866–1876. The Parnassians devoted themselves to objective poetry. The statement 'Le poète est le sculpteur', by Gautier, became, for them, an emblem for their poetic craftsmanship. Other members of this school were Catulle Mendès, Xavier de Ricart, Mallarmé, Verlaine, Sully Prudhomme.

PARNASSUS. Greek *Parna(s)sos*. A mountain in Greece, a few miles north of Delphi, sacred to the Muses. One of its peaks was sacred to Apollo, the other to Dionysus.

PÁRODOS. Greek, literally, the song accompanying the entrance of the chorus in a Greek tragedy.

PARODY. Greek *parōidía*, burlesque poem or song. A composition mimicking closely in rhythm, phrase, and theme a serious work, for example the parody of Swinburne in *Octopus* by A. C. Hilton:

> Strange beauty, eight-limbed and eight-handed,
>   Whence camest to dazzle our eyes?
> With thy bosom bespangled and banded
>   With the hues of the seas and the skies;
> Is thy home European or Asian,
>   O mystical monster marine?
> Part molluscous and partly crustacean,
>   Betwixt and between.

PARONOMASIA: PUN.   Greek *pará*, beside, *onomasia*, naming.
A play upon words for humorous or serious purposes.   The pun
may consist in the use of the same word with two meanings, as in:

> Old Gaunt indeed, and gaunt in being old

or in the use of two words spelled differently, pronounced the same
with a similarity of meaning.   In John Donne's *Hymn to God the
Father*, the word *Son* means both Christ and the sun, the word
done is a pun on the poet's own name:

> I have a sin of fear, that when I have spun
> My last thread, I shall perish on the shore;
> But swear by Thy self, that at my death Thy Son
> Shall shine as he shines now, and heretofore;
> And having done that, Thou hast done;
> I fear no more.

In *Cock and the Bull*, a parody of Browning, C. S. Calverley says,

> As we curtail the already cur-tailed cur
> (You catch the paronomasia, play 'po' words?)

PARTICLES.   Latin *particula*, diminutive of *pars, partis*, a part.
The short connecting words of language, as preposition, conjunction, interjection.   These are more plentiful in modern than in the
classical tongues, owing to our loss of the forms of case and tense.
In *Du Bartas*, Joshua Sylvester (1563–1618) tells how Adam
invented nouns and verbs for his own use:

> And then, the more t'enrich his speech, he brings
> Small particles, which stand in lieu of strings,
> The master members fitly to combine,
> As two great boards a little glue doth join.

In her *Life of Dr. Darwin*, Anna Seward, a friend of Dr. Johnson,
praises the way in which the eighteenth-century writers, 'sweep
from the polished marble of poetry and eloquence a number of the
sticks and straws of our language: its articles, conjunctions and
prepositions'.   Later, in *Table Talk*, Coleridge speaks of the
particles as 'the cements of language'.

PART-SONG.   A song, with or without instrumental accompaniment,
the parts (bass, tenor, alto, and soprano) of which are sung by
different voices, or groups of voices, so as to form a harmony.

PASQUINADE.   Italian *pasquinàta*, lampoon, pasquinade.   A
lampoon or piece of satire affixed to some public place.   The term
derives from the name Pasquino or Pasquillo, given to a mutilated
statue, exhumed at Rome in 1501, which was saluted on St. Mark's
Day in satirical Latin verses.   Later, pasquinades became common
in other countries of Europe.

PASSION.   Latin *passiōnem*, suffering, emotion.   Any intense emotion or agitation of mind, especially in tragedy.

> Only I discern —
> Infinite passion, and the pain
> Of finite hearts that yearn.
> Robert Browning, *Two in the Campagna*

PASSION PLAY.   A miracle play representing the Passion of Christ.   Performances of this play are given every tenth year at Oberammergau, a village in Upper Bavaria.

PASTICHE.   Late Latin *pasta*, paste.   A picture made up of fragments or pieced together or copied from an original.   Sometimes it is an imitation of the style of several artists mixed together to form a medley.   Also a literary composition made up from various sources. If satirical, it is a kind of parody.   Here is an example of pastiche in *Ancient Music* by Ezra Pound:

> Winter is icummen in,
> Lhude sing Goddamm.
> Raineth drop and staineth slop,
> And how the wind doth ramm!
> Sing: Goddamm.

PASTORALE.   Latin *pāstōrālis*, pastoral.   A musical composition, dealing with a pastoral subject, portraying pastoral scenes.

PASTORAL ELEGY.   *See* ELEGY.

PASTORAL IDYLL.   *See* IDYLL.

PASTORAL POETRY.   Latin *pāstōr-(em)*, shepherd, from *pāscĕre*, *pāst-*, to feed.   This is poetry which deals with the life of shepherds and rustics.   The Greek poet Bion in his lament for Moschus presented that poet under the guise of a shepherd.   Virgil followed this manner in his *Bucolics*.   George Loane, in *Short Handbook of Literary Terms*, outlines the growth of pastoral poetry briefly:

> Hence grew up the strange convention of writing about all
> sorts of persons as if they were shepherds and led a pastoral
> life.   Johnson's common sense revolted against it, and
> certainly such a spectacle as the melancholic landscape-
> gardener Shenstone warbling about his crook, his pipe, and
> his kids provokes mirth.   But the fact remains that some of
> the loveliest of English poems were written according to this
> convention, and we must accept the convention or lose great
> pleasure.   Milton's *Lycidas*, Shelley's *Adonais*, and Arnold's
> *Thyrsis* more than justify it.

In *Essays and Studies*, Swinburne said:

> There is grace ineffable, a sweet sound and sweet savour of things past, in the old beautiful use of the language of shepherds, of flocks and pipes; the spirit is none the less sad and sincere because the body of the poem has put on this dear familiar raiment of romance; because the crude and naked sorrow is veiled and chastened with soft shadows of a 'land that is very far off'.

'Perhaps the best pastoral in the language,' says Hazlitt, in his essay 'On Cowper and Thomson', 'is that prose-poem, Walton's *Compleat Angler.*' Burke maintained that Goldsmith's *Deserted Village* surpassed the pastoral poetry of Pope and Spenser.

In *Some Versions of Pastoral*, William Empson shows the various ways in which the pastoral form has been used in English literature.

PASTORELLA: PASTOURELLE. Latin *pāstōr-em*, a shepherd. A medieval lyric in which a knight pays court to a shepherdess, usually with no success. In Spenser's *Faerie Queene*, the Pastorella tells of a shepherdess loved by a shepherd and by Sir Calidore. She is carried off by brigands, rescued by Sir Calidore, and found later to be the daughter of Sir Bellamoure.

PATAVINITY. Livy, born at Patavium (Padua), was said to have some dialectal peculiarities in his writing, referred to as *patavinity*. The word came to mean provincialism in style.

PATHETIC FALLACY. This was first named by Ruskin in *Modern Painters* (1888):

> All violent feelings . . . produce in us a falseness in all our impressions of external things, which I would generally characterize as the 'Pathetic Fallacy'.

The commonest form is seen in the tendency of poets to ascribe human feelings to inanimate objects. Leigh Hunt noticed how the Greek pastoral poets made floods and flowers sympathize with human woe. Later poets were 'for ever hearing tongues in trees'.
In *The Giaour*, Byron says of a cypress:

> Dark tree, still sad when others' grief is fled,
> The only constant mourner o'er the dead!

PATHOS. Greek *páthos*, experience, suffering, emotion. The quality in writing which evokes pity or sadness. It is therefore an element of tragedy, removed itself from true tragedy. Dickens shows himself to be a master of pathos in *The Old Curiosity Shop*.

PATOIS.   French, origin unknown.   A dialect of common people, far removed from the literary language.

PATRON.   Latin *patrōnus*, from *patĕr*, father.   One who gives influential support to a person, a cause, or an art.   Lord Chesterfield received with neglect Johnson's 'Plan' of his Dictionary, but commended it upon its publication.   Thereupon, on 7th February 1755, Johnson wrote the famous letter:

> Is not a Patron, my Lord, one who looks with unconcern on a man struggling for life in the water, and, when he has reached ground, encumbers him with help?   The notice which you have been pleased to take of my labours, had it been early, had been kind; but it has been delayed till I am indifferent, and cannot enjoy it; till I am solitary, and cannot impart it; till I am known, and do not want it.

PATTERN.   Latin *patrōnus*, in sense of archetype, model.   In poetry, pattern is the verse form expressed both through the sense and through the sound and movement of the words.   In *Practical Criticism*, I. A. Richards makes this comment:

> The pattern is only a convenience, though an invaluable one; it indicates the general movement of the rhythm; it gives a model, a central line, from which variations in the movement take their direction and gain an added significance; it gives both poet and reader a firm support, a fixed point of orientation in the indefinitely vast world of possible rhythms; it has other virtues of a psychological order; but it has no compulsory powers, and there is no good reason whatever to accord it them.

PATTERN POEMS.   *See* CARMEN FIGURATUM, ALTAR POEM, *and* EMBLEM BOOK.

PAUSE.   Greek *paûsis*, from *paúein*, to make cease.   This is a break in the movement of verse.   It comes most often at the end of every line, but pauses within the line are one great element in the varied organic rhythm of poetry.   The opening lines of *Paradise Lost* show Milton's infinite variety in its use:

> Of Mans First Disobedience, | and the Fruit |
> Of that Forbidden Tree, | whose mortal tast
> Brought Death | into the World, | and all our woe, |
> With loss of *Eden*, | till one greater Man
> Restore us, | and regain | the blissful Seat, |

Sing | Heav'nly Muse, | that on the secret top
Of *Oreb*, | or of *Sinai*, | didst inspire
That Shepherd, | who first taught the chosen Seed, |
In the Beginning | how the Heav'ns and Earth
Rose out of *Chaos* |

PEDANTESQUE. Italian *pedante*, pedant. A style found, for
example, in Rabelais, which turns classical words into the native
forms. Here is a passage from Rabelais, translated by Thomas
Urquhart:

> If by fortune there be rarity or penury of pecune in our
> marsupies, and that they be exhausted of ferruginean metal
> for the shot, we dimit our codices, and oppignerate our
> vestiments, whilst we praestolate the coming of the tabellaries
> from the penates and patriotic lares.

George Loane expresses this more simply:

> If our purses lack money, we get rid of our books, pledge our
> clothes, and anticipate our patrimony.

PEDANTIC HUMOUR. Latin *paedagōg-(us)*, slave in charge of
children, preceptor, tutor. A vain and pretentious show of learning.
In *As You Like It*, Touchstone makes fun of William, a simple,
country fellow:

> Therefore, you clown, abandon — which is in the vulgar
> leave — the society — which in the boorish is company —
> of this female — which in the common is woman — which
> together is: abandon the society of this female; or, clown,
> thou perishest; or, to thy better understanding, diest; or,
> to wit, I kill thee, make thee away, translate thy life into
> death, thy liberty into bondage. I will deal in poison with
> thee, or in bastinado, or in steel. . . .

PEELERS. A nickname first given to the Irish constabulary founded
in 1814 by Sir Robert Peel. Later applied to the English police
(cf. Bobby).

PENNY-A-LINER. A writer paid at a penny a line, or at a low rate,
for work of no literary value. A hack writer for the press.

PENNY DREADFUL. A novelette of violence, mystery, adventure,
which is cheaply produced. It is also called a 'blood', equivalent
to the American 'dime novel'. The term, penny dreadful, is not
used today. It belongs to the late nineteenth and early twentieth
centuries. G. K. Chesterton wrote an essay *In Defence of Penny
Dreadfuls*.

PENTAMETER.   Greek *pentámetros*; *pénte*, five, *métron*, a measure.
A line of verse of five metrical feet.   The iambic pentameter is the
commonest in English poetry.

> This royal throne of kings, this scepter'd isle,
> This earth of majesty, this seat of Mars,
> This other Eden, demi-paradise,
> This fortress built by Nature for herself
> Against infection . . .   *King Richard II*

PENTHEMIMERAL.   Greek, literally, consisting of five halves.   In
Latin hexameters and pentameters, penthemimeral is applied to the
caesura in the middle of the third foot.

PENULT.   Latin *paenultimus*, nearly last.   The last syllable but one
of a word.   The penult of *geocentric* is *cen*.

PERFECT RHYME.   Rhymes in which the initial consonants of the
words differ, while the stressed vowel and succeeding consonants
are the same:

> The spider's touch how exquisitely fine!
> Feels at each thread, and lives along the line.
>   Pope, *An Essay on Man*

PERIOD.   Greek *períodos*; *perí*, around, *hodós*, a way.   A complete
sentence consisting of several clauses which are so arranged that the
sense is not finished till the close.   This is effective in rhetorical
language.   In the following lines from *New Timon*, Bulwer Lytton
describes William Pitt's method:

> We hear the elaborate swell of that full strain
> Linking long periods in completest chain;
> Staying the sense, from sentence sentence grows,
> Till the last word comes clinching up the close.

In his prose classic, *Of the Laws of Ecclesiastical Politie*, Richard
Hooker uses a periodic style.   Thomas Fuller, in *Church History of
Britain*, calls it 'long and pithy, the author driving on a whole flock
of several clauses before he came to the close of a sentence'.

PERIPETEIA: PERIPETY.   Greek, literally, sudden change.

> The moment when the action of the tragedy changes its course,
> a knot or complication having arisen in the relations of the
> characters which has to be unloosed.   With Euripides the
> *peripeteia* became more complicated, striking, and abrupt.
>   Paul Harvey, *Oxford Companion to Classical Literature*

PERIPETY.   *See* PERIPETEIA.

PERIPHRASIS. Greek *periphrasis*, roundabout speech; *peri*, about, *phrásis*, speech. A roundabout form of statement; a circumlocution. Here is an example in Micawber's letter to David Copperfield:

> Hiding the ravages of care with a sickly mask of mirth, I have not informed you, this evening, that there is no hope of the remittance! Under these circumstances, alike humiliating to endure, humiliating to contemplate, and humiliating to relate, I have discharged the pecuniary liability contracted at this establishment, by giving a note of hand, made payable fourteen days after date, at my residence, Pentonville, London.

PERORATION. Latin *perōrātiō*, *perōrāre*, to bring a speech to an end; *per*, through, *ōrāre*, to speak. The conclusion of a speech. A rhetorical performance.

PERSIFLAGE. Latin *sībīlāre*, to hiss, to whistle. French *persiflage*, from *persifler*, to banter. Flippancy, raillery, banter.

PERSONA. Latin *persōna*, actor's mask, a character represented by an actor, the part any one sustains in the world or in a book.

> I wandered lonely as a cloud
> That floats on high o'er vales and hills,
> When all at once I saw a crowd,
> A host, of golden daffodils;
> Beside the lake, beneath the trees,
> Fluttering and dancing in the breeze.

In this poem the *I* is not Wordsworth, but the *persona*, a projection of the poet into another person. The incident, which Wordsworth recorded in verse, occurred on 15th April 1802, when he was walking with his sister Dorothy from Ullswater to Dove Cottage.

PERSONIFICATION. Latin *persōna*, actor's mask, character acted, a human being; *personāre*, to sound through. The representation of inanimate objects or abstract ideas as persons, or endowed with personal attributes, as in, 'Let the floods clap their hands'.

Personification, which is a kind of metaphor, is one of the most frequent resources of poetry. I. A. Richards says, in *Practical Criticism*:

> There are indeed very good reasons why poetry should personify. The structure of language and the pronouns, verbs and adjectives that come most naturally to us, constantly invite us to personify. And, to go deeper, our attitudes, feelings, and ways of thought about inanimate things are moulded upon and grow out of our ways of

thinking and feeling about one another. Our minds have developed with other human beings always in the foreground of our consciousness; we are shaped, mentally, by and through our dealings with other people. No wonder then if what we have to say about inanimate objects constantly presents itself in a form only appropriate, if strict sense is our sole consideration, to persons and human relations.

> The fog comes
> on little cat feet.
>
> Carl Sandburg, *Fog*

PERSPECTIVE. Medieval Latin *perspectīva*, from *perspicĕre*, to see through. To have a true view of events and circumstances; to see them in proper relative proportion throughout a literary work.

PETRARCHAN SONNET. *See* SONNET.

PETRARCHISM. The style introduced by Petrarch, the Italian poet and humanist (1304–1374). He is today perhaps most famous for a long series of love-poems. Petrarch had a passion for formal perfection. In *The Arte of English Poesie*, 1589, Richard Puttenham says of the poets of the new courtly verse in England, 'Their conceits were lofty, their styles stately, their conveyance cleanly, their terms proper, their metre sweet and well proportioned, in all imitating very naturally and studiously their Master Francis Petrarcha.'

PHENOMENON. Greek *phainómenon*, from *phaínesthai*, to appear. A fact connected with the external form of things perceived by the senses or the mind. Something known by observation or experience. A rare, remarkable fact or occurrence.

PHILIPPIC. Greek *philippikós* (*Phílippos*, Philip). Any speech which denounces someone in harsh and bitter invective. The term derives from the orations of Demosthenes against Philip of Macedon; hence applied to Cicero's orations against Mark Antony.

PHILISTINE. Greek *Philístinoi*, Hebrew *p'lishtīm*, plural name of tribe, cognate with *Palestine*. One of the ancient inhabitants of south-west Palestine, enemies of the Israelites. Matthew Arnold singled out as Philistines those who believed that wealth indicated greatness, with no concern 'for art, beauty, culture, or spiritual things'.

PHILOSOPHY. Greek *philosophia*, love of wisdom. The study of ultimate realities and general principles; the system of theories on the nature of things or of rules for the conduct of life.

PHONETIC. Greek *phōnētikós*; *phōnētós*, to be spoken. Connected with, relating to, the sounds of human speech. *Phonetics* is a branch of linguistic science which deals with speech-sounds, and the way in which they are formed by the organs of speech.

PHONETIC ALPHABET. Greek *phōnētikós*, from *phōnē*, sound. Greek *álpha bêta*, A B; Hebrew *āleph*, ox, and *bēth*, house, from Phoenician symbols. In his preface to Professor R. A. Wilson's *The Miraculous Birth of Language*, Bernard Shaw expresses at length his own plan for a new English phonetic alphabet. He would discard useless grammar, and spell phonetically. 'There is nothing for it', he says, 'but to design twenty-four new consonants and eighteen new vowels, making in all a new alphabet of forty-two letters, and use it side by side with the present lettering until the better ousts the worse.' He concludes by saying that if the introduction of this alphabet costs a civil war he would not grudge it.

PHOTOGRAVURE. A hybrid, from Greek *phôs*, light, and French from *gravure*, engraving. A picture produced from a photographic negative transferred to a metal plate and etched in. A method of printing from etched copper plates.

PHRASAL VERB. The sense of a phrasal verb is completed by an adverb or a preposition, as *run out, fall in, jump up*.

PHYLACTERY. Greek *phulaktérion*, amulet. Vellum strips inscribed with passages taken from the Scriptures, enclosed in a leather case, and worn by the ancient Jews. There are two, one fastened to the forehead and the other to the arm, with leather thongs. The purpose of the phylacteries was to remind them to keep the law. It is also a term for an amulet or talisman.

PICARESQUE. Spanish *picaro*, rogue, knave. Resembling and related to rogues. A form of novel with a rogue for hero, who remains unchanged throughout, was invented in Spain in the sixteenth century. It became widely popular following the success of an anonymous work *La vida de Lazarillo de Tormes* (*c.* 1554). The first book of this type in English was *The Unfortunate Traveller, or the Life of Jack Wilton*, by Thomas Nashe (1594).

In *History of English Literature*, J. A. Jusserand says the picaresque hero is 'faithless, shameless, if not joyless, the plaything of fortune, by turns valet, gentleman, courtier, thief. We follow him in all societies. This hero has necessarily little conscience and still less heart.'

Gil Blas by Le Sage is the most famous picaresque story in French. Defoe portrays a picaroon in *Captain Singleton* and

Colonel Jack. The style is followed by Fielding in *Jonathan Wild* and by Smollett in *Ferdinand Count Fathom*.

PICAROON. Spanish *picaro*, rogue. A knave, thief, brigand. Also a pirate, corsair.

PICTORIAL METHOD. *See* PANORAMIC METHOD.

PIDGIN-ENGLISH: PIGEON-. A Chinese perversion of the English word 'business'. A jargon used in China, New Guinea, and the South Sea Islands between native inhabitants and Europeans. It consists of English words, oddly pronounced, with Chinese, Malay, Hindustani and other vernaculars arranged to the Chinese idiom.

PIERROT. French *Pierrot*, the stock character of French pantomime, diminutive of *Pierre*, Peter. Applied today, in English, to a wandering minstrel with a whitened face and a loosely fitting dress.

PINDARIC ODE. In English verse, the Pindaric Ode was invented by Abraham Cowley, named after the great Greek lyric poet Pindar. It is characterized by the varied number of feet in different lines, and the irregular position of the rhyming words. *Alexander's Feast* by Dryden is a fine example.

PIRACY. Greek *peirāteía*, piracy, from *peirāt-(és)*, pirate. To reproduce a published work in infringement of copyright. An edition of a book taken without leave from one country and edited in another is called a pirated edition. In *Five Hundred Years of Printing*, S. H. Steinberg says:

> Piracy was as old as the printing trade itself. It was in vain that, as early as 1525, Luther attacked these literary 'high-waymen and thieves', for the sure gain to be extracted from the reprint of marketable books was stronger than moral scruples. The Signoria of Venice was the first in 1492 to safeguard a printer against unauthorized issues of his books by others. The first effective dam against piracy was erected by the English Copyright Act of 1709. . . . The Berne Convention of 1886 established the principle of international reciprocity of rights. The Universal Copyright Convention of 1955, sponsored by UNESCO, has eventually provided a system of international copyright protection (from which only the Communist countries keep aloof).

PLAGIARISM. Latin *plagiārius*, kidnapper. To take and use another person's thoughts, writings, as one's own. 'Borrowing,' says Milton in *Eikonoklastes*, 'if it be not bettered by the borrower, among good authors is accounted plagiarie.' This partnership and community of goods has always been allowed to poets and other writers. It has been claimed that among the mighty plagiarists are Molière, Sterne, Dumas, and Disraeli.

PLAINSONG. Translation of medieval Latin *cantus plānus*, even, level singing.

> The large body of traditional vocal music of the Western Christian Church, composed in the medieval mode. Plainsong rhythm is the free rhythm of speech, arising from the unmetrical nature of the words to be recited in unison — psalms, prayers, and the like. The Ambrosian plainsong of Milan was gradually supplanted by the Roman form, which acquired the name of Gregorian chant in the sixth century A.D.
>
> Percy A. Scholes, *Oxford Dictionary of Music*

PLAINT. Latin *plangĕre*, to beat the breast; *planctum*, lament. A lamentation in verse.

PLANH. In the poetry of Provence, a song of mourning for a patron who has died. It praised his virtues beyond those of people who remain.

PLANOGRAPHY. Latin *plānus*, level, flat. Smooth-surface printing as distinguished from letterpress or intaglio printing. The most common method of planography for book production is called offset printing.

PLATITUDE. French, coined from *plat*, flat, dull. An empty, dull statement made as if it were important. In *Hamlet*, Polonius utters many platitudes when he says goodbye to his son Laertes:

> Give every man thy ear, but few thy voice;
> Take each man's censure, but reserve thy fancy.
> Costly thy habit as thy purse can buy,
> But not express'd in fancy; rich, not gaudy
> For the apparel oft proclaims the man . . .
> Neither a borrower nor lender be;
> For loan oft loses both itself and friend.

PLATONIC LOVE. 'Love of a purely spiritual character, free from sensual desire. *Amor Platonicus* was used by the Florentine Marsilio Ficino (1433–1499), synonymously with *Amor Socraticus*, to denote the kind of interest in young men which was imputed to Socrates; cf. the last few pages of Plato's "Symposium". As thus originally used it had no reference to women.' (*Oxford English Dictionary*)

PLATONISM.   Paul Harvey says that Plato's central conception is

> ... the existence of a world of ideas, divine types, or forms of material objects, which ideas are alone real and permanent, while individual material things are but their ephemeral and imperfect imitations.   Of this ideal world the Form of Good is the highest and brightest point.   Perfect virtue consists in wisdom and science — knowledge, that is, of the Good, which implies the effort to realize it.   This perfect virtue is given to very few.   Ordinary practical virtue consists in conduct in accordance with man's true nature, developed by education, which represents the constraint of the State's laws.

PLAY.   Anglo-Saxon *plegian*, to play.   A literary composition in dramatic form designed to be performed on a stage by actors.

> When learning's triumph o'er her barb'rous foes
> First rear'd the Stage, immortal Shakespeare rose;
> Each change of many-colour'd life he drew,
> Exhausted worlds, and then imagin'd new:
> Existence saw him spurn her bounded reign,
> And panting Time toil'd after him in vain.
>
> Samuel Johnson, *Prologue at the Opening of the Theatre in Drury Lane, 1747*

PLÉIADE, LA.   A group of French poets of the latter part of the sixteenth century, consisting of Pierre de Ronsard, Joachim du Bellay, Pontus de Thiard, Jodelle, Baïf, Belleau, and Dorat.   They had the highest esteem for the writers of antiquity, and united to bring French literature and language to a classical form.   The name was taken from the Pleiades, a constellation named for the seven daughters of Atlas, first given to a group of seven Greek poets, including Theocritus, Lycophron, and Aratus.

PLEONASM.   Greek *pleonázein*, to be superfluous.   The use of more words in a sentence than are needed to express the meaning. Redundancy of expression.   The pleonastic line is often used for poetic effect, as in Antony's speech to the crowd in *Julius Caesar*:

> For Brutus, as you know, was Caesar's angel:
> Judge, O you gods, how dearly Caesar loved him!
> This was the *most unkindest* cut of all;
> For when the noble Caesar saw him stab,
> Ingratitude, more strong than traitors' arms,
> Quite vanquish'd him.

PLOT. French *complot*, conspiracy. In *Aspects of the Novel*, E. M. Forster says:

> A story is a narrative of events arranged in time sequence . . .
> A plot is also a narrative of events, the emphasis falling on causality. 'The king died and then the queen died' is a story. 'The king died, and the queen died of grief' is a plot.

PODSNAPPERY. A type of self-importance and self-satisfaction. Mr. Podsnap is a character in Dickens's *Our Mutual Friend*, 'a too, too smiling large man with a fatal freshness on him'.

POEM. Greek *póēma* variant of *poiēma*, from *poieîn*, to make. A metrical composition expressing facts, thoughts, or feelings in words always rhythmical, usually metaphorical.

POETASTER. Greek *poētés*, *poiētés*, maker, poet; *-aster* suffix, expressing contempt. A paltry poet; a writer of inferior or trashy verse.

POETIC DICTION. Latin *dīcĕre*, to say. In his *Life of Dryden*, Dr. Johnson said:

> There was before the time of Dryden no poetical diction, no system of words at once refined from the grossness of domestick use, and free from the harshness of terms appropriated to particular arts. Words too familiar, or too remote, defeat the purpose of a poet. From those sounds which we hear on small or on coarse occasions we do not easily receive strong impressions or delightful images; and words to which we are nearly strangers, whenever they occur, draw that attention on themselves which they should transmit to things.

Wordsworth's choice and use of words was in deliberate dissent from Thomas Gray's statement that our poetry 'has a language peculiar to itself, to which almost everyone that has written has added something'. The opening lines of the Preface to the *Lyrical Ballads* gets to the heart of the matter, 'by fitting to metrical arrangement a selection of the real language of men in a state of vivid sensation'.

POETIC JUSTICE. Thomas Rhymer used this phrase in *Tragedies of the Last Age* (1678) to express the idea that the good are rewarded and the evil are punished. In the eighteenth century, John Dennis, supporting the idea, said that literature which was not 'a very solemn lecture' was either 'an empty amusement, or a scandalous

and pernicious libel upon the government of the world'.   In *The
Dunciad*, Pope recognized:

> Poetic Justice, with her lifted scale,
> Where, in nice balance, truth with gold she weighs,
> And solid pudding against empty praise.

POETIC LICENCE.   We accord to the poet the right to use certain
forms and structures that we should not approve in prose, such as
(*a*) archaisms, (*b*) contracted forms like *e'en*, *e'er*, (*c*) the giving of
full syllabic value to the final -*ed* in verbal terminations (as *seemèd*,
lookèd) where it would not normally be pronounced as a separate
syllable, (*d*) inversions, like 'Then *saw they* how there hove a dusky
barge' (*Morte d'Arthur*); to this we give the general name of poetic
licence.   Poetic licence does not extend to gross breaches of
grammar and idiom, to the distortion of the pronunciation of words
merely for rhyming purposes, and similar devices.

POETIC PROSE.   Elaborately constructed prose in which many of
the devices of poetry are used.   Examples are found in the work of
Pater and John Addington Symonds.   Here is the description of
love in W. S. Landor's *Pericles and Aspasia*:

> There is a gloom in deep love, as in deep water: there is a
> silence in it which suspends the foot, and the folded arms
> and the dejected head are the images it reflects.   No voice
> shakes its surface: the Muses themselves approach it with
> a tardy and a timid step, and with a low and tremulous and
> melancholy song.

James Joyce uses the complicated patterns of poetry in *Finnegans
Wake*:

> As my explanations here are probably above your under-
> standings, lattlebrattons, though as augmentatively uncom-
> parisoned as Cadwan, Cadwallan and Cadwalloner, I shall
> revert to a more expletive method which I frequently use
> when I have to sermo with muddle crass pupils.   Imagine
> for my purpose that you are a squad of urchins, snifflynosed,
> goslingnecked, clothyheaded, tangled in your lacings, tingled
> in your pants, etsiteraw etcicero.   And you, Bruno Nowlan
> take your tongue out of your inkpot!   As none of you knows
> javanese I will give all my easyfree translation out of the
> fabulist's parable.   Allaboy Minor take your head out of
> your satchel!   *Audi*, Joe Peters!   *Exaudi* facts!

POET LAUREATE.   Latin *laureātus*, crowned with laurel.   'The
title given to a poet who receives a stipend as an officer of the Royal
Household, his duty (no longer enforced) being to write court-odes.
The title formerly was sometimes conferred by certain universities.

The first poet laureate in the modern sense was Ben Jonson, but the title seems to have been first officially given to Dryden. The other laureates in chronological order are as follows: Shadwell, Tate, Rowe, Eusden, Cibber, Whitehead, T. Warton, Pye, Southey, Wordsworth, A. Tennyson, A. Austin, Bridges, Masefield.'

Paul Harvey, *Oxford Companion to English Literature*

POETRY. Greek *poiétria*, poetess; *poiëtês*, one who makes, an artificer, a poet. A good deal has been written about the nature of poetry.

Sir Philip Sidney said in *An Apologie for Poetrie*:

> Poesy therefore is an art of imitation, for so Aristotle termeth it in his word *Mimesis*, that is to say, a representing, counterfeiting, or figuring forth — to speak metaphorically, a speaking picture; with this end, to teach and delight.

In a letter to Richard West, Thomas Gray declared:

> As to matter of style, I have this to say: the language of the age is never the language of poetry; except among the French, whose verse, where the thought or image does not support it, differs in nothing from prose. Our poetry, on the contrary, has a language peculiar to itself; to which almost every one, that has written, has added something by enriching it with foreign idioms and derivatives: nay sometimes words of their composition or invention.

Wordsworth tells us in the Preface to the *Lyrical Ballads* how his poetry was written:

> I have said that poetry is the spontaneous overflow of powerful feelings: it takes its origin from emotion recollected in tranquillity: the emotion is contemplated till, by a species of reaction, the tranquillity gradually disappears, and an emotion, kindred to that which was before the subject of contemplation, is gradually produced, and does itself actually exist in the mind. In this mood successful composition generally begins, and in a mood similar to this it is carried on; but the emotion, of whatever kind, and in whatever degree, from various causes, is qualified by various pleasures, so that in describing any passions whatsoever, which are voluntarily described, the mind will, upon the whole, be in a state of enjoyment. If Nature be thus cautious to preserve in a state of enjoyment a being so employed, the Poet ought to profit by the lesson held forth to him, and ought especially to take care, that, whatever passions he communicates to his Reader, those passions, if his Reader's mind be sound and vigorous, should always be accompanied with an overbalance of pleasure.

In *A Defence of Poetry*, Shelley wrote:

> Poetry awakens and enlarges the mind by a thousand un-apprehended combinations of thought . . . The great secret of morals is Love; or a going out of our own nature, and an identification of ourselves with the beautiful which exists in thought, action, or person, not our own. The great instrument of moral good is the imagination. Poetry enlarges the circumference of the Imagination.

Wordsworth also said:

> The Poet binds together by passion and knowledge the vast empire of human society, as it is spread over the whole earth, and over all time . . . Poetry is the first and last of all knowledge, it is as immortal as the heart of man.

POETRY AND EXPERIENCE. In *New Bearings in English Poetry*, F. R. Leavis has said, 'Poetry can communicate the actual quality of experience with a subtlety and precision unapproachable by any other means.' We can only share this experience by an appreciation of the words, for it is the words which stand for all that the poet has felt, for all that has passed through his imagination. Although poetry and prose both use words, prose uses chiefly the meaning, whereas poetry uses *all* the qualities of words. Coleridge had this in mind when, writing of poetry, he said, 'Be it observed, however, that I include in the meaning of a word not only its correspondent object but likewise all the associations which it recalls.' These associations have been likened to the ripples caused when a stone is dropped into a pool; they can spread in widening circles to the limits of the reader's mind.

POETRY AND PROSE. In *Form in Modern Poetry*, Herbert Read says:

> Poetry is properly speaking a transcendental quality — a sudden transformation which words assume under a particular influence — and we can no more define this quality than we can define a state of grace. We can only make a number of distinctions, of which the main is the broad but elemental one between poetry and prose. I use the word 'elemental' deliberately, because I believe the difference between poetry and prose to be, not one of surface qualities, not of form in any sense, not even of mode of expression, but absolutely of essence. It is not a case of the mind, in need of expression, choosing between two ways — one poetry, the other prose. There is no choice for the particular state of mind in which poetry originates. It must either seek poetic expression, or it must simply not be expressed; for an altogether lower

tension, involving a different kind of mentality, must be substituted before the activity of prose expression can intervene.

Benedetto Croce says in *The Philosophy of Giambattista Vico*:

Poetry is produced not by the mere caprice of pleasure, but by natural necessity. It is so far from being superfluous and capable of elimination, that without it thought cannot arise: it is the primary activity of the human mind. Man, before he has arrived at the stage of forming universals, forms imaginary ideas. Before he reflects with a clear mind, he apprehends with faculties confused and disturbed: before he can articulate, he sings: before speaking in prose, he speaks in verse: before using technical terms, he uses metaphors, and the metaphorical use of words is as natural to him as that which we call 'natural'.

POETRY AND TRUTH. Old English (*ǧe*)*trēowe*, faithful, trusty, honest. In *The Emperor's Clothes*, writing on this subject, Kathleen Nott says:

Plato, for instance, thought that poets had inevitably a wrong relation to their subject-matter; that they were liars, because they treated the absolute and divine, too often, in terms of the temporal and fleshly. This is an attitude which continually recurs, in whatever disguises. At the other extreme, I. A. Richards makes a sharp opposition between the scientific and the emotive use of language which implies that whatever any poet is trying to tell us, it is not in any meaningful sense true or false; its value to us is not the value of a piece of information which might enable us to correct either our actions or our direction. Then there are all the rather more negative definitions: Sidney's, that poets are not liars because they 'nothing affirm', or Coleridge's 'willing suspension of *disbelief* for the moment which constitutes poetic faith', or Dr. Leavis's 'pseudo-statements' which seem to lie somewhere in between active deceit and suspension of disbelief. But on the whole the consensus of critical opinion has been against the idea of Art for Art's sake and in favour of the belief that some highly important relation always exists between poetry and 'truth' however difficult it may be to define.

POIEMA. *See* LOGOS.

POINT. The unit of measurement for type bodies, the unit being one point or 0·01383 inch in Britain and the United States. Twelve points make one pica. The Point System replaced the older names such as long primer, brevier, english, which had been used to distinguish type sizes. This type is nine point.

POINT OF ATTACK. This term, applied to the drama, means that moment in the story when the main action really begins. This may come at the very beginning or it may be set just before the catastrophe.

POINT OF SANITY. *See* NORM.

POINT OF VIEW. In *The Craft of Fiction*, Percy Lubbock says:

> The whole intricate question of method, in the craft of fiction, I take to be governed by the question of the *point of view* — the question of the relation in which the narrator stands to the story.

The various points of view he then examines have been summed up briefly in *Aspects of the Novel*, by E. M. Forster:

> The novelist can either describe the characters from outside, as an impartial or partial onlooker; or he can assume omniscience and describe them from within; or he can place himself in the position of one of them and affect to be in the dark as to the motives of the rest; or there are certain intermediate attitudes.

POLEMIC. Greek *polemikós*, *pólemos*, war. A vigorous dispute. The practice of controversy, especially in theology (theological polemics). Polemical works were written by Richard Bentley, Richard Porson, Swift, and Milton, whose *Areopagitica* is one of the most famous.

POLITICAL NOVEL. 'Politics in a work of literature', wrote Stendhal, 'is like a pistol-shot in the middle of a concert, something loud and vulgar, and yet a thing to which it is not possible to refuse one's attention.' After this shrewd remark, we should define the political novel as one in which we take political ideas or the political milieu to be dominant. In *Politics and the Novel*, Irving Howe says:

> The political novel is peculiarly a work of internal tensions. It deals with moral sentiments, with passions and emotions; it tries, above all, to capture the quality of concrete experience. Ideology, however, is abstract, as it must be, and therefore likely to be recalcitrant whenever an attempt is made to incorporate it into the novel's stream of sensuous impression.

One of the greatest of all political novels is Dostoevsky's *The*

Possessed. Others are Koestler's *Darkness at Noon*, Malraux's *La Condition humaine*, Orwell's *1984*, Silone's *Fontamara*.

POLYGLOT BIBLE, THE.   Greek *polúglōttos*, of many tongues; *polús*, many, *glôtta*, tongue.   Edited in 1654–1657 by Brian Walton (1600–1661), Bishop of Chester, and other scholars.   It contained parts of the *Vetus Latina*, of the Ethiopic and Persian versions, with Latin translations, and an *apparatus criticus*.

POLYPHONIC PROSE.   Greek *poluphōnía*, variety of tones or sounds.   Prose which has some of the qualities of verse, especially alliteration, assonance, and rhyme.   Amy Lowell's *Can Grande's Castle*, which appeared in 1918, is a good example of this form of prose.

POLYPTOTON.   Greek, literally, repetition of a word in different cases.   A figure of speech consisting in the repetition of a word in several of its grammatical forms in the same sentence, as in these lines of Sir Philip Sidney:

> Thou art of *blood*, joy not to make things *bleed*:
> Thou fearest *death*, think they are loath to *die*.

POLYSYLLABIC HUMOUR.   Greek *polú(s)*, many, much, *sullabé*, that which holds together.   The use of long words instead of simple short ones for amusing effect; for example, to call a lie a *terminological inexactitude*, or a conjuror a *prestidigitator*.   Dickens rather affected this kind of humour.

POLYSYNDETON.   Greek *polusúndeton*, bound together.   A figure which consists in the use of a number of conjunctions close together; usually the repetition of the same conjunction.

> He has out-soared the shadow of our night;
> Envy and calumny and hate and pain,
> And that unrest which men miscall delight.
>
> Shelley, *Adonais*

POMPOSITY.   Greek, *pompé*, solemn procession, parade; *pémpein*, to convoy, escort.   Language displaying bombast, turgidness; the use of exaggerated splendour.

PONS ASINORUM.   Latin, the bridge of asses.   A name given to the fifth proposition of the first book of Euclid, the first difficult theorem, which dunces rarely get over without stumbling.

PORTMANTEAU WORD.   French; *porter*, to carry, *manteau*, a cloak.   In *Through the Looking-Glass*, Lewis Carroll applied this term to his invented words composed of two words run together and having a combined meaning. 'Well', says Humpty Dumpty to Alice, explaining the meaning of some words in the poem 'Jabberwocky', ' "*slithy*" means "lithe and slimy". "Lithe" is the same as "active". You see it's like a portmanteau — there are two meanings packed up into one word.'

James Joyce made free use of portmanteau words in *Finnegans Wake*, as, for example, 'ordinailed ungles'.

POT-BOILER. A work of literature or art which is done merely to make a living. The writer or artist who does this work.

POULTER'S MEASURE. (Poulter stands for poulterer.) This was a fanciful name for a metre consisting of lines of twelve and fourteen syllables alternately.

In *The Steele Glas*, George Gascoigne wrote, 'Poulter's measure, which giveth xii for one dozen, and xiiij for another.'

PRAGMATISM. Greek *prāgmatikós*, versed in business; *prâgma*, *prâgmatos*, deed. The matter-of-fact treatment of things. In philosophy, the doctrine that estimates any assertion solely by its practical bearing upon human interests, not upon speculation or abstract thought. William James's method of approach to metaphysics was pragmatism, as shown in his works *Pragmatism* (1907), *The Meaning of Truth* (1909).

PRECIOUS. Latin *pretiōsus*; *pretium*, price. This term, ever since Molière, has been used to describe affectation, whether in manners or in style. It is precious to use archaic words such as *certes*, *parlous*, *perchance*.

PRÉCIS. French *précis*, precise. An abstract, a summary of a work.

PREFACE. Latin *praefātiō*; *prae*, before, *fārī*, *fātus*, to speak. Something written as an introduction to a literary work, usually explaining its subject, scope, and method. Shaw's Prefaces to the plays are notable among his writings.

PRELIMS: PRELIMINARY MATTER. Latin, *praelīmināris*, *prae*, before, *līmen* (-*inis*), threshold. The introductory matter in a book which precedes the text. The conventional order of the prelims is: half-title, list of other books by the same author, frontispiece, title-page, verso (with copyright notice, publishing history, publishers' address, printers' imprint), dedication, preface, list of contents, list of illustrations, introduction. The page-numbers of the prelims are always printed as roman numerals, to distinguish them from the text and to avoid the necessity of complete re-pagination should the author add new matter (e.g. to his preface) at the page-proof stage.

PRE-RAPHAELITE BROTHERHOOD. A group of young artists and writers who, about 1850, united to resist the conventions in art and literature of their day. They wished to follow art forms in use before the time of Raphael. They expressed their views in 'The Germ'. Members of the group were John Millais, Holman Hunt, Dante Gabriel Rossetti, William Rossetti, Thomas Woolner, Frederick Stephens, and James Collinson.

PRIMARY AND SECONDARY STRESS. The emphasis which falls in ordinary speech on a strongly stressed syllable in a word is the primary stress. The emphasis falling on a lightly stressed syllable in the same word is the secondary stress. Donne's lines

> This ease controules
> The tediousness of my life

show both primary and secondary stresses in the word *tédiousnèss*, the strong stress falling on the first syllable.

PROBLEM PLAY. A drama dealing with a social problem. In the nineteenth century, this form originated in France with such plays as *Le Demi-Monde*, *Le Fils naturel* by Dumas fils. Ibsen, in Norway, had considerable influence on the development of the type elsewhere, and especially in Britain. *Widowers' Houses* and *Mrs. Warren's Profession* by Bernard Shaw, John Galsworthy's *The Silver Box* and *Justice* are other examples directing attention to 'injustices and maladjustments and preventible evils of many kinds'. This new drama is also called the *thesis* or *propaganda play*.

PROCRUSTEAN. Greek *Prokroústēs*, literally, 'the Stretcher', the surname of Polypemon or Damastes, a mythical robber of Attica, who was killed by Theseus. He tied his captives on a bed, then stretched or chopped to make them fit. The term means trying to gain uniformity by violent methods.

PROEM. Greek *prooímion*, a prelude; *pró*, before, *oîmos*, path. An introduction to a book or other form of writing; a preface; a preamble.

PROLEGOMENON: PROLEGOMENA. Greek *prolégein*, to say in advance, to preface. An introduction, preface. Specifically, an introductory treatise on some special subject. For example, T. H. Green's *Prolegomena to Ethics*.

PROLEPSIS.   Greek *prólēpsis,* a taking beforehand, anticipation; *pró,* before, *lambánein,* to take.   The anticipatory use of an epithet. A figure of speech in which an anticipated event is referred to as though it had already taken place.   The device is shown in these lines from Keats's *Isabella*:

> So the two brothers and their *murder'd* man
> Rode past fair Florence.

PROLIXITY.   Latin *prōlixus,* flowing forth, from *liquēre,* to be liquid.   Lengthy, wordy, tedious description.   Verbosity.   In *Hamlet,* Polonius is often prolix:

> My liege, and madam, to expostulate
> What majesty should be, what duty is,
> Why day is day, night night, and time is time,
> Were nothing but to waste night, day, and time.
> Therefore, since brevity is the soul of wit,
> And tediousness the limbs and outward flourishes,
> I will be brief.

PROLOGUE.   Greek *prólogos; pró,* before, *lógos,* speech.   In Greek tragedy the part before the entrance of the chorus, setting forth, in monologue or dialogue, the subject of the drama.   The preface or introduction to a discourse or performance, especially the poem introducing a play.   David Garrick wrote in his *Apprentice*:

> Prologues precede the piece — in mournful verse;
> As undertakers — walk before the hearse.

PROOF.   French *épreuve,* trial, test.   Any impression taken from a printing surface for the purpose of inspection and correction.

PROPAGANDA PLAY.   *See* PROBLEM PLAY.

PROPERTIES.   Latin *proprietās,* ownership, property.   In logic, the term means qualities, characteristics, or attributes found in all examples of a group or class of objects or events.   In classical or traditional poetry, intrinsic characteristics.

PROPRIETY.   Latin *proprietāt(em),* property, peculiar nature or quality.   Conformity with good standards of taste and correctness. Conformity with what is suitable and appropriate at the moment, as shown in various forms of poetry.

PROSAIC.   Latin *prōsa* from *prorsus,* straightforward; *prō,* forward, *vertĕre, versum,* to turn.   Like prose, unromantic, commonplace, and dull; lacking in poetic beauty.

PROSCENIUM.   Greek *proskēnion*; *pró*, before, *skēnē*, stage.

The stage of a Greek or Roman theatre on which the actors stood, between the orchestra and the wall standing at the back.   In the modern theatre it is the front part of the stage between the curtain and the orchestra, also the curtain and the arch holding it, which divides the stage from the auditorium.   H. C. Wyld, *Universal English Dictionary*

PROSE.   Latin *prōsa*, in phrase *prōsa orātiō*, straight, direct, unadorned speech; from *prōrsus*, straightforward, direct for *prō versus*, turned forward.   Language, spoken or written, as in ordinary usage, not marked by metre or rhyme.

In *Table Talk*, Coleridge said:

I wish our clever young poets would remember my homely definitions of prose and poetry; that is, prose = words in their best order; poetry = the *best* words in the best order.

In *Preface to Fables*, Dryden wrote:

What judgment I had increases rather than diminishes; and thoughts, such as they are, come crowidng in so fast upon me, that my only difficulty is to choose or reject; to run them into verse or to give them the other harmony of prose.

Oscar Wilde, in *The Critic as Artist*, declared:

Meredith is a prose Browning, and so is Browning.   He used poetry as a medium for writing prose.

PROSE POEM.   A prose work of poetical style.   The prose poem first appeared in 1836 in *Gaspard of the Night* by Aloysius Bertrand. A few years later Baudelaire wrote *Little Poems in Prose*.

PROSODY.   Greek *prosōidía*, a song sung to accompaniment.   The study of versification, covering metre, rhythm, rhyme, and verse-forms.

PROSOPOPOEIA.   Greek *prosōpopoiía*, from *prósōpon*, a face, person, and *poieîn*, to make.   'A rhetorical figure by which (1) past events are described as though actually taking place, as by use of the historical present; or (2) dead persons are represented as present and speaking, and inanimate objects as though they had life and feeling; or (3) introduction of a dead person as alive, or of an absent person as present and speaking.'   H. C. Wyld, *Universal English Dictionary*.

PROTAGONIST.   Greek *prōtagōnistēs*, first actor in a drama.   The chief actor or character.   The Greek tragic poet was restricted to three actors, known as *protagonist, deuteragonist, tritagonist*: first, second, and third actor. When contests between actors were established, only the protagonists were considered.

PROTASIS.   Greek *prótasis*, a stretching forward; *pró*, before, *tásis*, a stretching. That which is put forward, a proposition.

In the Greek drama the first part of a play, in which the characters are introduced and the situation explained. The *protasis* is thus opposed to the *epitasis* and the *catastrophe*.

It is also the first subordinate clause of a conditional sentence, here opposed to *apodosis*.

PROTHALAMION.   A coined word from Greek *pró*, before, *thálamos*, bridal chamber. A 'spousal verse' written by Edmund Spenser in 1596 in celebration of the double marriage of the Lady Elizabeth and the Lady Katherine Somerset, daughters of the Earl of Worcester. Spenser invented the name on the model of 'Epithalamion'.

PROTHESIS.   Greek *próthesis*, a setting out, a placing before. The addition of an expletive letter or syllable at the beginning of a word to give emphasis or modify the meaning, as in *yclad, bemock*.

PROVERB.   Latin *prōverbium*, from *verbum*, word. A short familiar saying expressing a supposed truth or moral lesson. In the Old Testament the *Proverbs* consist of maxims attributed to Solomon and others.

PROVERBE DRAMATIQUE.   Alfred de Musset (1810–1857) applied this term to some of his plays in which the theme is pungently expressed in the title, e.g. *On ne badine pas avec l'amour* (One does not jest with love).

PROVINCIALISM.   A word or phrase peculiar to a province of a country. A limited intellectual outlook. Failure to consider questions from a national point of view. In *Life of Nathaniel Hawthorne*, Henry James said Thoreau was 'worse than provincial — he was parochial'.

PRUNING POEM.   In his essay 'The Poem as Hieroglyph', Joseph H. Summers quotes George Herbert's *Paradise* as a pruning poem:

> I blesse thee, Lord, because I GROW
> Among thy trees, which in a ROW
> To thee both fruit and order OW.

What open force, or hidden CHARM
Can blast my fruit, or bring me HARM
While the inclosure is thine ARM?

Inclose me still for fear I START.
Be to me rather sharp and TART,
Then let me want thy hand & ART.

When thou dost greater judgements SPARE
And with thy knife but prune and PARE
Ev'n fruitfull trees more fruitfull ARE.

Such sharpnes shows the sweetest FREND:
Such cuttings rather heal than REND:
And such beginnings touch their END.

He says:

> The second and third rhymes of each stanza are formed by
> 'paring' off the first consonant of the preceding rhyme. . . .
> The 'pruned' rhymes do compel the reader to 'see' what
> the poem is saying concerning the positive function of
> suffering. The meaning is traditional, of course. The fate
> of the 'unprofitable vineyard' was destruction rather than
> pruning. By changing the image from the vine to the
> English orchard, Herbert related the 'pruning' more
> immediately to his readers' experience, but the point is the
> same: the surgical knife is necessary for the order which
> produces fruit. . . . For the religious man of the seventeenth
> century 'end' nearly always implied purpose as well as
> finality. 'And such beginnings touch their END' means
> that God's pruning causes the fruits of righteousness which
> are the end of man's creation. It also implies that the
> cutting away of the fruitless branches images the final
> 'cutting away' of the body and the release of the soul at death.

PSALM. Greek *psalmós*, twanging of strings, from *psállein*, to
twitch. A devotional song or hymn, especially one of those included
in the Old Testament *Book of Psalms*.

PSALTER. Greek *psaltērion*, stringed instrument, used in Church
Latin and Greek for psalm-book. It has been replaced in its
original sense by the later borrowed *psaltery*. The Book of Psalms,
especially the Psalms arranged for use in daily service. Any special
version of the Psalms as *Latin, English Prayer-book*.

PSEUDEPIGRAPHA. Greek from *pseûdos*, a lie, falsehood, and
epigraphē, an inscription. 'A collective term for books or writings
bearing a false title, or ascribed to another than the true author;

specifically applied to certain Jewish writings ascribed to various patriarchs and prophets of the Old Testament.' (*Oxford English Dictionary*)

PSEUDONYM. Greek *pseudo-*, false, *ónoma*, name. An assumed name, as by an author. A nom-de-plume.

PSEUDO-STATEMENT. *See* POETRY AND TRUTH.

PSYCHIC DISTANCE. *See* DISTANCE.

PSYCHOLOGICAL NOVEL. Greek *psūkhē*, life, breath, soul. A novel which is concerned mainly with the mental and emotional lives of its characters. Outstanding examples are found in the work of James Joyce, Dorothy Richardson, D. H. Lawrence, Virginia Woolf.

PUDDER. *See* GOBBLEDYGOOK.

PUFFERY. Old English *pyffan*, imitation of sound expelling breath. Advertisement disguised as honest praise. Criticism by a clique or coterie overpraising the work of a friend in hope of a suitable reward. In Sheridan's play *The Critic*, the false critic is named Mr. Puff. This passage is taken from the play:

> Yes, sir, puffing is of various sorts; the principal are, the puff direct, the puff preliminary, the puff collateral, the puff collusive, and the puff oblique, or puff by implication.

PUN. *See* PARONOMASIA.

PURITAN. One of the party of English Protestants who seceded from the Reformed Church under Elizabeth, demanding that it should be purified from those unscriptural forms and ceremonies retained from the unreformed Church and interfering in religion. The Puritan acknowledged the sole authority of the 'pure Word of God' without 'note or comment'.

The term is not now used as one of abuse, but is applied to a person who observes the strictest morality.

PURPLE PATCH. Latin *purpura*, Greek *porphúrā*, name of the shellfish, also called *murex*, which gave the Tyrian purple dye. A heavily ornate passage in a literary composition, such as this from Oscar Wilde's *The Young King*:

> Facing the window stood a curiously wrought cabinet with lacquer panels of powdered and mosaiced gold, on which were placed some delicate goblets of Venetian glass, and a

cup of dark-veined onyx. Pale poppies were broidered on the silk coverlet of the bed, as though they had fallen from the tired hands of sleep, and tall reeds of fluted ivory bare up the velvet canopy, from which great tufts of ostrich plumes sprang, like white foam, to the pallid silver of the fretted ceiling.

PYRRHIC. Greek *purrhikhios*, from *purrhikhē*, said to be named from *Púrrhikhos*, the inventor of a war-dance of the ancient Greeks. A metrical foot used in the war-song, accompanying the dance, was called a *pyrrhic foot*, consisting of two unstressed syllables. This line is from Shelley's *Adonais*:

$$\text{Oh weep for Adona} | \overset{\smile}{\text{is}} \, \overset{\smile}{\text{the}} \, | \text{ quick dreams} \ldots$$

PYRRHIC VICTORY. One gained at too great a cost to the victor, like that of Pyrrhus, King of Epirus (318–272 B.C.) over the Romans at Asculum. He was said to exclaim, 'One more such victory and we are lost.'

Q

QUADRIVIUM. Latin, literally, a place where four ways meet, crossroads. In medieval times, the more advanced part of the university course of seven liberal arts, namely, the four subjects: *arithmetic, geometry, music,* and *astronomy.*

QUANTITATIVE VERSE. From Latin *quantus,* how much, how many. This verse in classical prosody depends upon the quantity of time required to utter a syllable; therefore, duration was more important than emphasis.

QUANTITY. Latin *quantitātem,* from *quantus,* how much, how many. 'In Greek and Latin prosody, syllables are classed as either long or short, according to the time taken in pronouncing them.' George Loane goes on to say, in *Short Handbook of Literary Terms:*

> Feet are defined as arrangements of long and short syllables, not, as in English, of syllables accented and unaccented; the nature of a syllable is thus called its quantity. Dryden and Cowper went so far as to say that they found every syllable as clearly long or short in English as in Latin or Greek; and Tennyson knew the quantities of every English word, except perhaps 'scissors'; but nobody has been able to write down the rules.

Tennyson expressed his views on English hexameters in these lines:

> These lame | hexam|eters the | strong winged |
>   music of | Homer!
> No — but a | most bur|lesque ‖ barbarous |
>   experi|ment.
> Was there a | harsher | sound ever | heard, ye |
>   Muses, in | England?
> When did a | frog coars|er ‖ croak upon |
>   our Heli|con?

QUART D'HEURE. French, literally, a quarter of an hour. In the French theatre, a brief play, a curtain-raiser.

QUARTO. Latin (*in*) *quarto,* (in) one-fourth. Folded into four leaves or eight pages (often written 4to). A book of sheets so folded in one of three standard sizes.

Some of Shakespeare's plays were printed separately in quarto.

238

Here the reference is actually to the size of the page, but in effect it refers to the first, second, third, etc., edition of the individual play.

QUATERNARIUS. Latin, consisting of four each. A metrical line of four iambic or trochaic feet.

> The year is going, let him go;
> Ring out the false, ring in the true.
>
> Tennyson, *In Memoriam*

QUATORZAIN. Latin *quattuordecim,* fourteen. French *quatorzaine,* a set of fourteen. A poem, consisting of fourteen lines, which does not follow the strict rules of the sonnet.

QUATRAIN. Latin *quattuor,* four. A stanza consisting of four lines, which may have various rhyme schemes. In English verse the quatrain is the commonest stanza form:

> I strove with none; for none was worth my strife;
> Nature I loved, and, next to Nature, Art;
> I warmed both hands before the fire of life;
> It sinks, and I am ready to depart.
>
> W. S. Landor, *Finis*

QUINARIUS. Latin, consisting of five. A metrical line of five iambic feet, as in blank verse.

> For you and I are past our dancing days.
>
> *Romeo and Juliet*

QUINTAIN. Latin *quintus,* fifth. A stanza consisting of five lines which may have variety of rhyme and length of line:

> Go, lovely Rose!
> Tell her, that wastes her time and me,
> That now she knows,
> When I resemble her to thee,
> How sweet and fair she seems to be.
>
> Edmund Waller, *Go, lovely Rose*

QUINTESSENTIAL WORDS. In *The Poetic Approach to Language*, V. K. Gokak says:

> Perhaps the best part of the vocabulary of poetic language consists of words which sum up the significance of the poems in which they occur in their entirety, and sometimes even of the personality of poets and their epochs. They seem to be quintessential words — the poems are but an expansion of the idea, the emotion and the image which they convey.

The word *melancholy* was current in Middle English (from Old French *melancholie*, from Latin *melancholia*, from Greek *melagkholia*, 'choleric humour', from *melan-*, stem of *mélas*, 'black'). It is used for the first time in Robert Mannyng's *Handlyng of Synne* (1303) in the sense 'the condition of having too much black bile'; the disease supposed to result from this condition. Burton's *The Anatomy of Melancholy* (1621) purposes to be a medical work, the author's intention being to describe the cause and cure of that melancholy which is 'an inbred malady in every one of us'.

Melancholy became a favourite theme with dramatists during the first decade of the seventeenth century. Shakespeare presented a study of it in *Hamlet* . . . In his madrigal, *When as she smiles* (1614), Drummond of Hawthorden writes: 'A sweet Melancholie my senses keepes'. In Milton's *Comus*, the Attendant Spirit starts his narration of how he heard the voice of the Lady lost in the forest, with the lines:

> I sate me down to watch upon a bank
> . . . and began
> Wrapt in a pleasing fit of melancholy
> To meditate my rural minstrelsie,
> Till fancy had her fill . . .

The two meanings of melancholy — 'sadness' and 'meditation' — converge in Keats. The word acquires a profound significance in his *Ode on Melancholy* . . .

Quintessential words are the flesh and blood of poetry — a harmony of image and emotion, of instinctive and intuitive perception.

QUIP. Short for the obsolete *quippy*, Latin *quippe*, forsooth. A smart repartee, a sarcastic remark, a fanciful conceit.

QUOTATION. Latin *quotāre*, to mark off chapters and verses by numbers, from *quotus*, how many. A passage quoted from a literary work. In *Modern English Usage*, H. W. Fowler says:

To each reader those quotations are agreeable that neither strike him as hackneyed nor rebuke his ignorance by their complete novelty, but rouse dormant memories.

Q.V. Latin *quod vide*, which see (in references).

R

RABELAISIAN. From the name of François Rabelais (*c.* 1490–1553). Resembling the exuberance of imagination and language of Rabelais, with the same coarseness of humour and human satire.

RAISONNEUR. *See* CONFIDANT.

RANGE. Old French *ranger*, earlier *rengier*, from *rang*, rank. The range or scope of writers varies greatly. In *The Art of Fiction*, Henry James wrote:

> Experience is never limited, and it is never complete; it is an immense sensibility, a kind of huge spider-web of the finest silken threads suspended in the chamber of consciousness, and catching every air-borne particle in its tissue.

In *Aspects of the Novel*, E. M. Forster, in his practical way, says:

> Then why is *War and Peace* not depressing? Probably because it has extended over space as well as over time, and the sense of space until it terrifies us is exhilarating, and leaves behind it an effect like music. After one has read *War and Peace* for a bit, great chords begin to sound, and we cannot say exactly what struck them. They do not arise from the story, though Tolstoy is quite as interested in what comes next as Scott, and quite as sincere as Bennett. They do not come from the episodes nor yet from the characters. They come from the immense area of Russia, over which episodes and characters have been scattered, from the sum-total of bridges and frozen rivers, forests, roads, gardens, fields, which accumulate grandeur and sonority after we have passed them. Many novelists have the feeling for place — Five Towns, Auld Reekie, and so on. Very few have the sense of *space*, and the possession of it ranks high in Tolstoy's divine equipment. Space is the lord of *War and Peace*, not time.

REALISM. Latin *reālis*, belonging to the thing itself (especially as used in medieval philosophy). In scholasticism, the theory that general ideas or universals have an existence independent of the individual mind, of which Thomas Aquinas was the chief exponent. Paul Harvey says, in *The Oxford Companion to English Literature*, 'Duns Scotus also maintained realism in an extreme form. Also in the arts a loosely used term meaning truth to the observed facts of life (especially when they are gloomy).'

REALISM OF PRESENTATION. In *An Experiment in Criticism*, C. S. Lewis defines this as:

> ... the art of bringing something close to us, making it palpable and vivid, by sharply observed or sharply imagined detail. We may cite as examples the dragon 'sniffing along the stone' in *Beowulf*; Layamon's Arthur, who, on hearing that he was king, sat very quiet and 'one time he was red and one time he was pale'; the pinnacles in *Gawain* that looked as if they were 'pared out of paper'; Jonah going into the whale's mouth 'like a mote at a minster door'; the fairy bakers in *Huon* rubbing the paste off their fingers; Falstaff on his death-bed plucking at the sheet; Wordsworth's little streams heard at evening but 'inaudible by daylight'.

REASON. *See* AGE OF REASON.

RECEIVED PRONUNCIATION. In the *Universal English Dictionary*, H. C. Wyld defines this as 'recognized as conforming to a standard, as being in accordance with common practice'.

RECENSION. Latin *recensiō*, from *recensēre*, to survey, review, revise. The revision of a text in a critical manner. A version of a text resulting from such revision.

RECESSIVE ACCENT: STRESS. Latin *recessus*, from *recēdĕre*, *recess-*, to recede, withdraw. In the speaking of poetry, an accent which falls on the first syllable of a word normally accented on the second syllable. This line from *Love's Labour's Lost* provides an instance of recessive accent:

> ⏑ ⁄ ⏑ ⁄ ⏑ ⁄ ⏑ ⁄ ⏑ ⁄
> The extreme parts of time extremely forms
> All causes to the purpose of his speed.

RECONDITE. Latin *recondĕre*, from *condĕre*, to put away, hide. This word stresses the idea of depth or profundity, especially with reference to knowledge beyond ordinary understanding.

RECTO. Latin *recto (folio)*, on the right, *folium*, a leaf or page. Any right-hand page of an open book, front of the leaf. Always the odd page.

REDACTION. French *rédaction*, editing. The process of editing, preparing a work for publication.

REDUCTIO AD ABSURDUM. Latin, an obviously absurd conclusion. The process whereby an argument or analogy is rendered absurd by its being stretched to a point where it ceases to be applicable.

REDUNDANT VERSE. *See* ACATALECTIC.

REDUPLICATION. Latin *reduplicātiō*; *duplicāre*, to double, from *duo*, two, *plicāre*, to fold. Repetition in word-formation. In *The English Language*, Ernest Weekley says:

> Another method of forming new words is by reduplication, either with variation of the vowel, e.g. *see-saw* (from the sawyer's movement), *shilly-shally* (from shall I?), or of the consonant, e.g. *roly-poly* (from *roll*), *namby-pamby* (from *Namby-Pamby*, the nickname of Ambrose Philips, an early eighteenth-century poetaster).

REFERENCE MARKS. Footnotes are often indicated by the following marks, which appear in the order shown: * (asterisk), † (dagger), ‡ (double dagger), § (section mark), ‖ (parallel), ¶ (paragraph mark). If more than six notes are required to a page, these signs can be doubled (**, ††, etc.) or trebled (***, †††, etc.). When a large number of reference marks are used, however, the more usual method of indicating them is by the use of superior figures. But the reference marks shown above are always used in mathematical works, to avoid any confusion with the workings.

REFERENTIAL LANGUAGE. *See* EMOTIVE.

REFLECTION. Latin *reflectĕre*, to bend back. The act of meditation, profound consideration. In the *Preface to the Lyrical Ballads to the Edition of 1815*, Wordsworth said:

> Reflection makes the poet acquainted with the value of actions, images, thoughts and feelings; and assists the sensibility in perceiving their connection with each other.

REFOCILLATE. Late Latin *refocillāre*, to revive, reanimate. To warm into life again. The word occurs in *Brief Lives* by John Aubrey when writing of William Prynne:

> His manner of studie was thus: he wore a long quilt cap, which came, two or three, at least, inches over his eies, which served him as an umbrella to defend his eies from the light. About every three houres his man was to bring him a roll and a pott of ale to refocillate his wasted spirits.

REFRAIN. Old French *refraindre*, to restrain, check; also to repeat. Low Latin from *refringĕre*, to break back. A refrain or burden is a phrase or line recurring usually after each stanza, sometimes within the stanza. It was common in the old ballads with the value of an incantation.

> This ae nighte, this ae nighte,
> — *Every nighte and alle,*
> Fire and fleet and candle-lighte,
> *And Christe receive thy saule.*
>
> When thou from hence away art past,
> — *Every nighte and alle,*
> To Whinny-muir thou com'st at last:
> *And Christe receive thy saule.*

The memorable feature of Spenser's *Prothalamion* is the refrain 'Sweet Thames, run softly, till I end my Song'; he uses a more subtle refrain in his *Epithalamion*, being many variations of:

> So I unto my selfe alone will sing;
> The woods shall to me answer, and my Eccho ring.

REGIONALISM. Latin *regĕre*, to direct. The representation in literature of a particular region, influencing the lives of the characters in the work. The novels of Thomas Hardy set in the countryside of Dorset, which he called Wessex, and the novels of the Five Towns of Arnold Bennett, set in the Potteries, are examples of regional literature.

RENAISSANCE: RENASCENCE. The great revival of learning under the influence of Greek and Latin art and literature, which began in Italy in the fourteenth century. It continued throughout Europe during the fifteenth and sixteenth centuries, emphasizing the vital importance of the intellect, and the conviction that human affairs do not become intelligible until they are seen as a whole.

REPETEND. Latin *repetendum*, (that) which is to be repeated. A recurring word or phrase. It refers to the repeated parts of a poem, a kind of refrain which may be varied in placing for dramatic effect. A striking example is the use of 'glittering eye' and 'skinny hand' by Coleridge in *The Rime of the Ancient Mariner*.

REPETITION. Latin *repetĕre*, to try again, from *petĕre*, to seek. One of the basic devices of art. It is used in musical composition, painting, poetry, and prose. Repetition sets up a tide of expectation, helps to give unity to a work of art. In poetry, devices based on repetition are the refrain, the repetend, alliteration, assonance, rhythm, and the metrical pattern.

REPLEVIN. Old French *replevir*, from *plevir*, to pledge. This rather unusual term is used in the title of a book published in 1958:

Landor. A Replevin, by Malcolm Elwin. The author explains that the word is really a legal term, and means an enquiry set on foot to secure the restoration to their owner of goods that are alleged to have been wrongly distrained. As a literary term, therefore, it is used to denote a critical enquiry into an author's works in order to secure the recognition that hitherto has been denied to him.

REPORTAGE. Latin *reportāre*, to bring back (a message). To make a report in the form of gossip, lacking careful thought and a true sense of perspective.

REPORTED SPEECH. *See* INDIRECT SPEECH.

REQUIEM. Latin, accusative of *requies*, rest. It is the first word of Introit in the Mass for the Dead, *Requiem aeternam dona eis, Domine*. A special mass for the repose of the souls of the dead. Also the musical setting for the requiem. At the funeral of Ophelia in *Hamlet*, the Priest says:

> No more be done:
> We should profane the service of the dead
> To sing a requiem and such rest to her
> As to peace-parted souls.

RESTORATION. The return of Charles II in 1660 re-established the monarchy in England. This period of literary history was marked by the event; the chief authors are Dryden, Congreve, Vanbrugh, Farquhar, Wycherley, Pepys, and Locke.

The term 'Restoration', as applied to English literature, is not confined to the later Stuart Period (1660–1688) but extends to the end of the seventeenth century. Allardyce Nicoll's *Restoration Drama* covers the years 1660 to 1700.

RÉSUMÉ. A summary, epitome, abstract.

REVIEW. Latin *revidēre*, to see again. A short account in which the writer gives his critical consideration of a literary composition, film, play, or musical performance.

A periodical consisting of articles on general and special problems, and of criticisms of books. Notable examples are *The Edinburgh Review*, and *Blackwood's Edinburgh Magazine*.

REVUE. A loosely constructed theatrical presentation consisting of scenes or spectacles often satirizing current events.

RHAPSODY. Greek *rhapsōidía*, from *rhapsōidós*, reciter, from *rháptein*, to stitch, compose songs. In Greek antiquities an epic poem, or part of it, which is of the right length for one recitation. Any wild, extravagant, or unconnected utterance or composition. A term brought into music by Tomaschek about 1813 and adopted by Liszt in 1853. It applies to an emotional piece of music.

RHETORIC. Greek *rhētorikē*; *rhětōr*, an orator, especially a professional one. The art of using language, as in a public speech, to persuade or influence others; eloquent and often heightened use of words.

> His legs bestrid the ocean; his rear'd arm
> Crested the world; his voice was propertied
> As all the tuned spheres, and that to his friends;
> But when he meant to quail and shake the orb,
> He was as rattling thunder.
>
> *Antony and Cleopatra*

RHETORICAL QUESTION. Greek *rhětōr*, an orator. A question put not to elicit an answer but as a more effective substitute for a statement:

> Hath not a Jew eyes? hath not a Jew hands, organs, dimensions, senses, affections, passions? . . . If you prick us, do we not bleed? if you tickle us, do we not laugh? if you poison us, do we not die? and if you wrong us, shall we not revenge?   *The Merchant of Venice*

RHOPALIC VERSE. Greek *rhópalon*, a cudgel, thicker towards one end. Verse of which each word contains one more syllable than the word before it. The Roman poet, Ausonius, composed a prayer in forty-two rhopalic hexameters beginning:

> Spes deus aeternae stationis conciliator.

RHYME: RIME. Greek *rhuthmós*, Latin *rhythmus*, measured motion, rhythm, cognate with *rhein*, to flow. Ernest Weekley says, 'The persistence of this form was partly due to association with Anglo-Saxon *rīm*, number; compare German *reim*, from French *rime*, but also associated with Old High German *rīm*, number, sequence. The half-restored spelling *rhyme* was introduced about 1600.' Rhyme is identity of sound between two words extending from the last fully accented vowel to the end of the word, as in *fair*, *chair*, or *smite*, *write*, or *ending*, *bending*. The identity of sound must not include the consonant coming before the last accented vowel: *seat* and *deceit* is not a true rhyme.

(1) One-syllable rhymes are called *male* or *masculine* or *single*.
(2) Two-syllable rhymes are called *female* or *feminine* or *double*.
(3) Three-syllable rhymes are called *triple*.

> Send her victorious
> Happy and glorious.

(4) Four-syllable rhymes are called *quadruple*.

(5) Rhyme coming in the middle as well as at the end of the same line of verse is called *middle*, *medial* or *internal* rhyme:

> We were the *first* that ever *burst*
> Into that silent sea.

(6) Alternate rhyme is the rhyme scheme of the stanza form *a b a b*.

(7) Enclosed rhyme is *a b b a*, as in Tennyson's *In Memoriam*.

(8) Nursery rhymes are brief verses for children, ranging from jingles to these lines of Blake printed in an edition of *Mother Goose*:

> A robin redbreast in a cage
> Sets all heaven in a rage.

In his *Life of Swift*, Sir Walter Scott said, 'Rhyme, which is a handcuff to an inferior poet, he who is master of his art wears as a bracelet'.

RHYME ROYAL. The seven-line decasyllabic stanza with the rhyme scheme *a b a b b c c*. In English poetry, Chaucer first used it in his *Compleynte unto Pite*:

> A compleynt had I, writen, in myn hond,
> For to have put to Pitee as a bille;
> But when I al this companye ther fond,
> That rather wolden al my cause spille
> Then do me help, I held my pleynte stille;
> For to that folk, withouten any fayle,
> Withoute Pitee ther may no bille availe.

It is probable that the name *rhyme royal* derives from the French *chant royal*, not from its use by James I of Scotland in *The Kingis Quair*. This stanza was used by Shakespeare in *Lucrece*, and by Wyatt, and Spenser.

RHYME SCHEME. The pattern of the rhymes in a stanza.

RHYTHM. Greek *rhuthmós*, measured motion; *rheín*, to flow. The measured flow of words and phrases in verse or prose. There is the rhythm achieved by the ordinary arrangement of stressed and unstressed syllables, producing something more or less mechanical, such as these lines by Browning in *How They Brought the Good News from Ghent to Aix*:

> I sprang to the stirrup, and Joris, and he;
> I galloped, Dirck galloped, we galloped all three;
> 'Good speed!' cried the watch, as the gate-bolts undrew;
> 'Speed!' echoed the wall to us galloping through!

The consonants here contribute a good deal to the metallic briskness of the passage. But it is obvious that the rhythm is, as it were, external and made to fit to a selected pattern.

In more complex poetry the rhythm is organic, and is part of the process of creating the poem. The poet who has been deeply moved is now translating the experience into an artistic form through the medium of words. These words will give substance to his thought and feelings and to the images which give the emotional colouring to those thoughts and feelings. Though the poet may be shaping the poem to conform to some established verse pattern, he will also make the words conform to the flow of his feelings. Obviously a sad experience will be expressed in a poem with solemn sounds, but the poet will get closer to the actual experience than that. The rhythm of the line will follow the very rhythm of his own feelings, an organic rhythm will be created, and as this is individual the poem will not repeat the exact rhythm of a fixed metre, but have the individual mark of the poet upon it. This is the touchstone of true poetry. It can be recognized by the rhythm which will be authentic, not imposed from the outside, but created by the inner compelling rhythm of the poet's experience.

Complexity of rhythm is shown in the following lines from Shelley's *Ode to the West Wind*:

> Make me thy lyre, even as the forest is:
> What if my leaves are falling like its own!
> The tumult of thy mighty harmonies
>
> Will take from both a deep autumnal tone,
> Sweet though in sadness. Be thou, Spirit fierce,
> My spirit! Be thou me, impetuous one!
>
> Drive my dead thoughts over the universe
> Like withered leaves to quicken a new birth!
> And, by the incantation of this verse,
>
> Scatter, as from an unextinguished hearth
> Ashes and sparks, my words among mankind!
> Be through my lips to unawakened earth
>
> The trumpet of a prophecy! O, Wind,
> If Winter comes, can Spring be far behind?

RIBBON EDGES. *See* CIRCUIT EDGES.

RIDDLE. Anglo-Saxon *rædels*, from *rædan*, to read. An obscure description of something which the hearer is asked to name. A puzzling question; a conundrum, enigma. Riddles were a popular literary form in Greek and Roman times, also in the Middle Ages. Perhaps the most famous riddle is the one put to Oedipus by the Sphinx. 'What animal walked on four legs in the morning, two a noon, and three in the evening?' Paul Harvey, continuing the story, tells us that Creon, the king of Thebes, promised his crown and his sister Jocasta in marriage to whoever should solve the riddle. This Oedipus did. He observed that man walked on all fours when a child, erect in the noon of life, and supported by a stick in old age. The Sphinx, on hearing this answer, dashed her head against a rock and expired.

RIME. *See* RHYME.

RIME COUÉE. *See* TAIL-RHYME STANZA.

RIME RICHE. French, literally, rich rhyme. Also known as *full* or *perfect* rhyme, *rime riche* occurs when the rhyming words are identical in sound, although the sense differs. An example occurs in Chaucer's *Troilus and Criseyde*:

> Have mercy, swete herte myn, Criseyde!
> And if that, in the wordes that I seyde,
> By any wrong, I wol no more trespace.

RISING ACTION. *See* FREYTAG'S PYRAMID.

RISING RHYTHM. When the stress falls on the last syllable of a metrical foot, the rhythm is called a *rising* one, as in these lines from Tennyson's *Ulysses*:

> Made weák | by time | and fáte, | but stróng | in wíll |
> To stríve, | to seék, | to fínd, | and nót | to yiéld. |

ROCKING RHYTHM. Anglo-Saxon *roccian*, to move jerkily. When the metrical stress falls between two unstressed syllables, the rhythm is called *rocking*. This line from Swinburne's *Hertha* is an example:

> To grow stráight in the stréngth of thy spírit,
> and líve out thy lífe as the líght.

ROCOCO. French, alteration of *rocaille*, rock-work, ornamentation of pebbles and shells. This style, which flourished in Europe from 1735 to 1765, has been described by Herbert Read as the 'last manifestation in Europe of an original style'. It has been regarded as an extension of baroque; is lively, sometimes frivolous; often the style of sophisticated living.

RODOMONTADE. The term is derived from the character of Rodomont, the boastful Saracen leader in Ariosto's *Orlando Furioso*. Vainglorious bragging or boasting.

I

ROMAIC. Greek *Rhōmaïkós*, Roman, used especially of the Eastern Empire. The modern Greek language.

ROMAN À CLEF. French, literally, a novel with a key. A novel in which real individuals appear under fictitious names. In *The Green Carnation*, for example, Robert Hichens caricatured Oscar Wilde and Lord Alfred Douglas. See also SCHLÜSSELROMAN.

ROMAN À DEUX SOUS. See PENNY DREADFUL.

ROMAN À THÈSE. See THESIS NOVEL.

ROMANCE. Latin *Rōmānicē scrībĕre*, to write in the vernacular, as distinguished from literary Latin, tongue. Old French *romans*, something written in the popular tongue, not in Latin; hence, a tale of chivalry. A medieval tale in prose or verse celebrating the adventures, in love and war, of some hero of chivalry. George Loane says, in *Short Handbook of Literary Terms*: 'As these tales are not a part of classical literature either in fact or in spirit, they fell into disfavour at the Revival of Learning. Montaigne never knew such time-consuming and wit-besotting trash of books as King Arthur, Launcelot du Lake, Amadis, and Huon of Bordeaux; give him Ovid.' To Roger Ascham, in *Toxophilus*, they are 'books of feigned chivalry, wherein a man by reading should be led to none other end but only to manslaughter and bawdry'.

Scott is the great reviver of the romance in verse and in prose, but the marvellous element has almost disappeared. Meredith's *The Shaving of Shagpat* is a unique modern imitation of the oriental tales which contributed to making the romances of the Middle Ages.

ROMAN FLEUVE. French, literally, a novel like a stream. Referring to the series of twelve novels collected under the title *Pilgrimage*, Leon Edel says, in *The Psychological Novel*, 'In 1928 Dorothy Richardson was still absorbed in her *roman fleuve*'. See also SAGA NOVEL.

ROMAN POLICIER. French, detective story. Ronald Knox said that at the heart of the classical detective story was the Great Detective. The Belgian-born novelist, Georges Simenon, revolutionized detective fiction by his tough and tolerant Inspector Maigret. In the *New Statesman*, Raymond Mortimer said:

> M. Simenon never makes a comment. He does not analyse his characters, which reveal themselves only in words and actions; he does not commit himself to any opinions . . . Though without Zola's grandiose sweep, he is a poet of the sordid. *See also* THRILLER *and* WHODUNIT.

ROMANTIC COMEDY. This originated in Spain, and was highly successful in France during the Romantic Revival. Phyllis Hartnoll says, in *The Oxford Companion to the Theatre*:

> It is marked by exaggeration and violence, and by an overpowering use of local colour, costume, and scenery. In the hands of a great poet it may give an illusion of greatness, but easily degenerates into melodrama.

ROMANTICISM. French *romantique*, from Old French *romant*, romance. The term is characterized by the qualities of remoteness, desolation, melancholy, divine unrest, passion, and the all-embracing power of the imagination. It is suggestive of strangeness and of adventure, of never-satisfied aspiration after the unknown or the unattainable.

Defining the Romantic Revival, in *The Oxford Companion to English Literature*, Paul Harvey says:

> This is a name given to a movement in European literature which marked the last quarter of the eighteenth century. The old narrow intellectual attitude gave place to a wider outlook, which recognized the claims of passion and emotion and the sense of mystery in life, and in which the critical was replaced by the creative spirit, and wit by humour and pathos.

In *English Literature*, A. C. Ward outlines the relationship between Romanticism and Classicism:

> That the spirit of ancient Greek literature and the ideals it expresses have irrigated and fertilized the modern mind to its incalculable profit is unquestionable; but it is also unquestionable that most of the profit which English literature owes to the classical tradition has come through Romantic writers.
>
> Where and when Romanticism has fallen into disrepute the cause lies in the extravagance and incapacity of undisciplined minor writers who exploit the sentimental, the sensational, the morbid, the occult, the erotic. These aspects of Romanticism appear severally in the works of lesser Elizabethan and later playwrights, in the gothic novels of the late eighteenth and early nineteenth centuries, and scattered over minor poetry at irregular intervals from the seventeenth-century Metaphysicals onwards. But modern English Romantic literature also embraces the simplicities of Nature in, for example, Gilbert White's prose and Wordsworth's verse, the lyrical harmony of Shelley, the restraint and form and finish of Keats's odes.

ROMAN TYPE. The plain ordinary type, in which the vertical strokes are upright, as distinguished from the sloping *italic*.

RONDEAU. French *rondeau*, earlier *rondel*: *rond*, round. A short poem consisting of thirteen lines divided into three stanzas, having only two rhymes throughout, and with the opening words used twice as a refrain. Voltaire popularized the rondeau. Here is an adaptation of one of his poems:

> You bid me try, Blue-eyes, to write
> A Rondeau. What! forthwith? — Tonight?
>   Reflect. Some skill I have, 'tis true;
>   But thirteen lines! — and rhymed on two! —
> 'Refrain,' as well. Ah, hapless plight!
> Still there are five lines — ranged aright.
> These Gallic bonds, I feared, would fright
>   My easy Muse. They did, till you —
>   *You* bid me try!
>
> 'That makes them eight. — The port's in sight:
> 'Tis all because your eyes are bright!
>   Now just a pair to end in "oo", —
>   When maids command, what can't we do!
> Behold! The Rondeau — tasteful, light —
>   You bid me try!'

RONDEAU REDOUBLÉ. This elaborate verse form consists of six quatrains with two alternating rhymes. It has a strict pattern, each line of the first quatrain serving, in order, as the last line of the four succeeding quatrains. The first half of the opening line is repeated as an unrhymed refrain at the end of the last stanza. The rhyme scheme is *a b a b, b a b a, a b a b, b a b a, a b a b, b a b a refrain*.

RONDEL. Old French *rondel*, *rond*, round. Dating back to the fourteenth century, it is a short poem of fourteen lines on two rhymes with a refrain, the first two lines of the opening quatrain recurring at the end of the second quatrain, and at the end of the poem. Sometimes the rondel is shortened to thirteen lines, as in *The Wanderer* by Austin Dobson:

> Love comes back to his vacant dwelling, —
>   The old, old Love that we knew of yore!
>   We see him stand by the open door,
> With his great eyes sad, and his bosom swelling.
>
> He makes as though in our arms repelling,
>   He fain would lie as he lay before; —
> Love comes back to his vacant dwelling, —
>   The old, old Love that we knew of yore!

Ah! who shall help us from overspelling,
That sweet forgotten, forbidden love!
E'en as we doubt in our hearts once more,
With a rush of tears to our eyelids welling,
Love comes back to his vacant dwelling.

RONDELET. French, diminutive of *rond*, round. A song with a refrain; a dance in a ring.

ROOFER. *See* COLLINS, WILLIAM.

ROSICRUCIAN. A member of a supposed mystic order, reputedly founded in 1484 in Germany by Christian Rosenkreuz, and known in seventeenth-century England as the *Rosy Cross.* The members were said to have magic and secret knowledge, such as the lengthening of life, the changing of metals, and power over the elements. No Rosicrucian society really existed. In the seventeenth century, religious reformers used the name, and spoke of mysticism and alchemy. In his historical novel, *John Inglesant*, J. H. Shorthouse says much on this subject.

ROTARY. Latin *rota*, wheel. A printing machine in which both the printing surface and the impression cylinder rotate.

ROUND CHARACTER. In *Aspects of the Novel*, E. M. Forster says:

> The test of a round character is whether it is capable of surprising in a convincing way. If it never surprises, it is flat. If it does not convince, it is a flat pretending to be round. It has the incalculability of life about it — life within the pages of a book. And by using it sometimes alone, more often in combination with the other kind, the novelist achieves his task of acclimatization, and harmonizes the human race with the other aspects of his work.

Among novelists who create round characters are Jane Austen, Fielding, Charlotte Brontë, Thackeray, Dickens, Tolstoy, and Dostoevsky.

ROUNDEL. Old French *rondel*, *rond*, round. A short poem consisting of three stanzas of three lines each, linked together with but two rhymes, and a refrain taken from the opening of the first line and rhyming with the second line. In this poem, Swinburne describes and illuminates the form:

> A Roundel is wrought as a ring or a starbright sphere,
> With craft of delight and with cunning of sound unsought,
> That the heart of the hearer may smile if to pleasure his ear
>   A roundel is wrought.

Its jewel of music is carven of all or of aught —
Love, laughter, or mourning — remembrance or rapture or fear —
That fancy may fashion to hang in the ear of thought.

As a bird's quick song runs round, and the hearts in us hear —
Pause answers to pause, and again the same strain caught,
So moves the device whence, round as a pearl or tear,
    A roundel is wrought.

ROUNDELAY. Old French *rondelet*. A short song with a refrain set to simple music.

RUBÁIYAT. Arabic *rubais*, quatrains. A collection of four-line stanzas, or quatrains, as in the translation by Edward FitzGerald of *The Rubáiyát of Omar Khayyám*, the Persian poet and astronomer.

RUBRIC. Latin *rubrīca*, red earth for colouring. Heading of chapter, also certain portions, written or printed in red, or in special lettering. Directions for conduct of divine service, properly in red, inserted in liturgical books.

RULING PASSION. Pope, in *Moral Essays*, was the first to use this phrase. He was defending Sir John Blunt, who declaimed against the corruption and luxury of the age, and was particularly eloquent against avarice. So Pope, feeling strongly, wrote:

    The ruling Passion, be it what it will,
    The ruling Passion conquers Reason still.

Macaulay says, in *Collected Essays*:

The silly notion that every man has one ruling passion and that this clue, once known, unravels all the mysteries of his conduct, finds no countenance in the plays of Shakespeare. The man appears as he is, made up of a crowd of passions which contend for the mastery over him, and govern him in turn.

RUNE. Old Norse *rūn*, mystery, dark secret. Any letter of the ancient Germanic alphabet, dating from as early as the second century A.D. The runic alphabet was formed by modifying the letters of the Greek or Roman alphabet so that they could be cut more easily upon wood or stone. Ancient Finnish and Scottish poetry was written in runes. The Anglo-Saxon poet Cynewulf used runic characters in his verse. Magic wands, weapons, and amulets, inscribed with runes, were used in incantations and for the casting of spells. Kipling composed some verses called *The Runes on Weland's Sword*.

RUNNING HEADLINE. *See* HEADLINE.

RUNNING RHYTHM. *See* COMMON RHYTHM.

RUN-ON LINE. A line of verse is said to be run-on when the sense runs over to the following line.

> My love is of a birth as rare
> As 'tis for object strange and high.
>
> Marvell, *The Definition of Love*

S

SAEVA INDIGNATIO. These, his own, words occur in Swift's epitaph: *Ubi saeva indignatio ulterius cor lacerare nequit:* 'Where fierce indignation can no longer tear his heart.' This indignation was the compelling force in his satire.

SAGA. Old Norse *saga*, story. A prose narrative written in Iceland or Norway during the Middle Ages. The Icelandic sagas are highly national and insular. They fall into two groups, the *Heimskringla* being the most notable in the historical group, and the *Laxdaela* the chief of the legends. We have a version of the latter in William Morris's *Earthly Paradise.*

SAGA NOVEL. A prose narrative portraying the life of a large family, presented through a series of novels, as in John Galsworthy's *The Forsyte Saga.*

SANSKRIT. In the language itself *samskṛta*, put together, perfected, from *sami*, together and *kṛta*, made. Compare *Prakrit*, the common language. The ancient, classical and sacred language of the Hindus, belonging to the Aryan family with the earliest records (*c.* 1500 B.C.). Hindu literature from the Vedas downward is composed in Sanskrit.

SAPPHICS. The four-line stanza utilizing a metre associated with the name of Sappho, the Greek poet. Restrictions were imposed by Horace as to the position of divisions of words — a division in the first three lines after the fifth or after the sixth syllable and the fourth syllable must be long. The Sapphic stanza has been imitated by poets writing in English, exemplified by Swinburne's *Sapphics*:

> All the night sleep came | not upon my eyelids,
> Shed not dew, nor shook | nor unclosed a feather,
> Yet with lips shut close | and with eyes of iron
> Stood and beheld me.

SAPPHIC STANZA. This is only one of the many metres that Sappho used. It consists of $- \cup - \bar{\cup} - \cup\cup - \cup - \bar{\cup}$ repeated three times, and followed by $- \cup\cup - \bar{\cup}$. It was used by Horace, who made some modifications.

SARCASM.   Late Greek *sarkasmós*, from *sarkázein*, literally, to tear flesh; to speak bitterly.   A taunting remark, sometimes ironical, always bitter or ill-natured (as irony need not be); its motive is to inflict pain.   Byron's portrait of Southey in *The Vision of Judgment* is a renowned example of sustained sarcasm.   Here are some lines coming near the end of that poem.   Southey has fallen into his lake.

> He first sank to the bottom — like his works,
>   But soon rose to the surface — like himself;
> For all corrupted things are buoy'd like corks,
>   By their own rottenness, light as an elf,
> Or wisp that flits o'er a morass.

SATANIC SCHOOL.   In the preface to *A Vision of Judgment*, Robert Southey invented this phrase with particular reference to Byron's poetry:

> The school which they have set up may properly be called the Satanic School; for though their productions breathe the spirit of Belial in their lascivious parts, and the spirit of Moloch in those loathsome images of atrocities and horrors which they delight to represent, they are more especially characterized by a Satanic spirit of pride and audacious impiety, which still betrays the wretched spirit of hopelessness wherewith it is allied.

Byron replied to this in the appendix to *The Two Foscari*, and also held the poet laureate up to derision in his satire, *A Vision of Judgment*, a travesty of Southey's poem.

SATIRE.   Latin *satura*, later *satira*, feminine singular of *satur*, full, sated, from *satis*, enough, sufficient, as in *satura lanx*, a full dish, from *sat-* enough; hence a medley such as the earliest satires were. Satire is the holding up of vice or folly to ridicule.   It often makes use of irony and sarcasm.   H. W. Fowler says that its motive is amendment, its province morals and manners, its method accentuation, and its audience the self-satisfied.   In his essay *Original and Progress of Satire*, Dryden says:

> Yet still the nicest and most delicate touches of satire consist in fine raillery . . . How easy is it to call rogue and villain, and that wittily!   But how hard to make a man appear a fool, a blockhead, or a knave, without using any of those opprobrious terms!   To spare the grossness of the names, and to do the thing yet more severely, is to draw a full face, and to make the nose and cheeks stand out, and yet not to employ any depth of shadowing . . . Neither is it true, that this fineness of raillery is offensive.   A witty man is tickled while he is hurt in this manner, and a fool feels it not.   The

occasion of an offence may possibly be given, but he cannot take it. If it be granted, that in effect this way does more mischief; that a man is secretly wounded, and though he be not sensible himself, yet the malicious world will find it out for him; yet there is still a vast difference betwixt the slovenly butchering of a man, and the fineness of a stroke that separates the head from the body, and leaves it standing in its place.

This 'fineness of a stroke' is shown in Pope's portrait of Addison, in *Epistle to Dr. Arbuthnot*:

Should such a man, too fond to rule alone,
Bear like the Turk, no brother near the throne.
View him with scornful, yet with jealous eyes,
And hate for arts that caus'd himself to rise;
Damn with faint praise, assent with civil leer,
And without sneering, teach the rest to sneer;
Willing to wound, and yet afraid to strike,
Just hint a fault, and hesitate dislike;
Alike reserv'd to blame, or to commend,
A tim'rous foe, and a suspicious friend.

In the preface, *The Battle of the Books*, Swift said, 'Satire is a sort of glass wherein beholders do generally discover everybody's face but their own'.

Examples of satire are *Hudibras*, by Samuel Butler (1612–1680), Dryden's *Absalom and Achitophel*, Swift's *Gulliver's Travels*, Pope's *Dunciad*, Byron's *Don Juan*, and *Erewhon*, by Samuel Butler (1835–1902).

SATYRIC DRAMA. The fourth play in the tetralogy of the ancient Greeks, a semi-mocking, semi-serious presentation of a legendary theme in honour of Dionysus, a god attended by satyrs. The only complete, extant, satyric drama is the *Cyclops* of Euripides.

SCALD: SKALD. Old Norse *skāld*. Origin unknown. A Scandinavian bard or minstrel.

SCANSION. Latin *scandĕre*, to climb, ascend; in *scandĕre versūs*, to measure verses by taking them foot by foot. The study of metrical form includes that of scansion. English verse rhythm depends upon the arrangement of stresses; stressed syllables being those we give more emphasis in natural speech. We should scan this line as follows:

The cur|few tolls | the knell | of part|ing day |

indicating the stressed and unstressed syllables as shown. With two syllables (the first unstressed, the second stressed) in each foot, and five feet in the line, we recognize the verse pattern as iambic pentameter. Other verse patterns are the trochaic (/ ⌣), and, with three syllable feet, anapaestic (⌣ ⌣ /) and dactylic (/ ⌣ ⌣). These, with the occasional feet — the spondee (/ /), and the pyrrhic (⌣ ⌣) — provide the possibility of infinite variety.

In scansion, a syllable is either stressed or unstressed. This does not take into account the varying weight of the words, from the merest breath of sound to the heaviest weight that a word can carry. So that along with, as it were, the basic pattern, or rhythmic norm, there is the emphasis of the sense (open to different interpretations), and the infinite variety of weight of words. *Lump* is a heavier word than *sun*, both contain the *u* sound, both would take a stress in a line. These lines from Coleridge show the difference of weight, though scansion can show stressed and unstressed syllables only:

> With heavy thump, a lifeless lump,
> They dropped down one by one

and

> The Sun's rim dips; the stars rush out:
> At one stride comes the dark.

The poet has an instinctive ear for language and he is weighing and measuring words habitually so as to give continuous verbal music to his verse.

SCATOLOGY. Greek *skôr*, *skat-*, dung. Obscene literature.

SCAZON. *See* CHOLIAMBIC.

SCENARIO. A sketch of the plot of a play, giving particulars of the scenes, situations, and the characters involved.

SCENE. Latin *scéna*, Greek *skēnĕ*, booth, stage. The stage of the ancient Greek or Roman theatre, strictly the stone or wooden background, the stage itself being the *proscenium*. The place of action in a play or story. A division of a play marked by a change of place, effected by the fall of the curtain, or by the entry or exit of ⌐n important character. The curtain was unknown in the Elizabethan theatre, and many plays had no divisions. In the Restoration theatre it rose at the end of the Prologue (which was spoken on the forestage) and came down at the end of the play. In the modern theatre, scene divisions are marked by the use of the curtain.

SCENE À FAIRE. French for obligatory scene (q.v.).

SCHLÜSSELROMAN. In the introduction to *Der Teufel im Winterpalais* by Werner Bergengruen, Kate Pearl says:

> This novel, published two years after Hitler's coming to power, was called in Germany a 'Schlüsselroman', a 'key novel', meaning a story in which the well-informed reader can identify the characters and action with real people and events of his own time, even if the period has been altered.

See also ROMAN À CLEF.

SCHOLASTICISM. The doctrines of the Schoolmen, chief of whom were Peter Lombard, Abélard, Albertus Magnus, Duns Scotus, Aquinas, and Ockham. These men flourished from the eleventh to the fifteenth century, and their theological and philosophical teaching tried to reconcile the pronouncements of Aristotle with the Christian faith. After Ockham (*d.* 1349), '*Doctor invincibilis*', the movement died away, losing all contact with the practical features of life. *See also* NOMINALISM.

SCHOLIUM. Greek *skholē*, leisure, discussion, place of learning. An explanatory note or comment; especially an ancient note upon a text of a Greek or Latin author.

SCHOOL OF NIGHT. A group of Elizabethan intellectuals consisting of Sir Walter Ralegh, Christopher Marlowe, George Chapman, Matthew Roydon, the mathematician Thomas Harriot, and others. They were suspected of being atheists, dedicated to the study of 'dark and prohibited subjects'. In 1594, Chapman wrote about this coterie in *Shadow of Night*, and Shakespeare makes this reference in *Love's Labour's Lost*:

> O paradox! Black is the badge of hell,
> The hue of dungeons and the School of Night;
> And beauty's crest becomes the heavens well!

SCHWÄRMEREI. German, the enthusiasm of a fanatic; excessive emotion.

SCIENCE FICTION. Stories and novels dealing, usually in a fanciful way, with space travel and other fascinations of science. Such fiction may have begun in the second century with Lucian's *Vera Historia*, in which the hero is whirled to the moon. In the seventeenth century Bishop Godwin wrote *The Man in the Moon*, and Cyrano de Bergerac dealt with the same subject.

Jules Verne with *Cinq semaines en ballon* and *Vingt mille lieues sous les mers* and H. G. Wells with *The First Men in the Moon* and *The Time Machine* established themselves as classic writers of science fiction. C. S. Lewis's *Out of the Silent Planet*, and Olaf Stapledon's *First and Last Men* are ingenious novels of the world of science.

SCILICET. Latin, to wit, for *scīre licet*, it is permitted to know. Namely; abbreviation: sc.

SCOFF: SCOP. Synonymous Old Norse *skop*, *skaup*; cognate with Anglo-Saxon *scop*, poet. An Anglo-Saxon minstrel, singing poems of heroic deeds.

SCOTTISH CHAUCERIANS. The fifteenth century in Scotland is described as 'the golden age of Scottish poetry', and James I, Henryson, Dunbar, and Gavin Douglas are declared to be the descendants of Chaucer. These Scottish Chaucerians show not only original talent but the power of assimilation, which discriminates them from Lydgate and Occleve.

SCREEN. Two pieces of glass, with fine lines crossing at right-angles to each other, through which copy is photographed in the production of a half-tone. On the resulting negative the tones in the original copy are represented by tiny dots of varying intensity.

SCRIBLERUS CLUB. Pope, Swift, Gay, Congreve, Arbuthnot, Parnell, Lord Oxford, and Atterbury were members of this club, founded about 1713. Martinus Scriblerus, of Münster in Germany, a man of capacity who had read everything but whose judgment was worthless, was the subject of *memoirs*, a satirical work directed against 'false tastes in learning', written mainly by Arbuthnot. This satire appeared in Pope's prose works in 1741.

SCRIPTORIUM. Latin *scriptor*, a writer. A room set apart in a monastery or abbey for the writing and copying of books.

SCRIVENER'S PALSY. Latin *scrībānus*, from *scrībĕre*, to write. Palsy, contraction of Old French and Middle English *paralisie*, for *paralysis*. Writer's cramp.

SECENTISMO. Italian, sixteenth, used for 1600s. A term used to indicate the flamboyant mannerism of the seventeenth-century Italian poet Marino and his followers. He was the author of an extremely long poem entitled *Adone*.

SECONDARY STRESS. *See* PRIMARY AND SECONDARY STRESS.

SEDULOUS APE. Latin *sēdulus*, from adverb *sēdulō*, honestly, Old Latin *se dolo*, without guile. One who plays the sedulous ape gains a literary style by diligent imitation. In *Memories and Portraits*, Stevenson said:

> I have thus played the sedulous ape to Hazlitt, to Lamb, to Wordsworth, to Sir Thomas Browne, to Defoe, to Hawthorne, to Montaigne, to Baudelaire and to Obermann.

SEMANTICS. Greek *sēmantikós*, significant, from *sēmaínein*, to show. The branch of philology concerned with meanings of words and with the development of the meanings of words.

SENARIUS. Latin, consisting of six each. A Latin verse of six iambic feet. Used in the rhyming couplets of French plays as the *alexandrine*.

> That, like a wounded snake, drags its slow length along.
> Pope, An Essay on Criticism

SENECAN TRAGEDY. William Beare says, in *The Oxford Companion to the Theatre*:

> For the Renaissance, Seneca, the Roman dramatist, was the model writer of tragedy. His plays were regularly constructed in five acts, according to the Horatian precept; they dealt with emotions and catastrophes which, if they seem to us overdrawn, were universally intelligible; even his rant and rhetoric appealed to the prevailing taste. His rattling line-by-line interchange of dialogue, his chorus, his tyrants, ghosts, and witches, his corpse-strewn stage all reappear in Elizabethan drama.

SENSIBILITY. Latin *sententia*; *sentīre*, to feel. The capacity and susceptibility to feel; exceptional openness to emotional impressions; responsiveness to aesthetic phenomena. The use of the term is exemplified in the title of Jane Austen's novel *Sense and Sensibility*, where each of the qualities is represented by one of two contrasted characters in the story. As Aldous Huxley says, in *Texts and Pretexts*:

> Experience is not a matter of having actually swum the Hellespont, or danced with the dervishes, or slept in a dosshouse. It is a matter of sensibility and intuition, of seeing and hearing the significant things, of paying attention at the right moments, of understanding and co-ordinating.

SENSITIVE. Latin *sensus*, from *sentīre*, to feel. Quick to detect, and to be moved by, stimuli communicated through the senses; ready and delicate in response to outside influences. Addison said, in the *Spectator*, 'Quick sensitiveness is inseparable from a ready understanding'. In *The Prelude*, Wordsworth proclaims:

A Sensitive being, a *creative* soul.

SENSUOUS. Latin *sensus*, from *sentīre*, to feel. The word *sensuous* was coined by Milton; he said, in *Tractate of Education*, 'To which Poetry would be made subsequent or indeed rather precedent, as being lesse suttle and fine, but more simple, sensuous and passionate'. Connected with experience derived from the senses. It is distinguished from *sensual* in that it conveys no sense of grossness or lewdness.

SENTENTIA. *See* APHORISM.

SENTENTIOUS. Latin *sententia-*, *sentīre*, to feel. Aphoristic, pithy, given to the use of maxims; affecting a terse impressive style.

SENTIMENT. Latin *sentīre*, to feel. Feeling, with a tendency to be influenced by emotion rather than by reason or by fact.

SENTIMENTAL COMEDY. A type of pathetic play which reflected the false sensibility of the rising middle class in the eighteenth century. This reaction from the comedy of the Restoration was introduced by Richard Steele's *The Lying Lover* (1703), and *The Tender Husband* (1705). Colley Cibber wrote similar comedies, including *The Careless Husband* (1705).

SENTIMENTALISM. Latin *sentīre*, to feel. The quality of excessive emotion. The affectation of fine feeling. In *Diana of the Crossways*, Meredith said, 'Sentimental people, in her phrase, fiddle harmonics on the strings of sensualism'.

SENTIMENTALITY. Late Latin *sentīmentum*, *sentīre*, to feel. The too-ready reaction to emotion. We are surrounded by various forms of stimulation, which encourage an immediate response to a situation unworthy of that emotional response. Here, of course, the cinema and the television take the lead. There is something extremely valuable in the slow generation of pity and terror in a Shakespearean tragedy, or in a long epic poem. When we find that we are moved by so-called tragic situations which are purely incidental, then the result is a weakening and dissipating of emotion.

SENTIMENTAL NOVEL. In eighteenth-century England, a narrative in which the sentiment is free from sentimentality. The story presents simple goodness, avoiding mawkishness by humour and pathos. Goldsmith's *Vicar of Wakefield* is a fine example.

Other notable novels of this kind are Maria Edgeworth's *Castle Rackrent*, and Henry MacKenzie's *The Man of Feeling*.

SEPTENARIUS: SEPTENARY. Latin from *septēnī*, seven each. A metrical line of seven feet. Macaulay uses this measure in *The Armada*:

> Look how the Lion of the sea lifts up his ancient crown.

The *septenary*, or seven-foot line, forms ballad metre when printed in alternate lines of four and three feet.

SEPTET. A poem or stanza of seven lines. The most common seven-line stanza is known as *rhyme royal*.

SEPTUAGINT. Latin *septuaginta*, seventy, from a weakened form of *septem*, seven. The Greek version of the Old Testament and the Apocrypha, so called because it is said to be the work of seventy, or rather seventy-two Jewish elders asked to do so by Ptolemy Philadelphus (284–247 B.C.). It was completed by them on Pharos, in seventy-two days. The name may come from the authorization by the seventy members of the Jewish Sanhedrin.

SERENADE. Italian *serenata*, an evening song, from *sereno*, the open air. A song written to be sung by a gallant under his lady's window. A poem in imitation of this song, such as Shelley's *Indian Serenade*.
    An early form of the instrumental symphony, associated with Haydn and Mozart.

SERENDIPITY. From *Serendip*, a former name for Ceylon, coined by Horace Walpole upon the title of the fairy tale *The Three Princes of Serendip*, the heroes of which 'were always making discoveries, by accidents and sagacity, of things they were not in quest of'.

SERPENTINE VERSE. A metrical line which begins and ends with the same word. This is in allusion to the representation of a serpent with its tail in its mouth.

> May, the white blossom, crowns Queen of the May.

SESQUIPEDALIAN. Latin *sesquipedālis*, of a foot and a half. Used humorously of words with many syllables.

SESTET, SEXTET. A poem or stanza of six lines; the term frequently refers to the second part of the Petrarchan sonnet.

SESTINA. Italian *sestetto*, from Latin *sextus*, sixth. A complicated verse form invented by the French troubadours of the twelfth century. It consists of six stanzas of six lines each, with a concluding tercet (a group of three lines). It may be unrhymed, or rhyme on two words throughout. The terminal words of the first stanza are all repeated as terminal words in the succeeding stanzas, and in the tercets, in a strict order which varies throughout. In the diagram below, each letter represents the terminal word of each metrical line, and each line of letters represents a stanza:

```
a b c d e f
f a e b d c
c f d a b e
e c b f a d
d e a c f b
b d f e c a
  e c a
```

The form has been used by Petrarch and Dante, also by Swinburne, Kipling, and Auden.

SETTING. The manner in which a poem is set to music. The way in which a play is put on the stage: scenery, costumes, properties.

SEVEN DEADLY SINS. These are Pride, Covetousness, Lechery, Anger, Envy, Gluttony, Sloth. They were often personified in medieval literature and appear in *Piers Plowman*, Chaucer's *Parson's Tale*, and Spenser's *Faerie Queene*.

SEVEN LIBERAL ARTS, THE. The subjects of the medieval *Trivium* (the lower division) — Latin grammar, logic, and rhetoric; and the *Quadrivium* (the higher division) — arithmetic, geometry, astronomy, and music.

SEXTET. *See* SESTET.

SHADOW SHOW. 'The shadow theatre', says George Speaight, in *The Oxford Companion to the Theatre*, 'is a puppet-show in which flat figures are passed between a strong light and a translucent screen; the audience, on the other side of the screen, sees their shadows passing across it. Limited of necessity to a highly stylized convention, the shadow show has proved itself an artistic medium of rare and delicate charm.'

SHAGGY DOG STORY. The idea in Greek *parà prosdokiān*, contrary to expectation. In *A Charm of Words*, Eric Partridge says, 'The most important feature of "shaggy dogs" is the unexpectedness of their endings, although that in itself is not enough to make a story "shaggy".'

In one sense the 'shaggy dog' forms a special aspect of the

catch-story; in another, of the ordinary witty story, exemplified perhaps first in the very ancient Greek example: 'A pert youth, meeting an old crone driving a small herd, cried, Good morning, mother of asses! — Good morning, my son!'

In the early days of broadcasting, A. J. Alan did much to popularize this kind of story. In *John Mistletoe* (1931), Christopher Morley tells briefly of 'a small hairy dog' — a story which may have fixed the name 'shaggy dog'.

SHAKESPEAREAN SONNET. S. S. Sopwith, writing of the Sonnets, in *English Sampler*, says:

> The innumerable sonnet-sequences of the Elizabethan Age find their climax in the sequence of one hundred and fifty-four sonnets of Shakespeare. These sonnets are not, like the others of the period, concerned with a lover's disdain, but they express the poet's love for his young patron, with all its joys and disillusionment, its distrust and jealousy; and into this tragedy of fading love enters an evil spirit — 'the dark lady of the Sonnets' — who tempts the poet's hero from his side.

The pattern of the Shakespearean sonnet in iambic pentameter consists of three quatrains followed by a couplet. The alternate rhyming of the quatrains gives the couplet the force of a climax, expressing the theme in the last two lines.

> Let me not to the marriage of true minds
> Admit impediments. Love is not love
> Which alters when it alteration finds,
> Or bends with the remover to remove:
> O, no! it is an ever-fixed mark,
> That looks on tempests and is never shaken;
> It is a star to every wandering bark,
> Whose worth's unknown, although his height be taken.
> Love's not Time's fool, though rosy lips and cheeks
> Within his bending sickle's compass come;
> Love alters not with his brief hours and weeks,
> But bears it out even to the edge of doom.
>　　If this be error and upon me proved,
>　　I never writ, nor no man ever loved.　　　*Sonnet* 116

SHANTY: CHANTY. French *chanter*, to sing. A sailor's song sung during heavy work.

SHELTA: SHELTER. Celtic. Origin of the name unknown. A kind of cryptic slang based on Old Irish Gaelic, still used by wandering gipsies and tinkers.

SHIBBOLETH. Hebrew *shibbōleth*, ear of corn, rustling stream (both from idea of growth).

> The Hebrew word used by Jephthah as a test-word by which to distinguish the fleeing Ephraimites (who could not pronounce the *sh*) from his own men, the Gileadites (Judges xii. 4–6). Hence a word or formula used as a test by which the adherents of a party, etc., may be distinguished from others.
>
> *Oxford English Dictionary*

SHORT COUPLET. A tetrameter couplet, which may be iambic or trochaic, such as the following:

> There is a lady sweet and kind,
> Was never face so pleased my mind;
> I did but see her passing by,
> And yet I love her till I die.

The short couplet may be called *octosyllabic* because each line contains eight syllables.

SHORT MEASURE (S.M.). A quatrain rhyming either *a b a b* or *a b c b*, in which the first, second, and fourth lines are iambic trimeter, and the third iambic tetrameter. This stanza is by Isaac Watts:

> There is a dreadful Hell,
> And everlasting pains;
> There sinners must with devils dwell
> In darkness, fire, and chains.

SHORT STORY. A brief narrative in prose. In general it goes back to earliest times, to legends and fairy tales, to the *Fables* of Aesop and *The Arabian Nights*. The medieval secular stories, Gower's *Confessio Amantis* and Chaucer's *Canterbury Tales*, owe much to the *Gesta Romanorum* and Boccaccio's *Decameron*. Short stories appeared inside the earlier novels, such as those of Defoe and Sterne. *Wandering Willie's Tale* from Scott's *Redgauntlet* is a famous example.

The modern short story was created by Edgar Allan Poe. Maupassant showed himself to be a master of this literary form, and he was widely imitated in England. Kipling developed the tale of adventure. Katherine Mansfield, D. H. Lawrence, Elizabeth Bowen covered a wide range. Prominent among later writers are Somerset Maugham, T. F. Powys, and A. E. Coppard.

SIC. 'Latin adv. = so, appended in brackets after a word or expression in a quoted passage as guarantee that it is quoted exactly, though its incorrectness or absurdity would suggest that it was not' (*The Concise Oxford Dictionary*).

SIGMATISM. *Sigma* is the Greek *s*. The marked use or repetition of *s*. Addison refers to the profusion of sibilant sounds in English when he says, 'the hissing so much noticed by foreigners'. Tennyson tells us that he controlled his use of sibilants by 'Kicking the geese out of the boat'. Milton sometimes allows the collision of *s* sounds, as in this line from *Paradise Regained*:

> And seat of *Salmanassar*, whose success . . .

In *Faustine*, Swinburne hisses with the adders:

> What adders came to shed their coats?
> What coiled obscene
> Small serpents with soft stretching throats
> Caressed Faustine?

John Thelwall (1764–1834) wrote *Song Without a Sibilant*, which begins:

> No, not the eye of tender blue,
> Though, Mary, 'twere the tint of thine,
> Or breathing lip of glowing hue
> Might bid the opening bud repine,
> Had long enthrall'd my mind.

SIGNATURE. Latin *signāre*, *-ātum*, to sign. The letter or figure placed by the printer at the foot of the first page of each sheet of a book. This is done as a guide in making up such sheets for binding in the correct order after folding. Printed signatures were first used by Johann Koelhoff at Cologne in 1472.

SIMILE. Latin *similis*, like. A simile makes an imaginative comparison for purposes of explanation, allusion, or ornament, introduced by a word such as *like*, *as*, or *such*. It can be simple, briefly expressed, or long and sustained, known then as the epic simile. To say that a girl looks like Helen of Troy is not a simile, but to say 'My heart is like a singing bird' is.

> Anon out of the earth a Fabrick huge
> Rose like an Exhalation, with the sound
> Of Dulcet Symphony and voices sweet.
>> Milton, *Paradise Lost*

> And silence, like a poultice, comes
> To heal the blows of sound.
>> Oliver Wendell Holmes, *The Music Grinders*

SIMILITUDE. Latin *similis*, like. The state of being similar or like. Comparison; parable; allegory. Bunyan on the title-page of his allegory, *Pilgrim's Progress*, declares, 'Delivered under the similitude of a dream'.

SINCERITY. Latin *sincērus*, clean, pure. The freedom from hypocrisy or false pretence. It is not always easy to explain just what sincerity is. In the most deeply sincere poetry the words produce overtones of emotion in the sensitive reader which cannot be fully analysed or explained. One may, however, compare two poems such as Milton's sonnet *On his Blindness* and Colley Cibber's *The Blind Boy* to show sincerity.

SIRVENTE. French *servir*, to serve. A form of poem or lay, usually satirizing figures of the time, employed by the troubadours of the Middle Ages.

SKELTONIC VERSE. The rough, stressed verse of John Skelton, the tutor to Prince Henry, later Henry VIII, and 'poet-laureate'. His poetry was called 'tumbling verse' by James VI of Scotland. His favourite metre was a 'headlong voluble breathless doggerel, which, rattling and clashing on through quick recurring rhymes . . . has taken from its author the title of Skeltonical verse' (Churton Collins).
He wrote justly of his own verse in *Colyn Cloute*:

> And if ye stand in doubt
> Who brought this ryme about,
> My name is Colyn Cloute.
> I purpose to shake out
> All my conning bag.
> Like a clerkly hag,
> For though my ryme be ragged,
> Tattered and iagged,
> Rudely rayne beaten,
> Rusty and mothe eaten;
> If ye take well therwith,
> It hath in it some pyth.

SKETCH. Latin *schedium*, extempore poem, from Greek *schédios*, extempore. A short musical or dramatic play. A brief, descriptive article. John Malcolm wrote *Sketches of Persia* (1827), and a collection of pieces by Dickens appeared in one volume as *Sketches by Boz* (1839).

SLACK, THE. The unstressed syllable or syllables in a foot of verse. The slack consists of the first two syllables in *sĕrĕnáde*.

SLANG. Originally a cant word; possibly cognate with 'sling', Old Norse *slyngva*, to throw, sling. In *Language*, Otto Jespersen says:
Slang words are words used in conscious contrast to the natural or normal speech: they can be found in all classes of society

in certain moods and on certain occasions when the speaker wants to avoid the natural or normal word because he thinks it too flat or uninteresting.

Logan Pearsall Smith, in *Words and Idioms*, wrote:

Slang words, being generally created, not to define a thing, but to say something funny about it, keep as a rule their slangy character; while those among the dialect terms which are genuine and useful definitions lose little by little their vulgar associations.

Here are a few examples: *bloke, cove, stiff, geezer, croaker*.

SLANT RHYME. One that is not a true rhyme, due to the poet's failing or his desire to create a particular effect.

SLAPSTICK. Knockabout comedy: slapdash methods. Originally, a slapstick was a wand made of two flat pieces of wood with a handle. It was used by the harlequin in a pantomime. When he struck one of his companions, the slapstick made a loud report.

SLICE OF LIFE. Edith Wharton says in *The Writing of Fiction*:

It seemed necessary to revert to the slice of life because it has lately reappeared, marked by certain unimportant differences, and re-labelled the stream of consciousness; and, curiously enough, without its new exponents' being aware that they are not also its originators. This time the theory seems to have sprung up first in England and America; but it has already spread to certain of the younger French novelists, who are just now, confusedly if admiringly, rather over-conscious of recent tendencies in English and American fiction.

The stream of consciousness method differs from the slice of life in noting down mental as well as physical reactions, but resembles it in setting them down just as they come, with a deliberate disregard of their relevance in the particular case, or rather with the assumption that their very unsorted abundance constitutes in itself the author's subject.

This passage, written in 1924, refers to *tranche de vie*, the unselective presentation of life with extreme realism. The writers in this style were Zola, Maupassant, Edmond and Jules Goncourt.

SLOGAN. Gaelic *sluagh-ghairm*; *sluagh*, host, army, *ghairm*, cry, shout. A Highland war-cry; the cry of a political or other party; a catchy phrase used in advertising. It is a substitute for the older *watchward, motto*.

SLOKA. Greek. A distich, two metrical lines of sixteen syllables. This is the chief verse form of the epics written in Sanskrit, the ancient and sacred language of India.

SLUG. A solid line of type cast by a composing machine in Linotype printing.

SMECTYMNUUS. The pseudonym used by five Presbyterian ministers in 1641 in their pamphlet against episcopacy. It was made out of their initials; their names were Stephen Marshal, Edmund Calamy, Thomas Young, Matthew Newcomen, and William Spurstow. Bishop Joseph Hall answered the attack, and Milton defended what these men had said.

SOBRIQUET: SOUBRIQUET. French. An epithet, a nickname.

SOCIETY FOR PURE ENGLISH, THE: S.P.E. This was founded in 1913. Henry Bradley, Robert Bridges, Walter Raleigh, and Logan Pearsall Smith were on the committee. Their object was to guide and help in the use and improvement of the English language, and the Society has issued many Tracts since 1919.

In 1712 Swift produced his *Proposal for correcting, improving and ascertaining the English Tongue* claiming:

> . . . that some method should be thought on for ascertaining and fixing our language for ever, after such alterations are made in it as shall be thought requisite. For I am of opinion, that it is better a language should not be wholly perfect, than that it should be perpetually changing . . . Provided that no word, which a society shall give a sanction to, be afterwards antiquated and exploded, they may have liberty to receive whatever new ones they shall find occasion for.

Unfortunately the death of Queen Anne stopped the scheme.

SOCK. Latin *soccus*, light shoe. The light shoe worn by actors in ancient comedy. Used for comedy and the comic style. *See also* BUSKIN.

SOCRATIC IRONY. *See* IRONY.

SOLECISM. Greek *soloikismós, soloikizō* from *sóloikos*, barbarous; said to come from the corruption of the Attic dialect among the Athenian colonists (*oikízein*, to colonize) of *Soloi* in Cilicia in Asia Minor. An offence against conventional grammar or idiom. A blunder in the manner of speaking or writing. An impropriety in good taste and conduct. In these lines from *Childe Harold*, Byron commits a solecism for the sake of the rhyme:

> And send'st him, shivering in thy playful spray
> And howling, to his Gods, where haply lies
> His petty hope in some near port or bay,
> And dashest him again to earth: — there let him lay.

SOLILOQUY. Late Latin *sōliloquium*, coined by St. Augustine, bishop of Hippo, on Greek *monologíā*, from *sōlus*, alone, *loqui*, to speak. Speaking one's thoughts aloud with none to hear or regardless of the presence of hearers. A declamation in this manner by a character in a play, as in the soliloquies of Shakespeare. *See also* MONOLOGUE.

SOLIPSISM. Latin *sōlus*, alone, *ipse*, self. The view that self is the only object of real knowledge or the only thing really existent. An extreme form of idealism.

SONG. Old English *singan*, to sing. Perhaps cognate with Greek *omphē*, voice. A lyrical poem intended to be set to music and sung. The first book of accompanied songs to be published is that of Don Luis Milan (1536), a Spanish lute-player. Here is the last verse of 'Who is Sylvia?' from Shakespeare's *Two Gentlemen of Verona*:

> Then to Sylvia let us sing,
> That Sylvia is excelling;
> She excels each mortal thing
> Upon the dull earth dwelling
> To her let us garlands bring.

SONNET. Italian *sonetto*, diminutive of *suono*, sound, Latin *sonus*. A poem of fourteen lines in pentameter verse form.

The Italian (Petrarchan or Regular) sonnet is divided by a pause into octave and sestet. The octave, consisting of two quatrains, rhymes *a b b a, a b b a*. The sestet, consisting of two tercets, rhymes *c d c, d c d*, or *c d e, c d e*.

In the English or Shakespearean sonnet, the lines are grouped into three quatrains and a concluding couplet, rhyming: *a b a b, c d c d, e f e f, g g*.

The Miltonic sonnet follows the Petrarchan in arrangement of the octave, but there is no division marked between the octave and sestet, the sense running from the eighth into the ninth line. The rhyming of the sestet is sometimes arranged *c d c d c d*, instead of *c d e c d e*.

The sonnet sequence, a collection of sonnets on the same theme, was originated by Sir Philip Sidney's famous series of sonnets known as 'Astrophel and Stella'.

SOPHISM. Greek, *sóphisma, sophízō*, instruct, from *sophós*, wise. A specious but fallacious argument, used either deliberately to mislead or to display ingenuity in reasoning.

SOPHIST. Greek *sophistēs, sophízō*, instruct, from *sophós*, wise. In ancient Greece, a paid teacher of intellectual and ethical matters; contrasted with 'philosopher', and frequently used as a term of disparagement.

> As swift to scent the sophist as to praise
> The honest worker or the well-turned phrase.
> C. A. Alington

SOPHISTICATION. Greek *sóphisma, sophízein*, to make wise; *sophós*, wise. The use of, or deception by, sophistry (specious but fallacious reasoning); the state of being involved or subtle, without directness, simplicity, or naturalness; experienced in the more artificial phases of life; worldly-wise.

SOTIE. French *sot*, fool, clown. The topical and satirical play of medieval France. Pierre Gringore is the best-known author of these plays, intended for amusement only.

SPANISH VERSE. Unrhymed trochaic tetrameter four-line stanzas. Instances of its use can be found in the later poetry of Heinrich Heine (1797–1856).

SPARE LYRICISM. Speaking of Canadian verse, Ralph Gustafson says:

> We are hitched to the seasons — four sharp ones with no south to melt into. After ice-lockings, we dive into spring. Conditions are good for spare lyricism, metaphysical wit for an essential stability; for the green from the white.

> Fled to the green suburbs, Death
> Lies scared to death under a heap of bones.
> Beauty buds from mire
> And I, a singer in season, observe
> Death is a name for beauty not in use.
> Irving Layton, *Composition in Late Spring*

SPASMODIC SCHOOL. Greek *spasmṓd-(ēs)*, of the nature of a spasm, from *spaşm-(ós)*, spasm, from *spá-(ein)*, to drag, tear. A term applied by W. E. Aytoun to a group of poets including P. J. Bailey, S. T. Dobell, and Alexander Smith. He ridiculed their poems in his mock-tragedy, *Firmilian, or the Student of Badajoz* (1854).

SPECTATOR, THE. A periodical produced by Steele and Addison from 1st March 1711 to 6th December 1712. It appeared daily, dealing with manners, morals, social affairs, and literature. One aim was to bring 'philosophy out of closets and libraries, schools and colleges, to dwell in clubs and assemblies, at tea-tables and in coffee-houses'. Papers presenting Sir Roger de Coverley are a notable feature. Its modern descendant, a weekly, is still a journal of some influence.

SPENSERIAN SONNET. Edmund Spenser told his own love story in the sonnet-sequence, the *Amoretti*. Also called the link sonnet, it has a rhyme scheme which links octave and sestet, and concludes with a rhymed couplet:

> *a b a b   b c b c*
> *c d c d   e e.*

Unrighteous Lord of Love, what law is this,
That me thou makest thus tormented be,
The whiles she lordeth in licentious blisse
Of her freewill, scorning both thee and me?
See! how the Tyrannesse doth joy to see
The huge massácres which her eyes do make;
And humbled harts brings captive unto thee,
That thou of them mayst mightie vengeance take,
But her proud hart doe thou a little shake,
And that high look, with which she doth comptroll
All this worlds pride, bow to a baser make,
And al her faults in thy black booke enroll:
  That I may laugh at her in equall sort,
  As she doth laugh at me, and makes my pain her sport.

SPENSERIAN STANZA. This stanza was invented by Edmund Spenser; in it he wrote *The Faerie Queene*. It consists of nine lines, eight five-foot iambic lines, followed by an iambic line of six feet, the alexandrine. The rhyme scheme is *a b a b b c b c c* (three sets of rhymes). Here is the description of Blandina:

Yet were her words and looks but false and fayned,
To some hid end to make more easie way,
Or to allure such fondlings whom she trayned
Into her trap unto their owne decay:
Thereto, when needed, she could weepe and pray,
And when she listed she could fawne and flatter;
Now smyling smoothly like to sommers day,
Now glooming sadly, so to cloke her matter;
Yet were her words but wynd, and all her tears but water.

Byron's *Childe Harold's Pilgrimage*, Shelley's *Adonais* and Keats's *The Eve of St. Agnes* are all written in the Spenserian stanza.

SPIRIT OF THE AGE. This is the feeling of the writers and artists of the day. In *A Defence of Poetry*, Shelley says:

> It is impossible to read the compositions of the most celebrated writers of the present day without being startled with the electric life which burns within their words. They measure the circumference and sound the depths of human nature with a comprehensive and all-penetrating spirit, and they are themselves perhaps the most sincerely astonished at its manifestations; for it is less their spirit than the spirit of the age.

Writing of William Godwin, Hazlitt said:

> The Spirit of the Age was never more fully shown than in its treatment of this writer — its love of paradox and change, its dastard submission to prejudice and to the fashion of the day. Five-and-twenty years ago he was in the very zenith of a sultry and unwholesome popularity; he blazed as a sun in the firmament of reputation; no one was more talked of, more looked up to, more sought after, and wherever liberty, truth, justice was the theme, his name was not far off: — now he has sunk below the horizon, and enjoys the serene twilight of a doubtful immortality.

SPONDEE. Greek *spondeîos* (*poús*, stem, *pod-*, foot), used in the slow solemn hymns sung at a *spondḗ* or drink-offering. In classical poetry, a foot consisting of two long syllables. In English verse, a metrical foot of two stressed syllables as in this line from Milton's *Paradise Lost*:

Rócks, cáves, | lakés, féns, | bógs, déns, | añd shádes | óf déath. |

SPOONERISM. From the name of the Rev. W. A. Spooner, Warden of New College, Oxford, who made many such slips. An accidental reversal of the initial sounds, or other parts, of two or more words, as in *Kinquering congs their titles take* for *Conquering Kings their titles take*. Other examples are *poured with rain* for *roared with pain*; *a well-boiled icicle* for *a well-oiled bicycle*. See also METATHESIS.

SPRUNG RHYTHM. A rhythm counted not by syllables and regular feet but by stresses (stress being the emphasis of the voice upon a word or syllable). If you imagine a line divided into feet, then one syllable would be stressed in each foot, but that syllable can either stand alone or be accompanied by a number of unstressed syllables (usually not more than four). As stresses, not syllables, make up the line, it may vary considerably in length.

Consider these lines from G. M. Hopkins's *The Wreck of the Deutschland*:

Thou hast bóund bónes and véins in me fástened me flésh
And áfter it álmost unmáde, whát with dréad . . .

each has five stresses, and would have the same value as this normal iambic line:

But sóft: methínks I scént the mórning aír.

STAGE DIRECTIONS. Notes added to the script of a play giving information about its performance, usually concerned with the movements of the actors, and with the scenery or the stage effects. Stage directions vary from the brief statement in *The Winter's Tale*, 'Exit, pursued by a bear' to the prolix information inserted in the text of his plays by Bernard Shaw.

STAGE TIME. The unity of time, derived from Aristotle's *Poetics*, observed by the French dramatists, but ignored by Shakespeare, stated that a play should represent what takes place 'within the limits of a single revolution of the sun, or nearly so'. Though Shakespeare speaks in *Romeo and Juliet* of 'the two hours' traffic of our stage', in the action of the play we see a great expanse of time. Stage time nearly always differs from real time.

STAND. A synonym for *epode*.

STANDARD ENGLISH. The form of English used, in Britain, with some slight variations according to the locality, by most cultured, English-speaking people. In *The Universal English Dictionary*, H. C. Wyld defines Received Standard English as one 'recognized as conforming to a standard, as being in accordance with common practice'.

STANZA. Latin *stantem*, *stāre*, to stand. Lines of verse grouped together to compose a pattern usually repeated throughout the poem. A stanza pattern is determined by the number of lines, the number of feet and stresses in each line, and the rhyme scheme. It is a melodic unit, often unaltered throughout, but slight changes are made for effect as in Coleridge's *The Rime of the Ancient Mariner*. Stave, another name for stanza, is associated with song.

STASIMON. Greek *stásimon*, stationary. In ancient Greek tragedy, a song of the Chorus, coming after the *párodos*, which continued without being interrupted by dialogue.

STATEMENT. Latin *stāre*, to stand. I. A. Richards uses this term in *Principles of Literary Criticism* to indicate discourse which can be verified scientifically.

STATIONERS' COMPANY. This was one of the Livery Companies of the City of London, incorporated by royal charter in 1557. At Stationers' Hall, the hall of this Company, every member had to enter in the register the name of any book he desired to print. During the seventeenth century, the Company's control of printing declined, but was revived under the Copyright Act of 1709.

STAVE. A verse or stanza of a poem. A set of lines for musical notation.

STEREOTYPE: STEREO. Greek *stereós*, solid; *túpos*, *túptein*, to strike. A duplicate printing-plate cast from a papier mâché or plastic mould.

STET. Latin word meaning 'let it stand', written in the proof margin to cancel an alteration. Dots are placed under the word which is to remain.

STICHOMYTHIA. Greek *stikhomūthia*; *stíkhos*, a line, *mûthos*, speech, talk. In Greek drama, dialogue consisting of single lines of verse spoken alternately, especially in disputes. It was sharpened by antithesis and rhetorical repetition. Examples occur also in Seneca's tragedies. The term is applied to modern imitations, as in these lines from T. S. Eliot's *Murder in the Cathedral*, when the Knights speak four harsh lines to Thomas à Becket:

> *First Knight.* Absolve all those you have excommunicated.
> *Second Knight.* Resign the powers you have arrogated.
> *Third Knight.* Restore to the King the money you appropriated.
> *First Knight.* Renew the obedience you have violated.

STILNOVISM. Italian, new style. *See* DOLCE STIL NUOVO.

STOCK CHARACTER. Old English *stocc*, trunk, log, stock. A familiar character, such as the hero, heroine, tyrant, and villain of nineteenth-century melodrama. Other examples are the *miles gloriosus* or braggart soldier, Bobadill, in Jonson's *Every Man in his Humour*; in Shakespeare, Falstaff, Juliet's Nurse; Sir Anthony Absolute in Sheridan's *The Rivals*.

STOCK RESPONSES. Old English *stocc*, trunk, log, stock. Latin *respondēre*, from *spondēre*, to pledge. In *Practical Criticism*, I. A. Richards says:

> These have their opportunity whenever a poem seems to, or does, involve views and emotions already fully prepared in the reader's mind, so that what happens appears to be more of the reader's doing than the poet's. The button is pressed, and then the author's work is done, for immediately the record starts playing in quasi- (or total) independence of the poem which is supposed to be its origin or instrument.

STORM OF ASSOCIATION. Wordsworth used this phrase when speaking of the power of inspiration, a kind of external force, which compelled the poet to write. Blake also experiencing the power of creation declared, 'Energy is Eternal Delight'.

STORY. Latin *historia*. R. L. Stevenson gives us this information:

> There are only three ways of writing a story: you may take a plot and fit characters to it; or you may take a character and choose incidents and situations to develop it, or . . . you may take a certain atmosphere and get action and persons to express and realize it.

STORY WITHIN A STORY. *See* FRAME STORY.

STREAM OF CONSCIOUSNESS. This phrase was first used by William James, and appeared in his *Principles of Psychology* in 1890. It is the technique for revealing thoughts and feelings flowing, in perpetual soliloquy, through the mind of the character. The method has been used by Dorothy Richardson, James Joyce, Virginia Woolf, and William Faulkner. Edith Wharton says, in *The Writing of Fiction*:

> The stream of consciousness method differs from the slice of life in noting down mental as well as physical reactions, but resembles it in setting them down just as they come, with a deliberate disregard of their relevance in the particular case, or rather with the assumption that their very unsorted abundance constitutes in itself the author's subject.

STRESS. Low Latin *strictiāre*, from *stringĕre*, to draw tight, to compress. The emphasis laid on a syllable or word. In verse, the emphasis required by the metre is the *metrical* stress. When the meaning demands stress not in accord with the metre, this change in the rhythmic pattern is called *sense*, *logical*, or *rhetorical* stress.

STROPHE.   Greek *strépho*, turn.   In Greek prosody, a stanza of a
   Greek choral song sung as the chorus moved in one direction.   It
   was followed by the *antistrophé*, a similar stanza, which was sung
   when the chorus turned and moved in the opposite direction.   The
   term is also applied to a stanza in which two or more series of lines
   correspond metrically to form divisions of the poem.   Ben Jonson's
   A Pindaric Ode on the Death of Sir Henry Morison is a fine example.
   This is the first stanza:

> It is not growing like a tree
> In bulk, doth make men better be;
> Or standing long an oak, three hundred year,
> To fall a log at last, dry, bald, and sere:
> A lily of a day,
> Is fairer far in May,
> Although it fall and die that night;
> It was the plant and flower of light.
> In small proportions we just beauties see;
> And in short measures, life may perfect be.

STURM UND DRANG.   German, literally, storm and stress.   The
   name was taken from the title of an absurd romantic drama, *Wirr-
   warr, oder Sturm und Drang* by Friedrich Klinger.   It was given to
   a period of literary ferment in Germany during the latter part of the
   eighteenth century.   Inspired by the fervent idealism of Rousseau,
   it was a revolt against the limitations of conventions, and was a
   recall to nature.   The movement was strongly nationalistic, and
   showed itself in Goethe's *Faust* and *Götz von Berlichingen*, Schiller's
   Die Räuber, Friedrich Müller's *Golo und Genoveva*, and *Die Soldaten*
   by Jakob Lenz.

STYLE.   Latin *stilus*, a pointed instrument for writing on waxed
   tablets; also, way of writing.   In his book *Style*, F. L. Lucas says:

> Our subject, then, is simply the effective use of language,
> especially in prose, whether to make statements or to rouse
> emotions.   It involves, first of all, the power to put facts
> with clarity and brevity; but facts are usually none the
> worse for being put also with as much grace and interest as
> the subject permits.   For grace or interest, indeed, if the
> subject is purely practical, like conics or conchology, there
> may not be much room; though even cookery books have
> been salted with occasional irony; and even mathematicians
> have indulged in jests, as of going to Heaven in a perpendicu-
> lar straight line.   But, further, men need also to express
> and convey their emotions; and to kindle emotions in others.
> Without emotion, no art of literature; nor any other art.

STYLE: STYLUS. Latin *stilus*, a pointed instrument for writing on wax-tablets; incorrectly spelt *stylus* by late writers; perhaps some meanings from Greek *stûlos*, a pillar. An ancient writing-implement, a small metal rod with pointed end for scratching letters on wax-covered tablets, plates of lead. The blunt end was used for obliterating.

SUBCONSCIOUS. Latin *sub*, below, under, beneath, *conscius*, knowing, aware of. Pertaining to conscious processes just outside personal awareness.

SUBJECTIVE WRITING. Latin *subiectus*; *subicĕre*, to subject, from *iacĕre*, to throw. Laying stress upon personal thoughts, impulses and feelings. The writing of Virginia Woolf, Dos Passos, the poetry of Rimbaud and Dylan Thomas are outstandingly subjective.

SUBLIME. Latin *sublīmis*, lofty. Characterized by extreme nobility and grandeur. Impressive, exalted, awe-inspiring. As though raised above the ordinary human qualities.

Longinus was the author of the remarkable treatise of literary criticism, *On the Sublime*.

SUBPLOT. A separate action in a story or play, usually contrasting with the main plot. Sometimes called a counterplot, it is important in many of Shakespeare's plays, for example, *King Lear, Hamlet, The Tempest*.

SUBSTITUTION. Latin *substituĕre*, to appoint under, from *statuĕre*, to appoint, set up. The use of a metrical foot other than the one fixed by the metre. The classical rule of equivalence makes two short syllables equal to one long. Therefore, in quantitative verse, dactyls, anapaests, spondees, amphibrachs may be substituted one for the other. When an iamb is substituted for a trochee or an anapaest for a dactyl, the result is a *reversed* or *inverted* foot, sometimes called *inverted stress* or *accent*. Perhaps the commonest substitution in English verse is the use of a trochee for an iamb at the beginning of a line, as here in Shakespeare's Sonnet 26:

Lórd ŏf | mỹ loŕe, | tŏ whóm | iñ váss | ălắge. |

SUBTOPIA. From Latin *sub*, below and *utopia*; 'near Paradise'. A term applied to urban and rural areas which have been spoilt by bad planning. It refers also to unsightly suburbs and ribbon development spoiling the countryside.

SUCCÈS DE SCANDALE. French. Success dependent upon a work's scandalous character.

SUCCÈS D'ESTIME. French. A success of esteem or approval, but not necessarily a profitable one; a very mild success.

Twilight Bar 'had what is called a *succès d'estime* — in other words, it was a flop'. Arthur Koestler, quoted in *Radio Times*, 22nd October 1964.

SUCCÈS FOU. French. Wild, enthusiastic success.

SUMMARY. Latin *summārium*, a summary. A brief account, an abridgement, an epitome.

SURPRISE ENDING. An unexpected twist at the end of a narrative. This occurs frequently in the short stories of O. Henry.

SURREALISM. French *surréalisme*, beyond realism. A recent movement among certain writers and painters, which originated in France. Paul Harvey says, in *The Oxford Companion to English Literature*, 'The former attempt expression by means of words set down without logical sequence; while the latter, led by the Spanish painter, Joán Miró, give weird distorted forms to ordinary objects'.

The prose of James Joyce in *Finnegans Wake* and some of the verse of Dylan Thomas and Edwin Muir have been called surrealistic.

SUSPENDED RHYME. *See* CONSONANCE.

SUSPENSE. Latin *suspendĕre*, to hang up. The state of expectation in that we want to know what happens next. It is an element of nearly all plays, and the author plays upon our anxious uncertainty. As E. M. Forster says, in *Aspects of the Novel*, 'There is nothing in us but primeval curiosity, and consequently our other literary judgments are ludicrous'.

In Milton's *Samson Agonistes*, Manoa declares:

Suspense in news is torture, speak them out.

The Messenger replies:

Then take the worst in brief, *Samson* is dead.

SUSPENSION OF DISBELIEF. In his *Biographia Literaria*, Coleridge spoke of 'that willing suspension of disbelief for the moment, which constitutes poetic faith'. He had in mind a remark made by Ben Jonson, in *Discoveries*, 'To many things a man should owe but a temporary belief, and suspension of his own judgment'. It is this 'willing suspension of disbelief' which makes us accept as real the creations of the imagination.

SWASH LETTERS. Flourished or calligraphic letters seen in certain italic capital letters of such founts as Caslon and Garamond.

SWEETNESS AND LIGHT. In *Culture and Anarchy*, Matthew Arnold says, 'The pursuit of perfection, then, is the pursuit of sweetness and light. . . . He who works for sweetness and light united, works to make reason and the will of God prevail.' This came to Arnold from a sentence in *The Battle of the Books* by Jonathan Swift, 'Instead of dirt and poison we have rather chosen to fill our hives with honey and wax; thus furnishing mankind with the two noblest of things, which are sweetness and light'.

SYLLABIC VERSE. The determining feature of syllabic verse is the number of syllables in the line, not the stress nor the quantity. In *Smooth Gnarled Crape Myrtle*, Marianne Moore uses this verse form. In the first stanza of thirteen lines the syllables number 6, 8, 9, 9, 6, 7, 5, 8, 8, 6, 7, 4, 6:

> A brass-green bird with grass-
> green throat smooth as a nut springs from
> twig to twig askew, copying the
> Chinese flower piece, — businesslike atom
> in the stiff-leafed tree's blue-
> pink dregs-of-wine pyramids
> of mathematic
> circularity; one of a
> pair. A redbird with a hatchet
> crest lights straight, on a twig
> between the two, bending the
> peculiar
> bouquet down; and there are . . .

SYLLABUS. Ernest Weekley says this is 'a ghost-word due to a misprint in the fifteen-century edition of Cicero — "indices . . . quos vos Graeci (ut opinor) *syllabos* appellatis" (*Ad Atticum*, iv. 4), where correct reading is *sittubas*, accusative plural of *sittuba*, Greek *sittúbē*, piece of parchment used as a label-tag of MS'. An abstract giving the main subjects of a course of teaching, of a lecture; a plan of hours of work. It is a summary of the decrees of the Roman Curia, especially the list of eighty heretical doctrines condemned by Pius IX in 1864.

SYLLEPSIS. Greek *súllēpsis*, a taking together, comprehension; *lambánein*, to take. A figure of speech in which the same word (verb or preposition) is applied to two others in different senses. Evelyn describes Charles I as 'circled with his royal diadem and the affections of his people'. In Goldsmith's essay, *The Important Trifler*, Beau Tibbs greets a friend, 'Where have you been hiding this half-century? Positively I had fancied you were gone down

to cultivate matrimony and your estate in the country.' Dickens
wrote, 'Miss Bolo went home in a flood of tears and a sedan
chair.'

SYLLOGISM. Greek *sullogismós*, a reckoning together, from
logízesthai, to reckon, from *lógos*, word, reckoning. Deduction,
from two propositions containing three terms of which one appears
in both, of a conclusion that is necessarily true if they are true.
'All men are mortal; all soldiers are men; Therefore all soldiers
are mortal.' *Mortal* is the *major term*, the first proposition is the
major premise; *soldiers*, the subject of the conclusion, is the *minor
term* and the preliminary proposition containing it is the *minor
premise*. The term common to both premises (*men*) is the *middle
term*.

SYMBOL. Greek *súmbolon*, token, watchword, from *sumbállein*, to
agree, literally, cast together. In *Dictionary of Art Terms*, R. G.
Haggar, defining this term, says:

> It is a recognizable equivalent or type of some person, object,
> or abstract idea by means of features associated in the
> popular mind with that person, object, or abstract idea.
> Thus in medieval art the saints are identified by the signs of
> their martyrdom; for example, the wheel of St. Catherine.
> It is also the expression of abstract ideas in terms of pattern,
> colour, line; the conveyance of abstract or spiritual ideas by
> means of natural objects. Symbols may be of many kinds:
> hieroglyphics, initials, emblems, allegories, fables, and (as in
> some modern art) enigmas. Some symbols closely approxi-
> mate to an idea or person and are easily recognized; others
> can be understood only by following some out-of-the-way
> association of ideas.

Blake made great use of symbols in his poetry, and Yeats
acknowledged his main symbols to be 'Sun and Moon (in all phases),
Tower, Mask, Tree . . .'

SYMBOLISM. Greek *súmbolon*, token, watchword, from *sumbállein*,
to agree. The characteristic of some writers to invest objects,
actions, or ideas with a symbolic meaning. The representation, not
literally, but by symbols. A symbol is something standing for
something else; the cross is a symbol of Christianity, the rose is a
symbol of beauty. .
Symbolism is also the name of a recent school of French poets,
including Mallarmé, Verlaine, and Rimbaud, who aimed at
representing ideas and emotions by suggestion rather than by direct
expression. They set symbolic meaning on objects, words, sounds,

and as extreme individualists showed their revolt against naturalism and realism. Mallarmé gives this definition:

> Nommer un objet, c'est supprimer la jouissance du poème, qui est faite du bonheur de deviner peu à peu; le suggérer, voilà le rêve. C'est le parfait usage de ce mystère qui constitue le symbole; évoquer petit à petit un objet pour montrer un état d'âme par une série de développements.

It has been claimed that the work of James Joyce, Gertrude Stein, Kafka, and T. S. Eliot is close to Symbolism.

SYMPLOCE. Greek, *sumplokē*, interweaving, plaiting together. A figure of speech consisting in the repetition at both the beginning and the end of a sentence of one word or phrase. It is a combination of *anaphora*, and *epistrophe*. Here is an example from Sir Philip Sidney:

> Such was as then the estate of this Duke, as it was no time by direct means to seek her, and such was the estate of his captive will, as he could delay no time of seeking her.

SYMPOSIUM. Greek *sumpósion*, convivial gathering of the educated. Literally, a drinking together, from Greek *pósis*, drinking. Friendly, philosophic discussion. An account of such discussion. A set of contributions on one subject from various writers.

SYNAERESIS. Greek *sunaíresis*, a taking, drawing, together. The contraction of two vowels or syllables. Slurring syllables, especially vowels, together, as: *flower, amorous, mouldering*.

SYNAESTHESIA. Greek *sún*, together, *aisthētikós*, *aisthánomai*, perceive. The close association of an image perceived by one of the senses with an image perceived by another. The sensory impressions belonging to sight, sound, and smell are intimately connected. Dr. Johnson once commented on the discovery made by a blind man that scarlet 'represented nothing so much as the clangour of a trumpet'. One of the best examples of *synaesthesia* occurs in Baudelaire's Sonnet *Correspondences* when he describes certain perfumes as 'soft as oboes, green as meadows'. Edith Sitwell makes free use of this device, and says in *Aubade*:

> Jane, Jane,
> Tall as a crane,
> The morning light creaks down again.

Here she suggests that the fitful uncertain quality of morning light makes a creaking sound.

SYNAL(O)EPHA. Greek *sunaloiphē*, contraction of two syllables. The elision of two syllables into one, especially the elision in a line of verse of the two vowels at the end of one word and the beginning of the next. In his dedication to the *Aeneid*, Dryden gives this example of *synaloepha* from Chapman's *Homer*:

> Apollo's priest to th' Argive fleet doth bring

and says it is 'to shun the shock of the two vowels immediately following each other'.

SYNCOPATE. Latin *syncopāre*, to faint away, from Greek *sugkopē*, a cutting short. To shorten a word by dropping a medial sound or syllable, as in *symbology* for *symbolology*, *Gloster* for *Gloucester*. (*Concise Oxford Dictionary*)
   To change musical rhythm by displacing either the beat or the normal accent.

SYNCOPATION. Greek *sugkopē*, a cutting short. In *Poetry Handbook*, Babette Deutsch says:

> This is the usual term for the concurrence of two different temporal patterns. It is evident where the speech rhythm of a line requires a different number of stresses from that required by the metrical scheme. Thus, this line of Milton's has the ten syllables of regular blank verse, which is iambic in character and normally has five stresses, yet it is natural to read the line with only four stresses:
>
> > Of púritie and pláce and ínnocénce.
>
> The musical effects of Marvell's lyric, *The Garden*, are in part due to syncopation. The duple rhythm established at the start,
>
> > How váinly mén themsélves amáze
>
> is occasionally counterpointed against a triple rhythm, as in the second line of this couplet:
>
> > Annihilating all that's made
> > To a green | Thought | in a green | Shade.
>
> A similar effect is obvious in these lines by Yeats:
>
> > A levelling, rancorous, rational sort of mind
> > That never looked out of the eye of a saint
> > Or out of drunkard's eye.
>
> The word accent and the sense stress in the first two lines are counterpointed against the normal iambic beat observable in the third half-line, with resulting syncopation.

SYNCOPE. Greek *sugkopē*, a cutting short; from *sún*, together, *kopē*, act of cutting. The omission of a letter or a syllable from within a word, as in *o'er* for *over*, *ta'en* for *taken*.

SYNECDOCHE. Greek *sunekdéchesthai*, to take with something else, understood along with. A figure of speech in which a part of an object or idea stands for the whole; or the whole stands for a part. For example: 'Give us this day our daily *bread*'. 'All *hands* to the pumps'. *England* for the *English XI*.

SYNONYM. Greek *sunónumos*, of like sense, with-name. A word having the same, or very nearly the same, meaning as another. The only practical use of synonym is to describe words of similar but not identical meaning, such as: *commence, begin*; *hide, conceal*; *wish, desire*; *benevolence, good-will*.

SYNONYMOUS PARALLELISM. Greek *sunónumos*, of the same name; *parállēlos*, beside one another. A couplet in which each line expresses the same idea in different terms:

> There is nothing hid that shall not be made manifest,
> No secret that shall not come to light.

SYNOPSIS. Greek *súnopsis*, *sún*, with, together, *ópsis*, a view. A collective or general view of any subject; a summary.

SYNOPTIC. Greek *sunoptikós*, taking a general view. Giving a general view of the whole. The *Synoptic Gospels*, those of St. Matthew, St. Mark, and St. Luke, which present similarity in matter and form, readily admit of being brought under *synopsis*.

SYNTAX. Greek, *súntaxis*, arrangement, grammatical construction. The arrangement and grammatical relation of words as parts of a sentence. Sentence construction.

SYZYGY. Greek *súzugía*, from *sún* and *zugón*, yoke, pair. In Greek prosody, a dipody, or combination of two feet.

T

TABLEAU. French *tableau*, picture. The representation of living persons suitably dressed and posed in fixed attitudes of some well-known picture, an historical scene, or part of a play. It is also called *tableau vivant*.

TABULA RASA. Latin, 'erased tablet'. Anthony Friedson says, 'In his *Essay on Human Understanding*, Locke defines what is really the opposite point of view to Plato's. He is the pioneer proponent of the *tabula rasa*. Locke regards the mind at birth as comparable to an empty cabinet with two compartments. As we live one compartment is filled with our *perceptions* and the other with our *sensations*. From these two combined we get our *idea*.'

TAGS. Hackneyed phrases or quotations. In *Modern Poetry*, Louis MacNeice said, 'The Eliot–Pound method allows of the bodily transference into a poem not only of tags from other poetry or prose, but of bits of public records, washing bills, statistics.'
This is shown in these lines from Ezra Pound's *Canto LXXXI*:

> Hast 'ou fashioned so airy a mood
>   To draw up leaf from the root?
> Hast 'ou found a cloud so light
>   As seemed neither mist nor shade?
>
>   Then resolve me, tell me aright
>   If Waller sang or Dowland played.
>
> Your eyen two wol sleye me sodenly
> I may the beauté of hem nat susteyne
>
> And for 180 years almost nothing.
>
> Ed ascoltando al leggier mormorio
>   there came new subtlety of eyes into my tent . . .

TAIL-RHYME STANZA: *RIME COUÉE*. The usual structure is *a a*⁴ *b*³ *c c*⁴ *b*³. A group of lines is followed by a shorter line, resembling a tail when compared with the others, rhyming with another short line.

TALE. Anglo-Saxon *talu*, speech, number. A fictitious narrative, told in prose or verse. It is often simple in theme, skilful in presentation. Famous examples are Chaucer's *Canterbury Tales*,

Swift's *A Tale of a Tub, Wandering Willie's Tale* in *Redgauntlet* by Sir Walter Scott, *Tales in Verse* by George Crabbe. The term, usually synonymous with *short story*, can refer to a novel, for example: *The Tale of Chloe* by George Meredith, and *A Tale of Two Cities* by Dickens.

TALENT. Greek *tálanton*, pair of scales, balance, sum of money representing a talent of silver. Archaic form *talássai*, to take upon oneself, undergo. Special gift or faculty, a marked aptitude. William Hazlitt says, 'Talent is the capacity of doing anything that depends on application and industry; it is a voluntary power, while genius is involuntary'.

TALL TALE. A narrative which is extravagant, excessive, and difficult to believe.

TASTE. Vulgar Latin *taxitāre*, from *taxāre*, to handle, to touch. The faculty of liking, of discerning excellence, especially in art and literature. 'Good taste', says Coleridge, in *Biographia Literaria*, 'must be acquired, and like all other good things is the result of thought and the submissive study of the best models.'

TAUTOLOGY. Greek *tautología*, saying the same; *tò autó*, the same, *légein*, to speak. Needless repetition of the same thing in different words; for example: 'My friends spoke all at once together.'

TELESTICH. Greek *têle*, *télos*, end, *stíkhos*, a row, a line of verse. A short poem in which the final letters of the lines, taken in order from the first line, spell a word or words.

TENOR. In *The Philosophy of Rhetoric*, I. A. Richards designated the two parts of a metaphor by the terms *tenor* and *vehicle*. A metaphor is a comparison; one part is the tenor, the other is the vehicle. When Macbeth says, 'Life's but a walking shadow', the word *life* is the tenor of the metaphor and *walking shadow* is the vehicle.

TENSION. From Latin *tendĕre*, to stretch. Following Anaximander, Heraclitus the Greek 'weeping philosopher' (*c.* 500 B.C.) maintained that the universe was a conflict of opposites controlled by eternal Justice. 'Men do not know how what is at variance agrees with itself. It is an attunement of opposite tensions, like that of the bow and the lyre.' Some critics hold that it is this attunement of mental and emotional tensions which gives form and unity to a work of art.

TERCET. Latin *tertius*, third. Three lines of verse which form a unit. The term applies especially to the terza rima stanza and to half the sestet of a sonnet. The following tercets are from *Ode to the West Wind*, in terza rima, by Shelley:

> O wild West Wind, thou breath of Autumn's being,
> Thou from whose unseen presence the leaves dead
> Are driven, like ghosts from an enchanter fleeing,
>
> Yellow, and black, and pale, and hectic red,
> Pestilence-stricken multitudes! O thou,
> Who chariotest to their dark wintry bed
>
> The wingèd seeds . . .

The term *triplet* applies to three lines which have the same rhyme. This example is from Tennyson's *Two Voices*:

> A still small voice spake unto me,
> 'Thou art so full of misery,
> Were it not better not to be?'

TERZA RIMA. Italian, literally, *third rhyme*. An Italian form of iambic verse consisting of stanzas of three lines, the middle line of each stanza rhyming with the first and last of the succeeding. Rhyme scheme: *a b a, b c b, c d c, d e d* and so on, giving the appearance of unending continuity to the poem. It closes with a quatrain rhyming *y z y z*, or with a rhyming couplet. The most famous example of this form is *La Divina Commedia* by Dante. It has been used in English poetry by Sir Thomas Wyatt, Byron, Shelley, Browning, and W. H. Auden. Here is the last part of the *Ode to the West Wind*, a poem in which Shelley shows his mastery of the use of interlocking tercets:

> O thou,
> Who chariotest to their dark wintry bed
>
> The wingèd seeds, where they lie cold and low,
> Each like a corpse within its grave, until
> Thine azure sister of the Spring shall blow
>
> Her clarion o'er the dreaming earth, and fill
> (Driving sweet buds like flocks to feed in air)
> With living hues and odours plain and hill;
>
> Wild Spirit, which art moving everywhere;
> Destroyer and preserver; hear, O, hear!

TETRALOGY. Greek *tetralogía*, series of four dramas. A group of four dramas competing for the prize at Athens at the festival of Dionysus in the fifth century B.C. Three of the plays, forming the *trilogy*, were tragic. The other play was satyric. Here the chorus was dressed to represent satyrs (woodland gods, half men, half beasts) attendants of Dionysus.

The term also applies to four connected dramas, as found in Shakespeare's historical plays — the three parts of *Henry VI* and *Richard III*. Another example is Wagner's *The Ring of the Nibelungs* consisting of *Rhinegold, The Valkyrie, Siegfried,* and *The Dusk of the Gods*.

TETRAMETER. Greek *tetra*, *téttares*, four, *métros* from *métron*, measure. A line of four metrical feet. Here is an example from *Ode* by Collins:

> There Hon | our comes, | a pil|grim grey, |
> To bless | the turf | that wraps | their clay, |
> And Free|dom shall | awhile | repair, |
> To dwell | a weep|ing her|mit there! |

TEXTURE. Latin *textūra*; *texĕre, textum,* to weave. The structural impression resulting from the manner of combining or interrelating the parts of a whole as in music, art, literary compositions. Speaking of metre, John Crowe Ranson uses the term *texture* to refer 'to the variations on the basic metrical pattern, or structure'.

THEATRE OF CRUELTY. Antonin Artaud, who coined this phrase in the 1920s, meant the theatre which demonstrated man's unavoidable enslavement to things and to circumstance. This must, 'because its theme is humanity's common fate, be the theatre of an audience's total involvement, a theatre of experience rather than a didactic or a moral theatre'. Artaud himself said, 'The audience will be involved in a true action affecting the mind, flesh, and spirit'.

A programme entitled *The Theatre of Cruelty* arranged by Peter Brook and directed by him, in association with Charles Marowitz, was presented by the New Lamda Theatre Club early in January 1964. It contained wordless gesture, lively improvisations, and revealed a puzzling attitude of mind which springs from distrust of words.

A dramatic critic of *The Times* said that David Rudkin's *Afore Night Come*, a key-work of the sixties, ranks as British drama's first fully-fledged contribution to the theatre of cruelty, showing ritual violence and shutting out individual thought-processes.

THEATRE OF SILENCE. In *Twentieth Century Drama*, Bamber Gascoigne says:

> In Paris in the late twenties it seemed that the style of Jean-Jacques Bernard would have a profound influence on modern drama. His theatre was based on the dramatic possibilities inherent in the gaps between bits of dialogue and was known as 'the theatre of silence'. It has since been almost entirely forgotten.

THEATRE OF THE ABSURD. In *The Theatre of the Absurd*, Martin Esslin gives this name to *avant-garde* plays of today. He says that such playwrights as Samuel Beckett, Jean Genet, Eugène Ionesco, and Harold Pinter are not bound by any of the old conventions of 'the well-made play'. Characters may appear in different guises, change personality, age, or sex; the play may have no fixed location of scene; the very sequence of time and the laws of physics may go by the board. At first sight one seems to be presented with a series of random events designed only to bewilder. We may suppose this to be one of the effects of surrealism on literature.

THEME. Greek *théma*, proposition, from *tithénai*, to put. The subject on which one speaks; the term is more often used to indicate its central idea. The theme of *The Trojan Women* is regret for war. Anouilh's *Ring Round the Moon* is evolved round the theme 'all is vanity'.

THEOGONY. Greek *theós*, god. An account of the origin and of the genealogy of the gods.

THESAURUS. Greek *thēsaurós*, store, treasure, storehouse. A repository of information. A lexicon, cyclopaedia. In a more specialized use, a work such as *Roget's Thesaurus*, a comprehensive dictionary of synonyms.

THESIS. Greek *thésis*, a placing, arranging. A proposition to be maintained; dissertation, especially one by a candidate for degree. Also the unaccented syllable in English scansion. (*Concise Oxford Dictionary*)

THESIS NOVEL: *ROMAN À THÈSE*. A novel which deals with a social or political problem. Well-known examples are Harriet Beecher Stowe's *Uncle Tom's Cabin*, Upton Sinclair's *The Jungle*, John Steinbeck's *The Grapes of Wrath*.

THESIS PLAY. *See* PROBLEM PLAY.

THREE UNITIES. *See* UNITIES.

THRENODY. Greek *thrēnōidía*; *thrênos*, lamentation, *ōidé*, song. A song of lamentation. In classical Greek poetry, a lament for the dead; a choral dirge.

THRILLER. A highly sensational and exciting novel, play, or film. Ian Fleming's James Bond novels are highly successful examples of this genre. It need not necessarily be a *roman policier* (q.v.), though there is sometimes a strong element of the whodunit (q.v.) present.

TILDE. Spanish, from Latin *titulus*, title, inscription. *Tilde* is the diacritic mark ~ placed above the letter *n* in Spanish to indicate a front nasal consonant sound (ny), as in *señor* (senᵞor), *cañon* (anglicized as *canyon*).

TIME NOVELS. These are modern novels of the stream of consciousness school, dealing with significant moments of time in the lives of the characters. The time sequence is of importance to such writers as Dorothy Richardson, James Joyce, Virginia Woolf, and Marcel Proust.

TIRADE. French *tirade*, a long speech, Italian *tirata*, a volley, *tirāre*, to pull, to fire. A volley of words. A long vehement speech of censure or reproof. Mr. Micawber's denunciation of Uriah Heep is an excellent example:

> I'll put my hand in no man's hand until I have — blown to fragments — the — a — detestable — serpent — HEEP! I'll partake of no one's hospitality, until I have — a — moved Mount Vesuvius — to eruption — on — a — the abandoned rascal — HEEP ... I — a — I'll know nobody — and — a — say nothing — and — a — live nowhere — until I have crushed — to — a — undiscoverable atoms — the — transcendent and immortal hypocrite and perjurer — HEEP!

TMESIS. Greek *tmêsis*, cutting, *témnein*, to cut. The separation of the parts of a word by the insertion of another word or words. Fowler gives the example: 'whatsoever things' is written *what things soever*.

TONE. Greek *tónos*, stretching, tension; from *teínō*, stretch. The author's prevailing spirit, mental attitude, moral outlook appearing in the work itself and determining its tone. F. R. Leavis, considering the tone of a lyrical poem, called it 'the manner of readin compelled upon one', and referred to these lines by Thomas Nashe in *In Time of Pestilence*:

> Brightness falls from the air;
> Queens have died young and fair;
> Dust hath closed Helen's eye.
> I am sick, I must die.
>> Lord have mercy on us.

TOUCHSTONE. A siliceous stone used for testing alloys of gold or silver. Figuratively, a test or standard. In *The Study of Poetry*, Matthew Arnold says:

> Indeed there can be no more useful help for discovering what poetry belongs to the class of the truly excellent, and can therefore do us most good than to have always in one's mind lines and expressions of the great masters, and to apply them as a touchstone to other poetry. Of course we are not to require this other poetry to resemble them; it may be very dissimilar. But if we have any tact we shall find them, when we have lodged them well in our minds an infallible touchstone for detecting the presence or absence of high poetic quality, and also the degree of this quality, in all other poetry which we may place beside them. Short passages, even single lines, will serve our turn quite sufficiently.

TOUR DE FORCE. French, literally, a feat of strength or skill. A work showing clearly the author's power and skill.

TRACT. Latin *tractātus*, a touching, handling; a treatment. A treatise. A short pamphlet on some religious or political subject. For example, the renowned *Tracts for the Times* were a series of tracts on religious subjects written by Newman, Keble, Pusey, and R. H. Froude, appearing from 1833 to 1841.

TRACTARIAN MOVEMENT. *See* OXFORD MOVEMENT.

TRAGEDY. Greek *tragōidía*, from *trágos*, he-goat, *ōidě*, song; *tragōidós*, tragic poet and singer, probably 'goat singer', because the singers were clothed in goat-skins, or because a he-goat was the prize. In his *Poetics*, Aristotle defined tragedy as 'an imitation of an action that is complete, and whole, and of a certain magnitude; for there may be a whole that is wanting in magnitude.' A serious play in which the chief figures by some peculiarity of character pass through a series of misfortunes leading to the final catastrophe. In *Principles of Literary Criticism*, I. A. Richards says:

> What clearer instance of the 'balance or reconciliation of opposite and discordant qualities' can be found than Tragedy. Pity, the impulse to approach, and Terror, the impulse to retreat, are brought in Tragedy to a reconciliation which they find nowhere else, and with them who knows what other allied groups of equally discordant impulses. Their union in an ordered single response is the *catharsis* by which Tragedy is recognized, whether Aristotle meant anything of this kind or not. This is the explanation of that sense of release, of repose in the midst of stress, of balance

and composure, given by Tragedy, for there is no other way
in which such impulses, once awakened, can be set at rest
without suppression . . .
But there is more in Tragedy than unmitigated experience.
Besides Terror there is Pity, and if there is substituted for
either something a little different — Horror or Dread, say,
for Terror; Regret or Shame for Pity; or that kind of Pity
which yields the adjective 'Pitiable' in place of that which
yields 'Piteous' — the whole effect is altered. It is the
relation between the two sets of impulses, Pity and Terror,
which gives its specific character to Tragedy, and from that
relation the peculiar poise of the Tragic experience springs.

TRAGEDY OF BLOOD. *See* TRAGEDY OF REVENGE.

TRAGEDY OF REVENGE. This was the name given to those
Elizabethan plays of which Kyd's *Spanish Tragedy* in 1592 was the
first. In *The Oxford Companion to the Theatre*, Phyllis Hartnoll
says:

Dealing with bloody deeds which demand retribution, their
motto was 'an eye for an eye and a tooth for a tooth', and
their sublimity could easily turn to melodrama; and indeed
in a cruder form the revenge motif underlay many of the
melodramas of the nineteenth century. In the range of
Shakespeare's plays *Titus Andronicus* may be considered the
lowest form of the Revenge Tragedy, *Hamlet* its perfect
flowering. Under the same heading come the great tragedies
of Webster and of Tourneur.

TRAGIC FLAW. The flaw or error in the tragic hero which brings
about his downfall. In the *Poetics* of Aristotle this is the much-
debated *hamartia*.

TRAGIC IRONY. *See* IRONY.

TRAGI-COMEDY. John Fletcher defines this term in his preface
to *The Faithful Shepherdess* (1610):

A tragi-comedy is not so called in respect to mirth and killing,
but in respect it wants deaths, which is enough to make it no
tragedy, yet brings some near it, which is enough to make
it no comedy . . .

A most perfect example of the type is Corneille's *Le Cid* (1636);
a prolific writer of tragi-comedies was another French dramatist,
Alexandre Hardy, his best being *Marianne* (1610).

TRANCHE DE VIE. *See* SLICE OF LIFE.

TRANSCENDENTALISM.   Latin *trans*, beyond, *scandĕre*, to climb.   The investigation of what, in human knowledge, is known by reasoning alone, independent of the experience of everyday life. In 1836, this idea was presented in R. W. Emerson's prose essay *Nature*, which signified his idealism: 'Nature is the incarnation of thought.   The world is the mind precipitated.'

TRANSFERRED EPITHET.   An adjective used with a noun to which it does not properly apply.   For example: 'The prisoner entered the *condemned* cell'.
      In this line in Keats's *The Eve of St. Agnes*:

> Noiseless as fear in a wide wilderness

it is not actually fear that is noiseless, but the movements of the person under the influence of fear.

TRANSLATION.   Latin *translātiōn-(em)*, a removing, transferring, from one place to another.   The turning from one language into another.   Voltaire said, 'Translations increase the faults of a work and spoil its beauties'.   In *The Aran Islands*, Synge tells us that a translation is no translation unless it will give you the music of a poem along with the words of it.   George Borrow considered that translation is 'at best an echo'.   Nevertheless, the 'Authorized Version' of 1611 is not only a translation of the Bible, but literature in its own right.

TRAVESTY.   *See* BURLESQUE.

TREATISE.   Old French *traitier*, from Latin *tractāre*, to drag, handle, use, reflect upon.   A formal work containing a methodical examination of the principles of the subject.   One of the most challenging in the eighteenth century was *Treatise of Human Nature*, a philosophical work of David Hume.

TRECENTO.   Italian *il Trecento*, three (for thirteen) hundred.   The fourteenth century as a period in Italian literature and art.   Dante, Petrarch, and Boccaccio belonged to this period.

TRIAD.   Greek *treis*, three.   In classical Greek poetry a group of three lyric stanzas, the strophe, antistrophe, and epode.   This way of writing was introduced by Stesichorus, and followed by Simonides and Pindar.

TRIBRACH.   Greek *tri*, three, *brakhús*, short.   A metrical foot of three short or unstressed syllables.   The *tribrach* rarely occurs in English verse.

TRILOGY. Greek *trilogía*, series of three tragedies. In Greek antiquities, a series of three tragedies performed at Athens at the festival of Dionysus. They were originally connected in subject. The term is applied to any series of three related works, such as Shakespeare's *Henry VI*, Arnold Bennett's *Clayhanger* series — *Clayhanger*, *Hilda Lessways*, *These Twain*.

TRIMETER. Greek *tri*, three, *métros* from *métron*, measure. A line of verse consisting of three metrical feet as in this stanza by Byron:

> The mon|arch saw | and shook, |
> And bade | no more | rejoice;
> All blood | less waxed | his look, |
> And trem|ulous | his voice. |

TRIOLET. This is an eight-line stanza with two rhymes. The first line is repeated as the fourth and seventh, and the second and the eighth lines are alike. This triolet is by Thomas Hardy:

> How great my grief, my joys how few,
> Since first it was my fate to know thee!
> — Have the slow years not brought to view
> How great my grief, my joys how few,
> Nor memory shaped old times anew,
>   Nor loving-kindness helped to show thee
> How great my grief, my joys how few,
>   Since first it was my fate to know thee?

TRIPLE METRE. One with three syllables to each metrical foot, as in Kipling's

> In the Name | of the Em|press, the O|verland Mail!

TRIPLE RHYME. A rhyme in which the stressed syllable is followed by two unstressed syllables. This rhyme is often used for a comic effect, as in these lines by R. H. Barham:

> Having reached the summit, and managed to cross it, he
> Rolled down the hill with uncommon velocity.

TRIPLET. Latin *triplus*, threefold, triple; *tres*, three. Three lines of verse which form a unit, especially when rhyming together. This distinguishes it from the *tercet* which applies to three lines that do not have the same rhyme, as in the halves of the sestet of the Petrarchan sonnet, or in the terza rima stanza. Here is an example of rhymed triplets from Elizabeth Barrett Browning's *A Vision o, Poets*:

> There Shakespeare, on whose forehead climb
> The crowns o' the world. Oh, eyes sublime,
> With tears and laughters for all time!

TRISTICH. Greek *tri-*, three, threefold, thrice. A group of three lines of verse; a stanza of three lines.

TRITAGONIST. Greek *tritagōnistĕs*; *trítos*, third, *agōnistĕs*, actor. In Greek tragedy, the third actor, introduced by Sophocles.

TRITE. Latin *trītus*, rubbed, from *terĕre*, to rub. Commonplace, hackneyed. Lacking novelty and freshness; e.g. a *trite* remark.

TRIVIA. Latin *trivialis*, commonplace, from *trivium*, from *tri* and *via*, a place where three ways meet, suitable for gossip. Trifles, trivialities.

TRIVIUM. Latin *trivium*, place where three roads meet. In medieval schools, this was the course of study consisting of the three liberal arts: Latin grammar, logic, and rhetoric. This led to the B.A. course of later universities.

TROBAR CLUS. Provençal, literally, close composition. In the twelfth century, Provençal troubadour poets, among them Peire d'Auvergne, Giraut de Bornelh, and Marcabru, writing on subjects including praise of the Crusades, used a difficult style called the *trobar clus*, so named to distinguish it from *trobar clar*, the clear direct way of expression.

TROCHEE. Greek *trokhaîos*, tripping, running. A metrical foot of two syllables with the stress on the first foot, $/\smile$, as in daily. These lines from Dryden are an example of *trochaic dimeter*:

> Hópe ĭs | bánĭshed, |
> Jóys ăre | vánĭshed, |
> Dámŏn, | mý bĕ|lóv'd, ĭs | góne!

TROPE. Greek *trópos*, turn, way; *trépō*, turn. The figurative, elaborate use of a word. Hamlet says that the title of the play *The Mousetrap* is to be understood 'tropically' (i.e. figuratively), which suggests that trope was used in this sense in Shakespeare's day. The term was used frequently in the eighteenth century, and applied to metaphor, simile, personification, and hyperbole. Tropes could be employed in forms of irony.

A trope was also a phrase or verse introduced into some part of the Mass of the medieval church.

TROPISMS. Greek *trópos*, turn. Recently, a reviewer in *The Times* defined *tropisms* as short passages of prose in which single situations

— a shopping expedition, a chat with a cook, the discovery of old age — are examined with a microscopic attention to detail that hypnotizes the reader as surely as a weasel can hypnotize a hen. In *Tropisms and the Age of Suspicion*, Nathalie Sarraute tells us that tropisms are 'still the living substance of all my books'.

TROUBADOUR.   French *troubadour*, Provençal *trobador*, from *trobar*, to find, invent, compose in verse.   A medieval lyrical poet of a school which flourished in Provence and the south of France during the late eleventh and down to the end of the thirteenth centuries. Among the most celebrated troubadours were Bertrand de Born, Pierre de St.-Rémy, and Arnaut Daniel, whose work showed the devotion to the subject of courtly love, expressed in a most intricate metrical form.

TROUVÈRE.   French *trouver*, to find, discover, think.   One of a school of court poets who flourished in northern France from the eleventh to the fourteenth century at the same time as the troubadours of southern France.   The *trouvères* wrote love lyrics, historical verse romances, and the *Chansons de geste*.

TRUNCATED LINE.   *See* ACATALECTIC.

TUMBLING VERSE.   *See* SKELTONIC VERSE.

TWELVE-LINE STANZA.   This stanza form has been used by Tennyson, Robert Browning, and Praed with a varied rhyme arrangement.   The stanza below is by a Canadian poet:

> In the air there are no coral-
>   Reefs or ambergris,
> No rock-pools that hide the lovely
>   Sea-anemones,
> No strange forms that flow with phosphor
>   In a deep-sea night,
> No slow fish that float their colour
>   Through the liquid light,
> No young pearls, like new moons, growing
>   Perfect in their shells;
> *If you be in search of beauty*
>   Go where beauty dwells.
>
>   Duncan Campbell Scott, *A Song*

TWO CULTURES, THE.   A controversy sparked off by the novelist and scientist C. P. Snow in the 1959 Rede Lecture at Cambridge.   Snow deplored the ever-widening gap between the humanities and technology, and the wilful and even proud ignorance of non-scientists in all things scientific. To Snow, no man can properly claim to be 'educated' unless he can understand, for example, the Second Law of Thermodynamics as well as being able to read and appreciate Shakespeare. The gap between 'the two cultures' is disastrous, he claims, not only for our own increasingly technological society, but for the world as a whole, since its perpetuation can do nothing but increase that other frightening gap — between the 'have' and 'have-not' nations of the world.

Snow's thesis precipitated a violent academic controversy, his chief antagonist being Dr. F. R. Leavis, who in the 1962 Richmond Lecture, also delivered at Cambridge and later printed in the *Spectator* and published in book form, said that Snow was in no position to set himself up as a bridge between the two cultures, and that Snow's literary style itself left a lot to be desired.

Snow has enlarged on his original theme in his *Science and Government* (1961) and the expanded version of the original lecture, *The Two Cultures: and a Second Look* (1964).

TYPE-FACE. The kind or style of type, as bold face, light face. The four important dimensions of type are: height to paper (0·918 inches) which is constant for all English and American types and blocks, though not for all Continental types; body height, which is measured in points; set, also measured in points; and x-height, which is the height of the printing part of such letters as x, w, a, r (i.e. all those letters without *ascenders*, as b, d, or *descenders*, as p, q).

TYPOGRAPHY. The art of printing from type. The style, design, arrangement, and general appearance of a piece of type composition.

U

UBI SUNT THEME. A number of medieval Latin poems open with the words *ubi sunt*, 'where are'. This theme, dealing with the transience of so many things in life, is found in François Villon's *Ballade*, with the memorable refrain, '*Mais où sont les neiges d'antan?*' 'The Ballad of Dead Ladies', Dante Gabriel Rossetti's translation of the poem, has this refrain:

> 'Where are the snows of yesteryear?'

ULSTER THEATRE. *See* IRISH DRAMATIC MOVEMENT.

UNCIAL. Latin *unciālis*, as in Late Latin *litterae unciāles*, letters an inch high, used by St. Jerome of very large letters. Written in the large characters used in manuscripts from the fourth to the ninth centuries A.D. uncial differs from the 'majuscules' and the cursive 'minuscules'.

UNDERSTATEMENT. *See* MEIOSIS.

UNIQUE. Latin *ūnicus*, one and no more, alone of its kind. Having no like or equal. Used in catalogues to indicate books of which only one copy is known, or of which no copy exists in similar condition.

UNITIES, THE. Latin *ūnitās*, from *ūnus*, one. The three principles of dramatic composition, the unities of time, place, and action, were expanded from Aristotle's *Poetics* by Italian critics in the sixteenth century. In *Tragedy*, F. L. Lucas tells us:

> Aristotle had in fact insisted only that the action must have an artistic unity, free of irrelevances. He had also remarked, without forming any theory about it, that the duration of plays was in practice generally limited to twenty-four hours or a little more. The Unity of Place he never mentions at all. The Greek theatre, with a chorus, and without a curtain, did in fact generally observe the Unities of Time and Place. Without a curtain the transitions would have been difficult; and with a chorus, it was unlikely that the same dozen old men should reappear, all together, now at Athens, now at Sparta, now at Thebes.

UNIVERSALITY. Latin *ūniversum*, combined into one. That quality of a work of art which gives it a universal appeal. Longinus said, 'We may regard those words as truly noble and sublime, which please all and please always'.

UNIVERSITY WITS.   The name given to a group of Elizabethan playwrights and pamphleteers.   The chief of these were Robert Greene, George Peele, Thomas Kyd, John Lyly, Thomas Nashe, and Thomas Lodge.   They were called the University Wits because as Allardyce Nicoll says in *British Drama*, 'All these men, with the doubtful exception of Kyd, had had a training at one of the universities'.

UNTRANSLATABLENESS.   Coleridge   wrote, in *Biographia Literaria*:

> In poetry, in which every line, every phrase, may pass the
> ordeal of deliberation and deliberate choice, it is possible,
> barely possible, to attain that *ultimatum* which I have ventured
> to propose as the infallible test of a blameless style, namely,
> its *untranslatableness* in words of the same language without
> injury to the meaning.

In *A Defence of Poetry*, Shelley said:

> Hence the vanity of translation; it were as wise to cast a violet
> into a crucible that you might discover the formal principle
> of its colour and odour, as seek to transfuse from one
> language into another the creations of a poet.   The plant
> must spring again from its seed, or it will bear no flower —
> and this is the burthen of the curse of Babel.

UPANISHAD.   Sanskrit *upa-nishád*, a sitting-down at the feet of an instructor.   In Sanskrit literature, one or other of the various speculative, mystical treatises dealing with the Deity, creation, and existence.   *Upanishad* forms a part of the Vedic literature.

UTOPIAN LITERATURE.   Greek *outópos*, no place, nowhere. Literature describing an ideally perfect place or ideal society.   The word *Utopia* is the title of a speculative political essay by Sir Thomas More, published in 1516.   He was influenced by Plato's *Republic*, and set the pattern for the imaginary place with a perfect social and political system.   Others who presented ideal societies were Tommaso Campanella in *Civitas Solis* (1623), Francis Bacon in *New Atlantis* (1627), Samuel Butler in *Erewhon* (1872), Edward Bellamy, *Looking Backward* (1888), and William Morris, *News from Nowhere* (1890).· In 1905, H. G. Wells wrote *A Modern Utopia*.

V

VADE-MECUM. Latin, go with me; *vădĕre*, to go, *me*, ablative of *ego*, I, *cum*, with. A handbook (or manual) carried constantly about the person for reference. The term 'companion' implies the same meaning.

VALUES. Latin *valēre*, to be worth, to have a specific value. That quality of anything which makes it desirable or useful. As I. A. Richards says, in *Principles of Literary Criticism*:

> All that the study of value can do is to point out the things which possess this property of goodness, classify them, and remove certain confusions between ends which are good in themselves and means which are only called good, because they are instrumental in the attainment of intrinsically good ends.

VARIABLE SYLLABLE. One which may be long or short, stressed or unstressed in the metrical line, according to the context or the pattern. It is also known as the *distributed stress* or the *hovering accent*. For example, this line from Milton:

Now came still Evening on, and Twilight gray.

VARIORUM EDITION. Latin *varius*, various, literally 'of various persons'. An edition containing notes by various commentators or editors (*editio cum notis variorum*). Also an edition noting all the changes made to a work throughout the course of its successive printings, e.g. *The Variorum Edition of the Poems of W. B. Yeats* (1957).

VATES. Latin *vātēs*, a foreteller, a soothsayer whose utterances were made in verse. From earliest times, a poet or bard, especially one who is divinely inspired. The most famous was the Sibyl. Herodotus mentions Amphilytus, and preserves the text of his oracle. Virgil in his *Fourth Eclogue* prophesies the birth of a boy, under whose rule the world will be at peace. The child was taken to be the expected offspring of Octavian and Scribonia, who proved, in fact, to be a daughter. Later the poem was read as a prophecy of the birth of Christ. This led Dante to choose Virgil as his guide in the *Divina Commedia*.

VAUDEVILLE. French, earlier *vau-de-vire*, in full *chanson du Vau de Vire*, a light popular song such as those ascribed to Olivier

Basselin, who lived in the valley of the Vire in Calvados, Normandy, in the fifteenth century. Later, it meant an amusing stage performance with songs and dances; a light, musical comedy; a variety or music-hall entertainment.

VEDA. Sanskrit *vēda*, knowledge, sacred book, from the root *vid-*, to know. One or other of the four ancient sacred books of the Hindus. Each book has the *Veda* in its title. *Rig-Veda* is the earliest, and consists of psalms or hymns, many in the form of an allegory. *Yajur-Veda* contains litanies and prayers; *Sāma-Veda*, hymns and chants; *Atharva-Veda*, incantations. Each *Veda* includes a *sanhita* (a collection of hymns) and a *Brahmana* (a body of precepts); also attached is a *Upanishad*, a treatise dealing with creation and existence.

VEHICLE. *See* TENOR.

VELLUM. French *vélin*, from Old French *vel*, calf. Fine parchment originally from the skin of a newly-born calf. Also a manuscript written on this. Vellum seems to show to better advantage some heavy type-faces, such as those used by William Morris for printing the Kelmscott Press books.

VERBOSITY. Latin *verbōsus*, from *verbum*, word. Wordiness, prolixity, long-windedness. For example, Johnson's dictionary definitions of *network* as 'anything reticulated or decussated with interstices between the intersections' and of a *cough* as 'a convulsion of the lungs, vellicated by some sharp serosity'.

VERISIMILITUDE. Latin *vērisimilitūdō*, from *vērisimilis*, likely to be true. Having the appearance of truth. This quality can be achieved in literature by skilful selection and presentation of the material of human life. *Vraisemblance*, the French equivalent, is frequently used.

VERISM. Latin *vērus*, true. The doctrine that literature or art should rigidly represent truth or reality even when it is sordid. A *verist* is one who believes in this.

VERNACULAR. Latin *vernāculus*, born in one's house, domestic, native; from *verna*, one born within the community. Now only used of language, idiom, word of one's native country. Language which is not of foreign origin; one which is distinguished from the accepted, literary language; for example, 'the vernacular poems of William Barnes'.

VERS DE SOCIÉTÉ. French, literally, society verse. Occasional verse, turning a compliment or touching off the manners and conventions of the day. Such verse, produced by George Wither, and the Earl of Rochester, is graceful, elegant, and witty. An example is Gray's *Ode on the Death of a Favourite Cat*. Here are the last two stanzas:

> Eight times emerging from the flood
> She mew'd to ev'ry watry God,
>   Some speedy aid to send.
> No Dolphin came, no Nereid stirr'd:
> Nor cruel *Tom*, nor *Susan* heard.
>   A Fav'rite has no friend!

> From hence, ye Beauties, undeceiv'd,
> Know, one false step is ne'er retriev'd,
>   And be with caution bold.
> Not all that tempts your wand'ring eyes
> And heedless hearts, is lawful prize;
>   Nor all, that glisters, gold.

VERSE. Latin *versus*, a furrow, a row, line, a metric line, literally turning (to the next line), from *vertĕre*, to turn. Metrical composition or structure. A metrical line of poetry. A stanza consisting of several lines. One of the short sections into which a chapter of the Bible is divided.

VERSE PARAGRAPH. A group of lines, often in blank verse, arranged to form in itself a unity. Verse paragraphs are most effectively used in Milton's *Paradise Lost*, and in *The Prelude* by Wordsworth.

VERS LIBRE. French, free verse. Verses in which various metrical forms, or various rhythms, are combined, or the ordinary rules of prosody are ignored. Ezra Pound wrote these lines:

> Go, little naked and impudent songs.
> Go with a light foot!
> (Or with two light feet, if it please you!)
> Go and dance shamelessly!
> Go with impertinent frolic.

VERSO. Latin *verso* (*folio*), with the page turned; *versus*, past participle of *vertĕre*, to turn, *folium*, a leaf or page. Any left-hand page of a book. Always the even page.

VESTURE. Latin *vestis*, garment. This term, which has a poetical significance, is used by Carlyle in a well-known passage of *The Hero as Poet*:

> Fundamentally indeed Poet and Prophet are still the same; in this most important respect especially, that they have

penetrated both of them into the sacred mystery of the Universe; what Goethe calls 'the open secret'! 'Which is the great secret?' asks one. — 'The *open* secret', — open to all, seen by almost none! That divine mystery, which lies everywhere in all Beings, 'the Divine Idea of the World, that lies at the bottom of Appearance,' as Fichte styles it; of which all Appearance, from the starry sky to the grass of the field, but especially the Appearance of Man and his work, is but the *vesture*, the embodiment that renders it visible.

VICTORIAN. Paul Harvey has said:

> An epithet applied to anything (spiritual or material) or to a person (author, artist, politician, etc.) considered typical of the reign of Queen Victoria. Among the characteristics of the age in allusion to which the term is sometimes used are its improved standard of decency and morality; a self-satisfaction engendered by the great increase of wealth, the prosperity of the nation as a whole, and the immense industrial and scientific development; conscious rectitude and deficient sense of humour; an unquestioning acceptance of authority and orthodoxy.
>
> *The Oxford Companion to English Literature*

VIDE ANTE. Latin = See before.

VIDE INFRA. Latin = See below.

VIDELICET. Latin *vidēre licet*, it is permitted to see. That is to say, namely, to wit. Generally used to introduce a fuller explanation of what has been stated. Abbreviation, viz., commonly spoken as *namely*: under the following plan, viz. that action be taken . . .

VIDE POST. Latin = See below.

VIDE SUPRA. Latin = See above: abbreviation, *v.s.*

VIEWPOINT. *See* POINT OF VIEW.

VIGNETTE. French *vignette*, an ornamental border; diminutive of *vigne*, vine, vineyard. The decorative or ornamental design in the form of vine leaves surrounding the capital letters of ancient manuscripts and books. Any kind of printers' ornaments as leaves, flowers, tail-pieces. More recently, any kind of woodcut, engraving, not enclosed within a border.

The word *vignette* is also used in the sense of a short essay, as in the title of Austin Dobson's *Eighteenth Century Vignettes*.

VILLAIN. Old French *vilain*, peasant, churl; whence Modern French *vilain*, low, ugly. A scoundrel, one likely to commit, or who has committed, serious crimes. In literature, one who opposes the hero. The villain may become the centre of interest, as Satan in *Paradise Lost*.

VILLANELLE. Italian *villanello*, rural, rustic. A light poem of fixed form, usually pastoral in subject matter, and lyrical in manner. There are five three-line stanzas and one of four, with only two rhymes throughout. The two lines of refrain are repeated at the end of the final quatrain. Here is *Villanelle* by W. E. Henley:

> A dainty thing's the Villanelle
>   Sly, musical, a jewel in rhyme,
> It serves its purpose passing well.
>
> A double-clappered silver bell,
>   That must be made to clink in chime,
> A dainty thing's the Villanelle;
>
> And if you wish to flute a spell,
>   Or ask a meeting 'neath the lime,
> It serves its purpose passing well.
>
> You must not ask of it the swell
>   Of organs grandiose and sublime —
> A dainty thing's the Villanelle;
>
> And, filled with sweetness, as a shell
>   Is filled with sound, and launched in time,
> It serves its purpose passing well.
>
> Still fair to see and good to smell
> As in the quaintness of its prime,
> A dainty thing's the Villanelle,
> It serves its purpose passing well.

VIRELAY. French *virelai*; *virer*, to turn, *lai*, a song. A French form of verse seldom used in English. It is composed of stanzas with long lines rhyming with each other and short lines rhyming with each other. The short lines of one stanza provide the rhyme for the long lines of the next. In the last stanza the short lines take their rhyme from the short lines of the first stanza. In this way every rhyme occurs in two stanzas.

VIRGULE. Latin *virgula*, diminutive of *virga*, twig, rod. A thin sloping or upright line occurring in medieval manuscripts. It was used as a mark indicating the caesura, or as a punctuation-mark, comparable to the comma, whence its meaning in Modern French.

VOCALIC ASSONANCE. This is a kind of near rhyme where the stressed vowels in the 'rhyming' words agree, but the consonants do not. It is used in early ballads. Here is an example from *Young Bekie*:

> O it fell once upon a day
> Burd Isbel fell asleep,
> And up it starts the Billy Blind,
> And stood at her bed-feet.

VOLAPÜK. World's speech. An artificial international language invented by J. M. Schleyer in 1879. Superseded by Esperanto, Ido, and similar inventions.

VOLTA. Latin *volvĕre*, to turn. The change in thought and feeling which divides the octave from the sestet in a carefully designed sonnet. It is exemplified in this sonnet by Shakespeare:

> When I consider every thing that grows
> Holds in perfection but a little moment,
> That this huge stage presenteth nought but shows
> Whereon the stars in secret influence comment;
> When I perceive that men as plants increase,
> Cheered and check'd even by the self-same sky,
> Vaunt in their youthful sap, at height decrease,
> And wear their brave state out of memory;
> Then the conceit of this inconstant stay
> Sets you most rich in youth before my sight,
> Where wasteful Time debateth with Decay
> To change your day of youth to sullied night;
> And all in war with Time for love of you,
> As he takes from you, I engraft you new.

VORTICISM. Latin variation of *vertex*, from *vort-*, *vertĕre*, to turn. In *Dictionary of Art Terms*, Reginald G. Haggar says:

> Vorticism is an advanced art movement, launched in 1912 by Wyndham Lewis, which stemmed from Cubism and, more particularly, Futurism with which it had much in common; it created a good deal of artistic disturbance by shock tactics, noisy manifestoes, and group activity.

The term *Vorticism* was put forward by Ezra Pound in 1913. The movement extolled the beauties of the machine: hard, angular, sharp-edged.

VOWEL RHYME. A form of rhyme in which any vowel sound is allowed to agree with any other. This is rarely used, though it appears in the verse of Emily Dickinson. This stanza is from *The Chariot*:

> We passed the school, where children strove
> At recess, in the ring;
> We passed the fields of gazing grain,
> We passed the setting sun.

VRAISEMBLANCE. See VERISIMILITUDE.

VULGARISM. Latin *vulgāris*, from *vulgus*, the common people. A vulgar, unrefined way of speech, closely connected with slang and colloquialism. Examples: He bashed the old geezer. The yob nicked a packet of fags.

Another vulgarism in speech is the conversion of the ph into p in *diphtheria* and *diphthong*.

VULGATE. Latin *Biblia Latina Vulgatae editionis*. An ancient Latin version of the Bible prepared by St. Jerome and others in the fourth century, and later twice revised. It is so called from its common use in the Roman Catholic Church.

W

WARDOUR STREET ENGLISH. A style which makes use of bogus archaisms such as *verily, perchance, vouchsafe.* Wardour Street is a London street formerly occupied by many antique dealers (both genuine and bogus). Today, however, Wardour Street is more famous as the centre of the British film industry, and its former meaning has ceased to have much validity.

WATER-LINES. Transparent perpendicular marks on paper, caused by the supports of the frame in which the paper is made. Water-lines are useful in determining the size of old books.

WATERMARK. Faint design seen in some paper when held against the light, indicating maker, size, etc.

WAX ENGRAVING. A method of obtaining printing plates by redrawing an illustration on a wax-coated plate of copper, from which an electrotype is made.

WAYZGOOSE: WAYGOOSE. A corruption of *wakegoose.* Anglo-Saxon *wacian, weccan,* cognate with *watch.* An entertainment given by master-printers to their workmen towards the end of August, when work by candle-light began. Later, an annual bean-feast held in the summer by the employees of a printing establishment, consisting of a dinner and a trip into the country.

WEAK ENDING. One that concludes a line of verse, but is unstressed in normal speech. The unstressed tenth syllable in a blank verse line. (An auxiliary with its verb, preposition with its noun, conjunction with its clause in the next line.)

> Say that I wish he never find more cause
> To change a master. O, my fortunes have
> Corrupted honest men!
>
> *Antony and Cleopatra*

>   nor set
> A mark so bloody on the business; but
> With colours fairer painted their foul ends.
>
> *The Tempest*

WELLERESQUE: WELLERIAN: WELLERISM. Typical of Sam Weller or his father, two famous characters in Dickens's *Pickwick Papers*.

> 'Vell, gov'ner, ve must all come to it, one day or another.'
> 'So we must, Sammy,' said Mr. Weller the elder.
> 'There's a Providence in it all,' said Sam.
> 'O' course there is,' replied his father with a nod of grave approval. 'Wot 'ud become of the undertakers vithout it, Sammy?'

WELL-MADE PLAY. In *The Oxford Companion to the Theatre*, Phyllis Hartnoll says:

> Eugène Scribe (1791–1861), French dramatist, was the originator and exponent of the 'well-made play'.
> His plays are constructed with the utmost neatness and economy. They are still interesting as examples of dramatic construction, though seldom revived nowadays. . . . He wrote successfully for a number of theatres for more than thirty years, and his example weighed heavily on the European theatre for long after his death.

WELTANSCHAUUNG. German, literally, ideology, outlook upon the world. A philosophical view of the world; dealing with and envisaging the events and experiences of human life.

WELTSCHMERZ. German, literally, world-pain; weariness of life, pessimistic melancholy. A feeling of uneasiness with the state of the world.

WESSEX NOVELS. Thomas Hardy used 'Wessex' to designate the south-west counties of England, principally Dorset, which are the scene of his novels, from *Desperate Remedies* (1871) to *Jude the Obscure* (1895). For the topography of the novels see Hermann Lea's *Thomas Hardy's Wessex*, which was written with the help of the novelist.

WESTERN. A film or novel dealing with cowboys, bandits, sheriffs, rustlers, and shanty towns, and set in the West of the United States, usually during the period when this region was being opened to permanent settlement, with its attendant lawlessness and violence. Sometimes referred to jocularly as a 'horse opera'.

WHEEL OF THINGS, THE. A law of universal change. The first song in Sophocles' *The Women of Trachis* advances as a counsel of hope 'the old Orphic or Pythagorean doctrine of the wheel of things; joy succeeds sorrow and sorrow succeeds joy:

> To all they come, sorrow and joy,
> In circling round, like the turning
> Paths of the Bear.'

WHODUNIT. From 'who done it?' which is the illiterate form of 'Who did it?' asking the question, 'Who committed the crime?' It is a crime story, usually concerned with murder and the search for the criminal, i.e. a specialized form of the *roman policier* (q.v.), which need not be restricted to murder, but covers the whole gamut of crime. *See also* THRILLER.

WIDOW. A short last line of a paragraph which appears as the first line of the next page in the book. Good typography requires that widows should be avoided.

WIT. Anglo-Saxon *witt*, understanding, sense, from *witan*, to know. Wit is more intellectual than humour, and depends upon ingenuity and swift perception of the incongruous. The word has changed its meaning since the seventeenth century when Dryden defined it as 'a propriety of thoughts and words; thoughts and words elegantly adapted to the subject'. On another occasion he said, 'Wit-writing (if you will give me leave to use a school distinction) is no other than the faculty of imagination in the writer'.

Sir Henry Craik observed that the object of seventeenth-century 'wit' was 'not to excite laughter but to compel attention'.

Coleridge, defining the term in *Literary Remains*, says, 'It arises in detecting the identity in dissimilar things'.

WIT-WRITING. *See* WIT.

WORD-PLAY. This includes verbal fencing, repartee; also play on words, puns, paradoxes.

WRITER'S BLOCK. Inability to complete work. Used by a publisher or printer of an author who fails to submit copy in good time.

X

XEROGRAPHY.   Greek *xērós*, dry.   'A non-chemical photographic process in which the plate is sensitized electrically and developed by dusting with electrically-charged fine powder.'   (*Chambers's Twentieth Century Dictionary*)   Xerography is increasingly used for reproducing rare books in limited numbers.

X-HEIGHT.   The height of lower-case letters, excluding descenders and ascenders, that is, the height of the lower-case x.

XYLOGRAPH.   Wood-engraving, especially of the fifteenth century. Also a decorative pattern obtained by a mechanical reproduction of the grain on the surfaces of wood.

Y

YELLOW-BACKS. Cheap editions of novels bound in yellow boards. They were the 'railway novels' of the last years of the nineteenth century.

YELLOW BOOK, THE. An illustrated quarterly which appeared from 1894 to 1897. Among the distinguished writers and artists who contributed to it were Aubrey Beardsley, Max Beerbohm, Henry James, Edmund Gosse, Walter Sickert.

YELLOW JOURNALISM. A name given to the sensational journalism of America which developed about 1880 under the influence of Joseph Pulitzer. The term is derived from the appearance in 1895 of a number of the 'New York World' in which a child in a yellow dress ('The Yellow Kid') was the central figure of the cartoon, this being an experiment in colour-printing designed to attract purchasers. (*Oxford English Dictionary*)

YELLOW PRESS. A term applied in England to sensational periodicals.

Z

ZEITGEIST. German, literally, spirit of the age. This is applied to the feeling and the reactions of the writers of the time.

ZEUGMA. Greek *zeûgma,* band, bond, from *zeúgnūmi,* I yoke. A figure of speech by which a verb or an adjective is applied to two nouns, though strictly appropriate to only one of them. In *syllepsis* the single word is in correct grammatical relationship with each of the other two and makes sense with each. A commonly recognized *zeugma* occurs in *Henry V* when Fluellen says:

> Kill the poys and the luggage.

Here the verb *kill* does not apply to *luggage.*

> See Pan with flocks, with fruits Pomona crown'd.
>
> Pope, *Windsor Forest*

BIBLIOGRAPHY

Abercrombie, Lascelles, *Principles of English Prosody* (Secker)

Barfield, Owen, *History in English Words* (Faber)

Baugh, Albert Croll, *A History of the English Language* (Routledge & Kegan Paul)

Berg, P. C., *Dictionary of New Words in English* (Allen & Unwin)

Bradley, H., *The Making of English* (Macmillan)

Brewer, E. C., *Dictionary of Phrase and Fable* (Cassell)

Brook-Rose, Christine, *A Grammar of Metaphor* (Secker & Warburg)

Brown, Ivor, *Say the Word* (Cape)

——, *No Idle Words* (Cape)

——, *Having the Last Word* (Cape)

Chase, Stuart, *The Tyranny of Words* (Methuen)

——, *The Power of Words* (Phoenix House)

Classen, Ernest, *Outlines of the History of the English Language* (Macmillan)

Collins, V. H., *The Choice of Words* (Longmans)

——, *One Word and Another* (Longmans)

Emerson, Oliver F., *The History of the English Language* (Macmillan)

Empson, William, *Seven Types of Ambiguity* (Chatto)

——, *The Structure of Complex Words* (Chatto)

Entwistle, W. J., *Aspects of Language* (Faber)

Firth, J. R., *The Tongues of Men* (Watts)

Fowler, H. W., *A Dictionary of Modern English Usage* (Oxford)

Gardiner, Alan, *The Theory of Speech and Language* (Oxford)

Granville, Wilfred, *A Dictionary of Theatrical Terms* (Deutsch)

Gray, L. H., *Foundations of Language* (Macmillan, N.Y.)

Greenough, J. B. & Kittredge, G. L., *Words and their Ways in English Speech* (Macmillan, N.Y.)

Groom, Bernard, *A Short History of English Words* (Macmillan)

Haliwell-Phillips, J. O., *A Dictionary of Archaic and Provincial Words* (Routledge)

Hartnoll, Phyllis, *The Oxford Companion to the Theatre* (Oxford)

Harvey, Paul, *The Oxford Companion to English Literature* (Oxford)

Henle, P., *Language, Thought, and Culture* (Ann Arbor)

Horwill, H. W., *A Dictionary of Modern American Usage* (Oxford)

Jesperson, Otto, *Growth and Structure of the English Language* (Blackwell)

——, *Essentials of English Grammar* (Allen & Unwin)

——, *A Modern English Grammar on Historical Principles* (Allen & Unwin)

Johnson, Samuel, *A Dictionary of the English Language* (Degg)

Jones, Daniel, *An Outline of English Phonetics* (Heffer)

Knights, L. C. & Cottle, B., *Metaphor and Symbol* (Butterworth)

Leavis, F. R., *Revaluations* (Chatto)

——, *The Great Tradition* (Chatto)

Lewis, C. S., *Studies in Words* (Cambridge)
McKnight, G. H., *Modern English in the Making* (Mayflower)
Nicoll, Allardyce, *The Theatre and Dramatic Theory* (Harrap)
——, *British Drama* (Harrap)
——, *World Drama* (Harrap)
Ogden, C. K. & Richards, I. A., *The Meaning of Meaning* (Routledge)
Onions, C. T., *An Advanced English Syntax* (Kegan Paul)
Orr, J., *Words and Sounds in English and French* (Blackwell)
Partridge, Eric, *Usage and Abusage* (Hamish Hamilton)
——, *From Sanskrit to Brazil* (Hamish Hamilton)
——, *The World of Words* (Hamish Hamilton)
——, *A Dictionary of Slang and Unconventional English* (Routledge)
——, *A Dictionary of the Underworld, British and American* (Routledge)
——, *A Dictionary of Clichés* (Routledge)
——, *Name into Word* (Secker & Warburg)
Pei, Mario Andrew, *The Story of English* (Allen & Unwin)
Potter, Simeon, *Modern Linguistics* (Deutsch)
——, *Language in the Modern World* (Penguin)
——, *Our Language* (Penguin)
Richards, I. A., *Practical Criticism* (Routledge)
——, *Principles of Literary Criticism* (Routledge)
——, *The Philosophy of Rhetoric* (Oxford)
——, *Speculative Instruments* (Routledge)
Robertson, Stuart & Cassidy, F. G., *The Development of Modern English* (Prentice-Hall)
Robinson, R., *Definition* (Oxford)
Roget, P. M., *Thesaurus of English Words and Phrases* (Dent; Longmans)
Ross, A. S. C., *Etymology. With Especial Reference to English* (Deutsch)
Russell, Bertrand, *An Inquiry into Meaning and Truth* (Allen & Unwin)
Sapir, Edward, *Language, An Introduction to the Study of Speech* (Harcourt)
Savory, T. H., *The Language of Science* (Deutsch)
Scott, A. F., *The Craft of Prose* (Macmillan)
——, *The Poet's Craft* (Cambridge)
Sheard, J. A., *The Words We Use* (Deutsch)
Skeat, Walter W., *An Etymological Dictionary of the English Language* (Oxford)
——, *Principles of English Etymology* (Oxford)
——, *A Glossary of Tudor and Stuart Words* (Oxford)
Smith, Logan Pearsall, *The English Language* (Oxford — Home University Library)
——, *Words and Idioms* (Constable)
Stanford, W. B., *Greek Metaphor* (Oxford)
——, *Ambiguity in Greek Literature* (Oxford)
Steinberg, S. H., *Five Hundred Years of Printing* (Penguin)
Ullmann, Stephen, *The Principles of Semantics* (Blackwell)
——, *Semantics. An Introduction to the Science of Meaning* (Blackwell)

Urban, W. M., *Language and Reality* (Allen & Unwin)

Ushenko, A. P., *The Field Theory of Meaning* (Ann Arbor)

Walpole, H. R., *Semantics. The Nature of Words and their Meaning* (Norton)

Ward, Ida C., *The Phonetics of English* (Heffer)

Weekley, Ernest, *The Romance of Words* (Murray)

——, *Words Ancient and Modern* (Murray)

——, *A Concise Etymological Dictionary of Modern English* (Secker & Warburg)

Whatmough, J., *Language. A Modern Synthesis* (Secker & Warburg)

Wrenn, C. L., *The English Language* (Methuen)

Wright, Joseph, *English Dialect Dictionary* (Frowde)

Wyld, Henry Cecil, *A Short History of English* (Murray)

——, *A History of Modern Colloquial English* (Blackwell)

——, *The Universal Dictionary of the English Language* (Routledge)

Yamaguchi, H., *Essays towards English Semantics* (Tokyo)

Yule, G. U., *The Statistical Study of Literary Vocabulary* (Cambridge)

INDEX OF AUTHORS QUOTED